W9-BDV-448

DATE DUE

Does the Constitution Follow the Flag?

DOES THE CONSTITUTION FOLLOW THE FLAG?

The Evolution of Territoriality in American Law

Kal Raustiala

OXFORD
UNIVERSITY PRESS
2009

OXFORD
UNIVERSITY PRESS

Oxford University Press, Inc., publishes works that further
Oxford University's objective of excellence
in research, scholarship, and education.

Oxford   New York
Auckland   Cape Town   Dar es Salaam   Hong Kong   Karachi
Kuala Lumpur   Madrid   Melbourne   Mexico City   Nairobi
New Delhi   Shanghai   Taipei   Toronto

With offices in
Argentina   Austria   Brazil   Chile   Czech Republic   France   Greece
Guatemala   Hungary   Italy   Japan   Poland   Portugal   Singapore
South Korea   Switzerland   Thailand   Turkey   Ukraine   Vietnam

Published by Oxford University Press, Inc.
198 Madison Avenue, New York, New York 10016
www.oup.com

Library of Congress Cataloging-in-Publication Data
Raustiala, Kal.
Does the constitution follow the flag? / Kal Raustiala
    p.   cm.
Includes bibliographical references and index.
ISBN 978-0-19-530459-6
1. Conflict of laws—Jurisdiction—Unites States.   2. Unites States—Foreign
relations—Law and legislation.   3. Effectiveness and validity of law—Unites States.
4. Exterritoriality.   5. Aliens—Legal status, laws, etc.—United States.
6. Americans—Legal status, laws, etc.—United States.
I. Title.
KF413.J87R38   2009
342.73'0413—dc22   2009003557

9 8 7 6 5 4 3 2 1

Printed in the United States of America
on acid-free paper

PREFACE

This book is about the way that geography shapes legal rules and understandings—and how fundamental changes in American power and in world politics have challenged and sometimes altered the traditionally territorial system of American law. Do U.S. laws stop at the water's edge? If not, do they operate differently beyond American territory? At one level, these questions are narrow and lawyerly, and there is indeed a large legal literature on these topics. At another level, however, the nature of the connection between law and land raises profoundly significant political, economic, and social questions.

Many of us have watched footage of Cuban refugees swimming ashore in Florida, desperately trying to reach land before American officials can grasp them. Under what is known as the "wet foot–dry foot" policy, touching the territory of the United States—the dry soil itself—is critical to the legal determination of their status: the difference between a new life in the United States and a forced return to Cuba. This is a dramatic example of the power of territory, but not an unusual one. The laws of Japan differ from those of the United States, and hence even in a supposedly "flat" and globalizing world Americans in Japan expect to be subject to Japanese law. The spatial dimension of law exists even within the United States: Nevada permits acts banned in Utah, and thus crossing the state line alters what is and is not legal. In a deep sense legal power is defined territorially, and has been since the sovereign state came into being in seventeenth-century Europe. The basic jurisdictional principle is a simple one: where you are determines what rules you are governed by.

Yet, perhaps precisely *because* this principle of territoriality is so commonplace, it is rarely examined and surprisingly ill defended. Unlike sovereignty—the subject of yards of shelf space in any good library—territoriality has not been the topic of much debate outside of geography departments. Writing in the mid-1990s, the influential political scientist John Ruggie declared that "it is truly astonishing that the concept of territoriality has been so little studied by students of international politics."[1] Fifteen years later it remains little studied.

This is one reason events that force attention to the territorial nature of legal rules cause so much disagreement and confusion. Consider the current debate over the rights of suspected terrorists held in the American naval base in Guantanamo Bay, Cuba. In recent years the federal courts have grappled with the question of whether these detainees have any constitutional rights at all, or whether instead they are, as critics charge, trapped in an offshore "legal black hole."

The answer turns very much on how we understand the fundamental geography of American law. As I will demonstrate, such questions are not new and they surface more frequently than one might imagine. Whether U.S. law applied in occupied Mexican cities, federal territories in the West, "Indian country," or offshore consular courts; whether it restricts law enforcement abroad, regulates foreign stock manipulators, or governs military dependents in overseas bases—these and other issues have repeatedly arisen throughout American history. The complex, interdependent world we live in today has simply multiplied and deepened the challenges to territoriality; it has not created them.

This book has several aims. The first is to explain why territoriality is a significant concept and why the American legal system, like other legal systems, has traditionally been presumptively territorial. I say "presumptively" because territoriality is not an ironclad principle, nor is it unchanging. But it is essential to the understanding of sovereignty that has been in place more or less since the Treaty of Westphalia in 1648. Territoriality grounds political power in control over space. Because jurisdiction is a foundational concept in law, legal rules are an excellent window on the evolution of territoriality. I focus in this book on American legal rules not because the paradigm of territoriality is unique to the United States— territoriality is a fundamental principle of the international system—but because the United States is enormously significant and because, as an American professor of law, it is the legal system I know best.

My second aim is to trace, in very broad brushstrokes, the evolution of territoriality in American law from the founding era to today. Territoriality has always been an important principle, but as a practice, as well as a principle, it has a complicated past (and an even more complicated present). It arises in myriad ways, such as whether the Environmental Protection Agency can regulate polluters in Canada, whether U.S. antitrust law applies to foreign firms affecting U.S. markets, or whether FBI agents must read *Miranda* warnings to suspects abroad. These varied issues are not new or unknown, but to date they have been addressed separately. This book shows that all share a common core in our assumptions about, and responses to, the territorial nature of sovereignty.

My final aim is to advance several claims about the evolution of territoriality. First, extraterritoriality has shown surprising continuity in its purpose even as its form has changed. Extraterritoriality meant very different things to nineteenth-century lawyers than it does to contemporary lawyers. But despite dramatic changes in form, the primary function of extraterritoriality has remained much the same. That function, I argue, is to manage and minimize the legal differences entrenched by Westphalian sovereignty.

Second, extraterritoriality is paralleled by what I call *intraterritoriality*. Just as extraterritoriality has long been a way to conceptually redraw maps, to redefine what is inside and outside the scope of a sovereign's law, intraterritoriality has served to delineate differences within national borders, particularly as the United States grew in size and power. Intraterritorial doctrines, such as the claim that some constitutional rights do not apply in some American territory, reflect the tension between the demands of liberal constitutionalism and the imperatives of global power politics. This tension was dramatically evidenced when, as a rising great power, the United States acquired an overseas empire a century ago. But it continues to play out today, as the debate over Guantanamo amply illustrates.

Throughout this book I pay close attention to the international context, and particularly to the changing global role of the United States. As a weak power, the United States showed solicitude for traditional Westphalian principles of territoriality. As a superpower, it was far more willing to bend and even break established doctrine. This transformation, and related shifts in international politics and economics, helped to shape the kinds of territorial claims that were made, even if the fundamental aim of these claims—to manage and sometimes manipulate legal differences—remained broadly constant.

In short, this book offers a framework that connects a disparate set of territorial rules and practices and explores their purpose and function. My overarching goal is to make sense of a world in which the United States applies its law to some actors in some places while denying it to other actors in other places. I do not claim to offer a comprehensive theory of the evolution of territoriality; the topic is too complex to be explained satisfactorily by a few master variables. Instead, I have written an account that I hope brings clarity to the topic, that links its political and legal as well as domestic and international aspects, and that helps to ground current debates in an historical context.

ACKNOWLEDGMENTS

The genesis of this book rests with a student's question, many years ago, about how the doctrines of jurisdiction within international law fit with the constitutional treatment of Puerto Rico. From there I began to read more about the American imperial adventure of the early twentieth century and, increasingly, to see the parallels between these older historic episodes and the then-emerging effort to detain foreign nationals outside American territory in the wake of the 9/11 attacks. Soon, and with the urging of others, I began to think about a book on these topics.

Over the many years that I explored these issues I have incurred numerous debts, but have also had the great pleasure of working with many excellent scholars and students. At Princeton, where I spent the 2002–3 academic year in the Law and Public Affairs Program at the Woodrow Wilson School, I began the early stages of this project. I thank Princeton for its support and in particular thank our leader at LAPA, Chris Eisgruber, who inculcated a wonderful spirit of inquiry and gave us substantial freedom to think and write. Visits at Harvard Law School, Columbia Law School, and the University of Chicago Law School gave me new colleagues to engage and many new ideas. And with the support of my Dean at UCLA, Michael Schill, I convened a small interdisciplinary workshop on territoriality at UCLA in 2006, which provided me a wealth of new issues to consider. Over the last few years I have presented aspects of this project at many institutions around North America, including Princeton, Columbia, Harvard, Hofstra, Berkeley, Chicago, Duke, SMU, the University of British Columbia, Georgetown, Penn, the RAND Corporation, and UCLA. I thank the many participants at all these talks for their helpful and constructive feedback.

An early and brief version of my argument appeared as part of a volume edited by Miles Kahler and Barbara Walter, titled *Territoriality and Conflict in* an *Age of Globalization* (Cambridge University Press, 2006). The meetings leading up to the publication of *Territoriality and Conflict* were uniformly excellent and thought provoking, and the editors helped steer the project in the right direction. Some of the arguments in this book, in particular those concerned with Guantanamo, also appeared in a 2005 article titled "The Geography of Justice" in the *Fordham Law Review*.

I owe particular debts to a few hardy souls who took time out of their busy lives to read various chapters of the manuscript: John Agnew, Peter Andreas, Jack Beard, Gary Born, Christina Burnett, Bill Dodge, Eleanor Fox, Maximo Langer, Hiroshi Motomura, Gerry Neuman, Anthony Pagden, Tonya Putnam, Eileen Scully, Clyde Spillenger, and Detlef Vagts. I very much apologize if I have inadvertently left anyone out. My editor at Oxford University Press, Dave McBride, was uniformly encouraging throughout the process. I especially want to thank the two excellent outside reviewers, Jack Goldsmith and Bob Keohane, who not only read the entire manuscript but gave me detailed and constructive (as well as unblinded) comments. I owe much as well to my long-time friend and mentor Anne-Marie Slaughter, who in this project, as in others, gave me excellent and comprehensive feedback and advice. I have immense respect for all these individuals, and their careful reads have made a major difference in the quality of this book.

Finally, I was fortunate to have a very able set of research assistants. Those who worked in part on this book include Ranee Adipat, Betsy Bennion, Lindsey Carlson, David Ginn, Wesley Gorman, Tom Hale, Michael Hughes, Justin Kachadoorian, and Venkatesh Vijayaraghavan. I am very grateful for their assistance. It goes without saying, but I will say it anyway, that any errors in the book remain my own. Most of all, I want to thank my wife, Lara Stemple, for her encouragement and support—not to mention her always-constructive commentary. I know she is as happy as I am to see this book completed.

CONTENTS

Does the Constitution Follow the Flag?

1

TERRITORIALITY IN AMERICAN LAW

In 1899 the English writer Rudyard Kipling penned a poem entitled "The White Man's Burden." The phrase is now famous, though few probably know that Kipling was its author. Fewer still know the full title: "The White Man's Burden: The United States and the Philippine Islands." Kipling published the poem to implore the United States, which had just defeated Spain in a war, to assume control of Spain's former colonies. By the end of the nineteenth century the United States had grown into an economic giant and had shown itself capable of vanquishing a once great European nation. Now, Kipling suggested, it was time to step into its natural role as an imperial power. His final verse made clear the stakes:

> Take up the White Man's burden—
> Have done with childish days—
> The lightly proferred laurel,
> The easy, ungrudged praise.
> Comes now, to search your manhood
> Through all the thankless years
> Cold, edged with dear-bought wisdom,
> The judgment of your peers!

Many Americans at the time agreed that victory in the Spanish-American War of 1898 demonstrated that the United States was now a world power of the first rank. Yet as the poem suggests, they were not entirely sure about ruling Spain's former colonial islands. Even if the United States did follow the lead of other great powers and build an overseas empire, it was unclear exactly how its colonies should be governed. Were the islands acquired from Spain subject to the same laws as ordinary American territory, or could the United

States rule offshore territories differently simply because they were offshore? In short, as contemporaries put the question, did the Constitution follow the flag?

This debate consumed the American public and elites alike. It became a central theme in the 1900 presidential contest between Republican incumbent William McKinley and Democratic challenger William Jennings Bryan. The Democratic Party platform emphatically declared an anti-imperial stance: "We hold that the Constitution follows the flag, and denounce the doctrine that an Executive or Congress deriving their existence and their powers from the Constitution can exercise lawful authority beyond it or in violation of it...Imperialism abroad will lead quickly and inevitably to despotism at home."[1] Lined up against this view were those who believed that legal rights were geographically limited and did not apply fully—or at all—beyond the states of the Union. For these individuals, America's sovereign borders were not the same as its constitutional borders. In short, they believed that the flag could be planted well out of reach of the Constitution.

At stake in this debate was the ability of the United States to participate in an age of great empires. As proponents of empire knew, if the Constitution indeed followed the flag, any American empire was going to remain very small. To govern distant Asian and Latin American colonies consistent with constitutional principles was widely thought to be out of the question. At stake as well was the self-conception of the United States as a constitutional republic. Was the United States like other great powers, all of whom had embraced imperialism? Or did the Constitution provide powerful limits on "despotic" rule that could not be circumvented simply by (re)drawing lines on maps and declaring some areas to be beyond the reach of the Bill of Rights?

Almost exactly a century after McKinley bested Bryan, ensuring the creation of an overseas American empire, the United States, in the wake of the September 11, 2001 attacks, transferred the first of what would become hundreds of suspected terrorists to the American naval base at Guantanamo Bay, Cuba. The base, itself a vestige of the Spanish-American War, was chosen in part because government lawyers believed it was beyond the reach of the federal courts.[2] In 2005 the *Washington Post* reported that the United States was also operating a secret network of detention centers abroad.[3] These "black-site" prisons were believed to be the site of highly coercive interrogation by the Central Intelligence Agency and were located, the *Post* said, in Eastern Europe.

The revelations about the clandestine prisons rocked Europe. The Bush administration had already faced severe criticism over the use of Guantanamo, and the extension of this policy of offshore detention inflamed key allies. At the same time Senator John McCain, himself a victim of torture during the Vietnam War, introduced a measure to bar cruel treatment by American officials anywhere in the world. The McCain Amendment stated that "nothing in this section shall be construed to impose any geographical limitation on the applicability of the prohibition against cruel, inhumane, or degrading treatment or punishment." In response, Secretary of State Condoleezza Rice declared that as a matter of policy, existing legal restrictions extended extraterritorially to "U.S. personnel wherever they are."[4] McCain's bill, however, sought to make this restriction legally binding.

The resulting furor over the propriety—or necessity—of cruel and degrading treatment of suspected terrorists obscured an important issue. Why exactly was the Bush administration flying suspected terrorists overseas in the first place? Was it because the executive branch could escape the bounds of American law by acting outside American territory? Critics in Europe and elsewhere were calling Guantanamo a "legal black hole," beyond the reach of American and international law.[5] Was Guantanamo really a lawless zone?

Geography matters for these questions because the organizing principle of modern government is *territoriality*. Territoriality refers to the organization and exercise of power over defined blocs of space.[6] At the core of contemporary statehood is the idea, often associated with the Treaty of Westphalia in 1648, that each sovereign state has its own discrete and exclusive territory. Under this view, legal rules and rights are generally seen as tied to territorial borders. The debates over whether the Constitution followed the flag to the Philippines, or to Guantanamo, are debates over whether, and if so how, the law of the United States is congruent with its sovereign territory.

As a governing principle, territoriality is so intuitive that we rarely question it. That states have borders, and that these borders determine the limits of their sovereign domain, is a widely accepted proposition in the modern world. Territoriality consequently lies at the core of most legal systems, including that of the United States. It is the most widely accepted form of jurisdiction.[7] Yet territoriality is not an inviolable principle, and domestic law is not always perfectly congruent with national borders. There are two fundamental ways that the connection between law and land can be stretched, or broken, both of which are extensively explored in this book. One occurs when domestic law extends beyond sovereign borders. This is commonly called *extraterritoriality*. The other, which is less well known, takes place when domestic law is restricted to certain national territory; in other words, when different areas within a sovereign state have distinct legal regimes. I call this *intraterritoriality*.

Asserting jurisdiction over an actor inside the territory of another state is an instance of extraterritoriality. For example, when the Supreme Court held in 1992 that insurance brokers in London were subject to U.S. antitrust law, it reinforced the (once controversial) principle that the regulatory power of the United States extends not just within the nation, but throughout the globe.[8] Extraterritoriality of this kind is common today; many domestic statutes, whether they relate to drug smuggling or stock market regulation, apply extraterritorially to foreigners and citizens alike. These laws aim to *police* activities that occur offshore, yet affect markets or individuals at home.[9]

Americans abroad have sometimes enjoyed another, more unusual form of extraterritoriality: the fictional *projection* of U.S. territory abroad. As a result of what were known as "capitulations," in the era before the Second World War Americans were shielded from local law in certain non-Western countries, such as China. They were instead subject to U.S. law, adjudicated by U.S. diplomats or judges. In a related fashion, many postwar treaties have guaranteed a regime of extraterritorial legal rights for U.S. military forces stationed abroad. In both these instances, domestic law was extended extraterritorially in order to insulate American citizens from foreign law.

Guantanamo involves a third type of extraterritoriality: the reach of constitutional rights. Whether the U.S. Constitution *protects* those who are outside American borders is at the core of the fracas over Guantanamo. Historically this question arose most frequently in the extraterritorial courts of the capitulation system. Did the Americans who were tried in a U.S. court in China have the same constitutional rights as Americans tried at home? Today it is clear that Americans are protected against the federal government by the Constitution when abroad, and so the question arises primarily with regard to the extraterritorial interrogation, detention, and trial of foreigners. Whether, and to what degree, the Constitution protects noncitizens abroad remains a vexing and uncertain issue.

Intraterritoriality, too, comes in different versions. One is very familiar to Americans: federalism, which divides the United States into fifty states and a federal government. From the perspective of international law these state lines disappear, but internally legal rules plainly differ from state to state. State law is not the focus of this book, however.[10] Instead, my interest is in the territorial scope of federal law. How and why federal law varies within the sovereign borders of the United States, as well as outside those borders, is a central topic in the chapters to come.

For example, it is relatively common for federal legislation that polices acts and actors within the United States to vary depending on location. Special legal rules apply to the District of Columbia, for instance, or to certain federal lands. In general, this form of intraterritoriality is uncontroversial. Much more controversial is whether constitutional rights also vary from place to place within the United States, or whether the Constitution inevitably and fully follows the flag. As we have seen, this question was at the heart of the fervent debate over American empire that arose a century ago.

This book makes two chief arguments about the geographic scope of American law, each of which I develop in more detail below. The first concerns extraterritoriality. Extraterritoriality has appeared in many different forms throughout history. All of these forms, however, exhibit a common theme: they are efforts to manage, minimize, or sometimes capitalize on legal differences. These legal differences are a direct result of the territorial basis of sovereign rule, which has been the organizing principle of the international system for centuries. To address the differences inherent in territorial sovereignty powerful states have long used various strategies, ranging from conquest to cooperation. Imperialism mitigated difference by colonizing foreign places; international agreements by consensually negotiating shared rules. Whether focused on policing, projecting, or protecting, extraterritoriality provides a kind of middle ground between these two extremes, enabling the United States to unilaterally manipulate legal difference so as to better serve its interests.

The second argument is that American law has long employed intraterritoriality as a way to facilitate the growth and power of the United States. The United States comprises a complicated mix of territory, including the fifty states, federal territories such as Puerto Rico, and "Indian country." Within the states constitutional rights apply fully. But throughout much of American history only a limited set of rights have applied in other U.S. territory. In other words, just as the map of American law is larger than the map of American territory—that is, some domestic law extends extraterritorially—the map of legal rights is smaller than the map of American territory. Intraterritoriality is in a sense a mirror of extraterritoriality. Extraterritoriality generally serves to mitigate difference. By contrast, intraterritoriality generally serves to establish difference.

Throughout the book I contend that we cannot understand the evolution of extraterritoriality and intraterritoriality in U.S. law without understanding the broader international context. American notions and doctrines of territoriality were themselves drawn from international law. Yet these notions and doctrines evolved over time to reflect American national interests. As the United States grew from a weak state to a global superpower, and as the nature of world politics itself changed, principles of both extraterritoriality and intraterritoriality have been transformed. Some territorial principles, however, have proven useful even in their original form even in the twenty-first century, and so remain robust, if increasingly anachronistic.

In short, in practice territoriality has neither been static nor treated as a given. Instead, it has been stretched and pulled over time in an effort to achieve national ends within the existing international order. When U.S. regulatory regimes and American firms were threatened by a more interdependent postwar economic system, for example, extraterritoriality was used to level the legal playing field. Likewise, when the U.S. government sought a freer hand when governing distant, foreign populations in places like the Philippines, intraterritoriality was used to limit the reach of constitutional rights. Legal "maps" have been drawn and redrawn even as sovereign borders remained unchanged.

The task of this chapter is to both introduce and explain these arguments and to lay a foundation for the rest of the book by summarizing the historical relationship between territoriality and sovereignty. What is sometimes called the "Westphalian system" is the basis of the contemporary sovereign state. The sovereign, territorial state has a long history in Europe, but for the rest of the world it was more common to be part of a larger empire. The international rules governing territoriality differed depending on what kind of state was involved. Among European sovereigns strict territoriality reigned and extraterritoriality was only very rarely permissible. Vis-à-vis other nations, by contrast, conquest and extraterritoriality were often legitimate and frequently utilized options.

To understand the evolution of extraterritoriality and intraterritoriality, therefore, we have to first understand the history of territorial sovereignty. This history is significant because American legal thought and doctrine drew deeply upon international rules and principles. Though presented only in broad brushstrokes, this history helps orient the remainder of the book. From territoriality came extraterritoriality; and from empire came both concepts of intraterritoriality and, eventually, the consolidation of Westphalian territoriality as the organizing principle of the entire world. After presenting this historical background I then lay out in more detail the chief arguments of the book. This chapter concludes with a brief overview of the remaining chapters.

Westphalia and the Rise of the Territorial State

Although many forms of political order have existed in times past, the dominant form today is the sovereign, territorial state.[11] There are few realistic alternatives to territorial governance in the realm of contemporary politics, and many theories of international politics assume that the territorial state is the only, or only significant, actor on the world stage.[12] Indeed, every existing state in the world today is territorial. In a sense this is true by definition: sovereign states are defined under international law as territorial entities. There nonetheless is a widespread belief today that territoriality is under siege. Some see the relentless rise of a borderless, globalized world that is dismantling traditional sovereignty.[13] In this supposedly "flat world," to use New York Times columnist Thomas Friedman's famous phrase, political boundaries matter little and economic and social forces move freely. Cyberspace is thought to even more directly challenge territoriality; some theorists argue that the Internet "radically subverts a system of rule-making based on borders between physical spaces . . . [and] territorially defined rules."[14] These claims contain elements of truth, but are strongly overstated. Sovereign borders still matter greatly for economic and political life. And territoriality even rules the virtual world; the Internet is subject to the control of sovereign states and increasingly "bordered" in its structure.[15]

The degree to which territoriality is loosening its grip is a topic that will arise in later chapters. Here it is sufficient to note that as a political reality, territorial governance remains robust and is remarkably total. Virtually every patch of ground on Earth save Antarctica is allocated to some sovereign state. States today generally accept the sanctity of these borders, even if occasional and sometimes violent disputes arise over their precise location within a riverbed or across a bay. And sovereign territoriality is enshrined in major international institutions, such as the United Nations. In short, there is "virtually universal recognition of territorial sovereignty as the organizing principle of international politics."[16]

Yet the world was not always neatly organized in this way. Many older systems of rule were not territorial at all.[17] The sovereign territorial state is essentially a European invention, but even in Europe it is only a few centuries old. Medieval Europe lacked sovereign, territorial states as we know them today. The medieval order instead comprised multiple, layered centers of political power as well as diverse sources of legitimation, allegiance, and identity.[18] Both secular and ecclesiastical forms of rule were important, and clearly demarcated borders that divided the various medieval rulers from one another did not exist.

One result was that a ruler's jurisdiction often overlapped with that of other potentates or joined noncontiguous areas. (Today we generally think noncontiguous territories, aside from islands, are anomalous and odd. Examples exist, such as Alaska or Kaliningrad, but they are rare.) Political authority in the medieval era was consequently "both personalized and parcelized within and across territorial formations."[19] More fundamentally, the idea that law was geographically bounded was only loosely accepted, if it was accepted at all. Indeed, it was a "well-established mediaeval idea that man took his own law with him when he went to strange lands."[20] Law was primarily tied to persons, not places.

The idea of law tied to persons rather than places dates back even further than the medieval period. As U.S. Supreme Court Justice Robert Jackson wrote in 1950, it "was old when Paul invoked it in his appeal to Caesar."[21] Influential early-twentieth-century English jurist J. L. Brierly noted decades before Jackson that the original conception of international law was personal. It was "only the rise of the modern territorial State that subjected aliens—even when they happened to be resident in a State not their own— to the law of that State. International law did not start as the law of a society of states each of omnicompetent jurisdiction, but of States possessing a personal jurisdiction over their nationals . . ."[22] Roman law, for instance, theorized that foreigners exist under a separate legal system, the *jus gentium*, rather than the *jus civile* of Roman citizens.[23] After the fall of the Roman Empire, and the rise of feudalism in Europe, the blending of territorial and personal notions of jurisdiction in international legal doctrine became greater.

The important point is that this complicated system of governance and authority began to change in the seventeenth century. To understand later changes in American law, we must understand how the United States adopted and understood the system of territorial sovereignty that prevailed by 1776.

The Treaty of Westphalia in 1648, which brought to a close the bloody Thirty Years' War in Europe, is generally seen as the central milestone in the shift to territorial sovereignty. Much of the Westphalian peace was devoted to reallocating land among minor Northern European princes. (The lasting significance of this aspect of the Westphalian settlement is limited, though some 3 centuries later Adolph Hitler complained in *Mein Kampf* about the treaty's territorial divisions of what is now Germany.) Of far greater consequence was the recognition and entrenchment of important principles about sovereignty and territorial rule. The Westphalian conception of statehood was revolutionary in that it drew all legitimate political power into a single sovereign who controlled absolutely a defined territory and its associated population. After Westphalia "the preeminence of the principle of territoriality in public international law became gradually entrenched in Europe."[24] The sovereign now had exclusive authority to enforce the law within that territory. Jurisdiction based on personality declined, and "the theory that a person who moved to another territory did not carry his personal laws with him, but became subject to the laws of that territory," gained support.[25]

In the Westphalian system, then, political borders clearly defined *outside* from *inside*. As John Marshall, the first chief justice of the United States Supreme Court, summarized the core principle in the early nineteenth century, "the jurisdiction of the nation within its own territory is necessarily exclusive and absolute. It is susceptible of no limitation not imposed by itself."[26] Again, this form of territorial sovereignty is an ideal, not a reality: as later chapters will make clear, the personal law of the medieval period was never fully extinguished, and the territorial sovereignty of many states was sometimes violated by stronger powers.

Scholars today debate whether the Treaty of Westphalia actually represented such a sharp break with the governance systems of the past. Many contend that its importance and novelty are overstated or misconstrued. Aspects of Westphalian sovereignty existed before Westphalia, pre-Westphalian principles and practices continued afterward, and some aspects of Westphalian statehood were not consolidated until late in the eighteenth century.[27] As far back as 1555, for example, the Treaty of Augsburg introduced the principle of *cujus regio, ejus religio*, which held that each ruler determined the religion in his land. This principle was an important steppingstone to the creation of territorial sovereignty, because it allocated power over religion to a ruler, and divided that power territorially. Likewise, the rise of capable and independent city-states in Italy and Northern Europe also helped create the proto-territorialist view that "certain places could be more or less immune from the authority structures that dominated elsewhere."[28]

Consequently, it is fair to say that territoriality did not arise suddenly with the Treaty of Westphalia. The set of agreements and understandings encompassed by the phrase *Westphalian* nonetheless flagged an important if imprecise shift in world history. It did so both by seconding and reinforcing the principles of the earlier Augsburg treaty, and by reorganizing the political map of Europe and building on the practices of the early city-states. Although imprecise like much shorthand, Westphalia has thus become a useful marker for a new political order within Europe, an order that eventually spread throughout the globe.

The distinctive feature of Westphalian statehood, in short, is that it divides the world into mutually exclusive territorial entities. (As a result, I will often refer to *Westphalian* or *strict* territoriality to signify the idea of mutually exclusive territorial control.) Westphalian territoriality, in turn, provided the bedrock principles for the development of modern international law. Writing in the 1950s, political scientist John Herz argued that from territoriality

> resulted the concepts and institutions which characterized the interrelations of sovereign units, the modern state system . . . only to the extent that it reflected their territoriality and took into account their sovereignty could international law develop. For its general rules and principles deal primarily with the delimitation of the jurisdiction of countries. . . . Sovereign units must know in some detail where their jurisdictions end and those of other units belong; without such standards, nations would be involved in constant strife over the implementation of their independence.[29]

What Herz is saying in this passage is that once sovereignty in the sense of supreme, final authority became a core attribute—or ideal—of statehood, it was necessary to define clearly where one sovereign's authority began and another's ended.[30] Territorial borders provided this definition.

The animating vision behind the shift to territorial division was stability and peace. Europe in the seventeenth century was plagued by bloody wars of religion. The Thirty Years' War had killed an astonishing 30 percent of the population of the continent. Clearly demarcating one sovereign from another, and giving each absolute authority within a circumscribed territory, minimized the potential for violent conflict—though, as history illustrates, it by no means eliminated it. Territoriality also provided an efficient way of communicating the authority of a sovereign, and of enforcing sovereign power. It was an effective "geographic strategy to control people and things by controlling area."[31]

From the seventeenth century onward territoriality became increasingly dominant in Europe, even as other dimensions of sovereignty were altered. For example, the French and American revolutions and the rise of nationalism reoriented ideas of sovereignty away from a discrete, individual sovereign—a king—and toward a particular people that enjoyed a shared (or sometimes constructed) history, culture, and language.[32] The rise of popular sovereignty did not, however, alter the fundamentally territorial nature of the Westphalian sovereign state. Arguably it reinforced it; as the English historian Eric Hobsbawm argues, "the equation nation = state = people, and especially sovereign people, undoubtedly linked nation to territory, since the structure and definition of states were now essentially territorial."[33]

Westphalian sovereignty also endorsed the view that states were juridically equal. Many thinkers have analogized states to individuals, arguing that a small state was no less sovereign than a large state.[34] Others have grounded sovereign equality in reciprocity. For example, F. H. Hinsley argued that "a state which claims to be free of limit and control within its community is bound in logic to concede the same freedom to other states in theirs."[35] However justified, sovereign equality is today an ideal of long standing. Sovereign equality becomes important in the context of legal doctrines concerning extraterritoriality, which were later (though not always) applied to strong states as readily as weak states.

Sovereignty is also a "ticket of general admission to the international arena."[36] Once a state is recognized as sovereign, it can conclude international agreements, engage in armed conflict, and so forth. Perhaps most attractively, sovereignty provides a sort of shield for states against influence by outsiders. In reality, of course, states are routinely influenced by events beyond their borders, and in the contemporary world their domestic laws and practices are increasingly subject to scrutiny by the outside world.[37] The acceleration of interdependence in the postwar era and the ascendancy of international human rights law have made this abundantly clear even for the most powerful states. But as a formal matter, under traditional Westphalian principles, no other sovereign state can legitimately intrude into the internal territory of another. This idea reached its zenith in American law in the late nineteenth century.

Embassies and Extraterritoriality

The sharp territorial distinctions created by this new conception of territorial sovereignty posed some challenges. One was how sovereign states would communicate with one another. Well before 1648 rulers had exchanged ambassadors. But because one consequence of the Westphalian revolution "was an increased emphasis upon the supremacy of national law, not merely over the natural born subjects of the king, but over all who dwelt within the limits of the territorial state, irrespective of their nationality," it was necessary to develop a set of legal principles governing the rights and privileges of ambassadors when they arrived in a foreign state.[38]

Ambassadors were, after all, representatives of other coequal sovereigns. To subject them to the rule of another sovereign appeared to elevate one sovereign over another. Yet as individuals residing within the territorial limits of a sovereign, under the Westphalian system ambassadors ordinarily would fall under the jurisdiction of that sovereign. The international law of ambassadors, which emerged from this quandary, reflected the juxtaposition of the functional need for emissaries with the supreme power within a defined area assumed by Westphalian territoriality.

The solution to this quandary was an idea central to this book: extraterritoriality. "In an effort to preserve the sanctity of the rights of embassy," writes one historian, "the fiction of exterritoriality [*sic*] was gradually and unconsciously built up."[39] In effect, embassies became small plots of foreign territory projected into the domain of the host state. Sovereigns would "assume or pretend that the ambassador and the precincts of his embassy stood as if on the soil of his homeland, subject only to its law."[40] These special extraterritorial zones allowed each sovereign to maintain their territorial sovereignty, while simultaneously enabling interaction between them. Akin to a medieval traveler, the ambassador's home law traveled with his person.

Consequently, in many respects the development of extraterritoriality was an outgrowth of Westphalian territoriality. As Garrett Mattingly writes in his definitive history of Renaissance diplomacy, referring to the Treaty of Augsburg's then-novel principle that a sovereign determined the religion of his domain, "By arrogating to themselves supreme power over men's consciences, the new states had achieved absolute sovereignty. Having done so, they found that they could only communicate with one another by tolerating within themselves little islands of alien sovereignty."[41] By the American Revolution this approach was well established. In the 1812 case of the *Schooner Exchange v. M'Faddon*, for instance, the Supreme Court noted that the world was "composed of distinct sovereignties, possessing equal rights and equal independence." But, the Court asserted, for reasons of practicality "all sovereigns have consented to a relaxation in practice, in cases under certain peculiar circumstances, of that absolute and complete jurisdiction within their respective territories which sovereignty confers."[42]

As later chapters will detail, the concept of extraterritoriality was eventually extended well beyond the case of the ambassador. The longstanding practice of extraterritorial jurisdiction over the nationals of Western powers who resided within "uncivilized" nations (about which I will say more in a moment) mimicked the ambassadorial approach but applied it to ordinary citizens. Much later, during the Cold War, the concept was applied to nearly all American offshore military forces. Likewise, extraterritoriality was eventually extended to the police powers of the state, as in the practice—embraced by the United States in the postwar period—of asserting jurisdiction over foreign actors for their acts that cause harm at home. Whether (fictionally) projecting domestic territory into other sovereign's domain or policing offshore activities that have transboundary effects, extraterritoriality has proven a useful tool for states eager to assert or maintain control over persons and actions beyond their borders.

Until the postwar era, however, extraterritoriality among acknowledged sovereigns was limited to the necessary case of ambassadors. Non-Western states like China and Morocco were subjected to other forms of extraterritoriality, but among the Western powers territoriality was respected. Indeed, by the nineteenth century the territorial nature of sovereignty was unquestioned. As a leading authority on international law wrote, reflecting the prevailing views of the era, each sovereign state "possesses and exercises exclusive sovereignty and jurisdiction throughout the full extent of its territory... No state can, by its laws, directly affect, bind, or regulate property beyond its own territory, or control persons that do not reside within it, whether they be native-born subjects or not."[43] This view was well established in the United States as well as in Europe. Indeed, strict territoriality "prevailed as dogma for most of American constitutional history."[44]

The Age of Empire

As this discussion suggests, despite being central to the international order, for a long time sovereignty applied only to a small set of nations. Sovereignty was fundamentally a European construct. In the nineteenth century, and even into the twentieth, the European powers generally did not consider non-Western polities to have met the prevailing "standard of civilization." In this regard, the United States was an exception; as a land of European settlement, governed by white Christians, it was treated as a sovereign state from 1776 onward. Sovereignty and territoriality became applicable to many societies around the world, however, only after a long and often violent process of colonization and decolonization.

The dominant political form in most of the world before the twentieth century was empire. Territorial conquest was not unique to the European encounter with the rest of the world; within Europe, states would often acquire territory from one another as a result of military victory. But although European states might gain or lose bits of territory in war, as France and later Germany did with Alsace-Lorraine, the game was still played among sovereigns. Outside Europe, things were different. Given the great disparities in military power between the European powers and the local groups they encountered, territorial conquest and imperial rule were often decisive and lasting.[45]

The first wave of European empire building occurred in the sixteenth and seventeenth centuries, and led to the establishment of the vast Spanish, Portuguese, French, and British empires. By 1830, however, many of these colonies were free, in particular those in the Western Hemisphere. The United States was the most prominent, but Haiti, many of Spain's Latin American possessions, and Brazil also became independent in this period. In the late nineteenth century a new wave of European imperialism took place. This wave was swifter and more total than the first. For example, in the century before 1880, new colonies were formed at the rate of five per decade; after 1880, the rate of colony formation rose to twenty per decade.[46] By the end of the nineteenth century most of Africa and much of Asia had been partitioned by the European powers. These vast empires coexisted with the high point of strict territoriality among Western sovereigns.

In Jared Diamond's famous words, "guns, germs, and steel" supplied the Europeans' overwhelming power advantage.[47] But internally, an ideological and legal framework for imperialism permitted European states to square their commitment to sovereignty with their thirst for colonies.[48] What was known as the "standard of civilization" kept outside the circle of sovereign states most non-Western political entities. A non-European state could be deemed civilized only if its internal legal structure resembled those in Europe—if, in essence, a foreigner in that state would be treated in roughly the same manner he or she was accustomed to at home. Over time, a few nations successfully "civilized," as Japan did just before World War I. But such cases were rare, and the distinction between civilized and uncivilized states was in practice very important.

The standard of civilization was grounded in race, history, and culture, but it was also grounded in the international law of the day. Alternatively, one could say that international law was grounded in the standard of civilization. International law was conceived by Europeans to be the shared law of civilized states; it was an "intrasociety" rather than international or interstate law. For example, a leading international law treatise of the nineteenth century asked rhetorically, "Is there a uniform law of nations? There certainly is not the same one for all the nations and states of the world. The public law, with slight exceptions, has always been, and still is, limited to the civilized and Christian people of Europe or to those of European origin."[49] This view made it easy for empire to coexist with Westphalian territoriality and to become a viable and even valorized form of rule. Today, by contrast, no political entity openly declares itself to be an empire, though some, such as China and Russia, retain the look and feel of traditional empires. (Many critics say the same about the United States, though for different and usually more metaphoric reasons.)[50]

Empire also had important implications for the geographic reach of legal rules. Empire served, as did extraterritoriality, as a means to minimize or negate legal difference across countries. This minimization of difference in turn served to better achieve the national interest of the conquering state. Controlling a foreign territory directly as a colony offered legal certainty in comparison to the vagaries of arms-length trading. Thus Britain sought to rule India in part because India, vast as it was, "was a captive market that could not be trusted with self-rule lest tariffs follow in its wake...Lancashire industry and British rule in India were thus bound together by an extraordinary symbiosis."[51] Likewise, for commercial endeavors involving foreign direct investment, imperial rule provided greater certainty of property rights than did arms-length relations between rulers.

This is not to say that empires possessed uniform legal systems; rather, "geographical differentiation is critical to empires."[52] Metropole and colony were often legally distinct, with separate rules and rights. The key point is that those legal differences relevant to the interests of the conqueror could be minimized via conquest; other legal differences, which might benefit the conqueror, could be retained or created. This pattern was certainly true of the United States. As later chapters will describe, in the American experience the tensions between imperialism and constitutionalism helped develop and cement constitutional doctrines that reflect what I have called intraterritoriality. Intraterritoriality entailed the differentiation of legal rights and privileges within sovereign borders of the state, differentiation that corresponded to location, distinguished core from periphery, and, ultimately, aided the growth and exercise of American power.

Intraterritorial distinctions, in turn, provided a foundation for differentiating the constitutional rights that protected overseas Americans from the constitutional rights that protected overseas aliens. From the geographic differentiation inherent in empire, in other words, we can trace, albeit unevenly, a route to the American naval base at Guantanamo Bay and the "legal black hole" it has come to represent around the world.[53]

"Extrality" and Informal Empire

Despite the prevalence of empire, the West did not colonize all weaker nations.[54] In some cases, such as the Ottoman Empire, there was a long history of European traders operating within another independent civilization.[55] Similarly, Western powers could not, or chose not to, subdue and rule China, Thailand, or Japan. Instead, they sought alternative ways to accommodate their growing desire for commerce with their need for order and security for their citizens abroad. "Unequal treaties," sometimes known as capitulations, were commonly negotiated in the nineteenth century to solve this problem. These agreements coupled open trade to extraterritorial rights for sojourning Westerners.[56] Nations like China abhorred these coercive treaties, rightly seeing their extraterritorial provisions as a humiliation, but they lacked the power to resist.

The unequal treaties generally had three elements: unilateral most-favored-nation clauses, a lack of tariff autonomy for the non-Western partner, and what was known as consular jurisdiction for Westerners. Unilateral most-favored-nation clauses ensured "equality in exploitation": whatever rights one Western power received had to be granted to all.[57] Restrictions on tariff autonomy ensured that goods could move in and out freely. Consular jurisdiction was perhaps the most unusual feature of these treaties. It referred to extraterritorial jurisdiction by foreign diplomatic officials, or consuls. These consuls adjudicated both criminal and civil matters involving their citizens abroad.

The United States and most other Western powers established this form of extraterritorial jurisdiction widely in the Islamic world and throughout Asia. The aim was to ensure that Westerners—mostly traders but also government officials, missionaries, and various drifters—did not have to obey unfamiliar and "barbaric" laws and negotiate arcane legal systems when in places like Shanghai or Constantinople.[58] Here we circle back to the extraterritoriality pioneered for ambassadors; much like ambassadors in "ordinary" sovereign nations, citizens of Western powers in Asia and the Middle East enjoyed a form of extraterritorial protection. Extraterritoriality provided a way for Western citizens to reside outside the West yet enjoy near-total immunity from local law.[59] As in the Middle Ages, law followed persons rather than places.

"Extrality" as it was colloquially known at the time, reached its apogee at the turn of the twentieth century. In some rare instances Western powers even created international zones (as in the case of Tangier) or international settlements (as in the case of Shanghai). These were areas carved out and administered directly by the foreign powers. The International Zone of Tangier, for example, was remarkably elaborate, with some 150,000 inhabitants, a legislative assembly, and an independent legal system with judges drawn from an array of Western states.[60] As later chapters will detail, in the years before World War I the American presence in China became so large that Congress went so far as to create a U.S. District Court for China that sat in Shanghai.[61] This extraterritorial American court lasted until the 1940s.[62] Hence for almost a century American citizens, whether missionaries or merchants, were not subject to Chinese law, but instead to an odd array of American laws.

The Consolidation of the Territorial State

Imperialism and unequal treaties were central to the international order in the centuries before 1945. Paradoxically, it was through imperialism that Westphalian territoriality slowly and unevenly spread to the rest of the globe. As former colonies became independent they often assumed the attributes of sovereign states. Over time, the number of such newly independent states grew, with the vast majority of the world's states becoming sovereign in the massive wave of decolonization that occurred after the Second World War. In an unraveling of remarkable swiftness the great Western empires came apart, and from some 50 member states in 1945 the United Nations encompassed over 150 by 1980. This unprecedented tripling of the world's states in little more than four decades represented the consolidation of Westphalian territoriality on a global scale.

Many factors lay behind this transformation in governance. By the Versailles Settlement of 1919 it was plain that the normative backdrop that fostered imperialism had begun to change. Notions of self-determination and democracy had gained sufficient strength that empires, capitulations, and international zones were all on the wane. Woodrow Wilson's famous Fourteen Points, of which point 5 called for "free . . . adjustment of all colonial claims, based upon a strict observance of the principle that in determining all such questions of sovereignty the interests of the populations concerned must have equal weight with the equitable claims of the government whose title is to be determined," garnered great attention, putting further pressure on the European powers to begin relinquishing their empires. And the increasingly powerful United States, which possessed only a small overseas empire but a giant manufacturing base, made clear during the Second World War that the postwar international order was going to be very different with regard to imperialism. Soon the old imperial preference schemes, which discriminated against trade with areas outside an empire, began to be dismantled.

But it was hardly ideas or American pressure alone that changed the nature and role of empire. Military and economic changes after 1945 affected the will of great powers to control contested territories as well as their ability to do so. Militarily, the control of large territories "decreased in value as a security asset. As the world moved to bipolarity and the Cold War, and as nuclear weapons and advanced weaponry changed the modes of warfare, imperial reserves of troops and resources became less important for the great powers."[63] The economic value of overseas territories also declined, though the causal relationships are complex. The resurgence of a liberal economic system meant that states could increasingly trade for what they once acquired through possession. Technological change added further pressure; as the economies of the Western democracies became less resource intensive, and more information and innovation intensive, the incentives for direct imperial control faded still further.

Whatever the cause, by 1945 a new age had arrived. The charter of the new United Nations endorsed the concept of sovereign equality, declared respect for the principle of equal rights and self-determination, and protected from interference those "matters which are essentially within the domestic jurisdiction of any state." The result was a system aimed at stabilizing the international order, limiting conflict, and protecting the sanctity of Westphalian territoriality. In this context the dismantling of European empires gathered speed, and in a soon only scant remnants—Gibraltar, Puerto Rico, French Polynesia—remained. Yet decolonization was not just about the end of direct territorial rule. As British historian John Darwin notes, it instead represented "the demolition of a Europe-centred order in which territorial empire was interlocked with extraterritorial 'rights.' The bases, enclaves, garrisons, gunboats, treaty ports, and unequal treaties . . . that littered the Afro-Asian world were as much the expression of this European imperialism as were the colonies and protectorates coloured red, blue, yellow, or green on old imperial maps."[64]

In sum, empires and extraterritoriality were closely linked. Both were transformed by the events of the twentieth century. And together, they played a striking and somewhat counterintuitive role in the legal regime of Westphalian territoriality that has prevailed over the last several centuries. On their face, both seem straightforward violations of the core notion of exclusive territorial sovereignty. Indeed, extraterritoriality appeared to be a vestige of the personal, status relations that marked law in the feudal era.

Yet these practices also reinforced the centrality of sovereignty and territory to the Westphalian conception of the state. States that were truly sovereign—that met the standard of "civilization" decreed by Europeans—did not permit extraterritorial courts on their territories. The nonwhite, non-Christian countries that accepted, or were forced to accept, extraterritorial courts were considered to be outside international society and hence outside the realm of international law. Although atavistic, empire and extraterritoriality reinforced the norm that among juridical equals, at least, Westphalian territoriality prevailed. It was this complex set of views that formed the basis, as the next chapter will describe, of the early American approach to territoriality.

Extraterritoriality and Intraterritoriality in American Law

This brief history of territoriality and extraterritoriality has stressed several important points: the rise of territoriality as the core organizing principle of sovereign statehood; the resulting incentives to develop various forms of extraterritoriality; the centrality of imperialism to the evolution of extraterritoriality and intraterritoriality; and the eventual consolidation of Westphalian territoriality around the globe in the postwar era. This summary omits many significant details, but it provides an essential foundation for the more extensive discussion of American understandings of territoriality in the chapters to come. With this framework in mind, in the remainder of this chapter I develop the major arguments of this book.

Extraterritoriality and the Minimization of Difference

The extraterritorial jurisdiction created by the capitulations so common before the Second World War was neither a historical quirk nor a mere expression of power. Extraterritoriality was instead a way to control and manage the interests of Western powers in foreign lands. Like empire, it was both a reaction to and a stimulus for rising interdependence in a world of disparate legal systems. When Western powers could not (or chose not to) conquer an alien land, they frequently used extraterritoriality to foster trade and protect their citizens. This form of extraterritoriality was certainly coercive—the unequal treaties were called capitulations for a reason—yet they fell well short of conquest and colonization. The aim was far narrower: to insulate Western citizens from the allegedly barbaric and bizarre legal systems of nations like China.

This insulation permitted Westerners to gain access to the riches of these societies without submitting to unwanted legal risks. Indeed, many of the unequal treaties of the era specified that extraterritorial rights were to be abandoned if adequate legal reform took place. An 1883 treaty between Korea and Great Britain, for instance, stated that "the right of extraterritorial jurisdiction over British subjects in Corea [sic] granted by this Treaty shall be relinquished when, in the judgment of the British Government, the laws and legal procedure of Corea shall have been so far modified and reformed . . . "[65] Following the same principle, when a European power assumed rule over an area deemed uncivilized, it typically suspended the extraterritorial privileges accorded to nationals of other Western powers.[66] Legal harmonization civilized and thus destroyed the basis for extraterritoriality.

Extraterritoriality was, in short, a strategy to manage and minimize legal difference. Absent legal difference, it had no role. In essence, it projected a small realm of domestic law into a (weaker) foreign power's territory as a way to inoculate one's citizens against the strange, the different, and the dangerous.

Seen this way, extraterritorial jurisdiction is really one of several strategies sovereign states historically have pursued to structure their relationships with alien powers. Empire was an extreme strategy—territorial conquest allowed the imperial power to control the foreign society and usually create whatever legal system it desired. The creation of extraterritorial consular courts was a more narrowly targeted approach that simply facilitated the presence of foreign nationals and the associated commerce (and proselytizing) they engaged in. The United States's use of such courts was thus not aberrational, but rather part of an established practice by great powers. The creation in 1906 of the U.S. District Court for China, discussed in depth in later chapters, was an unusually institutionalized version of this strategy, but was also not unprecedented.

During the Cold War both unequal treaties and empire largely disappeared as ideals of sovereign equality, and self-determination took root. The postwar management of difference instead occurred through other pathways, some of which existed prior to 1945 but which became much more significant after 1945. The best known is the use of international institutions. After the war, an intricate and dense web of international treaties and their associated international organizations served to harmonize or minimize legal difference via negotiated agreements.[67] States bargained over shared rules, replacing heterogeneity with some measure of homogeneity. Likewise, the development of transnational networks of national officials, who use the tools of modern communication and transportation, has served in the postwar era to coordinate and harmonize domestic policies in more flexible ways.[68]

These two forms of postwar difference management—treaties and networks—have been widely studied and analyzed. What is less commonly acknowledged is that extraterritoriality is, *mutatis mutandis*, a third strategy. Though dead in its traditional form of extraterritorial jurisdiction in uncivilized nations, extraterritoriality reappeared in the postwar world in two new guises, both developed and employed extensively by the United States. The first was the "status of forces agreement," or SOFA, and the second was "effects-based" regulatory jurisdiction.

The extensive postwar use of SOFAs grew out of America's dramatic postwar rise as a hegemonic power. Seeking for the first time a permanent global military presence, the American military retained or established hundreds of bases around the world aimed at containing the growing Soviet threat and protecting vital American assets and allies. Accompanying these forward bases were extraterritoriality agreements for American armed forces members. These SOFAs, many of which remain in force today, typically decree that certain infractions committed by American military personnel fall under the jurisdiction of U.S. military courts rather than local courts. Even when local courts take command of an investigation or trial, some special rules may apply for specified American personnel. Like "traditional" extraterritoriality, this form projected not only American law but American legal institutions into the domain of another state.

The agreement with Japan, for instance, for a long time required the U.S. military to hand over American service members to Japanese authorities only after they were charged with a crime, a right that Japanese citizens do not enjoy. Other SOFAs are similar. In form, these accords very much resemble the extraterritoriality obtained via the unequal treaties of the nineteenth century, though they are less sweeping in scope—only members of the armed forces are covered—and more narrow in the legal insulation they provide. Due to the vast postwar presence of overseas American troops, however, many more individuals have been subject to extraterritoriality under SOFAs than had been subject to traditional extraterritoriality via the unequal treaties. The importance of SOFAs continues today; the most contentious example is the high-profile negotiation, just completed at the end of 2008, between Iraq and the United States. At the heart of the conflict was the question of extraterritorial jurisdiction over American troops and contractors.[69]

Postwar extraterritoriality also took the form of regulation aimed at policing extraterritorial acts and actors. Indeed, the extension of domestic economic, environmental, and other regulatory laws to overseas acts and actors is what most lawyers today think of when they hear the word *extraterritoriality*. Like the SOFA, this form of extraterritoriality was novel. Throughout its history the United States had refrained from regulating acts that occurred in the territories of other sovereigns, consistent with the reigning principle of strict territoriality. Nineteenth-century lawyers believed it was a violation of sovereignty to assert jurisdiction in this manner.

In the postwar era, however, the United States began to routinely police foreign actors who somehow affected American markets or other domestic interests. Postwar courts (as well as Congress and the executive branch) embraced this more expansive understanding of jurisdiction, which, as I will describe in later chapters, advantaged an economically dominant state such as the United States. At the heart of the new approach was the concept of transboundary effects. If some act overseas affected American markets or interests, that effect gave rise to jurisdiction.

Effects-based extraterritoriality was unilateral and often conflictual. It was aimed not at weak or allegedly uncivilized states but largely at the Western allies of the United States. And it was based on statutes, not treaties. Like the outpouring of new international institutions after 1945, effects-based jurisdiction reflected the burgeoning growth of the regulatory state as well as the rise of extensive economic interdependence in the West. Absent a thick web of regulation at home, there was little cause to extend state power abroad. Absent interdependence, there were few effects to justify claims of extraterritorial jurisdiction.

SOFAs, capitulations, and the effects doctrine all illustrate a central point. Over the course of American history the practice of extraterritoriality has shifted in form but not function. The Westphalian paradigm purposefully granted each sovereign exclusive control over its domain; the very point of the rule of *cujus regio, ejus religio* was to align religious differences spatially—Catholics here, Protestants there—and therefore compartmentalize them. When sovereigns interact, however, these differences in domestic law become apparent and often prove costly, and the costs of the barriers grow as interdependence grows. As America's place in the world system changed, and as that system itself changed, territoriality and extraterritoriality were manifested in new ways. There is, nonetheless, an underlying logic to these extraterritorial practices. As in the past, extraterritoriality today typically flattens the legal differences that are fundamentally embedded in Westphalian territoriality.

Intraterritoriality and the Constitution

Throughout American history citizens and leaders have debated not only the geographic reach of the law that *polices* individuals, but also the reach of the law that *protects* individuals. That federal criminal and regulatory laws applied throughout the sovereign territory of the United States has never been in doubt. (Whether this policing function could reach outside the borders of the United States, as just discussed, was a more contentious story.) Most vexing of all has been the territorial reach of the constitutional rights that protect individuals against the federal government.[70] Is the map of the United States and of the Bill of Rights identical? Or are there gaps, where the United States rules but the Constitution does not reign?

Whether there are internal demarcations with regard to legal rights is a question of *intraterritoriality*. (Whether these rights extend abroad is a question of extraterritoriality.) Intraterritorial distinctions were at the heart of the debate over the acquisition of overseas colonies in 1898, the episode that gave rise to the title of this book. But similar questions arose about federal territories on the mainland, such as the Northwest Territory. The same was true of lands controlled by Indian tribes, who were often referred to by the Supreme Court as "domestic dependent nations" and yet were sometimes treated like foreign sovereigns. As a matter of international law, the sovereignty of the United States over all these areas was and remains uncontroverted; what was at issue was whether there were internal borders that determined where (and how) the fundamental laws of the United States applied.

In the infamous antebellum case of *Dred Scott* the Supreme Court declared that constitutional rights, including the right to property, followed the flag into any and all American territories. (The issue was slavery, though the principle enunciated had broader implications.) Many earlier cases, however, had suggested otherwise, and by the post–Spanish-American War *Insular Cases*—the series of decisions by the Supreme Court in the early twentieth century regarding Puerto Rico, the Philippines and other distant island possessions—the Court had rejected the reasoning of *Dred Scott* in favor of a "fundamental rights" approach. The *Insular Cases* held that, aside from certain fundamental rights that always applied within American territory, Congress possessed the power to determine what rights applied to what territory within the borders of the United States.

Rather than apply everywhere in equal measure, in other words, like water filling a canyon, U.S. law has differed depending on place. Throughout American history there has been a core in which all constitutional rights have applied and a periphery—federal territory, occupied enemy lands, Indian country, and the like—in which only a subset applied. These intraterritorial distinctions helped to ensure that the liberal regime of rights that distinguished American constitutionalism at home did not overly hobble or inhibit American interests abroad. They generally gave flexibility to the executive branch, enabled American expansion, and fed the global growth of American power.

Questions of intraterritoriality also fed into questions of extraterritoriality. The long-standing belief that constitutional protections did not apply extraterritorially was bolstered by judicial decisions entrenching intraterritorial distinctions. If the Bill of Rights did not fully apply within the United States, many reasoned, surely it did not fully apply outside the United States either. Thus the *Insular Cases* enabled American empire by limiting the reach of the Constitution.[71] They also became essential elements in later rulings that preserved some traditional territorial limitations on constitutional rights.

Whether the Constitution followed the flag, in other words, not only had meaning for America's formal empire—the narrow but highly significant question at the heart of the *Insular Cases*—but also for the projection of U.S. military and police power in the postwar era. Consider the vast, informal postwar empire of military bases established to project American power around the globe. These bases were full of U.S. citizens, both members of the armed forces and civilians. It was easy to believe that constitutional rights did not apply to these Americans overseas if some of those same rights did not apply even within U.S. territory.

In the 1950s, however, the Supreme Court rejected this view and expanded the extraterritorial reach of the Constitution. Today it is well accepted that the Bill of Rights protects U.S. citizens against their government wherever those citizens might be found. Despite this change, however, older intraterritorial precedents have never been expressly overruled. The strange result is that American citizens enjoy the full protection of the Bill of Rights if they are tried by the U.S. government at a military base in Japan. But they may not if they are tried by the government in the federal territory of Puerto Rico.[72]

More puzzles exist. The *Insular Cases* declared that the Constitution only partly followed the flag to certain offshore colonies of the United States. Is Guantanamo Bay akin to these colonial possessions, or is it more like a foreign base leased from Germany? More profoundly, do any constitutional rights protect foreigners overseas? This last question is not only germane to the struggle against al Qaeda and other terrorist groups; the widespread deployment of American law enforcement officials overseas in recent decades raises it on a regular basis. Contemporary courts have grappled, for example, with the question of whether a foreigner interrogated in a foreign city by the FBI has the right to remain silent in an interrogation, or whether the Fourth Amendment's restrictions on search and seizure apply to non-citizens abroad as well as at home.

Each of these issues, which are discussed in later chapters at length, implicates the relationship between law and land. The detention of foreign nationals at Guantanamo is certainly the most famous contemporary example. But as the Supreme Court noted in the 2008 case of *Boumediene v. Bush*, in which it declared that the right of habeas corpus applies to foreign detainees held at the island base, Guantanamo has many unique attributes that render it virtually U.S. territory. The larger issue is whether the Constitution controls the actions of American officials when they act outside of land over which the United States is sovereign or, as in Guantanamo, de facto sovereign. Does the right of habeas corpus, or to receive *Miranda* warnings, apply in Bagram Air Base in Afghanistan as well?[73] What about the streets of Karachi or Rome? These questions, which appear with increasing frequency in the twenty-first century, force us most dramatically to interrogate the assumptions and traditions of Westphalian territoriality.

Shaped by War and Trade

Throughout the pages that follow I stress the central role of international relations in shaping the evolution of territoriality in American law. Of particular importance is the changing role of the United States within the international order: the implications of its rise from a nation on the fringe of world politics to a hegemonic "hyperpower" with global ambitions and reach.

The growing power of the United States had two major, relevant effects. First, power promoted expansion, and expansion helped to entrench doctrines of intraterritoriality. Forced to reconcile its constitutional past with its great power future, the United States looked to intraterritoriality as a way to limit the costs of the former so as to better realize the latter. Second, power emboldened the United States to exercise extraterritoriality not only within weak societies—such as China and Morocco—but also within other Western powers. This shift was in turn facilitated by important changes in world politics itself, most notably the "complex interdependence" that increasingly characterized the states of the West during the Cold War.[74]

Both these claims sound in a long-standing, though hardly dominant, tradition of political inquiry that looks to the international plane to explain the domestic plane. In the 1970s Peter Gourevitch famously argued that "political development is shaped by war and trade."[75] Not only are political movements and cleavages explicable in terms of international pressures and norms, he suggested, but domestic institutional development is often a product of global forces. Using the jargon of international relations theory, which views the relationship between domestic factors and world politics as the "second image," Gourevitch surveyed what he called the "second image reversed."[76] It is easy to see, for instance, how the rise of Nazism within Germany helped spawn the Second World War. The "second-image reversed" perspective looks in the opposite direction to show how systemic pressures not only drive states to adopt certain foreign policies—this is a fundamental tenet of realism—but also shape their internal structures and politics in profound ways.

Outside of a few obvious areas such as trade politics, most studies of American development have nonetheless failed to seriously consider the significance of the global context. Students of U.S. politics "continue to pay nearly exclusive attention to domestic institutions and policies."[77] Likewise, few works of legal history directly explore how international forces have shaped the development of American law. Nonetheless, like domestic politics, domestic law is often subject to powerful pressures from abroad. This point is most apparent when one considers the impact of the remarkable growth of American power over two centuries. As a young and vulnerable state, the United States of the eighteenth and early nineteenth centuries was naturally drawn to Westphalian principles. Sovereignty was seen as a crucial shield, and exclusive territorial control a bulwark against foreign invasion and influence. Even as the United States grew into an economic giant after the Civil War, it took a cautious approach with regard to other great powers and in regions outside the Western Hemisphere.

As the United States harnessed its latent power at the turn of the twentieth century, however, it began to play a much more formative role in world politics.[78] Westphalian doctrines in turn grew less appealing, becoming nettlesome obstacles to the projection of American power and ideals. New and sometimes controversial forms of extraterritoriality better served the interests of the United States. These new forms were pioneered in the 1940s, a time when the United States wielded unparalleled political, military, and economic resources.

Yet it was not just that the United States went from weak to strong state; it was that the evolution of the international system itself altered the incentives and constraints the United States faced. Postwar effects-based extraterritoriality illustrates this dynamic well. The effects doctrine pioneered by American courts permitted the government and private litigants to police foreign actors whose acts created harmful effects within the United States. American firms were increasingly interested in competing on world markets, and they (and responsive federal regulators) sought to ensure that their foreign competitors faced similar regulations. A rapidly reintegrating world economy highlighted the growing disjuncture between national laws and global markets. Empire was an unrealistic and undesirable strategy to diminish legal difference. But extraterritoriality and international treaty making were attractive solutions that the United States in particular made vigorous use of.

Meanwhile, other international changes created a more permissive environment for extraterritorial claims by the United States. As I have discussed, in the nineteenth century such claims were viewed as dangerous incursions into another sovereign's domain. Yet by the 1950s the United States had embraced extraterritoriality, even when aimed at other great powers. Partly this reflected American hegemony. Yet the postwar order was also more forgiving of such incursions: the dramatic decline of territorial warfare, the onset of the Cold War, and the intricate institutional enmeshing of the Western powers stand in stark contrast to the endemic great power conflict and imperialism of the nineteenth century. In this new, more interdependent context the United States had little fear of serious conflict with its allies. As a result, although postwar assertions of extraterritoriality were greeted with alarm by America's allies, there was no longer much concern that they would harm elemental political relationships.

These specific claims, and analogous ones, will be developed in chapters to come. The key point here is simply to flag the central importance of the United States's rise to power within the international order. Absent careful attention to the global context, we cannot understand the unusual evolution of territoriality in American law.

Outline of the Book

This introductory chapter has laid the theoretical and historical foundation for the story of territoriality in the United States told in the next six chapters. Chapter 2 commences with an investigation of the constitutional design of 1789. Westphalian territoriality provided the template for the new nation. Yet the early decades of the United States presented a wide range of interesting territorial questions, some related to expansion—such as the constitutionality of the Louisiana Purchase—and others to military occupation and control. One of the most infamous judicial decisions of the era was *Dred Scott*, which raised the central question of the reach of the Constitution's prohibitions into the federal territories. In general, the early and antebellum periods illustrate the power of ideas of *strict territoriality*, which were present in a host of legal domains. But these periods also marked the early articulation of intraterritorial distinctions as the United States expanded westward.

Chapter 3 picks up the thread after the Civil War and focuses on two chief developments: the burgeoning establishment of extraterritorial courts in Eastern societies and the dramatic move to imperialism occasioned by the Spanish-American War of 1898. The most interesting extraterritorial court was the remarkable U.S. District Court for China. The China court, which answered to the Ninth Circuit Court of Appeals, heard thousands of cases over its history. Chapter 3 also looks closely at the *Insular Cases*, the group of two dozen early-twentieth-century rulings on the constitutionality of empire and the legal rules governing American colonies. These rulings definitively grounded the idea of intraterritoriality, and their principles continue to cast a heavy shadow over contemporary debates.

Chapter 4 turns to the mid-twentieth century and explores the decline of strict interpretations of Westphalian territoriality and the rise of effects-based extraterritorial jurisdiction in an age of rapid economic change. Effects-based jurisdiction was first applied by the United States in the context of antitrust law, but quickly spread to other regulatory laws, a broad area that, by the 1950s, had become centrally important to domestic legal systems throughout the developed world. It is here that the newly dominant United States most rattled contemporaries by unilaterally bending traditional territorial doctrines in new ways.

The postwar era also witnessed another novel form of extraterritoriality, the status of forces agreement. The Cold War witnessed an unprecedented global deployment of U.S. military forces. This story is the heart of chapter 5. American forces abroad, numbering in the hundreds of thousands, were typically shielded from local law by agreements that shared some features of the nineteenth-century capitulations. This remarkable deployment also brought many American civilians and dependants overseas, leading to one of the landmark territorial decisions of the twentieth century and the first ever articulation of the principle that constitutional rights protect Americans beyond U.S. borders as well as within them.

How broadly this principle of extraterritorial constitutional rights applied is a central concern of chapter 6. That American law could police acts abroad was increasingly accepted in the postwar era. At the same time, however, whether American law also protected actors abroad became increasingly contested. In this period a wide range of U.S. law enforcement agencies began to work offshore, tracking the rise of transnational criminal networks, global drug markets, and other aspects of the "dark side" of globalization. This push toward overseas policing forced the federal courts, increasingly solicitous of defendants' rights in the 1960s, to consider just where the Bill of Rights stopped. A few lower courts upheld the extraterritorial application of constitutional rights for foreign nationals. But in 1990 the Supreme Court ruled otherwise, casting significant doubt on the idea that the Constitution's protections had global application.

Chapter 7 brings the story back to our own era with an exploration of territoriality in the twenty-first century. The 9/11 attacks and the resulting armed conflicts in Iraq and Afghanistan have led to a range of territorial quandaries, including the law applicable to private military companies working overseas for the United States. The best-known quandary concerns the rights of foreign detainees held at Guantanamo, a detention center chosen precisely because it was thought to be beyond the reach of the federal courts—a question that nonetheless has come before the courts time and again in the first decade of the twenty-first century. The Supreme Court's landmark decision in *Boumediene v. Bush* undermined much of the basis of this policy but left many questions undecided. The detention and interrogation of suspected terrorists in offshore sites has forced U.S. courts and officials to consider anew whether, and to what degree, the Constitution followed the flag.

Chapter 8 brings these varied threads together by exploring more deeply the arguments laid out in this chapter and considering some of the other pressing issues at stake in the debate over the geographic ambit of American law. Territoriality in many ways remains vibrant, but it is also in undeniable tension with an increasingly interdependent world. The offshoring of government activities—exemplified by Guantanamo—has surfaced this tension in ways not witnessed since the early-twentieth-century debates over the Constitution, the flag, and the nascent American empire. Nearly a decade into the twenty-first century, the United States remains caught between its constitutional traditions and its global ambitions.

In Recent Years offshore prisons and trials have become signature strategies of the United States, made more attractive to the government by the continuing power of territoriality. At the same time, however, aspects of territoriality have undergone substantial change. Many things unknown a century ago, such as subjecting firms in foreign countries to domestic regulation, are now commonplace.

Indeed, in the 1990s political scientist John Ruggie famously argued that territoriality was becoming "unbundled"—that it was ceding ground, as it were, to functionally-defined modes of political authority such as the European Union that transcend the Westphalian territorial paradigm.[79] Crude versions of this view are increasingly commonplace as globalization accelerates and challenges traditional territorial concepts. Thus a globalized world has hyperbolically been said to be a borderless, or "flat," world.[80] The Internet, thought to be the harbinger of a radically nonterritorial form of community and governance, has likewise led to claims (even more overheated) of the demise of territoriality.

Globalization, the Internet, and even the rise of international human rights law have certainly made the legal differences among sovereign states more legible. By forcing states to engage their respective differences—whether through economic competition, negotiations over new norms, or jurisdictional conflict—these processes have highlighted the many barriers and differences among states.[81] They have led to conflict over national rules, which has in turn accelerated the development of international treaties, institutions, and networks. Yet these are not the only ways to reconcile legal differences across nations. The extraterritorial extension of domestic law has many attractive features, not least that it requires some market presence by outsiders but little assent from other governments. Hence it is a particularly useful strategy for a hegemonic and wealthy power in a relatively peaceful world.

As this suggests, the relationship of the United States to territoriality in recent decades is deeply influenced by its anomalous and outsized global role. Some observers suggest that the contemporary world has undergone a "Westphalian flip," in which the United States enjoys a quasi-monopoly on the use of force internationally and other states are increasingly subject to international scrutiny over their domestic domains.[82] If so, extraterritoriality will prove only more attractive in years to come. Indeed, the United States may well have achieved, in historian Charles Maier's words, "a postterritorial ascendancy—one in which it seems to transcend fixed borders and can project power, exert influence, and enjoy prestige far beyond traditionally bounded jurisdictions."[83] Along the way, however, the United States has had to grapple with the degree to which its fundamental legal commitments, as well as its military, criminal, and regulatory powers, reach beyond its borders. That story is the focus of this book.

2

TERRITORY AND THE REPUBLIC

The American Revolution birthed a new nation that, although small and weak, would eventually come to dominate world politics. The events of 1776 foreshadowed a range of future rebellions by peoples who chafed under imperialism and sought ultimately to control their own political destiny. In North America, as in the many independence movements since, the rebels aimed to do so by claiming and defending a distinct territory and declaring themselves a new state.

The American Revolution was unusual, however, in that the new United States did not simply occupy territory that had been previously ruled by an existing Westphalian sovereign. The United States was instead surrounded by a vast expanse of land largely ungoverned (in the view of Europeans) by any other political entity. The nation began as thirteen colonies on the Atlantic coast, but over the next two centuries it enlarged its territory dramatically through a combination of conquest, purchase, and treaty. This story is central to American history, and the "extraordinary geographic expansion of the United States is critical to understanding the rise of the nation as a world power and global empire."[1]

This chapter explores how the concept of territoriality was manifested and interpreted in early American law. The founding generation "was intensely interested in the geographic extent of the American polity."[2] How was this intense interest manifested? In what ways were established ideas about Westphalian territoriality reflected in the new Constitution? What legal questions did geographic expansion raise? In short, this chapter explores how eighteenth- and early-nineteenth-century Americans understood and interpreted the links between sovereignty and soil.

For several reasons the United States is particularly interesting in this regard. Federalism entails a central distinction between state and federal territory. For most of American history federal territory was substantial in size and, in large part due to conflicts over slavery, highly charged politically. How, if at all, constitutional protections differed in the states versus the territories was a question that would over time foment dramatic debate. The United States also contains many Indian tribes. Indian lands were incorporated through both treaty and conquest, and American constitutional law has long treated the native tribes as semiautonomous and even sovereign in some respects. The existence of tribal land adds another layer of complexity to territoriality in the American experience. And though born of rebellion against colonial rule, the United States itself embarked on an imperial adventure at the close of the nineteenth century. Vestiges of that imperial effort persist to this day, and they continue to pose hard questions about the geographic scope of legal rules. Each of these features—federalism, the presence of Indian nations, and imperialism—raised quandaries about the relationship between territoriality and sovereignty for a nation committed not only to prevailing ideas about Westphalian statehood, but also to the rule of law, inalienable rights, and limited government.

In the main, the early American republic hewed closely to the Westphalian vision of territoriality mapped out in the previous chapter. Sovereign jurisdiction was treated as exclusive and congruent with demarcated political borders. This idea was reflected in a wide array of legal doctrines and judicial decisions, which drew on international law frequently and emphasized the limits posed by sovereign borders. This jurisdictional congruence was particularly true of the nineteenth century.[3] Consequently—notwithstanding some important anomalies—the era can reasonably described as one of "strict territoriality."

The early history of the United States also illustrates an important distinction between external, sovereign borders and internal, constitutional borders. What this distinction meant was that territory unequivocally under U.S. control was nonetheless not always subject to the full sweep of U.S. law, particularly constitutional law. These intraterritorial distinctions proved very important and arose time and again in the nineteenth century.

"Free and Independent States"

The Declaration of Independence famously proclaims several truths to be self-evident. But it also declares the former British colonies to be free and independent states. As such, the Declaration asserts that "they have full Power to levy War, conclude Peace, contract Alliances, establish Commerce, and to do all other Acts and Things which Independent States may of right do."[4] This feature—that the new North American state(s) had the power to perform all "Acts and Things which Independent States may of right do"—reflects the profound ways in which the founding generation drew on prevailing conceptions of sovereignty and international law in creating their new nation.[5]

The acts the Declaration refers to were the acts of sovereign states, as defined by the international law of the time. In other words, the colonists sought to create a sovereign entity akin to, and equal to, those that existed in eighteenth-century Europe. They assumed that the United States would possess a defined territory, the borders of which other sovereigns would respect, and that it would control absolutely governance within that territory. Territorial sovereignty was thus the model upon which the framing generation based their aspirations.

Europe largely reciprocated. The 1783 Treaty of Paris, which ended the Revolutionary War, declares that "his Britannic Majesty acknowledges the said United States . . . to be free sovereign and independent states."[6] As this passage suggests, at the time it was thought by some that each of the thirteen colonies was an individual sovereign state, though in general, as in the Treaty of Paris itself, the discrete colonies let the central government handle foreign affairs. (Indeed, the peace treaty of 1783 is not between Britain and thirteen American states but rather between Britain and "the United States.") Among themselves, however, the colonies placed great importance on their independence from one another. As a result, many believed that the situation in North America could, without careful attention, come to resemble the power politics that characterized eighteenth-century Europe.[7] Alexander Hamilton, for example, warned in *Federalist 13* that "the entire separation of the States into thirteen unconnected sovereignties is a project too extravagant and too replete with danger to have many advocates."[8]

Hamilton was probably right. After the dismal experience of the Articles of Confederation, in which each colony had substantial autonomy and the central government only quite limited and feeble powers, the 1789 Constitution was drafted. The division of sovereignty between the states and the federal government consumed substantial attention. But the constitutional framers also considered the role of territoriality in the new political order. Their understanding of the role of territory in structuring sovereign power surfaced in several ways.

First, the Constitution presupposes a territory—it is a constitution for a Westphalian state. More specifically, it makes two express references to territory. The Territory Clause declares that: "The Congress shall have the Power to dispose of and make all needful Rules and Regulations respecting the Territory or other Property belonging to the United States. . . . " At the time only a small part of the vast territory to the west of the Atlantic coast belonged to the United States. The framing generation feared that, but for the creation of a well-ordered union, this terrain might well become "an ample theater for hostile pretensions."[9] As I discuss later in this chapter, the Territory Clause became central to disputes over whether the Constitution followed the flag into federal territory. "Though noticeably terse when it comes to territorial acquisition and governance," the Constitution also creates a mechanism for expansion.[10] The second reference to territory, Article IV, declares that "New States may be admitted by Congress into this Union." This process had a precedent in the Northwest Ordinance of 1787, and was used frequently over the next two centuries as the United States grew from 13 to 50 states. The assumption for much of American history was that federal rule under the Territory Clause was temporary, even if, as in the case of Oklahoma, the transition from federal territory to state might take a century or more. (That assumption, which also dates to the Northwest Ordinance, would be rebutted in the *Insular Cases*, discussed in the next chapter.) A geographically delimited "seat of government" over which Congress has exclusive governance powers.—the federal District of Columbia—was also created by Article I.

The Constitution contemplates its reach beyond American territory in more subtle ways. Article I grants Congress the power "to define and punish Piracies and Felonies committed on the High Seas," implying some degree of jurisdiction beyond the U.S. territorial borders. By definition, the high seas are not within any state's sovereign domain. Piracy was a serious problem at the time of the American founding, and international law permitted states to exercise what today would be called *universal jurisdiction* over pirates.[11] Universal jurisdiction meant that all states had the power to capture and try pirates found on the high seas. The important point here is that in allocating this power to Congress, the Constitution acknowledges that Congress's powers—and the enforcement powers of the United States—may reach beyond American territorial borders.

Later amendments also implicated the geographic dimensions of legal jurisdiction. The Thirteenth Amendment, enacted after the Civil War, declared that "[n]either slavery nor involuntary servitude . . . shall exist within the United States, or any place subject to their jurisdiction." Likewise, the Eighteenth Amendment, enacting Prohibition, banned the sale, manufacture, export, and import of liquor within the United States, as well as in "all territory subject to the jurisdiction" of the United States. Later disputes debated what the precise scope of these prohibitions was: did they extend to American ships on the high seas, or foreign ships in American waters?

Thus early American elites paid substantial attention to territoriality. And as judicial decisions from the early nineteenth century show, they fully grasped and incorporated into their jurisprudence the core principles of Westphalian territorial statehood described in chapter 1. In 1812, for instance, in the case of *The Schooner Exchange v. M'Faddon*, Chief Justice John

Marshall provided a pithy summary of ideal typic territorial sovereignty: "the jurisdiction of the nation within its own territory is necessarily exclusive and absolute. It is susceptible of no limitation not imposed by itself."[12] This statement was typical of the era, and the case law of the time is replete with analogous phrasings. Such absolutist language about territoriality was unsurprising. Like many new and weak states throughout history, the United States was drawn to a strict interpretation of the principles of Westphalian sovereignty. The freedom from external control that strict territoriality entailed was attractive given the new American state's structural position in the international system. America was weak, and there were many European powers that could credibly threaten to intrude on the domestic domain of the United States.

The United States was particularly concerned by the prospect of incursions by the major hegemonic power of the day, Great Britain, which remained present just to the north of the new nation. Secretary of State John Calhoun's statement in 1844, meant to ward off British interference in criminal matters, was emblematic:

> We hold that the criminal jurisdiction of a nation is limited to its own dominions and to vessels under its flag on the high seas, and that it cannot extend it to acts committed within the dominion of another without violating its sovereignty and independence. Standing on this well-established and unquestioned principle, we cannot permit Great Britain or any other nation . . . to infringe our sovereignty and independence by extending its criminal jurisdiction to acts committed within the limits of the United States.[13]

As the relative power of the United States grew, of course, the nation would change course, and increasingly favor extraterritorial jurisdiction and intervention abroad as a way to enhance its political and economic interests. By the middle of the twentieth century the United States and Great Britain had reversed roles; it was now America that was seen as the infringer, the overweening power bent on imposing its domestic law on others, and Britain that protested and filed *demarches*.

The nonintervention principle inherent in Westphalian territoriality was thus very attractive to the early United States. And the corollary principles— that the United States could not impose its own rule within the territory of other sovereigns, for instance—were not especially troubling. At the time, the only groups likely to suffer at the hands of the United States were Indian tribes. Although the Indians were in some cases militarily formidable, they lacked Westphalian sovereignty under the international law of the time.

In short, territoriality and expansion were central issues in the early history of the United States. Robert Kagan goes so far as at argue that "inducements to expansionism were embedded in the new republic's legal and institutional structures."[14] Whether territorial acquisition was truly in the nation's DNA from the start, it is clear that many Americans saw expansion as not only desirable but inevitable. Indeed, no less a figure than John Quincy Adams wrote, with regard to European claims over the rest of North America, that "it is a physical, moral, and political absurdity that such fragments of territory, with sovereigns at fifteen hundred miles beyond sea, worthless and burdensome to their owners, should exist permanently contiguous to a great, powerful, enterprising, and rapidly-growing nation."[15] Adjacent territories would inevitably be absorbed as the United States grew. How this expansion would comport with the American constitutional order was less clear.

Manifest Destiny and Territorial Expansion

In the nineteenth century the power to conquer territory was, as a matter of international law, a power possessed by all sovereign states. The United States claimed the right of conquest as a natural corollary of its sovereign status. It also claimed the related right of discovery, which, though central to earlier European imperial efforts, was decreasingly important as the globe gradually became fully mapped and governed. Perhaps the most famous American articulation of the discovery principle was by the Supreme Court in the 1823 case of *Johnson v. M'Intosh*.[16] In that case, which addressed a dispute over land title, Chief Justice Marshall surveyed the prevailing international legal doctrines relating to territorial acquisition.

According to Marshall, whose history was already questionable at the time he wrote, among the "great nations of Europe" "discovery gave title to the government by whose subjects, or by whose authority, it was made, against all other European governments . . . the exclusion of all other Europeans, necessarily gave to the nation making the discovery the sole right of acquiring the soil from the natives."[17] As this passage reflects, international law at the time was a law among nations, and the nations that counted were Christian, European powers. The law of discovery operated only vis-à-vis Europeans. The "natives" were left outside the system.

The United States, being a white Christian nation, was plainly civilized by the standard of the day. Consequently, Marshall argued that this legal rule applied to the United States after independence from Britain. America "maintain[s], as all others have maintained, that discovery gave an exclusive right to extinguish the Indian title of occupancy, either by purchase or by conquest . . ."[18] Yet despite this seemingly straightforward proclamation by the Supreme Court, in the early 1800s serious doubts persisted about the constitutional status of territory acquired by the United States, whether through conquest, discovery, or purchase. The fact that European powers might have generally understood international law to bestow rights of discovery and conquest on sovereign states did not in itself resolve questions about the *constitutionality* of acquisition by the United States. An early exemplar of the debate over the legality of acquisition—indeed, it precedes the decision in *Johnson v. M'Intosh* by nearly two decades—was the 1804 Louisiana Purchase.

The Louisiana Purchase was and remains the largest addition to the territory of the United States. The acceptance of Napoleon's offer to sell Louisiana seems in retrospect to have been an unimpeachable decision. Even at the time American leaders "from every region of the country and representing every political stripe shared a common belief that most if not all of North America, including Canada, Mexico, and the islands of Cuba and Puerto Rico, formed the 'natural' dominion of the United States."[19] At the same time, the republican vision of many early American elites was predicated on the virtues of small, well-connected communities.[20] This alone made the acquisition of the vast Louisiana territory politically problematic. But there were legal concerns as well. Indeed, then-president Thomas Jefferson was dubious that the Constitution permitted such a purchase. As he wrote to a close friend, "The general [federal] government has no powers but such as the constitution has given it; and it has not given it a power of holding foreign territory, and still less of incorporating it in the Union. An amendment of the constitution seems necessary for this."[21]

Within the executive branch the constitutionality of territorial expansion was hotly debated. Some in the cabinet disagreed with Jefferson's skepticism. They argued, prefiguring Marshall's words some 20 years later in *Johnson v. M'Intosh*, that under international law the United States had an inherent right to acquire territory, just as any sovereign state did. But Jefferson was initially unpersuaded, for this did not really address the question of whether American law allowed the purchase. Jefferson went so far as to draft two alternative constitutional amendments that would have clarified the legality of the purchase. He nonetheless recognized that amending the Constitution was a difficult endeavor and one probably not— at least as a political matter—necessary. Indeed, Jefferson ultimately placed pragmatism and the quest for American geopolitical power over any legal qualms he had. As he wrote at the time, "the less that is said of my constitutional difficulty, the better . . . It will be desirable for Congress to do what is necessary in silence."[22]

The legal and political issues that arose with regard to Louisiana would afflict later acquisitions of overseas territories, such as the acquisition of the Philippines and other former Spanish colonies in the early twentieth century. And as was true of the Philippines, many in the early nineteenth century thought that the inhabitants of Louisiana were intellectual and cultural inferiors who could not be trusted to rule themselves in accordance with republican principles. Jefferson himself told Congress that the local Creoles were such a childlike people that "our principles of popular government are utterly beyond their comprehension."[23] Here we see an early articulation of the tension between global ambition and constitutional tradition. We also see the articulation of a position that would later prove critical to the development of intraterritorial distinctions: the idea that certain peoples, because they lacked the skills and habits necessary to participate in a liberal constitutional order, were perhaps best ruled by the United States as subjects, rather than citizens.

To be sure, the debate over the constitutionality of territorial acquisition faded quickly after 1804. Indeed, the United States went on to acquire Florida from Spain in 1819. Shortly after this the Supreme Court spoke directly to the constitutionality of expansion, stating emphatically that "the Constitution confers absolutely on the government of the Union, the powers of making war, and of making treaties; consequently, that government possesses the power of acquiring territory, either by conquest or treaty."[24] By the 1850s Congress even authorized the acquisition of uninhabited high seas "guano islands"—islands (often mere rocks) with large guano, or bird dropping, deposits, which were valuable at the time as a source of fertilizer. Amazingly, some seventy such far-flung islands were acquired by the United States under this act.[25]

With the constitutionality of territorial expansion settled, several ancillary but nonetheless deeply important questions arose repeatedly in the nineteenth century. What would the citizenship of the inhabitants of new territories be? Could the nation absorb large populations of other races and languages? And, most relevant for this book, did the Constitution bind the government within new territories, and if so, how?

The last question was the most nettlesome and contentious. In broad terms, two chief camps existed in the nineteenth century. Some looked to the state-centric orientation of the constitutional text, as well as the explicit creation of the District of Columbia outside of any state, to argue that the Constitution, in particular its protections, had no meaningful applicability beyond the defined territory of the states. The states were, in other words, constitutionally distinct from the federal territories. Others, such as Marshall, believed that the Constitution applied throughout the sovereign territory of the United States, including states, territories, and the District of Columbia.[26] "Our great republic," Marshall contended in a decision from 1820, "is composed of states and territories. The District of Columbia, or the territory west of the Missouri, is not less within the United States than Maryland or Pennsylvania."[27] But even proponents of this more expansive position could not resist drawing an intraterritorial line somewhere, and for much of American history the Indians were on the wrong side of it.

Indian Country

North America was hardly empty when the first Europeans arrived. The international legal doctrines of discovery and conquest, and of *terra nullius*, were used to justify and entrench forcible control over Indian lands. The questions of native sovereignty and rights had nonetheless bedeviled European legal theorists for some time, starting with the Spanish jurists Vittoria and De Las Casas.[28] The Indian polities the Spanish encountered, for example, satisfied some essential criteria of sovereignty as it was then understood in international law. By the mid-nineteenth century these criteria had shifted, and the prevailing "standard of civilization" in international law excluded any polity that lacked European-style laws and political structures from recognition as a fellow sovereign state. But before the nineteenth century this concept had not yet arisen in its full form. Why then were the Indian tribes not treated as sovereign states? "The general answer was that sovereignty implied control over territory"—and territorial control was something the Indians often appeared to lack.[29]

That said, the fledging United States often negotiated agreements with Indian tribes and, in many instances, the federal government recognized that Indians possessed a form of sovereignty as well as property rights in their land. This was reflected in the fact that settlers frequently purchased land from Indians in the years before the Revolutionary War, as in the famous, if somewhat apocryphal, sale of Manhattan to the Dutch for twenty-four dollars in trinkets.[30] This practice of recognizing some version of Indian property rights continued after the war of independence, though acquisition of property by Americans became more coercive: the Indians had largely sided with the British in the war, and this fed opposition to Indian land rights of any kind. Indeed, the newly independent American colonies tried to claim that the Indians had lost all rights to their land as a result of the war. In 1783 the Continental Congress sent an emissary to the major Indian nations to announce this new state of affairs. "As we are the conquerors," he declared to the assembled leaders, "we claim the lands and property of all the white people as well as the Indians who have left and fought against us."[31]

Reality and statecraft, however, quickly intruded. The United States found it convenient to continue to sign treaties with tribes concerning territorial control, and private citizens continued to purchase land from Indians. The uncertain legal status of the tribes led to a concomitant unclarity about the status of their territory. Was Indian territory within American borders foreign or domestic, or something in between? Indian nations were plainly not organized like European states; yet, just as the Spanish had discovered much earlier, they were hardly unorganized groups of individuals either.

The early-nineteenth-century Supreme Court case of *Cherokee Nation v. Georgia.* is emblematic of these quandaries. The case arose because the Cherokees had resisted various power and land grabs by the state of Georgia; one Cherokee, Corn Tassel, was then captured by Georgia in Cherokee territory and executed. The tribe argued that Georgia's acts violated the various treaties the Cherokees had with the United States. In *Cherokee Nation* the Supreme Court first took up the question of whether the tribe was a "foreign state." This issue was crucial; if the Cherokees were not a foreign state the Supreme Court did not have jurisdiction over the case. The question was not an easy one. Indian tribes had been treated as akin to foreign states since the settlement of America by whites. The many treaties with the tribes, said the Court, "recognize them as a people capable of maintaining the relations of peace and war." Moreover, the "acts of our government plainly recognize the Cherokee nation as a state."[32] So as a matter of practice it was clear that, for the most part, the tribes had been treated *as if* they were sovereign states.[33]

That said, the Cherokees, like all Indian tribes in North America, were plainly different from other Westphalian sovereigns, such as France or England. As the Court noted,

[t]he condition of the Indians in relation to the United States is perhaps unlike that of any other two people in existence. In general, nations not owing a common allegiance are foreign to each other ... But the relation of the Indians to the United States is marked by peculiar and cardinal distinctions which exist no where else. The Indian territory is admitted to compose a part of the United States. In all our maps, geographical treatises, histories, and laws, it is so considered. In all our intercourse with foreign nations ... [Indians] are considered as within the jurisdictional limits of the United States ... They occupy a territory to which we assert a title independent of their will.[34]

The Indian tribes, in other words, lacked essential characteristics of territorial sovereignty. Tribal territory was American territory as far as the outside world was concerned. As the opinion stressed, "in all our maps" it was "so considered." These facts made abundantly clear that Indian land was, vis-à-vis the outside world, American land. "As a state," wrote another justice in a concurring opinion, the Cherokee "are known to nobody on earth, but ourselves, if to us; how then can they be said to be recognized as a member of the community of nations?"[35] In short, the Indians were not a foreign state. Two justices of the Supreme Court, one of them the famed jurist Joseph Story, dissented from this position. Their disagreement hinged on a core conceptual question: What is the essential nature of a state? Quoting the eminent eighteenth-century Swiss philosopher Emerich de

Vattel, the dissenters argued that under the law of nations the term *state* referred to a group of persons that governs itself without any dependence on a foreign power. Connection to a greater power did not matter; "[t]ributary and feudatory states do not thereby cease to be sovereign and independent states, so long as self-government and sovereign and independent authority are left in the administration of the state."[36] In short, for the dissenters self-determination was the key to statehood, and the Cherokees possessed self-determination. Hence they were in fact a foreign state. The majority in *Cherokee Nation* did not necessarily disagree that the tribes possessed self-government—after all, they called the tribe "a distinct political society." But that, they believed, was insufficient. A state possessed territorial sovereignty; the Cherokees did not.

A year later the Supreme Court faced a very similar situation in *Worcester v. Georgia*. This time, however, the plaintiff was a white missionary, arrested by Georgia for residing on Cherokee land without a license from the state. Samuel Worcester's argument closely tracked that in *Cherokee Nation*. The Supreme Court couched the issue as one of extraterritoriality. "The extra-territorial power of every legislature being limited to its own citizens or subjects, the very passage of this act is an assertion of jurisdiction over the Cherokee nation . . . "[37] In saying this, the Court was underscoring the importance of Westphalian territoriality: a state could not act beyond its sovereign borders, save only with regard to its own citizens. Certainly it could never act within another sovereign's domain. The Court then argued that the Cherokee Nation was like a sovereign state in some respects. The tribe possessed "territorial boundaries, within which their authority is exclusive" and controlled the land they lived on. Moreover, "the treaties and laws of the United States contemplate the Indian territory as completely separated from that of the states."[38] As a result, the laws passed by Georgia could not reach into Cherokee territory. They were extraterritorial in nature and, therefore, invalid.

How was it possible that the Cherokee Nation was a state for some purposes but not for others? Though it might appear so, the justices in *Worcester* were not directly overruling their decision a year earlier in *Cherokee Nation*. Rather, they were muddling toward a position that the tribes were neither fish nor fowl, but instead something unique. In *Worcester* they were primarily concerned with establishing the power of the federal government over relations with the Indians (and keeping the states out of Indian affairs). But to construct a ruling that kept Georgia's law out, the Supreme Court had to stress the state-like qualities of the tribes.

At the same time, the sovereignty of Indian tribes was decidedly not Westphalian. Thus despite language stressing the exclusive authority of the Cherokee Nation, the federal government could intervene in Indian lands when it wanted. The bottom line seemed to be that Indian tribes were states as far as the power of other states of the union were concerned, but they were not states as far as the federal government's power was concerned. Read together, the two decisions enhanced the power of the federal government, and diminished that of both the tribes and the state of Georgia. Indeed, throughout history the United States has asserted—and the federal courts have supported—the notion that the power of the federal government over the tribes, like the power over federal territory generally, is "plenary."[39] Congress could, as a result, adopt a criminal code that applied to Indians and to others within "Indian country"; seize traditional native lands without just compensation; and even terminate the legal existence of a tribe.[40] Tribal sovereignty existed, but it was more vestigial than vital. Consequently, the tribes were, in an artful if obfuscating phrase from *Cherokee Nation*, "domestic dependent nations."[41]

What did this odd phrase mean? First, that the tribes were plainly located within American territory: they were *domestic* nations. But at the same time, Indian land was distinctive. Vis-à-vis other sovereign states, such as France or Britain, the tribal lands were sovereign American territory. Yet Indian territory was not—as a matter of domestic law—fully within the United States either. This was the "dependent nations" portion of the phrase. This puzzle—was Indian territory, inside the United States or outside?—would continue until the present day. And, as in so many other arenas, the United States would manipulate the distinction between inside and outside, between constitutional core and constitutional periphery, so as to suit its particular interests in a given dispute.

In 1884, for example, the Supreme Court faced a seemingly simple question: was an Indian, "merely by reason of his birth within the United States" a citizen of the United States?[42] The question referred to the Fourteenth Amendment, which states that "all persons born or naturalized in the United States and subject to the jurisdiction thereof" are American citizens. Enacted after the Civil War, the amendment is commonly understood to establish that American citizenship stems not from blood ties, but from the territorial location of one's birth. The antebellum case of *Dred Scott*, discussed below in this chapter, had infamously held that Americans of African lineage were not citizens. Hence the intent of this aspect of the Fourteenth Amendment was to reverse that ruling and establish that all those born within the borders of the United States were citizens, simply by virtue of the territorial location of their birth.

But was the clause intended to include citizens of foreign states who happened to give birth while on U.S. soil? Many thought not; that interpretation was endorsed in the 1872 *Slaughter-House Cases*, in which the Supreme Court announced that "[t]he phrase, 'subject to its jurisdiction' was intended to exclude from its operation children of ministers, consuls, and citizens or subjects of foreign States born within the United States."[43]

Nonetheless, it would seem clear that any person who was not a foreign citizen and was born within the sovereign borders of the United States necessarily was an American citizen. And *Cherokee Nation* had made it clear that the Indian tribes were indeed within U.S. sovereign borders. Putting these two cases together, it seemed clear that Indians were natural-born citizens.

Yet the Supreme Court held that Indians born on American soil were not citizens. Once again the justices struggled to draw lines around the tribes, lines that simultaneously placed them inside and outside the United States. The Court again declared that "the Indian tribes, being within the territorial limits of the United States, were not, strictly speaking, foreign states." They were, however, "alien nations, distinct political communities."[44] Indians were thus within the United States for some purposes, but not for others. As this saga illustrates, even in the era of "strict" territoriality, territoriality was not truly strict. Indians were plainly born within the geographic borders of the United States, but they nonetheless fell outside the bounds of the Fourteenth Amendment.

In any event, as the military power of the United States grew, the federal government no longer feared the tribes. By 1849 the Bureau of Indian Affairs was transferred out of the War Department and into the Interior Department. And soon the United States ceased negotiating treaties with Indian tribes altogether. In debating the issue in 1871 a senator from California noted that "eighty or a hundred years ago, perhaps, when there were great confederated nations upon our borders, not entirely on soil owned by ourselves, we might [negotiate treaties] with them in order to keep peace; but now the whole thing is changed. We have absorbed the whole of the territory over which they roamed; it now belongs to us, not to them."[45] Today tribal sovereignty continues to exist more in name than deed. When useful, the tribes have been considered coequal sovereigns, as when the Supreme Court ruled that prosecution by a tribal government and the federal government does not constitute double jeopardy.[46] But more frequently tribal sovereignty has been treated as something that operates vis-à-vis tribal members, if at all. This conception of sovereignty is, in Westphalian terms, truly anomalous.

Governing the Territories

The relentless territorial expansion of the United States in the nineteenth century not only wiped out Indian tribes; it quickly became an object of struggle between the North and South. Any new territory inevitably had to be allocated to be either "slave" or "free." Hence, for much of the antebellum era territorial expansion was intimately tied up with the struggle over slavery.[47] Territorial expansion also raised complex questions about American law and its territorial scope, questions that were not unrelated to slavery though they sounded in broader themes of constitutionalism. The fundamental issue, as always, was where—if anywhere—the geographic limits of the legal system rested.

Many of the controversies triggered by territorial expansion stemmed from a distinction between the rules of international law and those of constitutional law. As a matter of international law, all territory within the borders of the United States was American sovereign territory. Whether a particular parcel of land was acquired by purchase or conquest, or how it was governed internally, was immaterial in terms of international law; other foreign states generally respected the new political borders that resulted from such acquisitions. Just as the states of the union were (and remain) formally meaningless under international law, so, too, were the distinctions between federal territories and the various states meaningless to foreign nations. Vis-à-vis the rest of the world, the United States was and is sovereign over all its territory equally.

But internally, as a constitutional matter, the status of new territories was less clear. Did a different legal order apply in the territories than in the states, one that gave the federal government more power and flexibility? The jurisprudence surrounding "Indian country" certainly suggested that some American territory could be ruled distinctively. And the text of the Territory Clause suggested a similar result: it seemed to grant Congress a wide, perhaps even open-ended, range of governance powers within federal territory. But even if that view was correct—and it was certainly disputed—did that mean Congress had an entirely free hand in federal territory?

The controversies over federal power in Indian country touched on this debate in different ways. But the inquiry also arose in the context of war and occupation. During the Mexican War of 1846–1848, for instance, American troops occupied and governed parts of Mexico. Did such military occupation mean that the occupied Mexican territory was now "within" the United States for constitutional purposes?

The 1850 case of *Fleming v. Page* raised this question directly. *Fleming* involved goods shipped from the U.S.-occupied Mexican port of Tampico to Philadelphia. The Constitution's Uniformity Clause requires that all duties "be uniform within the United States." As a result, once a shipment entered the United States, no further duties could be assessed. *Fleming* asked whether customs duties were properly assessed on goods shipped from Tampico to Philadelphia. In other words, the parties disputed whether the occupied port was effectively American or foreign territory for the purpose of assessing customs duties. Was Tampico more like New York, or more like Paris?

To answer this query, the Supreme Court first looked to international law, declaring that "[t]he United States, it is true, may extend its boundaries by conquest or treaty, and may demand the cession of territory as the condition of peace."[48] But it quickly turned to domestic law. Under American law sovereign boundaries can be extended, the Court said, "only by the treatymaking power or the legislative authority." The ability to add territory "is not part of the power conferred on the President by the declaration of war." Hence although Tampico was governed by American troops, that fact alone did not render it U.S. territory. The troops still "were in an enemy's country, and not their own." Anything more required an affirmative act by Congress.

Even earlier, the Marshall court had decided a case stemming from the War of 1812 and the brief British occupation of Maine.[49] This case posed essentially the reverse of *Fleming*. What if a foreign power temporarily conquered and occupied an American city? Would the city now be treated as foreign land? The answer was yes: the port city of Castine, Maine was held to be British, not American, territory for the purposes of the customs laws. As was noted in subsequent judicial decisions, putting these two situations together yielded an unusual pattern. Temporary British governance of the American port of Castine was sufficient to create "foreignness," whereas temporary American governance of Tampico was insufficient to render it domestic territory. Perhaps not coincidentally, this pattern maximized customs revenue for the American government. The decision in *Fleming* also reflected prior cases involving American control over foreign territory. A case from the 1820s, for example, had explored the acquisition of Florida. Long Spanish territory, Florida was ceded to the United States in 1819. In *American Insurance Co. v. Canter* the Court adjudicated whether Florida came fully within the laws of the United States via the treaty of cession with Spain, or whether further action was required.[50] This issue— was American sovereignty sufficient to bring the Constitution and other laws of the United States to bear in a territory, or was a further, affirmative act required?—was one that would arise repeatedly in American history.

As in *Fleming*, the answer was that bare sovereign control was not sufficient to extend the full force of American law. A clear act by the political branches was needed. In reaching this conclusion, however, the Supreme Court drew an important distinction between territorial conquest of Indian lands and territorial acquisition by treaty with another Westphalian state. "It is obvious," the Court wrote, "that there is a material distinction between the territory now under consideration [Florida] and that which is acquired from the aborigines, (whether by purchase or conquest) within the acknowledged limits of the United States." In both cases the sovereignty of the United States over the territory was not in doubt. But for "territories previously subject to the acknowledged jurisdiction of another sovereign . . . the government and laws of the United States do not extend to such territory by the mere act of cession."[51] As was repeatedly stressed in later cases, such as *Fleming*, Congress must choose to extend those laws.

This distinction between previously Indian territory and previously Spanish territory was grounded in respect for other territorial sovereigns and drew on principles of international law. International law established that states had some discretion in retaining the laws of a prior sovereign after conquest or accession. This principle is reflected in the law of occupation, which directs conquering states to retain as much of prior sovereign's law as is feasible. The rules were different for land taken from "savages," who were thought to have primitive, barbaric legal systems whose rules would never be retained.[52]

Looked at *in toto*, these early decisions on territorial acquisition seemed to assert that whether a particular geographic location was within or without the United States was a question that had, in essence, two answers. Consider the case of Tampico, the Mexican port occupied by the American military. Vis-à-vis the outside world, the United States was the occupying power and possessed all the powers of governance that flowed from effective military control, powers that were well-established under international law. But as a constitutional matter, Tampico was not within the United States, because Congress had not acted to bring it within the United States. Consequently, Tampico was foreign territory for one purpose, and American for another.

This notion—that territory could be sovereign American soil for some purposes, yet still be foreign for others—was very similar to that articulated in contemporaneous Indian country cases like *Worcester* and *Cherokee Nation*. Indian lands were, as far as the outside world was concerned, fully within the sovereign borders of the United States. Yet Indian country was foreign territory for some internal purposes. The state of Georgia, for instance, could not extend its law into Indian country; the Cherokee, like all Indian tribes, were "a distinct community occupying its own territory."[53] That distinctiveness nonetheless evaporated with regard to the outside world. As the Supreme Court made clear, as far as "all maps and geographical treatises" were concerned, Cherokee lands were American lands.

The geographic scope of American law varied, in sum, based on whether the question was one that was international or domestic in nature. From the vantage point of the outside world, the sovereignty of the United States enjoyed the greatest territorial ambit. But as an internal matter, American land was differentiated intraterritorially: there was a core where the Constitution and all laws applied fully, and there was a periphery where American law applied only partially. Whether Indian country, federal territory, or annexed offshore colony, these peripheral areas were undoubtedly under American sovereignty as far as the rest of the world was concerned. But their constitutional status, as an internal, domestic matter, was distinctive. This intraterritorial distinction was grounded in constitutional law, not international law. This approach to territoriality, which proved very useful, would be recalled and repeated in years to come.

Dred Scott

Once called "the most disastrous opinion the Supreme Court ever issued," the case of *Dred Scott* is generally thought of today in terms of citizenship, slavery, and racism.[54] Yet the disposition of the case turned closely on questions of the geographical scope of American law. And, ironically, though done in the service of protecting the institution of slavery, the Supreme Court's reasoning on the territorial limits of American law would today be considered progressive, for the Court held that the federal government did not gain extra-constitutional powers simply because it was operating beyond the borders of the states of the Union. As recent commentators have pointed out, the connections between *Dred Scott* and the rights of foreign detainees in Guantanamo—connections that are somewhat opaque at first glance—are surprisingly strong.[55]

Dred Scott also illustrates how territorial expansion in the antebellum years was generally viewed through the prism of slavery. The acquisition of the Hawaiian Islands, for example, was held up for decades because of concerns that Hawaii would have become a slave state under the terms of the Missouri Compromise of 1820.[56] The South generally sought to acquire new territory thought suitable for slave plantations, whereas the North preferred locations like Canada and Alaska. Each understood that the designation of slave or free in a new territory could alter the delicate balance between North and South, because it was generally believed that every territory would eventually become a state. What was less clear was what happened when a slave traveled into a free state or free territory. Did the slave remain a slave? In other words, did the property rights of slave owners have extraterritorial effect? This was the issue at stake in *Dred Scott*.

Dred Scott was a slave owned by John Emerson of Missouri, then a slave state. In 1836 Scott moved with Emerson to the free state of Illinois, and then to the Wisconsin Territory, where the Missouri Compromise prohibited slavery. After a number of years Scott moved back to Missouri. Following a convoluted series of events, he filed suit for his freedom in federal court. The core of his claim was that his time outside the South had made him free. To decide whether this was true, the Supreme Court focused on whether Congress had acted validly when banning slavery in the federal territories via the Missouri Compromise. The Territory Clause granted Congress the power to make "any needful rules" for the territory of the United States. But it was uncertain what limits existed on this power. Was Congress bound, in legislating for the territories, by the rest of the Constitution, including its provisions on the protection of property?

This general issue had been long debated politically, most famously by Daniel Webster and John Calhoun. Webster took a geographically restricted view of the matter and asserted that the Constitution was made for the states alone. It could not be extended wholesale to the territories, and at a minimum did not so extend automatically. Calhoun countered that the Constitution applied fully wherever the United States was sovereign. To press his case, Calhoun contended that obviously Congress could not do as it pleased in the territories. He asked rhetorically, "Can you establish titles of nobility in California?" (California was not then a state). Nobility was trivial, but the major point was that Congress was not ordinarily thought to have the power to establish an official religion in the territories, or suppress free speech. Given this, Calhoun asked, "[I]f all the negative provisions extend to the territories, why not the positive?"[57] This argument of the bitter following the sweet, as it were, proved difficult for opponents like Webster to counter.

In addressing the merits of Dred Scott's claim of freedom the Supreme Court first considered the meaning of the Territory Clause. Despite its seemingly clear and broad language, the clause was intended, the majority argued, for a very narrow purpose. It was only to "transfer to the new government the property then held in common by the States" during the Articles of Confederation period. The Territory Clause referred not to "territories" in general but to "the Territory of the United States— that is . . . a Territory then in existence." The reference to the authority to make needful rules and regulations referred only to "other property," somewhat implausibly construed to mean things like ships and weapons.

The Supreme Court then considered whether as a general matter the Constitution was geographically limited to the states. Like Calhoun, the majority argued that the rights embodied in the Constitution applied throughout American territory. They believed that Congress could not deny the population the right to bear arms, or quarter troops in the homes of the people, in any land that was within the sovereign borders of the nation. In a like manner, the due process clause of the Fifth Amendment extends to the whole of the United States, whether a given territory is organized into a state or kept under the control of the federal government. Because slaves were property, and because Congress could not strip a citizen of his property without due process of law,

> [t]he Act of Congress which prohibited a citizen from holding owning property of this kind [a slave] in the territory of the United States north of the line therein mentioned, is not warranted by the Constitution, and is

therefore void; and that neither Dred Scott himself, nor any of his family, were made free by being carried into this territory.[58]

Congress, in short, had no power to subvert the constitutionally-guaranteed property rights of citizens simply because it was legislating for the federal territories rather than the states.

In deciding *Dred Scott* this way the Supreme Court took sides in the long-running debate over the geographic scope of American constitutionalism. Yet it also weighed in on the future of American empire. The decision cast considerable doubt on the ability of the United States to acquire colonies or, for that matter, any territory not destined for statehood. The majority emphatically declared that "no power is given to acquire a Territory to be held and governed permanently in that character."[59] The federal government "has no power of any kind beyond [the Constitution]; and it cannot, when it enters a Territory of the United States, put off its character, and assume discretionary or despotic powers which the Constitution has denied to it." In other words, no legal black holes. No territory could be acquired that would allow the federal government to do things it could not do "at home."

That view, like much else in *Dred Scott*, would later be repudiated. But the idea that the Bill of Rights bound Congress in the territories in the same way it did in the states was endorsed in several subsequent decisions. There was certainly disagreement about whether the Constitution applied *ex proprio vigore*—of its own force—or whether Congress simply lacked the power under the Territory Clause to violate constitutional prohibitions.[60] But the end result was essentially the same: constitutional restrictions applied equally throughout American territory. Hence the intraterritorial distinction drawn in earlier cases (as well as in later cases) between territory where the Constitution applied in full and territory where it applied less completely—between constitutional core and periphery—was rejected in *Dred Scott*.

To be sure, this did not end the debate over the Constitution's reach into the territories. Many of the so-called organic acts that created territorial governments—which, as creatures of Congress, enjoyed only whatever powers Congress expressly delegated—stated that the power of the governments to legislate was extended to all rightful subjects of legislation "not inconsistent with the Constitution and laws of the United States."[61] Were constitutional restrictions plainly operative, this caveat would be unnecessary. The Supreme Court also expressed some uncertainty in later years. It noted, for instance, in one of the many Mormon Church cases that Congress, in legislating for the territories, was surely subject to fundamental limits on governmental power reflected in the Bill of Rights. But, said the Court, this was true only by inference, rather than "any express and direct application" of constitutional provisions.[62] As this suggested, precisely why the Constitution possessed the geographic scope it did was undertheorized and uncertain.

Reconstruction and the Occupation of the South

As the disputes over the status of the captured ports of Tampico, Mexico and Castine, Maine in the early nineteenth century illustrated, military conquest—whether by the United States or of United States territory by a foreign power—raised hard questions about the contours of the sovereign borders of the nation, and hence hard questions about the reach of American law. International law traditionally viewed the occupier as a kind of trustee who was, when possible, to retain preexisting local law. This principle was consistent with the views of the early nineteenth century Marshall Court, which had held that territory acquired in a peace treaty was not automatically subject to the Constitution. The United States instead had the option to keep the existing (foreign) law in place. *Dred Scott*'s expansive view of the Constitution's geographic reach seemed at odds with this approach, which was vibrant in the decades both before and after *Dred Scott* was handed down. But the justices in *Dred Scott* never spoke directly to the issue of occupation.

As a result it was unclear whether this broad set of principles and rules meant that the Constitution had no power whatsoever in foreign areas occupied by American military forces. The resolution of the Civil War offered the even more unusual situation of conquest by the United States of territory already within American borders. The Northern armies frequently resorted to martial law and to military commissions as a means to control the local populace in the South. These measures were often inconsistent with conventional understandings of constitutional rights. Yet they were nonetheless applied within a region that was unquestionably within the sovereign territory of the United States.

The most famous Civil War case implicating these questions revolved around a man named Lambdin Milligan. Milligan was imprisoned in 1864 by the Union Army and tried by military commission in Indianapolis. In *Ex parte Milligan*, the Supreme Court considered whether the Constitution restrained the actions of the military vis-à-vis citizens such as Milligan. The government argued that the protections of the Bill of Rights were not intended to apply in armed conflict. These "are all peace provisions of the Constitution and, like all other conventional and legislative laws and enactments, are silent amidst arms, and when the safety of the people becomes the supreme law."[63] The Supreme Court disagreed.

It noted that military commissions draw their power and authority from the laws of war. But these laws "can never be applied to citizens in states which have upheld the authority of the government, and where the courts are open and their process unobstructed." In short, because the civilian courts were open and functioning, and because Indiana was not a war zone, Milligan's trial by military commission was ruled unlawful.

The saga of Lambdin Milligan became prominent again nearly 150 years later in the wake of the 9/11 attacks. When President George W. Bush announced in 2001 his intention to create military commissions to try numerous suspected terrorists, many lawyers looked to *Milligan*, and its Second World War counterpart, the 1942 case of *Ex parte Quirin*, for guidance as to how the federal courts might treat the commissions.[64] Civil libertarians decried the military commissions' lack of protections for the accused and cited *Milligan* to suggest that such courts are likely unconstitutional, at least if they are constituted on the territory of the United States. Proponents looked to the later *Quirin* case, which also involved an American citizen, to suggest that military commissions were entirely permissible when used against unlawful enemy combatants.

Although Milligan's trial in Indiana captured the lion's share of attention, military commissions were used widely in the rebellious South. For example, when the Union armies in 1862 occupied New Orleans, by far the largest city in the South, a military commission sentenced to death a man named William Mumford for tearing up an American flag and throwing it to a mob.[65] Cases like this raised much the same question as *Milligan*: how could military rule and military justice, which so often was inconsistent with the Bill of Rights, exist on U.S. territory?

The Supreme Court, in a later case concerning military rule in New Orleans, contended that the answer was that Southern states were in fact conquered territory and therefore subject to the laws of war and the international law of occupation, not American law. International law displaced constitutional law. In the Supreme Court's words,

> Although the city of New Orleans was conquered and taken possession of in a civil war waged on the part of the United States to put down an insurrection and restore the supremacy of the National government in the Confederate States, that government has the same power and rights in territory held by conquest as if the territory had belonged to a foreign country and had been subjugated in a foreign war. In such cases the conquering power has a right to displace the preexisting authority and to assume to such extent as it may deem proper the exercise by itself of all the powers and functions of government ... There is no limit to the powers that may be exerted in such cases, save those which are found in the laws and usages of war.[66]

In short, New Orleans was no different, at least for legal purposes, than the conquered Mexican port of Tampico decades earlier. The international law of occupation was the paramount set of legal rules. And New Orleans was within U.S. control but not subject to the U.S. Constitution. This ruling not only reinforced the emerging use of intraterritorial distinctions and fore-shadowed later uses of international law to displace constitutional law. Its claim of power flowing from territorial conquest—and its claim that this power is unbridled by ordinary limitations of constitutional law—would later be echoed by the executive branch with regard to another belligerent occupation, that of Berlin after 1945.[67]

State Jurisdiction and Conflicts of Law

Controversies concerning the legal status of Indian country, the conquered South, and the law applicable to federal territory plainly implicated foundational ideas about territoriality and sovereignty. Territoriality was understood to be strict, in that the prevailing rules and norms of the day prohibited extraterritorial claims by one sovereign against another. But territoriality was also manipulated: Indian country was sometimes foreign and sometimes domestic; federal territory was sometimes subject to constitutional strictures and sometimes not; and conquered territory was governed by the United States but the United States was, in this context, not governed by the Constitution.

These issues were central to nineteenth-century understandings of territoriality. Less obviously and dramatically, ordinary civil litigation also provides an important window into how nineteenth-century jurists, government officials, and litigants thought about territoriality and the geographic scope of legitimate state authority. Across the board, these ordinary rules highlighted the enduring force of Westphalian territoriality.

A central example is jurisdiction. In a lawsuit a court must decide whether it has "personal jurisdiction" over the defendant—control over that particular defendant, in addition to jurisdiction over the matter in question. What is important for this book is that the canonical nineteenth-century cases concerning personal jurisdiction focused nearly exclusively on territorial considerations. Indeed, these cases reflected and underscored the remarkably widespread influence of international legal conceptions of territoriality, both in the importance they placed on sovereign borders and in their concern for the exclusive nature of sovereign power within its territorial metes and bounds.

The classic case in this regard, well known to every American lawyer, is *Pennoyer v. Neff*.[68] Decided in 1877, *Pennoyer* argued that the "authority of every tribunal is necessarily restricted by the territorial limits of the State in which it is established." Moreover, "any attempt to exercise authority beyond those limits would be deemed . . . an illegitimate assumption of power, and be resisted as mere abuse."[69] As support for this argument, the Supreme Court looked to two established principles of international law. International law was an appropriate source of normative guidance in this case, *Pennoyer* contended, because the several states of the Union, although not in every respect independent, "possess and exercise the authority of independent states" and "the principles of public law to which we have referred are applicable to them." In other words, they retain aspects of sovereignty, and vis-à-vis each other are akin to states in the international system.

The first principle was that "every State possesses exclusive jurisdiction and sovereignty over persons and property within its territory." This principle is familiar: it is a rearticulation of the basic Westphalian vision of sovereignty. The other principle was a direct corollary of the first: "no State can exercise direct jurisdiction and authority over persons or property without its territory . . . the laws of one State have no operation outside of its territory, except so far as is allowed by comity."[70] Any attempt, said the court, by a state to extend laws extraterritoriality is an encroachment upon the sovereignty possessed by others. This notion, too, reflects familiar Westphalian ideals; it is a necessary concomitant of the exclusivity announced in the first principle.

The close connection to the ideals of Westphalian sovereignty was not inadvertent. The justices who wrote *Pennoyer* leaned heavily on Joseph Story's influential treatise on "conflicts of law." The field of conflicts, as its name suggests, is focused on how a court ought to adjudicate between the law of two sovereigns when both have some connection to the case at bar. In the nineteenth century, conflicts of law were governed for the most part by principles of territoriality. The location of an act was thought to determine the applicable law. The rationale for this reliance on territorial location "was simple: because sovereignty is defined by territorial control, any other principle would be a source of friction and discord 'inconvenient to the commerce and general intercourse of nations.' "[71] Consistent with the original vision of the Westphalian Peace, this territorial principle "limited states' lawmaking competence so that conflict was practically impossible."[72]

To be sure, territorial location was not always decisive in the nineteenth century; exceptions existed, and in practice it was often difficult to determine exactly where an event occurred. But territoriality was the dominant approach, and remained so until the arrival of a powerful set of critiques in the early twentieth century. As one recent survey notes, this was true in a very wide range of legal doctrines. Throughout the nineteenth and early twentieth centuries domestic courts were quite limited in their ability to adjudicate disputes involving conduct that taken place outside their borders. The territorial nature of this limitation had many manifestations: the dominance of the doctrines of *lex loci declicti* (the law of the place of the wrong) and *lex contractus* (law of the contract) in choice of law, the presumptive territorial limits of prescriptive jurisdiction, the breadth of the act of state doctrine, and the great stinginess with which *res judicata* and collateral estoppel were applied across borders . . . [By the twentieth century] jurisdiction increasingly turned less on the place of service and more on the quantity and quality of contacts between the defendant and the forum.[73]

As this passage indicates, in the nineteenth century Westphalian territoriality was extremely influential in many areas of American law, though it eventually grew less influential. The debates over intraterritoriality and extraterritoriality that animate this book raised particular questions, but these questions were grounded in a much wider worldview that grew out of the fundamental principles of international order.

The Territorial Rights of Aliens

At the heart of intraterritoriality was the idea that a legal core, within which national law applied fully and completely, could be distinguished from a legal periphery. This intraterritorial approach helped determine *where* the law applied, but not always to *whom* it applied. Did citizens and aliens have the same set of rights? Debates over the rights of aliens date back to the framing generation. Debate over the Alien and Sedition Acts in the late eighteenth century, for example, turned in part on whether friendly aliens were understood to be protected by the newly created Bill of Rights.[74] Some argued that all friendly aliens fell within the Constitution's scope. James Madison, to take one notable example, argued that "if aliens had no rights under the Constitution, they might not only be banished, but even capitally punished, without a jury or other incidents to a fair trial."[75] Opponents of this view saw the Constitution as a compact among distinct parties (perhaps the states, perhaps a certain people or peoples) that therefore did not extend to all individuals. As we will see, this difference in views over the nature of the Constitution—was it purely territorial in its force, or did it apply to a special group of persons only?—would reappear throughout American history.[76]

The general approach throughout much of American history followed Madison. The Bill of Rights applied to aliens and citizens alike within American borders.[77] This territorial approach was of a piece with the strict territoriality found in so many other areas of American law, and was firmly established in a series of late-nineteenth-century disputes over the rights of

Chinese migrants. As the Supreme Court announced in one such decision, "the rights of the petitioners are not less because they are aliens and subjects of the emperor of China."[78] The Fourteenth Amendment's provisions "are universal in their application, to all persons within the territorial jurisdiction."[79]

A few years later the Supreme Court further bolstered this position, declaring that the Fifth and Sixth Amendments were applicable to "all persons within the territory of the United States."[80] There were (and are) important exceptions, however, to the view that the Bill of Rights applied equally to every person within the United States. One is that the federal government's power over immigration also entails a power to expel foreigners.[81] The result is a system that permits largely unfettered discretion in the process of admitting or expelling aliens, but requires fair treatment while the aliens are within the United States. The analogy might be to a private residence, in which the owner has complete control over the flow of visitors but treats all guests equally while within her home. This "guest theory" became important in later disputes over what rights of noncitizens abroad the United States government need respect.

The second exception relates more closely to questions of territoriality. Although presence on American territory is in theory the source of the constitutional rights aliens enjoy, not all aliens physically present in the United States are deemed to be legally present. Some migrants are deemed to be, for legal purposes, *at the border* even though they are plainly *within the border*. Because legally they are merely at the border, courts have held that they lack the full panoply of constitutional rights. (Indeed, the executive branch has frequently argued that aliens at the border lack any rights whatsoever.) This "entry fiction" is common—many of us have witnessed it at airports, where arriving foreign passengers, clearly on American soil, pass through customs and immigration checkpoints before "entering" the United States—and it produces surprising results at times.

In the 1980s, for example, Cubans who had arrived on the shores of the United States as part of the Mariel boatlift were granted "parole" into the United States. Parole in this context means they were literally allowed into Florida but were not deemed to have been legally admitted. Some committed crimes, and after serving their sentences were imprisoned indefinitely. A federal court held that this indefinite imprisonment was legal because the detainees, as aliens who had never properly "entered" the United States, had no constitutional due process rights at all.[82] In other words, even though the Cubans were actually present on American territory, they were treated as if they were held on the high seas or another extraterritorial location—which, under principles of strict territoriality, meant they lacked any constitutional rights. The entry fiction highlights the flexibility with which American law has manipulated categories of inside and outside for instrumental purposes. And it underscores how significant territorial presence is to the constitutional rights of individuals.

In sum, as was true in so many other areas of the law, with regard to aliens prevailing principles of Westphalian territoriality entailed the belief that location determined legal rules. What constituted "inside" and "outside," however, was sometimes stretched for strategic purposes. The Constitution, in turn, contained a bundle of rights that for the most part did not expressly indicate that they applied only to citizens. Put together, these principles meant that aliens within the United States generally enjoyed the same rights as citizens. Yet this generous approach was tempered by a harsh concomitant principle. Foreigners seeking to enter American territory were at the mercy of the federal government, which fully controlled the levers of legal entry as an "incident" of sovereignty. Those deemed to be outside American territory lacked any constitutional protections.

This principle of distinction was not unique to the nineteenth century. Indeed, the Supreme Court noted in 2001 that "the distinction between an alien who has effected an entry into the United States and one who has never entered runs through immigration law."[83] What has changed is the degree to which the boundary between inside and outside, between foreign and domestic, has shifted and blurred. Increasingly, the American border lies in *other nation's* sovereign territory, as when travelers "clear" U.S. customs and immigration while still in a foreign airport, or lies *within* American sovereign territory, as when Congress passed new legislation in the 1990s allowing the "expedited removal" of aliens found within 100 miles of the border. As one commentator has observed, "[T]he border itself has become a moving barrier, a legal construct that is not tightly fixed to territorial benchmarks."[84] This border manipulation, an intraterritorial act of line-drawing, will receive greater attention in later chapters.

The Territorial Paradigm in Early America

From the American Revolution to the Civil War the United States underwent dramatic territorial change. Through a series of purchases and conquests, the geographic scope of the United States expanded west to the Pacific, north to the Arctic, and south to the Caribbean. This enormous expansion forced upon the nation a series of questions about how its law connected to land. From its beginnings, the United States assumed the Westphalian territorial paradigm described in chapter 1. Westphalian territoriality was "deeply rooted in the constitutional system of the United States."[85] This territorial paradigm was not developed *de novo*; it was entrenched in and central to the international order of the day.

As a weak nation, with an uncertain relationship to the great powers of the day, the early United States was unsurprisingly drawn to the principle of complete sovereign control within demarcated geographic borders. Yet territorial sovereignty quickly generated challenges in the American context, most related to the problem of interposing an unusual republican constitution with geopolitical rivalries and Westphalian precepts. Doing so required some theory of the territorial dimensions of governance. American elites had to decide whether the limitations enshrined in the Constitution applied wherever the federal government acted, or instead were intended only for a particular place and a particular people.

The latter question—was the Constitution created for a particular people?—was asked in the nineteenth century, and the answer was generally negative. An expansive view of constitutional rights was a signature feature of American constitutionalism. This view was consistent with Westphalian territoriality—every person on American soil, whether citizen or alien, has the same set of rights—even if it is not necessarily entailed by it. The former question, whether the Constitution was written for a particular geographic place, continues to be a burning issue today.

Whether the Constitution was written for a particular place has both intraterritorial and extraterritorial elements. Throughout the antebellum era, as this chapter has illustrated, American law drew a distinction between territory that was clearly within U.S. control vis-à-vis the outside world, and territory that was subject to the full range of constitutional rights and limitations. In other words, two different borders existed, two distinct maps. One limned sovereignty (sometimes temporary, as in military occupation) and the other, drawn more narrowly, constitutionalism.

The brief and limited erasure of intraterritorial distinctions occasioned by *Dred Scott* was definitively brought to an end by the creation of a formal overseas empire after 1898. At the end of the nineteenth century the United States followed the path of other European powers not only in acquiring an overseas empire, but also (and earlier) in seeking extensive extraterritorial rights for its citizens in foreign locales that were deemed uncivilized by the West. This form of extraterritoriality reached its zenith with the creation of the U.S. District Court for China in 1906. This practice of extraterritoriality created yet another map—one in which American legal power extended into foreign societies, but was, as we will see, not governed by the Bill of Rights. These topics of imperialism and extraterritoriality are the focus of the next chapter.

3

THE IMPERIAL CONSTITUTION

"As near as I can make out the Constitution follows the flag—but doesn't quite catch up with it."[1]

—*Elihu Root, commenting on the Insular Cases*

On May 9, 1880, on an American ship named the *Bullion* docked in the harbor of Yokohama, Japan, John Ross stabbed his crewmate Robert Kelly to death with a knife.[2] As was the common practice at the time for Westerners who committed crimes in Asia, Ross did not face trial for murder before local Japanese authorities, nor did Japanese law influence the outcome of the case in any way. Rather, Ross's trial was conducted by Thomas van Buren, the local American consul in Kanagawa, Japan.

The trial occurred under consular jurisdiction (described in chapter 1 in this volume), a form of extraterritoriality that was commonly asserted in the past by European great powers in states they deemed "uncivilized." Japan, though soon to join the ranks of the civilized nations, was at the time of Robert Kelly's death compelled to afford the Western powers a free hand in adjudicating the crimes of their countrymen within Japan. The American consular court in Kanagawa convicted John Ross of murder and sentenced him to death. Although Ross was in fact British, the court held that because he was a seaman on a U.S. vessel he was subject to the jurisdiction of the United States. Ross's death sentence was ultimately commuted to life imprisonment by President Rutherford B. Hayes. Apparently unsatisfied, in 1890 Ross brought a challenge to his murder conviction that rose to the Supreme Court.

In the late nineteenth century the connections of American citizens to foreign places and foreign markets were rising rapidly. Extraterritorial jurisdiction was a European practice of long standing, but it became much more significant and extensive in the late nineteenth century.[3] Ross's case directly raised the question of the legality of such jurisdiction, not in terms of international law (that was generally unquestioned at the time), but in terms of domestic law. His case thus implicated the extraterritorial reach of constitutional rights at a time when imperialism was undergoing a major resurgence and the United States was assuming a more prominent place in international affairs than ever before.

This chapter explores the meaning and transformation of territoriality in American law from the Civil War to the First World War. During this period the United States became a great power and wielded increasing influence around the globe. From its beginnings America was a nation of substantial promise. But for most of the nineteenth century American power was either constrained by its distance from the centers of world politics or consumed by internal war. Exacerbating these factors was the narrow range and small size of the American state, which meant that America's economic might was not translated into political power.[4] Only in the years after Reconstruction did the United States begin to harness the hitherto latent power it possessed, and to engage more closely and forcefully in international relations.

Even then the United States remained a remarkably insular nation. Real change began only in the 1890s as the federal government began to grow and harness the resources of the American economy. Technological innovation played an important role in connecting these resources to the long-standing impetus to expand outward. The rise of the steamship, for example, allowed the United States to more readily access both Europe and the Far East, making the nation both more trade dependant and more open to the acquisition of distant colonies. As one advocate of American imperialism declared at the time, "Distance and oceans are no arguments . . . Hawaii and the Philippines are not contiguous! Our navy will make them contiguous."[5]

That the United States had a permanent consul in 1880s Japan—and a ready supply of American plaintiffs and defendants—was testament to this rising involvement in overseas affairs and the relative ease with which Americans could now trade, travel, and proselytize throughout the globe. By the early twentieth century the United States was a formidable player in the geopolitical great game.

A pivotal moment in the march to great power status was the Spanish-American War of 1898, in which the United States not only defeated a European power but acquired its far-flung colonial possessions in the bargain. With the decisive entry of American forces in the First World War, the transition was complete. Along the way, however, the United States faced a series of vexing questions that pitted the nation's commitment to limited government and constitutionalism, on the one hand, against the desire for global power and the fever for imperialism on the other. The acquisition of overseas colonies raised the question of the territorial reach of the constitution most dramatically. Whether the Constitution followed the flag— whether the boundaries of American sovereignty and of American constitutionalism were identical—was a crucial issue in the presidential election of 1900 and, for years later, within the Supreme Court. Yet prior to this period, as John Ross's appeal to the Supreme Court evidences, questions concerning the spatial dimensions of legal power and legal rights frequently arose.

Though diverse, these events and questions can be divided into two broad categories. One, as illustrated by John Ross's appeal to the Supreme Court, was whether the Constitution's protections applied extraterritorially. This issue obviously grew in importance as the United States began to exert more power and influence outside North America. A second, related issue was raised in the previous chapter: whether American law applied equally throughout its sovereign territory. In other words, the first question asked whether the Constitution's full scope was limited to American territory. The second asked whether *within* American territory distinctions could be drawn between different types of territory—what I have called intraterritoriality.

In both instances we see the federal judiciary interpreting American law instrumentally, in a manner that generally enhanced the autonomy and power of the United States government. With regard to extraterritorial jurisdiction, the federal government sought maximum flexibility and efficiency in its unusual overseas courts. Constitutional rights, of course, are costly and often burdensome. With regard to intraterritoriality, the federal government sought the freedom to colonize and control distant lands without the bringing along all the complex fetters of American legal rights. The tension between an emerging globalism and American constitutionalism is a major focus of this chapter.

Extraterritorial Courts and the Territorial Constitution

Japan had been opened to the West for less than 30 years at the time of John Ross's trial in Kanagawa. For centuries the ruling shogunate had largely closed the Japanese islands off from the rest of the world. Only a tiny number of Chinese and Dutch traders had been allowed within Japan, and their activities were closely circumscribed. This all changed in 1853 as American warships, commanded by Commodore Matthew Perry, steamed into what was then Edo (now Tokyo) Bay.[6] Perry bore a letter of introduction from President Millard Fillmore and demanded to negotiate with the emperor's high officials. The Japanese, intimidated by the technological and military prowess suggested by the steam-powered "black ships" of the Americans, eventually acquiesced. Perry's treaty, the Convention of Kanagawa, forced Japan to cede trading rights to the Americans. Other nations soon followed the American lead, and Japan, forcibly thrust out of its remarkable isolation, began its rapid ascent toward modernization and Westernization.

Japan soon faced an influx of foreign ships and goods. Many traders put down roots in the major Asian ports of call, and small communities of foreigners took root. As noted earlier, as the European powers expanded their influence throughout the globe they routinely demanded, and received, the right to have their citizens subjected only to their own law when they were living or working in foreign and exotic locales. Western nations considered the systems of justice in many non-Western nations to be unfamiliar, inadequate, and unfair. The solution was to apply Western law outside the West. In most cases of extraterritorial jurisdiction the system received "consent" from the host state in the form of a treaty. The 1830 treaty between the United States and the Ottoman Empire (known then as "the Sublime Porte") for example, read as follows:

> If litigations and disputes should arise between the subjects of the Sublime Porte and citizens of the United States, the parties shall not be heard, nor shall judgment be pronounced, unless the American dragoman be present ... [Americans,] when they may have committed some offence, they shall not be arrested and put in prison by the local authorities, but they shall be tried by their minister or consul, and punished according to their offence, following, in this respect, the usage observed towards other Franks.

The Ottoman treaty was typical of those Western powers negotiated with various non-Western polities ("Franks" referred simply to all Westerners). The practice of extraterritorial jurisdiction began, in the case of the United States, even before the Constitution was written: the first such treaty was negotiated in 1787, with Morocco.[7] Treaties awarding similar rights throughout the Islamic world—Algiers, Tunis, Muscat, Persia, and others—followed in quick succession and were in turn followed in the mid-nineteenth century by a set of Asian treaties also embodying similar rules and practices. Although not imperial in the formal sense, these arrangements for extraterritorial jurisdiction have been properly understood as manifestations of empire, albeit informal empire. Empire, in Michael Doyle's words, "is a relationship, formal or informal, in which one state controls the effective political sovereignty of another political society."[8]

During much of the nineteenth century informal imperialism was common; protectorates were a familiar strategy that allowed European powers to exert significant commercial control while avoiding the burdens of actual occupation. This strategy of "annexation without sovereignty" disentangled legal control (and responsibility) from political and economic influence.[9] Consular jurisdiction was similar; it allowed a measure of control and presence that fell between full imperial control and "ordinary" sovereign relations. So widespread were such informal imperial practices that some analysts even argue, analogizing empire to an iceberg, that focusing solely on formal colonization misses the vast majority of the action.[10]

Kanagawa

The jurisdiction of the American court that convicted John Ross was established by a treaty negotiated in 1857, just 4 years after the arrival of Perry's black ships in Edo Bay. The Japanese treaty was similar to that with the Sublime Porte. It declared "Americans committing offences in Japan shall be tried by the American consul general or consul, and shall be punished according to American laws."[11] As a result, whether an American committed a crime against another American, or against a Japanese subject, he or she faced only American law and American authorities.

The connection between this form of extraterritoriality and pre-Westphalian legal concepts was noted in Chapter 1. Writing in 1907, the editors of the *American Journal of International Law* noted that such "extraterritorial jurisdiction is a survival of, or a reversion to, the time when sovereignty was personal rather than territorial, when there was a king of the English rather than a king of England."[12] Extraterritorial consular courts were thus odd animals in a Westphalian world. They were the product of a dynamic and expanding European presence around the globe, the felt exigencies of an increasing focus on world trade, and the disdain European powers had for non-Western societies. Though they were rationalized on the basis of primitive, alien legal systems, extraterritorial courts nonetheless were distinct from domestic Western courts. They typically rendered rough justice via simple procedures. The American versions, for example, had no indictment by a grand jury and no trial by a petit jury.[13] As John Ross's story illustrates, they often were simply one man, the local consul, rendering a decision on the spot, sometimes with the assistance of associates chosen for the occasion. (In Ross's trial there were four such associates chosen.) The consuls were executive branch officials, not members of the judiciary.

Americans abroad were often unhappy not only with the limited procedures and protections offered, but also the underlying law that the consular courts applied. Shortly after Ross's appeal to the Supreme Court, in fact, several American residents in Japan petitioned Congress to modify by legislation the laws applied by the extraterritorial courts. The residents' complaints were varied, but focused—ironically, given that the official rationale for extraterritorial jurisdiction was the barbaric and unfair justice meted out by uncivilized states—on the antiquated and unfair rules of the common law imposed upon them. "For us," they pleaded, "there is no statute of frauds; there is no insolvency legislation ... imprisonment for debt has not been abolished ... we have no statute of limitations ..."[14]

Ross's case did not focus on the substantive law applied by the American consular court; murder was much the same in Japan as in the United States. Rather, Ross challenged the constitutionality of his conviction by such an odd judicial body. Specifically, he claimed that "so far as crimes of felonious character are concerned, the same protection and guarantee against an undue accusation or an unfair trial, secured by the Constitution to the citizens of the United States at home, should be enjoyed by them abroad."[15] Such a truncated process of conviction for a capital crime would never be allowed to stand were it to occur within the borders of the United States. Hence, he asserted, it must be overturned in his case as well, because the Constitution guarantees the rights of all Americans without qualification. In other words, Ross asserted that the Constitution applied in the same way to Americans abroad as well as at home—that it was, in essence, a document with global reach.

The Supreme Court was, to say the least, highly unreceptive to this claim. The justices declared,

> By the Constitution a government is ordained and established "for the United States of America," and not for countries outside of their limits. The guarantees it affords ... apply only to citizens and others within the United States, or who are brought there for trial for alleged offences committed elsewhere, and not to residents or temporary sojourners abroad. *The Constitution can have no operation in another country.* When, therefore, the representatives or officers of our government are permitted to exercise authority of any kind in another country, it must be on such conditions as the two countries may agree ...[16]

Ross's argument was, as a result, wholly without merit. The Constitution had no role in his trial, and he enjoyed none of the rights guaranteed by it while he was outside the sovereign territory of the nation.

Indeed, the decision painted Ross's complaint as not only legally without merit but even a bit ungrateful. Although the Supreme Court conceded that an American accused of crime in a foreign land subject to extraterritorial jurisdiction "is deprived of the guaranties of the constitution against unjust accusation and a partial trial," it averred that "in another aspect he is the gainer, in being withdrawn from the procedure of their tribunals, often arbitrary and oppressive, and some times accompanied with extreme cruelty and torture."[17]

That there was a third choice between prosecution by the Japanese and simplified consular procedures—jury trial subject to the Bill of Rights—was dismissed largely on the grounds of expediency and practicality. Applying the full panoply of constitutional protections to the accused was something that the United States was plainly not required to do. The Court suggested it might even be seen as a violation of the treaty between American and Japan, because the United States could practice only what Japan had agreed to. In any event, to question the constitutionality of the consular process was, the opinion implied, oxymoronic; the Constitution applied only within the sovereign territory of the nation, not beyond it.

Ross thus laid out a clear and—with one major exception addressed shortly—relatively coherent vision of strict territoriality. This vision was "strict" in that it hewed closely to the Westphalian ideal that geographic borders determined legal jurisdiction. It was a vision that claimed to respect other sovereign states in their respective territories—and, as with Japan, even to respect the agreements negotiated with uncivilized states—and limited the Constitution's reach to U.S. territory. Even though under the international law of the day (and still true today) a vessel might be construed to be an outpost of American sovereign territory, the court made clear that such "territory" was not the same as "the actual sovereign borders of the United States."

Of course, this theory of strict territoriality was not at all strict in one significant respect. In *Ross*, as in many similar cases, the United States was clearly acting extraterritorially. And not only did it act outside its borders, it did so within the territory of another state. The extensive jurisdiction of the consular court in Kanagawa appeared to be a blatant violation of Westphalian sovereignty. It certainly *would* have been a violation had the events described occurred in France rather than Japan. But because Japan was not yet a full member of international society, it was not thought to be a violation of its sovereignty to project foreign (e.g., American) law into Japanese territory.[18]

Moreover, the extraterritorial arrangements of the pre-Second World War era were grounded in treaties—the so-called unequal treaties, or capitulations. As these names suggest, in reality these treaties were hardly consensual. But they technically expressed the consent of nations such as Japan and China. Certainly the existence of the 1857 treaty guaranteeing the right of the U.S. government to adjudicate cases against Americans in Japan made the issue of extraterritoriality seem to be one of sovereign consent. So although the federal government clearly acted abroad when convicting Ross, it did so only with the active consent of the local sovereign. Spun this way, the practice of extraterritorial courts for Westerners in Asia seemed but a small step beyond the long-entrenched practice of embassies. As noted in chapter 1, Western states had long ago developed elaborate rules of ambassadorial immunity and extraterritoriality.[19]

Although the ambassadorial system is broadly analogous, there are some noteworthy differences. For one, ambassadorial immunity was and is generally reciprocal. States swap ambassadors, and each major power has many embassies within its territory. Extraterritoriality, by contrast, was decidedly one-sided: Japanese and Chinese in the United States—of which there were many in the late nineteenth century—certainly did not enjoy immunity from American law, but Americans enjoyed immunity from Japanese and Chinese law. The ambassadorial system also was not maintained by coercion, as was often true of extraterritorial jurisdiction. And the rules governing ambassadors were the product of centuries of practice, accreted into a set of norms embodied in customary international law. These rules were, as a result, largely uniform and universal.

Extraterritoriality was instead a product of treaty law, and therefore more heterogeneous: its content was essentially whatever the Western power(s) could effectively negotiate with the host state, and it became more draconian over the course of the nineteenth century as the relative power of the West grew even larger.[20] Consequently, the notion that the practice of extraterritorial jurisdiction over foreign nationals was a freely consented to deviation from the normal rules of Westphalian territorial sovereignty required a sizable leap of logic.

But there was another problem with the Supreme Court's conception of strict territoriality, however; and it is one less easily dismissed by reference to sovereign consent or analogous practices within the West. Regardless of Japan's status as a sovereign state, how was it possible for the United States to exercise judicial power—or any governmental power—outside American territory if the Constitution literally "had no operation" beyond those borders? The Constitution creates the federal government and defines its powers. As a result, either Thomas van Buren, the American consul, was acting *ultra vires* or the Constitution empowered him to act—in this case, to implement a treaty arrangement between the United States and Japan and to try and convict Americans sojourning, and murdering—in Japan. And if the Constitution empowered him to act while in Japan, then plainly it could not be true that it "had no operation" within another country.

This issue was ignored in the Supreme Court's decision in *Ross*, though it arose repeatedly in the decades after. If the Constitution did operate globally, it would seem to follow that the scale and scope of governmental power wielded by American officials when they were outside the borders of the United States was keyed somehow to the Constitution. The Constitution itself certainly did not say or imply that the powers wielded by the federal government were greater beyond the territory of the United States, or somehow different. And when it came to affirmative federal powers no one apparently thought that the restrictions of the Constitution evaporated at the border, such that the president could, for instance, begin handing out otherwise prohibited titles of nobility willy-nilly. This was the "bitter and the sweet" problem John Calhoun had raised in his famous debates with Daniel Webster over federal power in the western territories.

The decision in *Ross* also seemed to reflect, at least implicitly, a view of the Sixth Amendment as an individual right. This is certainly the prevailing view today. Conceptualizing the dispute over John Ross's trial as one that turned on the right of an individual may have naturally led the Court to an inquiry over whether the particular individual before the Court was "covered" by the right. If the right to a jury trial is instead understood as a structural constraint on government action, rather than an individual right of the accused, the extraterritorial location of the trial appears far less important. This conception of the Sixth Amendment has been mostly famously articulated by constitutional scholar Akhil Amar. Amar suggests that the requirement of a trial by jury is akin to the command of bicameralism and presentment. "[A] judge acting without a jury was simply not a court capable of trying a defendant, just as the Senate acting without the House is not a legislature capable of passing laws."[21] In other words, just as the Senate convening in Mexico could not bypass bicameralism and pass laws on its own, so, too, could a judicial official not convict a criminal absent adherence to the ordinary constitutional rules. This approach to the question would have resulted in a very different answer than the one John Ross received.

In any event, these thorny conceptual concerns did not appear to trouble the Supreme Court. And the decision in *Ross* certainly made it easier for the United States to control its citizens abroad and, as a result, to continue its march toward greater involvement in world trade and politics. In this sense the decision was an enabling one for a nation increasingly interested in playing a major role on the world stage. It facilitated the growth of an informal empire. And it made sure that the unusual restraints on governmental power that were built into the American constitutional order did not overly fetter the projection of American power, and American commerce, around the globe. As we will shortly see, the American imperial adventure of the end of the nineteenth century dramatically changed the stakes involved in such questions of constitutionalism and imperialism. The cession of Spain's colonies to the United States at the end of the Spanish-American War thrust large and populous colonies in the hands of the federal government, and equally large constitutional debates soon followed.

In short, *Ross* is frequently held to be a defining case for the nineteenth-century vision of strict territoriality.[22] The language—that the Constitution can have no force outside the United States and was intended only for the United States—is forceful, blunt, and proved widely influential. American extraterritoriality in Japan was, ironically, abolished just a few years after *Ross*. The United States surrendered extraterritorial jurisdiction on July 17, 1899; the first criminal trial of an American by Japanese courts was, even more ironically, a murder committed by a U.S. sailor that very day.[23] Yet the legacy of the decision lasted much longer. It took 70 years, but the Supreme Court would eventually overrule *Ross* and its vision of strict territoriality for the Bill of Rights, calling the decision "a relic from another era."[24]

The U.S. District Court for China

Like Japan before the arrival of Perry's black ships, China traditionally sought to control trade with the West by tightly limiting access to its markets and people. For many years foreign commerce could take place only through the port of Canton. Western dissatisfaction with this system was high, and was compounded by the fact that the Chinese weren't especially interested in buying Western goods.

Indeed, China was uninterested in the West generally. When Lord Macartney was sent by King George III of Great Britain as an ambassador to the Chinese emperor, the Chinese were indifferent. The emperor demanded that Macartney kowtow; Macartney refused, and when pushed he insisted that a Chinese official of equal rank kowtow before a portrait of George III that he happened to take with him on the voyage. What actually ensued in the emperor's chambers is not clear (it's easy to imagine Macartney caved), but the emperor ended the meeting by stating, "[W]e have never valued ingenious articles, nor do we have the slightest need of your country's manufactures."[25] Only after Britain forcibly coerced China to accept broader trade in opium—something the British grew in India, and the Chinese public grew to like—did the trading system begin to change. The Opium Wars of the 1840s and 1850s both underscored European military supremacy and coercively opened China to the rest of the world.

The United States was a part of this general expansion of trade in the East, and in 1844 it signed the Treaty of Wanghia, guaranteeing trading rights as well as extraterritorial jurisdiction for Americans. Americans could now trade freely in Canton as well as four other previously closed ports. (The Treaty of Wanghia was the model for Matthew Perry's later negotiation of the Treaty of Kanagawa.) Caleb Cushing, the American negotiator of the treaty, wrote to Secretary of State John C. Calhoun that he had "obtained the concession of absolute and unqualified extraterritoriality" from the Chinese.[26] Extraterritorial jurisdiction in China was seen as essential for the usual reasons: Westerners found the Chinese practices of collective guilt and punishment repugnant, as they did some of their punishments. Strangulation was but one method of execution in nineteenth-century China: others included death by slicing and beheading. These penal methods, coupled to unusual and barbaric (to Western eyes) procedures of justice, were used as justification for the development of extraterritorial jurisdiction—once the Western nations could project sufficient power to force the Chinese to submit.

In short, after the 1844 treaty, Americans in China, mostly concentrated in Shanghai, faced extraterritorial consular courts much like the one that convicted John Ross.[27] These courts were quite active, especially after the turn of the century. By the early twentieth century, however, concerns over corruption and the quality of justice in the consular courts, coupled to the burgeoning American population in China, led the federal government to do something unusual.

Somewhat remarkably, Congress created the "United States District Court for China." The court, which commenced operation in 1906, was a federal court, but the judges were not Article III judges and they lacked life tenure. The court, however, answered to the Ninth Circuit and had jurisdiction over the whole of China and Korea, though it was headquartered in Shanghai. Shanghai was a center of foreign commercial activity in China then as now, and there were somewhere between 500 and 1,000 Americans residing in Shanghai at the turn of the century. (By the 1930s there were over 10,000 Americans throughout China, though Shanghai remained the primary outpost.)[28] Many of these expatriate Americans were religious missionaries, but their ranks included traders, sailors, and prostitutes.

The model for the new extraterritorial American court was an existing British body called His Britannic Majesty's Supreme Court for China. Like the British court, the American court would, it was hoped, regularize and professionalize the process of justice in Asia, while also providing a "civilizing" model for the Chinese themselves. The result was a major incursion by the British and Americans into what is a traditionally sovereign function. Indeed, the United States District Court for China held in an early case that

the Emperor of China exercises nominal sovereignty over all Chinese territory including that occupied by the nationals of the United States and Great Britain, yet the jurisdiction of these two countries over their own citizens who reside in China is, for all practical purposes, as full and complete as if China were in fact territory belonging to these nations.[29]

The judges on the U.S. District Court for China applied an unusual mix of common law and federal law to the civil and criminal cases they adjudicated. In defining applicable federal law they in part drew on existing codes for the Alaska Territory and for Washington, DC. The jurisdiction of the court was both geographic and nationality based. As the statute creating the district court declared, anyone could be a plaintiff, but the defendant must be American citizen or subject. The American consuls in China continued to address smaller claims and petty crimes, which could be appealed to the district court, but the larger cases now went directly to the district court. The latter was active; by 1922 the District Court for China had heard nearly 2,000 cases, an average of 125 per year.[30]

Despite its designation as a federal court, and the greater congressional oversight that followed, the United States Court for China did not offer appreciably greater constitutional guarantees than those offered by the garden-variety consular court that convicted John Ross. Indeed, the court expressly allied itself with the strict territorial vision developed by the Supreme Court in *Ross*. An unexceptional criminal case from the 1920s, *U.S. v. Furbush*, illustrates the parallels.

Like *Ross*, *U.S. v. Furbush* involved murder and American sailors.[31] Henry Furbush, the accused, was an engineer aboard an American vessel called the *Edgehill*, docked outside Shanghai. After a night of drinking in Shanghai bars Furbush ended up at a cabaret called the El Dorado, where he shot to death an unnamed customer. Furbush's defense largely consisted of claiming that he was too drunk to recall any of the events. The district court found Furbush guilty of murder in the second degree, and sentenced him to life imprisonment in the Philippines, then an American possession. A week later Furbush challenged his conviction on the grounds that he, like Ross, had been denied a proper jury trial and therefore his Sixth Amendment rights had been violated. Furbush was aware of the prior ruling, but noted that unlike in *Ross*, the District Court for China had "extended" Alaska Territory and District of Columbia law to Americans in China. This, he believed, changed the constitutional calculus. If American substantive law was extended extraterritorially, then, he argued, the Constitution's protections must necessarily follow.

The reply from the court drew directly on the Supreme Court's decision in *Ross*. "The fundamental fallacy" in Furbush's argument, it declared, "lies in the assumption that the Federal Constitution has been extended to China." The China court cited the emphatic language from *Ross* about how the Constitution can have no operation in another country. (The court took no notice of the irony that the oath it demanded of attorneys who appeared before it stated, "I solemnly swear that I will support the Constitution and the laws of the United States of America."[32]) It was true that the laws of the United States had been extended in some sense to

China. But the Constitution had no operation in China, the district court argued, because the laws of the United States apply (or "were extended") to Americans in China only in a very limited sense.

This argument was subtly different from that in *Ross*. Whereas the Supreme Court in *Ross* appeared to claim that the Constitution *could not* operate in another country—for to do so would trench upon the sovereignty of the other state—the U.S. Court for China seemed to believe that Congress *could* extend the Constitution to China, but simply chose not to. Congress, in implementing the Treaty of Wanghia, had stated in 1848 that "such jurisdiction in criminal and civil matters shall, in all cases, be exercised and enforced in conformity with the laws of the United States, which are herby, so far as is necessary to execute said treaty, extended over all citizens of the United States in China . . . so far as such laws are suitable to carry said treaty into effect." Because the Constitution per se was not mentioned by the implementing legislation, the court believed the Bill of Rights simply did not apply to Americans in China.

The China court thus defined the rights of accused Americans abroad solely in terms of congressional action. Congress did not affirmatively and expressly extend the Constitution; hence Henry Furbush lacked any constitutional right to trial by jury. The reasoning tracked that employed by the Supreme Court in the early 19th century, as described in the preceding chapter; and essentially the same reasoning appears in the various *Insular Cases*, discussed in the next section of this chapter, which grew out of the acquisition of overseas colonies after the defeat of Spain in 1898. The decision in *Furbush* stood for the duration of the extraterritorial court's existence. In fact, the United States Court for China failed to empanel a single jury in its several decades of operation, despite many requests to do so by defendants.

The flexibility this doctrine granted the federal government was striking. Eager to see America retain access to the emerging markets of Asia, and concerned that the United States not be fettered by rules more restrictive than those enjoyed by other Western powers, the federal government sought to keep the extraterritorial courts efficient, effective, and free of nettlesome rights and restrictions. The courts were pliant partners in this arrangement. Despite the occasional effort at invoking the Bill of Rights, as in *Furbush*, the *Ross* rule of strict territoriality persisted for decades.

Despite its active docket, the United States District Court for China ground to an end with World War II, and was formally disbanded in 1943. For many years before that the Chinese had bridled at the imposition upon their sovereignty the American court, and its sister extraterritorial courts throughout the nation, represented. As chapter 1 described, the interwar period brought a new set of ideas to the fore that made extraterritorial jurisdiction, unequal treaties, and imperialism increasingly untenable. Self-determination, championed by President Woodrow Wilson, seemed thoroughly at odds with extraterritorial jurisdiction, and the Chinese, like the Japanese before them, certainly considered themselves fully civilized and resented the imposition extraterritoriality represented.

That said, it took time for the norms supporting the practice of extraterritorial jurisdiction to fall into full disfavor around the globe, and the China court remained active throughout the 1920s.[33] Indeed, the American consular court in Morocco, the final outpost of American consular jurisdiction, was still handling over one hundred cases a year well into the 1950s.[34] But with Moroccan independence in 1956, this era of American extraterritoriality was over.

Imperial America

The United States was expansionist throughout the nineteenth century—devastatingly so, to the native tribes of North America—but it was not an imperial power in the traditional sense. The United States eschewed formal empire, preferring the less sweeping incursions represented by the U.S. District Court for China. The nation did of course acquire new territories as it expanded westward, but these were geographically contiguous rather than overseas, populated possessions. That pattern of growth changed dramatically at the end of the nineteenth century, when the United States, following the lead set by the European great powers, rapidly acquired several overseas territories as a result of its victory in the Spanish-American War of 1898.

In 1898 empire as a political form was nearing the peak of its second great wave. Throughout the nineteenth century the European powers, most prominently Great Britain, took control of vast territories from Africa to Asia. Aided by weapons technology, mass armies, and fast steamships, the European powers easily subdued most of the societies they encountered. Some colonies welcomed the status—in the 1840s the Dominican Republic tried, unsuccessfully, to give itself to Britain, France, Spain, and the United States—but regardless most found resistance futile, especially when faced with the Maxim machine gun.[35] England controlled India, much of South and East Africa, Nigeria, Malaya, and Canada and Australia. The French focused on North and West Africa and Indochina, the Belgians on the Congo, Germany on South-West Africa (today Namibia), and so forth.

Nineteenth-century empire had strategic, economic, religious, and civilizing aims, though the degree to which it realized those aims was perhaps as highly contested at the time as they are now. Geopolitical rivalry among the great powers certainly played a role in promoting colonization, though Germany, one of the greatest powers of the late nineteenth century, acquired only a minimal overseas empire.[36] The notion that expansion added rather than sapped national power informs a long tradition of realist thinking, a tradition that continued into the Cold War when many feared the effects of Soviet expansion on American security.[37] Yet many at the turn of the last century were skeptical of the wisdom of imperial expansion. In Britain the nineteenth-century prime minister William Gladstone famously championed the idea—to little avail—that colonies were more burden than boon. Gladstone echoed a long line of liberal thinkers who doubted whether conquest really paid. Perhaps most notable was Adam Smith, who in the *Wealth of Nations* had concluded that colonies often contribute little or nothing to national wealth or security.

The economic rationale for empire was undermined in part by the dramatic rise in free trade that took place in the late 1800s. In many respects the era was the first great wave of globalization, a wave that crashed with the onset of the First World War.[38] But before that crash levels of trade, migration, and foreign investment were extremely high and the world was more and more interconnected economically. Controlling foreign territory via empire clearly gave Western powers secure access to crucial goods and services. But in a relatively open economy one could trade for items produced in other places, without the costs of direct coercive rule. The British free trader Richard Cobden declared in 1856 that "it would be a happy day when England has not an acre of territory in Continental Asia."[39]

There were moral concerns as well. Noted conservative Edmund Burke opposed British rule in India out of respect for the importance of local rule and tradition. Similar views were held by Adam Smith and Jeremy Bentham. For the most part, however, these justice-based critiques of colonization (which often were critiques about particular modes of imperialism, rather than of the idea of foreign rule itself) were more salient in the first half of the nineteenth century than the second.[40]

By the 1860s formal empire was again ascendant. Prevailing theories of racial superiority made subjugation by the West seem natural and inevitable. Moreover, empire was increasingly seen as a force for good: the West would Christianize the heathens, introduce commerce, and improve their lives. France, for instance, believed firmly in the value of its *mission civilisatrice*. Empire would bring grandeur, yes, but if France could control North and West Africa and bring it civilization, "who could say this was a poor use of force?"[41] Lord Curzon, the British viceroy in India from 1899 to 1905, echoed this view, claiming that "the British Empire is under Providence the greatest instrument for good that the world has seen."[42] In this climate it is unsurprising that the United States, though itself a former colony, would find the acquisition of an empire irresistible.

Island Hopping

Overseas expansion was nonetheless a divisive issue in American politics throughout the nineteenth century.[43] For most of this period the United States did resist the urge to obtain distant colonies, and focused instead on contiguous westward expansion and the "closing of the frontier." In general, nineteenth-century America suffered from what Fareed Zakaria has dubbed "imperial understretch." Despite its remarkable economic size—by 1885 it had the largest manufacturing output in the world—the United States played a very minor role in world politics and had little interest in overseas territory.[44] The one exception, before the burst of imperial growth at the end of the century, involved an odd commodity, one highly valued in the nineteenth century but today mostly viewed as a nuisance: bird droppings, or guano.

Guano was a fertilizer highly prized by American farmers. Facing shortages, in the 1850s Congress passed the Guano Islands Act, which empowered Americans to discover unoccupied "guano islands" and claim them for the United States.[45] Under the terms of the act such an "island, rock, or key may, at the discretion of the President, be considered as appertaining to the United States." What the term *appertaining to* meant was not clear. But it did not mean that the United States had to keep the island in perpetuity; as the act stated, the islands could be let go "after the guano shall be removed from same."[46] This acquisitional neologism led to much confusion over the legal status of the acquired guano islands. As a State Department memo from the 1930s aptly characterized the situation, "the only conclusion that can be fairly drawn . . . is that no one knew what the Guano Act really did mean."[47] Nonetheless, some seventy such overseas islands were claimed for America at the height of the guano craze.

The one judicial attempt to divine the legal meaning of the Guano Islands Act came in the 1890 case of *Jones v. United States*, which was handed down the same year as John Ross's appeal of his murder conviction in Japan. It also involved, somewhat improbably, both a man named John Ross and a murder in an exotic locale. Unlike *In re Ross*, however, the murder in *Jones* involved an axe rather than a knife—though in yet another strange convergence, an extraterritorial axe-murder would be the crime at the center of the 1957 landmark decision that overturned *In re Ross* and the regime of strict territoriality for constitutional rights it signified.

In *Jones* the Supreme Court was faced with the question of whether the federal government had jurisdiction over murders and other serious crimes committed on guano islands claimed by Americans under the Guano Act. The defendants argued that because the islands were not properly absorbed into the United States, but were instead only "appertaining" to it, Congress had no jurisdiction under international law. As a result, they believed, the United States could not police activities there: the statute criminalizing murder on the guano islands was invalid. The Supreme Court unanimously rejected this contention. The Court announced that not only was the impermanent title claimed by the United States contemplated by international law but that, in any event, claims of sovereignty over territory were questions for the political branches to determine. The particular guano island in question, off the coast of Haiti, "was at the time under the sole and exclusive jurisdiction of the United States . . . and recognized and considered by the United States as appertaining to the United States, and in the possession of the United States, under those laws."[48] Congress's criminal jurisdiction over the murder was, as a result, unquestioned.

In the end, the guano islands episode was a trivial chapter in the story of American overseas expansion. But the legal term *appertaining* would, in slightly altered form, become a significant part of the jurisprudence of the early-twentieth-century *Insular Cases*. The notion of an island or other landmass appertaining to the United States, rather than being a part of the United States, proved very appealing in the context of imperial expansion.

At about the same time as the guano craze, the U.S. became interested in a much more valuable set of islands: Hawaii. Americans had been deeply involved in the Hawaiian economy for much of the nineteenth century. Indeed, attempts were made to annex Hawaii as early as the 1850s.[49] Many were attracted to Hawaii's climate, which was tropical yet tolerable in an age before air-conditioning, and to its strategic location in the heart of the Pacific. The influence of the United States on Hawaii grew dramatically in 1898 when the United States annexed the islands and made them a federal territory. The annexation followed a series of machinations sufficiently sordid that the United States formally apologized to the native Hawaiian people a century later.[50]

The United States had, like many other states, recognized the Republic of Hawaii as an independent state during much of the nineteenth century. But as American business interests in Hawaii grew, however, there was agitation for change. Eventually the American ambassador conspired with local American residents to overthrow the Hawaiian government. The independent Republic of Hawaii was founded in 1893 with Sanford Dole, an American born in Hawaii, as president. The Republic of Hawaii was soon annexed by the United States and Dole installed as territorial governor. Hawaii remained federal territory for nearly six decades. As both the guano and Hawaiian islands episodes illustrate, by the late nineteenth century the United States was increasingly interested in distant offshore islands. Acquiring and controlling such islands soon became a major part of American foreign policy.

America's Rise and Spain's Decline

As the Monroe Doctrine evidenced, the United States had long asserted influence over Latin America; its ambitions outside North America were not limited to guano islands and Hawaii. American elites coveted Cuba, for example, believing it a natural addition to the nation. President Franklin Pierce had even tried to purchase the island from Spain in 1854. Thus the imperial expansion of the late 1890s did not come out of nowhere. Indeed, for some scholars "what is puzzling about the Spanish-American War of 1898 is not why it happened, but why it was so long in coming."[51] The United States had possessed the wealth and population to create a navy and an army that could exert extensive power overseas for some time. Until the end of the nineteenth century, however, it had never converted that latent power into meaningful force. In part this disjuncture was the result of America's "statelessness"—the "absence of a powerful central administration and of a national 'state elite' to run it."[52] The result was a nation that was widely thought to possess enormous potential, but—much like Brazil today—was not yet considered a great power.

The Spanish-American War was thus a striking moment in America's trajectory toward global dominance. Historian Ernest May wrote that "1898–99 marked the emergence of the United States as a great power."[53] The United States had not directly engaged a European power militarily since the War of 1812 against the British. The defeat of Spain—an aging and faded power, but a power nonetheless—was surprisingly easy. The United States Navy, led by Commodore George Dewey, attacked and readily defeated Spain in the Philippines. In Cuba the fighting was swift and not especially bloody. Only some four hundred American soldiers perished. The ready capitulation of Spain demonstrated the prowess of the United States, and did so at a time when the reigning global hegemon, Britain, was facing the limitations of its own power in the Boer War.[54] Victory also permitted, and indeed encouraged, the United States to engage in the imperial politics so endemic to the European powers of the era.

The successful prosecution of the war had a significant effect aside from signaling the extent of the United States's new ambitions: the peace treaty gave the United States control over many of the former Spanish island colonies. Spain resisted ceding some, such as the Philippines, but the United States prevailed and in the process gained control of a large chunk of Asia. This newfound imperial role was decidedly controversial at home. Could a former rebellious colony embrace the colonization of others? Should the republic become an empire? Books such as *Imperial Republic* (1899) suggested the United States could and should, but many political elites of the era remained opposed to the notion and were concerned about the implications for domestic governance.[55]

Beyond the political ramifications of ruling distant, overseas islands the acquisition of the Spanish colonies raised contentious legal questions. The most burning of these related to the territorial scope of the Constitution. Did the Constitution apply to these new territories, whose inhabitants were decidedly not Anglo-Saxons and did not speak English? Were the territories destined to become states? If the Constitution did not apply in these territories, what exactly was the status of these new possessions and their populations?

These legal questions were, of course, not wholly new. The Northwest Ordinance of 1787 had declared that Congress was to administer federal territories "for the purpose of temporary government" and it guaranteed the civil liberties of the territorial inhabitants. Territories were often understood in early American history to be proto- or apprentice states; they were, as the Supreme Court suggested in *Loughborough v. Blake*, "in a state of infancy advancing toward manhood" and would assume complete equality with the existing states of the union once they were fully grown.[56] And the antebellum case of *Dred Scott* had argued that the constitutional protections for property flowed immediately into whatever territory was under the sovereignty of the United States.[57] Several early-nineteenth-century cases supported a similar argument about the Constitution's congruence with the United States's sovereign borders.

Yet the situation presented by the acquisition of the Spanish colonies was novel. In stark contrast with the Nebraska or Ohio territories, for example, the islands contained very large populations of Asians and Spanish speakers. Unlike the Indian tribes of North America, these groups were unlikely to simply be pushed off by white settlers into some less desirable region. For a society like turn-of-the-century America, largely enthralled by a racism that seems shocking today, this prospect raised enormous concerns. In addition, the new territories were not geographically contiguous. They had hot, tropical climates that many contemporaries believed made them unsuitable for immigration by peoples of Northern European descent. In other words, they would likely remain non-Anglo-Saxon indefinitely.[58]

Many Americans were consequently chary about embracing these new territories as their own in a full sense. But the fever for imperialism burned high. Once the United States possessed Puerto Rico, Cuba, Guam, and the Philippines there seemed little reason to give them up. Cuba was a significant exception; the independence of Cuba had been a chief rationale for the war with Spain.[59] Nonetheless, when the American occupation ended in 1902, the new Cuban constitution included a provision dubbed the Platt Amendment, which permitted the United States to intervene at any time for "the preservation of Cuban independence, the maintenance of a government adequate for the protection of life, property, and individual liberty."[60]

At roughly the same time, the United States leased a seemingly innocuous "coaling station" on the southeastern end of Cuba. The coaling station turned out to be of much greater historical significance than the Platt Amendment. Guantanamo Bay was sizable—about twice the size of Manhattan—and strategically situated. It provided an excellent harbor for the growing American naval operations in the Caribbean. The terms of the Guantanamo Bay lease, which formally retain "ultimate sovereignty" for Cuba but indefinitely grant the United States "complete jurisdiction and control," were unusually favorable for the United States. Indeed, they were originally drafted as an act of Congress in 1901, while the United States still governed Cuba.[61]

Although Cuba was in many respects turned into a nominally-independent offshore protectorate, the United States was less sure about how to treat the other former Spanish islands. The Philippines, the largest of the new possessions, in particular vexed the political establishment of the time. Given their location in the Far East there was little prospect of statehood for the islands. Elites regularly described the inhabitants as illiterate and primitive; William Howard Taft, for example, described the Filipinos as an "ignorant, superstitious people," though well-intentioned and kind.[62] Many saw the notion of citizenship for the Filipinos, and likewise the Puerto Ricans, as impossible. The Democratic Party Platform in the election of 1900 baldly stated that "the Filipinos cannot be citizens without endangering our civilization; they cannot be subjects without imperiling our form of government."[63] Thus the acquisition of the Philippines "was understood by contemporaries on both sides of the [imperialism] debate, as it is readily understood today, to be a turning-point in our history."[64]

McKinley considered several options. One was to return the Asian islands to Spain, which seemed to contemporaries both unsporting and, given the widespread beliefs about despotic Spanish rule, tantamount to returning the Filipinos to virtual slavery. A second option was independence, but this was widely viewed at the time as untenable and likely to lead to civic disorder and breakdown. (Filipino insurgents fought for several years seeking independence, and the resulting bloody war consumed many civilian lives and saw brutal methods used by the American army.) A third option was to hand the islands to some other European power, but opponents feared this could sow considerable discord among the great powers and foment further war. The fourth, and in the end the least unattractive, option was continued possession of the Philippines by the United States.[65] The uncertainty over what course the country would choose led Rudyard Kipling to pen the famous poem that opens this book. "Take up the White Man's Burden," Kipling importuned the hesitant Americans.

Kipling's urging reflected the concern many Americans had about the effect of imperialism on the nation. Prominent professor William Graham

Sumner gave an address at Yale in 1899 in which he declared that "expansion and imperialism are at war with the best traditions, principles, and interests of the American people." Imperialism would threaten, if not destroy, "the scheme of a republic which our fathers formed."[66] Economic issues loomed large as well. It was widely feared that free trade between the lush Philippines and the United States would bankrupt American farmers.[67]

Although these concerns were widespread, many Americans disagreed and saw empire as natural and right, and even deserved. The nation had survived a civil war, and now had handily defeated a European power— albeit one teetering on the edge of political irrelevancy. The United States could now take its rightful place at the table among the great powers. For the United States to join in the imperial adventure of the time seemed, to many contemporaries, entirely apt. "God has not been preparing the English-speaking and Teutonic peoples for a thousand years for nothing," said Senator Beveridge of Indiana. "No! He has made us the master organizers of the world to establish a system where chaos reigns. He has made us adept in government that we may administer government among savage and servile peoples."[68]

With the overseas territories full of "savage and servile peoples" in hand—and new ones, such the Panama Canal Zone, being quickly added—a burning question of the day concerned what the precise status of these possessions was.[69] Could their governance differ from that in contiguous territories like California? In short, "did the Constitution follow the flag?"

The Insular Cases

Alexis De Tocqueville, a great student of American life, famously declared that "scarcely a political question arises in this country that does not sooner or later resolve itself into a legal question." The politics of empire proved no exception. It did not take long for the question of the constitutional status of the new American colonies to come before the Supreme Court. When it did, it capped a surprisingly heated and often bitter controversy that consumed substantial legal and political energy. As one close observer wrote in 1926,

> It is difficult to realize how fervent a controversy raged some twenty-five or more years ago over the question of whether the Constitution follows the flag. This question ... divided not only courts, judges, and lawyers, but public opinion generally. It led to a flood of controversial literature, to phrase-making in and out of Congress, and to a bitterness which almost threatened to resemble the controversies over the Fugitive Slave Law and the Missouri Compromise ... The election of 1900 largely turned upon the so-called issue of imperialism.[70]

A leading newspaper columnist of the day, Finley Peter Dunne, used his fictional Irish bartender Mr. Dooley to poke fun at the burst of enthusiasm over empire and the attendant confusion over its implications. Mr. Dooley's friend Mr. Hennessey, referring to President McKinley, declared, "I know what I'd do if I were Mack. I'd hist a flag over th' Ph'lipeens, an' I'd take in th' whole lot iv him." "An yet," replied Mr. Dooley, "tis not more thin two months since ye larned whether they were islands or canned goods."[71]

The rapidity with which the United States embraced the acquisition of a sprawling overseas empire may have partly accounted for the utter confusion over how to integrate these new colonies into the prevailing constitutional framework. Politicians debated the merits of empire, whereas prominent legal lights of the day—including Christopher Columbus Langdell, the former dean of Harvard Law School, and Abbott Lowell, the future president of Harvard University—wrote long articles analyzing their constitutional dimensions. And although historians continue to dispute the degree to which the 1900 presidential election in fact turned on the new-found embrace of imperialism, the issue was clearly a major one. Indeed, the Democratic Party platform of 1900 stated in no uncertain terms, "We hold that the Constitution follows the flag, and denounce the doctrine that an Executive or Congress deriving their existence and their powers from the Constitution can exercise lawful authority beyond it or in violation of it."[72]

Congress was involved in the debate from the start. On January 11, 1900, the *New York Times* ran this headline, seemingly stripped from the pages of today's satirical newspaper *The Onion*: "Status of New Possessions: House Committee Named to Ascertain If They Are in Fact Parts of the United States."[73] The political branches were unable to decisively answer the question, however. Eventually, as Tocqueville suggested it would, the judiciary stepped into the fray. The set of Supreme Court decisions known as "the Insular Cases" addressed the legal status of the new overseas territories. There were approximately twenty such cases, decided between 1900 and 1922, with the majority handed down between 1901 and 1904.[74] Arguably the most significant was the early case of *Downes v. Bidwell*.[75]

The question in *Downes* was in many respects familiar: was a newly acquired territory—in this case, the island of Puerto Rico—within "the United States" for the purposes of the customs and tariffs laws? The same central issue had arisen when the British temporarily conquered Castine, Maine, in the War of 1812 and when the United States conquered and governed Tampico, Mexico, after the 1845 Mexican-American War. At root, this dispute required the Supreme Court to decide where the borders of the United States lie. Were the sovereign borders of the nation, as recognized by the international community, congruent with the constitutional borders of the American political and legal system? Or was there some transitional region between the truly foreign and the truly domestic?

The larger question at stake was whether the American legal system was to going to foster or fetter imperialism. As the McKinley administration argued, "We must look at the situation as comprehending a possibility— I do not say a probability, but a possibility—that the question might be as to the powers of this government in the acquisition of Egypt and the Soudan [sic], or a section of Central Africa, or a spot in the Antarctic Circle, or a section of the Chinese Empire."[76] If domestic law required that all these places be treated as akin to the continental states, a foreign policy like that of Great Britain or France was, as a political matter, impossible for the United States to implement.

Issues of great geopolitical important thus lurked behind the seemingly-quotidian dispute in *Downes*. Technically, the case arose as a dispute involving imported oranges. In 1900 Samuel Downes brought a shipment of oranges from Puerto Rico into New York, where he was forced to pay duties on the grounds that Puerto Rico was a foreign country. Downes, with the assistance of the well-known New York lawyer Frederick Coudert, sued to recover the duties, arguing that they violated the constitutional require-ment that duties be uniform throughout the United States. The mundane nature of the case did not mask the true stakes. Reports of the time describe that unprecedented crowds gathered before the Supreme Court when the decision was announced. "The bare rumor that the court would render its decision" in *Downes*, said the *New York Times*, was sufficient to draw a huge crowd that "realized that no such momentous issues affecting the growth and progress of the nation were likely again to come before the tribunal . . . and every man who was fortunate enough to gain access to the chamber during the delivery of the opinions appreciated that he was witnessing one of the most tremendous events in the nation's life."[77]

In the face of this pressure, and generally "unwilling to throw water on the imperialist fires burning in the nation," the Supreme Court splin-tered.[78] The political frame of the debate in *Downes*—did the Constitution follow the flag?—was troubling to many of the justices. "The governing jurisprudence of the day," wrote legal scholar Owen Fiss many years later, "could not admit of the possibility of ever separating the flag and the Constitution." Moreover, social contract theory and the ideal of limited government ruled the day; the infamous *Lochner* decision, which struck down workplace hour regulation, was just a few years away. And yet, as Fiss pointed out, there was "nothing consensual about American domin-ation over the Philippines or Puerto Rico"—nor was federal power over the territories limited.[79] The McKinley administration also made clear that this might not be the last overseas colony the United States acquired—the riches of the "Soudan" beckoned. Hence the Court's ruling against Mr. Downes was, in the end, widely seen as one that bent principle in favor of political expediency.

The controlling opinion, though adhered to by only one justice, contained a long historical exegesis of prior judicial decisions concerning the constitutional treatment of the territories. Despite its highly checkered reputation, the obvious case on point was *Dred Scott*, and indeed it was cited frequently by all sides throughout the *Insular Cases*.[80] Some of the justices acknowledged that taken at face value, *Dred Scott*'s holding that the constitutional guarantee of property extended into federal territory strongly suggested that the Constitution did follow the flag. This, all agreed, would mean the end of American imperialism, for no one at the time thought it possible that these tropical, Spanish-speaking island populations could be fully protected by the Constitution.

Some justices argued, however, that subsequent events had destroyed the value of *Dred Scott* as a precedent, and empire—and intraterritorial differentiation—was consequently possible. As the ever witty Mr. Dooley put it at the time, Justice Brown, who advanced this argument in *Downes v. Bidwell*, must have thought to himself, "Again we take th' Dhred Scott decision. This is wan iv th' worst I ever r-read. If I cudden't write a better wan with blindhers on, I'd leap off th' bench. This horrible fluke iv a decision throws a gr-reat, an almost dazzlin' light on the case. I will turn it off."[81]

With the nettlesome precedent of *Dred Scott* summarily dispensed with, *Downes v. Bidwell* announced an unusual holding that resurrected the Guano Islands Act of the nineteenth century. "We are therefore of opinion," the Court concluded, "that the island of Porto Rico is a territory appurtenant and belonging to the United States, but not a part of the United States within the revenue clauses of the Constitution."[82] Puerto Rico was thus American territory, owned and controlled by the federal government, but it was not part of the United States for constitutional purposes. It was, in a telling phrase used by the Court, "foreign in a domestic sense."

This reasoning meant that the constitutional rule that all duties and imposts must be uniform throughout the nation did not apply. On its own, that holding was significant, if not completely startling: earlier cases had held that militarily occupied foreign territory was not within the United States, and it was not a tremendous leap—though it was a leap nonetheless—to hold that an American colony acquired via conquest from a foreign power was also outside the United States. But prior federal territories had not always been viewed this way. And, most notably, the *Downes* court itself had announced the same day, in a companion case, that the ratification of the peace treaty with Spain had caused Puerto Rico to cease to be a foreign country.[83] Indeed, as the decision in *Downes* itself pointed out, with considerable understatement, "[t]he decisions of this court upon this subject have not been altogether harmonious."

The "Occult" Doctrine of
Incorporation

The most influential and significant legacy of *Downes* was not about duties on Puerto Rican oranges. It was instead a concept. The case introduced into the legal lexicon the concept of "territorial incorporation."[84] Justice Edward White argued in a much discussed concurring opinion that Congress possessed the power to decide whether or not a given territory was incorporated into the United States. Incorporation in turn shaped the legal rules applicable to the territory. As the last chapter described, prior commentators had debated whether the United States consisted, for legal purposes, solely of the states or whether the territories, too, were part of the polity and fully protected by the Constitution. The first view recognized the existence of federal territories, but argued that the federal government's authority over them rested on the fundamental powers inherent in sovereignty or the particularities of the Territory Clause. The Constitution, as a result, was not generally a restraint when governing the territories. The second view was familiar from *Dred Scott*.

The significance of *Downes* was its articulation of a "third view," in the words of Abbott Lowell, in which Congress had discretion over the Constitution's reach.[85] To establish the discretionary power to incorporate a territory, White looked first to existing rules of international law. He argued that the law of nations traditionally provided every sovereign government with the inherent power to acquire territory, including by conquest. Quoting Halleck's then-influential treatise on international law, and in particular its provisions on belligerent occupation, White noted that a conquering nation can choose to govern a conquered nation according to the conquered nation's own laws.

Yet if the conqueror "incorporates them with his former states, giving to them the rights, privileges, and immunities of his own subjects," that choice of extending the conquering state's law is permissible as well.[86] So, too, can the conqueror grant to the conquered a lesser set of rights, if the people conquered are considered savages. (This distinction between the legal options applicable to territory seized from sovereigns and to territory seized from "savages" was not new: almost a century earlier the Marshall Court, in the 1819 case of *American Insurance Co. v. Canter*, had advanced essentially the same principle).[87] In short, White contended that international law established that a state had a range of options with regard to what set of legal rules would govern a newly acquired territory. The United States, as a sovereign state under international law, thus had the power to decide whether or not the Constitution was "extended" to new territories.

This was consistent with the idea, one of long standing, that Congress possessed plenary power over the federal territories. If a territory was incorporated by Congress, or the Constitution extended, the Constitution operated more or less as it did in the states themselves. Territories in which the Constitution was not extended, by contrast, enjoyed only those rights guaranteed by the Constitution that were deemed fundamental. White's opinion in *Downes* offered no comprehensive list of fundamental rights; nor were the concepts of incorporation or extension themselves particularly well-defined.[88] The central implications of this approach, however, were clear. Though plainly sovereign American territory, Congress could draw intraterritorial distinctions between one territory and another.[89]

This approach had a major impact on American legal thinking, and soon migrated from the intraterritorial context to the extraterritorial. It was later picked up by the United States District Court for China, as evidenced by the Shanghai murder case of sailor Henry Furbush described above. The District Court for China fended off Furbush's constitutional claim by noting that Congress had not extended the Bill of Rights to China, but rather had only extended certain aspects of American law.

The *Insular Cases* came as a surprise to some contemporary observers. In a lengthy survey of the constitutional powers of Congress over federal territory undertaken just before the *Insular Cases*, legal scholar Henry W. Bikle summarized the law thusly: "It is a significant fact that in no case in regard to jurisdiction within the territory of the United States has a limitation of the power of Congress over personal or proprietary rights been held inapplicable."[90] Existing precedents, he ventured, "make it improbable that the Court will hold any general provision limiting the power of Congress over personal and proprietary rights inapplicable in any part of the possessions of the United States."[91] This cautionary lesson in legal prediction underscores the great uncertainty that existed at the time over how best to work the transition from republic to empire. And predictions like Bikle's were in part reflective of the widespread opposition in Congress to American empire. Senator George Vest, for instance, put forward a resolution in 1898 denying to the federal government the power to acquire territory to held or governed permanently. "The colonial system of European nations," he said, "cannot be established under our present Constitution."[92]

The legal system put into place by the *Insular Cases* was also difficult to fathom. The oddity of the reasoning was encapsulated in Justice White's statement in *Downes* that overseas islands such as Puerto Rico were "foreign to the United States in a domestic sense."[93] This strange phrase, like the equally odd, if not oxymoronic, appellation of the Indian tribes as "domestic dependent nations," illustrated how difficult it was to square Westphalian territoriality with American constitutional jurisprudence *and* the desire for imperial expansion. If Puerto Rico and the other overseas lands were not foreign territory, were they not by necessity American territory? Was there some middle category? Apparently there was: territory could be American as far as other sovereigns were concerned yet, for the purposes of domestic law, remain foreign. Like Indian country, this kind of territory was distinctive internally, even if undifferentiated to the outside world.

The *Insular Cases* also reinforced the notion that military occupation by the United States was not tantamount to sovereignty. In *Neely v. Henkel*, also handed down in 1901, the justices held that although Cuba was occupied by and governed by the United States, it was nonetheless "foreign territory" because the United States was not a successor in title to the island (as was the case with Puerto Rico). As a result Cuba "cannot be regarded, in any constitutional, legal, or international sense, a part of the territory of the United States." As a result, the writ of habeas corpus, trial by jury, and other constitutional protections for the accused did not apply. These provisions, said the court, "have no relation to crimes committed without the jurisdiction of the United States against the laws of a foreign country."[94] Military governance, in short, might mean complete American control, but it did not mean constitutional control. This principle would of course be revived in the years after September 11, 2001.

These principles, and others, clearly raised hard questions about the relationship between the Constitution and American sovereignty. Some found it hard to see why *all* the powers, but only *some* of the rights, applied in a geographic region that Congress chose not to incorporate. Indeed, the dissenters in *Downes* were highly skeptical of the concept of territorial incorporation, calling it an "occult" notion with little foundation in American political theory or legal text. For the dissenters, the idea that Congress could extend the basic laws of the United States as a matter of choice misunderstood the nature of American constitutionalism. It substituted imperial power for republican principles. As Justice John Harlan later wrote, the concept of incorporation

assumes that Congress, which came into existence, and exists, only by virtue of the Constitution, can withhold fundamental guarantees of life and liberty from peoples who have come under our complete jurisdiction . . . over whose country we have acquired the authority to exercise sovereign dominion. In my judgment, neither the life, nor the liberty, nor the property, of any person, within any territory or country over which the United States is sovereign, can be taken . . . by any form of procedure inconsistent with the Constitution of the United States.[95]

But this was not the position taken by the majority of the Supreme Court. So did the Constitution follow the flag? It seemed it did not, though the various decisions, with their myriad tensions, fomented some debate on that score. Perhaps the best, and certainly the wittiest, assessment came from Elihu Root, then secretary of war. When asked to sum up the early decisions of the

Supreme Court on American empire, Root opined that the Constitution does indeed follow the flag, "but it doesn't quite catch up."[96]

"A Home Stayin' Constitution"

Another famous quip of the period declared that the Constitution may not follow the flag, but the Supreme Court surely followed the election returns.[97] In the election of 1900 McKinley, the Republican incumbent, assisted by Theodore Roosevelt, the hero of the Spanish-American War, handily defeated the Democratic Party challenger and oratorical firebrand William Jennings Bryan. Bryan ran on a platform of anti-imperialism and opposition to the gold standard. Both positions ran counter to the rising internationalism of the day. The gold standard was the lubricant that permitted a level of international economic integration previously unheard of. And, by the turn of the century, every major European power possessed a panoply of overseas territories.

Many Americans, newly cognizant of their growing power, sought their place among the great states of the day. McKinley's victory was seen as a vindication of this new and muscular foreign policy. For the Republicans, the Spanish-American War gave America "a new and noble responsibility . . . to confer the blessings of liberty and civilization upon all the rescued peoples." Roosevelt, McKinley's candidate for vice president, proclaimed further that "[t]he young giant of the West stands on a continent and clasps the crest of an ocean in either hand. Our nation, glorious in youth and strength, looks into the future with eager eyes and rejoices as a strong man to run a race."[98]

The Supreme Court thus tracked this new political movement, though there some dispute over whether the *Insular Cases* had actually supported or rejected the argument that the Constitution followed the flag.[99] (Thus Elihu Root's line that the Constitution followed the flag "but it doesn't quite catch up" was both funny and insightful.) The doctrine of incorporation facilitated the imperial ambitions of turn of the century America while retaining a veneer of commitment to constitutional self-government. Consequently, incorporation was not just a formalistic legal doctrine; it had potent implications for America's new role as a great power. As an editorial in a Chicago newspaper put it, the nation had now taken "a new place in the world." America "had thrown off its swaddling clothes" and come forth as a "full-powered" sovereign able to conquer and rule colonies at will.[100]

Throughout the *Insular Cases* the justices appeared concerned with how best to avoid fettering the imperial ambitions the nation possessed or might develop in the future. Justice Brown surfaced these concerns most clearly, writing in *Downes* that "a false step at this time might be fatal to the development of what Chief Justice Marshall called the American Empire."[101] Later cases likewise suggested that applying the Constitution fully to the new overseas colonies would inevitably constrain America's ability to engage to acquire an empire. Extending constitutional rights into all sovereign territory would mean that if "the United States, impelled by its duty or advantage, shall acquire territory peopled by savages," it would have to extend trial by jury and other significant constitutional rights. "To state such a proposition," the Supreme Court argued, "demonstrates the impossibility of putting it into practice."[102]

The *Insular Cases* are little remembered today. They nonetheless played a critical role in America's move toward empire. Ruled by the federal government, the residents of the "unincorporated" territories enjoyed only the most basic protections. The federal government had a far freer hand in ruling the colonies than it enjoyed in the contiguous territories. Moreover— and, in the wake of the Civil War, perhaps quite crucially—the unincorporated territories could be let go without sundering the Union.[103] The bond to the nation was not permanent. The American experiment with imperialism could, if need be, remain just that.

The Canal Zone

In 1903, with the *Insular Cases* still being hotly contested, the United States negotiated a treaty with the new Republic of Panama—or, to be precise, with a man named Philippe Bunau-Varilla, "envoy extraordinary" of the new Panamanian state. The Hay-Bunau Varilla Treaty further extended the reach of the United States and cemented its plans to control the sea lanes and maritime traffic of the Americas. The treaty granted control of a narrow but crucial patch of land stretching from the Atlantic to the Pacific:

> The Republic of Panama grants to the United States in perpetuity the use, occupation and control of a zone of land and land under water for the construction, maintenance, operation, sanitation and protection of said Canal...Panama grants to the United States all the rights, power and authority...which the United States would possess and exercise if it were the sovereign of the territory within which said lands and waters are located to the entire exclusion of the exercise by the Republic of Panama of any such sovereign rights, power or authority.[104]

Only two weeks before, the Republic of Panama did not exist. Panama had previously been a province of Colombia, but landowners in the region sought independence. The United States had long eyed the narrow neck of land as a suitable spot for an "isthmian canal" that would bridge the two oceans and enable ships to sail rapidly from New York to San Francisco. When plans for a canal across Nicaragua failed, the United States sought to have the canal built in the region of Panama. Congress passed the Panama Canal Act in 1902, authorizing the president to acquire from Colombia the rights to build a canal and control the immediate surrounding lands. When the Colombians balked, President Theodore Roosevelt, a proponent of maritime power and avid reader of Alfred Mahan's influential 1890 treatise *The Influence of Sea Power upon History*, did not stand idly by. Roosevelt encouraged the Panamanians to revolt and sent in the United States Navy for support.

Once Panamanian independence was assured, the United States quickly recognized the new government and negotiated the Bunau-Varilla Treaty. The language of the agreement was quite similar to that of the contemporaneous lease with Cuba for the strategic harbor at Guantanamo.[105] Indeed, in both cases the United States permitted formal independence of the partner state but retained total control of a crucial strategic overseas territory. Like the unequal treaties of the nineteenth century, this veneer of consent allowed the United States to maintain that it was not colonizing, but merely cooperating with, other nations. Many contemporaries nonetheless saw through this veneer and believed that the Roosevelt administration had acted wrongly, if not illegally in obtaining the Panama canal. Indeed, in a telling story, Roosevelt at one point asked his cabinet whether he had successfully defended himself against critics of his Panama policy. "Have I answered the charges?" Roosevelt asked, after a long disquisition on the topic of the canal. As was often the case, the quick-witted Elihu Root jumped in. "You certainly have, Mr. President," Root apparently said. "You were accused of seduction and you have conclusively proved that you are guilty of rape."[106]

As in the *Insular Cases* two core questions arose. Was the canal zone foreign or domestic? Either way, what laws applied to it? A tariff dispute again brought these issues to the fore. In 1904 Roosevelt decreed that full tariffs applied to goods imported into the canal zone, even if the goods came from Panama itself.[107] To make clear that the zone was a microcosmic overseas outpost of America, he also declared that the domestic postage rate would apply to letters sent from the zone to the United States (or vice versa), but foreign rates would apply for a letter going from the zone into Panama. These rules, though not contradicted by the Hay-Bunau Varilla Treaty, precipitated a crisis with the Panamanians—so much so that Roosevelt ultimately relented.

Nonetheless, the Supreme Court in 1907 did not hesitate to describe the canal zone as "belong[ing] to this nation," and for the most part that was the view taken elsewhere in the federal government.[108] Roosevelt created a governing commission for the canal zone in 1904 and instructed it to "make all needful rules."[109] He stressed that existing law should more or less continue in force, but that there were "great principles of government which have been made the basis of our existence as a nation which we deem essential to the rule of law" and these must have force within the zone.[110] These "great principles" included the right to due process of law, the right to property, and various criminal procedures—though trial by jury was not among them. By 1914 Woodrow Wilson, then president, created a permanent administration for the canal zone and a set of overseas district courts that would answer to the Fifth Circuit. Thus from the Wilson administration onward the basic judicial structure of the canal zone court was much like that of the U.S. District Court for China.

By the 1940s, with empire building largely behind the nation, the federal courts were less inclined to see the canal zone as constitutionally anomalous.[111] The result was a somewhat confused series of rulings about the reach of the Constitution's protections. In a World War II–era case the district court for the canal zone held the Fifth Amendment due process clause applicable to the acts of the canal zone governor.[112] Yet in the 1970s the federal courts made clear that the Bill of Rights did not fully extend into the canal zone. A man named Michael Scott, convicted of dealing cocaine, appealed on the grounds that his Fifth Amendment rights had been denied at trial, and that "a citizen of the United States charged with a violation of a federal law in a United States court is constitutionally entitled to the benefit of a grand jury."[113] The Fifth Circuit replied flatly that "the constitution does not require the extension of all protections of the bill of rights to territories governed by the United States."[114]

Scott's citizenship did not matter to the court; aliens and citizens were treated alike because "it is the territorial nature of the Canal Zone and not the citizenship of the defendant that is dispositive."[115] This position—that location determined the scope of an individual's rights, and that offshore locations received a lesser quantum of rights—was of course the ground norm animating cases from *In re Ross* through the United States District Court for China to the *Insular Cases*. But as later chapters will describe, by the 1970s, when the Fifth Circuit made this claim, much had changed with regard to the overseas rights of citizens.[116]

The canal zone's unusual status also raised other interesting questions. Were the children born to "Zonians" ordinary citizens of the United States? For nearly all intents and purposes this issue was insignificant. In 1904 Congress had declared those born in the zone to American parents to be citizens. But the Constitution establishes a special rule for presidents: they must be "natural born citizens." When one of the most famous Zonians, Senator John McCain, ran for president in 2008 this issue suddenly bubbled up. While few doubted that McCain would be treated as eligible for the presidency, the question was harder than it appeared. (In an ironic twist of fate, the issue of foreign-born presidents had last been discussed in the context of the father of McCain's chief rival for the Republican nomination, Mitt Romney. George Romney, former governor of Michigan, and presidential aspirant in the election of 1968, had been born in Mexico to American parents.)[117]

American control of the canal zone lasted nearly a century. The Carter administration eventually negotiated treaties relinquishing the canal, though many in Congress were unwilling to let it go. Indeed, one commentator at the time noted that "the future of the Panama Canal has become the most controversial issue in American foreign policy since the Vietnam War."[118] But the canal zone, which thrust American power and control right through the center of another sovereign state, was by the 1970s an anachronism of world politics. Of the great American imperial rush of the early twentieth century, only Guantanamo Bay, with its controversial naval base, and Puerto Rico, in a kind of limbo between colony and commonwealth, remain today as potent symbols of the era.

The Aftermath of Empire

The fever for imperialism cooled in the United States after World War I. Though the *Insular Cases* had made the world safe for American empire—or perhaps more accurately made America safe *from* empire—the United States soon took a different tack. Woodrow Wilson made national self-determination a central plank in his efforts to remake world politics, and the United States increasingly opposed European empires as a violation of free trade principles and American interests. The extraterritorial courts in Asia and the Middle East were generally wound down by the 1930s. And during the Second World War Franklin Delano Roosevelt made clear to the Allies that the old days of empire were fading. Strategically, America saw its future not in imperialism but in an open liberal order that it could construct and lead.[119]

The United States generally put its money where its mouth was. The Philippines, the most distant and populous of the American overseas possessions, was granted independence in the wake of the war—and a bloody insurgency. Some might say that the United States retained a postwar imperial presence in the Philippines, only with a lighter hand: in addition to great political influence, the United States retained massive military bases on the islands throughout the Cold War, including Subic Bay, long the home of the U.S. Navy's Seventh Fleet. Likewise Germany and Japan hosted enormous overseas military bases after the formal American occupations ended. The result was a postwar network of bases that circled the globe, and a military presence that was akin to that of the British Empire at its height, but lacked the attendant structures of local governance that the British maintained.

Securing strategic naval bases was a major impetus for the burst of empire building at the turn of the century, and this goal continued to motivate American grand strategy throughout the twentieth century.[120] Thus one way to view the twentieth century is as a period in which the United States transformed a small, traditional empire into a large, untraditional and informal one. "One need not send out ships, seize territories, and hoist flags to construct an empire," eminent Cold War historian John Lewis Gaddis wrote in 1997. "[S]urely American and Soviet influence, throughout most of the second half of the 20th century, were at least as ubiquitous as that of any earlier empire the world had ever seen."[121]

Both formal and informal U.S. imperialism were facilitated by geographic distinctions about the reach of American law. Intraterritoriality permitted and fostered formal empire; extraterritoriality, coupled with the strict territoriality of constitutional rights, maximized informal control and influence. As American constitutionalism increasingly clashed with ascendant global predilections the United States found territorial differentiation a very useful tool.

Extraterritoriality was not absent from the new postwar order, however. New forms of extraterritoriality emerged to replace the old forms; these forms were far more suited to the open liberal trading system America and its allies had created and, moreover, reflected the dramatic extent of postwar U.S. hegemony. The extraterritorial expansion of domestic statutes, which increasingly governed economic life at home, is the topic of the next chapter.

4

THE FALL AND RISE OF EXTRATERRITORIALITY

T he opening decades of the twentieth century were a period of great change in international politics. The First World War led not only to a reallocation of territorial possessions—the empires of the great powers had reached their zeniths—but also to a reallocation of power in world politics. Leadership began to flow from Great Britain, the "weary titan," to the comparatively wealthy and vibrant United States.[1] The newly formed League of Nations sought to manage international conflict but, with the United States refusing to join, was soon overwhelmed by rising violence. Nations turned inward, no longer willing to pursue the economic interdependence of the late nineteenth century. In E. H. Carr's famous words, a "twenty years' crisis" began at the close of the "war to end all wars"; the crisis culminated in the onset of another, even deadlier, war in 1939.[2]

These were also decades of ferment at home. The Progressive movement was recasting American politics, while the voting franchise expanded. At the same time the federal government was becoming a much more significant force in American life. The role of the federal government had long been limited. What scholars call the administrative state was quite small until the early twentieth century.[3] By the 1940s, by contrast, the federal government comprised a rich and powerful array of agencies and departments, many devoted to regulating economic and social relations. These regulatory agencies, and the laws they implemented, provided a new frontier in the development of norms and rules of territoriality.

The onset of comprehensive national regulation had many causes. Industrialization, the nationalization of the economy, and the Depression and its associated political upheaval—all these and more contributed to a remarkable shift in the role of government. In a wave of lawmaking that began in the 1890s, and accelerated dramatically with the New Deal, the

United States promulgated a myriad of new laws aimed at subjecting economic and social activity to government power.[4] One of the first examples of this new genre of statutes was the Sherman Anti-Trust Act of 1890. "Trusts" were a form of conglomerate common in the late nineteenth century. The Sherman Act was aimed at "trust busting"; that is, the breaking up of monopolistic enterprises and cartels. The act declared that "every contract, combination in the form of trust or otherwise, or conspiracy, in restraint of trade or commerce among the several States, or with foreign nations, is declared to be illegal."[5] Although the primary focus was the national market, cartels involving foreign nations were also forbidden. But could an act of Congress police the behavior of foreigners *outside* the United States? Or was domestic law restricted only to regulating acts by foreigners that occurred within the territorial borders of the nation?

These questions were sharply posed in the early twentieth century by a dispute involving two American banana companies operating in Central America. In adjudicating this conflict, the Supreme Court issued the first of what would become many judgments on the territorial limits of domestic regulation. As previous chapters have detailed, federal courts had considered the territorial scope of U.S. law many times before, such as whether overseas colonies were "within the United States" for customs purposes. Disputes over the geographic reach of the Sherman Act, however, were among the first involving major federal legislation.

At the start of the twentieth century, when the banana conflict took place, domestic legislation was understood through the dominant conceptual prism of Westphalian territoriality. As a result, one sovereign's power simply could not legitimately reach into the geographic domain of another. Hence the notion that domestic statutes could police acts that occurred within the territories of foreign states was met with considerable skepticism. Of course, there were sizable exceptions to this principle: not only formal empire, but also extraterritorial consular jurisdiction. As recounted in the previous chapter, this form of extraterritoriality was still quite active at the time of the banana dispute. But extraterritorial courts, like empire itself, gradually became discredited in the early twentieth century. Outside of a few locales, traditional extraterritoriality was essentially dead by 1945.

Yet just as one form of extraterritoriality was waning, another was waxing. By mid-century, the executive branch, Congress, and the courts were all seeking to extend the reach of a burgeoning array of domestic statutes to acts and actors overseas. This new form of extraterritoriality rapidly became a common part of American jurisprudence, and was in many respects more encompassing and powerful than the old extraterritoriality. Like the old, the new extraterritoriality deliberately extended American law beyond the borders of the United States in an effort to minimize the effects of legal difference. This time, however, domestic legal rules penetrated the borders of acknowledged and coequal sovereigns, not merely weak semisovereign powers. By the 1960s the idea that United States law was limited to American territory would seem quaint, almost a relic from another era.

This chapter charts the rebirth and reconfiguration of extraterritoriality in the mid-twentieth century. In order to understand the rise of the new extraterritoriality, one must appreciate not only its unusual predecessor, consular jurisdiction, but also several major domestic and international trends: the rise of the regulatory state; the rebirth of interdependence after 1945; the embedding of peaceful relations among the democratic powers; the decline of "classical legal thought" in American jurisprudence; and the extraordinary role played by the United States in postwar politics. Together, these features facilitated a new understanding of the relationship between sovereignty and territory. The demise of traditional imperialism was a central focus of the Roosevelt administration in their planning for the postwar order. The decline of the old extraterritoriality was a necessary concomitant of this effort. Nonetheless, though opposed to empire, the United States did not retreat into a purer form of strict territoriality after victory over the Axis powers. Instead, it reinvented and recast extraterritoriality for a new era.

The new extraterritoriality rested on a simple notion: acts that had tangible impacts within its borders could be regulated by the United States, wherever they might have originated. This effects-based approach in turn rested on a crucial fact: postwar America's unparalleled economic dominance. Because its economic power was so great—the United States accounted for nearly half of global manufacturing activity in 1945—foreign firms found the American market irresistible.[6] But entry into the American market created legal vulnerability, because it was the presence of assets within the reach of federal courts that generally gave the new extraterritoriality its practical bite. Less fearful of international conflict, and more engaged in global economic competition, an increasingly powerful United States creatively flexed its jurisdictional muscles in what, to many of its closest allies, was an alarmingly aggressive and unilateral fashion.

This shift from old to new extraterritoriality is largely one of means rather than ends. Like the old extraterritoriality, the new aimed to manage and minimize legal difference. It sought to make trade and commerce easier and smoother by bringing American law to others while bringing others' products to America. Extraterritorial regulation was thus an attractive complement to the dense network of American-created postwar international institutions that has captured the attention of so many analysts of world politics.[7] These institutions were vehicles for cooperation as well as power. They sought to harmonize domestic rules on largely American terms. Like them, but even more so, extraterritoriality permitted the United

States to achieve some measure of international harmonization on terms of its choosing.

Postwar American hegemony, in short, was manifested not only in military power and economic influence, but also in an expansive understanding of the reach of domestic law—an understanding that honored American anti-imperialism while it simultaneously extended American legal rules throughout the globe.

"A Rather Startling Proposition": Antitrust and the Birth of the American Regulatory State

Contemporary governments regulate a large part of the national economy in nearly every industrialized society. In the early twentieth century, however, the regulatory state was relatively new and unformed. True of many nations, this was particularly true of the United States, which long had viewed the prospect of a powerful central government with suspicion.[8]

One of the earliest federal regulatory efforts in the United States involved a peculiarly American interest: antitrust law. The United States has long been unusual in its commitment to regulating competition among economic entities. A recent history of antitrust policy recounts that before 1945, "businesses operating across national borders lived with a basic contradiction: the laws of most industrial countries tolerated and even encouraged cartels, whereas the statutes of the United States, the world's largest economy, banned them."[9] At first, the contradiction was not especially problematic. The Sherman Act was used only intermittently in its early years. The earliest cases involved straightforward American defendants, such as the Knight sugar company, which controlled nearly all of the sugar refining in the United States.[10] In time, however, the gap between American and foreign law would become wider and more costly, and American plaintiffs would increasingly seek to reduce its impact.

In 1909 the American Banana Company sued the United Fruit Company in federal court, arguing that it had been injured by anticompetitive actions undertaken at the behest of United Fruit. The twist was that these actions had occurred in Central America, in territory that was, at various times, under the control of Costa Rica, Panama, and Colombia. According to the American Banana Company, United Fruit had persuaded the Costa Rican government to seize part of a banana plantation and to interfere with shipments and supplies. The firm argued these acts constituted an illegal restraint of trade under the Sherman Act.

The American Banana Company's claim was rebuffed initially. Citing various old precedents, the Second Circuit declared that it could not pass judgment on the acts of another sovereign. The Supreme Court, hearing the case on appeal, took a different tack, though with the same unhappy result for the American Banana Company.[11] Justice Oliver Wendell Holmes began his decision by acknowledging the various harms suffered by American Banana. These harms were serious and, most important, were plainly of the sort contemplated by the Sherman Anti-Trust Act. However, Holmes stated, "it is obvious" that the case depends on "several rather startling propositions." Foremost among these was that "the acts causing the damage were done, so far as it appears, outside the jurisdiction of the United States, and within that of other states. It is surprising to hear it argued that they were governed by an act of Congress."[12]

Holmes found this claim startling because it was at odds with the prevailing vision of strict territoriality, which, as previous chapters have detailed, was then well-reflected in international and domestic law. Indeed, just a few years earlier the Supreme Court had declared that "[n]o law has any effect, of its own force, beyond the limits of the sovereignty from which its authority is derived."[13] This flowed directly from Westphalian principles of international law: it "was an axiom of international jurisprudence," said the Court in yet another case from the era, that "the laws of a country had no extra-territorial force."[14] As a result, the Supreme Court declared that United States courts lacked jurisdiction over the banana dispute because American law did not, and could not, reach into the territory of another sovereign state.

The Supreme Court nonetheless was well aware that there were exceptions to this axiom. It conceded that "no doubt in regions subject to no sovereign, like the high seas, or to no law that civilized countries would recognize as adequate, such countries may treat some relations between their citizens as governed by their own law, and keep to some extent the old notion of personal sovereignty alive."[15] But the case before them was different. In saying this, the *American Banana* court was referring to cases involving piracy and slave trading on the high seas, and to the various extraterritorial consular courts still quite vital in 1909.

The Supreme Court believed that these extraterritorial courts, like the U.S. District Court for China, which had just recently been established, were based on distinctive principles. Although these courts plainly involved the extension of American law abroad, they were situated in what Americans (and Europeans) of the day considered uncivilized countries that possessed inadequate and even barbaric laws. In such aberrant situations it was reasonable, the justices suggested, for a civilized state such as the United States to extend its own law into the territory of another nation for the protection of its citizens. This extension was entirely consistent with the international law of the day.

The dispute among the American fruit companies, by contrast, was a different matter. It took place in Latin America, a region that had long been independent of European empires and whose states were fully sovereign. As Justice Holmes described as far as sovereign states were concerned:

> The general and almost universal rule is that the character of act as lawful or unlawful must be determined wholly by the law of the country where the act was done . . . For another jurisdiction, if it should happen to lay hold of the actor, to treat him according to its own notions rather than those of the place where he did the acts, not only would be unjust, but would be an interference with the authority of another sovereign, contrary to the comity of nations, which the other state concerned justly might resent.[16]

Holmes was certainly correct that in the early twentieth century, jurisdiction was thought to be highly territorial. That said, there were a few exceptions besides the extraterritorial courts. It was not unknown, for instance, for states to criminalize or regulate certain acts that occurred on the high seas but nonetheless had effects within their borders. The *American Banana* court itself cited one such case, an 1869 Massachusetts manslaughter conviction of several residents of Maine. The Mainers collectively assaulted and starved a resident of Massachusetts while aboard a ship on the high seas.[17] The victim survived the attack, but died shortly after in Massachusetts. The Massachusetts police charged the perpetrators under a state statute that specifically criminalized manslaughter that begins beyond the state's borders but ends in Massachusetts.

The notion that crimes committed on the high seas could be tried in local courts was of course a necessity, as there were no courts on the high seas. As the Massachusetts Supreme Court noted in the maritime manslaughter case, since "the most ancient times of which we have any considerable records, the English courts of common law took jurisdiction of crimes committed at sea, both by English subjects and by foreigners."[18] Hence although interesting cocktail party examples, cases of this sort did not meaningfully contravene the prevailing principles of Westphalian territoriality. The high seas were distinctive: there was no sovereign on the oceans and hence no sovereign power to intrude upon. This situation was thoroughly unlike that presented in the dispute between United Fruit and American Banana.

Consequently, when the *American Banana* court wrote that "for another jurisdiction, if it should happen to lay hold of the actor, to treat him according to its own notions rather than those of the place where he did the acts, not only would be unjust, but would be an interference with the authority of another sovereign," it was distinguishing the accusations against the United Fruit company from the many high seas cases of ancient vintage. It was one thing to apply American law to an ungoverned zone such as the oceans—especially when a failure to apply the law would leave murderers unpunished. It was a quite another to apply that law to an act occurring within the territorial borders of a coequal sovereign.

The Supreme Court was articulating a view very common at the time. The 1920 edition of Lassa Oppenheim's influential treatise on international law, for instance, stated baldly that "no right for a state to extend its jurisdiction over acts of foreigners committed in foreign countries can be said to have grown up according to the Law of Nations."[19] Indeed, the justices seemed to believe that such assertions of extraterritorial jurisdiction were an affront to the very nature of sovereignty. In this sense the reasoning in *American Banana* was closely aligned with prior Supreme Court decisions such as *In re Ross*. *Ross* had held that American constitutional protections did not extend beyond the sovereign borders of the nation, and certainly did not and could not extend into another sovereign's realm. As in *Ross*, Westphalian territoriality served as the foundation for the reasoning in *American Banana*.

American Banana also espoused an important interpretive principle, one that would receive attention throughout the twentieth century even as the federal courts dramatically expanded the extraterritorial reach of American statutes. Despite statements about the axiomatic nature of Westphalian territoriality, the Supreme Court believed that Congress could, if it chose, violate international law and extend domestic extraterritorially.[20] But this power had to be wielded very gingerly. Because of the importance of sovereignty, the *American Banana* court argued that when there was doubt about congressional intentions, a federal statute must be construed as territorial. In Holmes's words, "all legislation is prima facie territorial in nature."[21] The claim that territoriality ought to be a judicial default in the interpretation of statutes was hardly novel; *American Banana* itself cited an 1856 English admiralty decision stating that "in endeavoring to put a construction on a statute, it must be borne in mind how far the power of the British Legislature extends, for unless the words are so clear that a contrary construction can in no way be avoided, I must presume that the Legislature did not go beyond this power."[22]

This interpretative principle is now called the "presumption against extraterritoriality." It means that federal courts assume that Congress legislates with domestic acts and effects in mind unless Congress says otherwise. Today the presumption is frequently overcome, sometimes because Congress does make clear its intent to regulate extraterritorially and sometimes because courts simply soften the test. And the federal courts occasionally have applied the presumption to U.S. statutes in situations in which there was no conflict whatsoever with foreign law.[23] At times judges have even ignored the presumption entirely.[24] Lawyers continue to argue over why and when it is invoked. But in the early twentieth century the presumption was taken quite seriously, and litigants had to provide substantial evidence to rebut it.

American Banana is often read as a "conflicts of law" case, in which the Supreme Court had to choose between two potentially applicable bodies of law emanating from two sovereigns. Standard conflicts problems include what law to apply in a case involving an American worker injured in Saudi Arabia by a truck owned by the Arabian American Oil Company, and whether Swiss law or New Jersey law governs a charge of bribery by a New Jersey firm operating in Switzerland.[25] The standard view of scholars of conflicts is that *American Banana* simply reflected the prevailing conflicts theory of the time, which, like the international and constitutional law of the time, was highly territorial.[26]

As discussed in chapter 2, the prevailing nineteenth-century conflicts theory was based on the Westphalian principle that, as Justice Story wrote in his influential commentaries on American law, "every nation possesses an exclusive sovereignty and jurisdiction within its own territory." Moreover, Story argued, it would be "wholly incompatible with the equality and exclusiveness of the sovereignty of all nations, that any one nation should be at liberty to regulate either persons or things not within its territory."[27] The first part of this statement neatly encapsulates Westphalian territorial sovereignty; the second is a logical corollary of the first. The centrality of territoriality in nineteenth-century international law doctrine was thus echoed in conflicts doctrine; indeed, it seems far more likely that the conflicts doctrine of the time simply reflected prevailing international legal concepts rather than the reverse.

In any event, the animating idea in all these bodies of law is the same: sovereigns controlled absolutely their territories, and no other sovereign could, as a result, extend their laws into that territory absent very special circumstances. This idea reached "its zenith" in *American Banana*.[28]

The Decline of Territorialism

The *American Banana* decision is almost universally cited as an example of traditional territorial thinking. The decision stood for some time, but the strict territoriality it embodied did not last long. In an autarkic world, in which nearly all economic activity occurs within sovereign borders, it might be possible to limit regulatory statutes of the sort represented by the Sherman Act to the domestic domain. But in a more interdependent global economy, in which goods and markets cross borders readily, such a rule has, or is thought to have, perverse and damaging effects. To fail to apply the Sherman Act to cartels that occur outside American borders might disadvantage local producers vis-à-vis foreign ones. It might even incentivize cartels to relocate abroad in order to escape liability. And it might harm American consumers, who would pay higher prices if the overseas monopolists were not controlled.

As we will see, these concerns, and others, helped stimulate a dramatic shift in legal doctrine. Of course, if other states had similar antitrust laws, and applied them similarly to cartels and other anticompetitive acts, this would greatly limit the damage from a strictly territorial rule of statutory interpretation. Global legal harmonization, in other words, would permit territorial jurisdiction to more easily coexist with economic interdependence. Alternatively, governments could negotiate an international antitrust treaty, and perhaps create an international antitrust agency to enforce its rules. In 1909, however, the United States was a regulatory outlier. Very few states had laws governing anticompetitive behavior, and there was no international antitrust agreement or agency. (Indeed, neither exists today). At the beginning of the twentieth century, antitrust regulation was an American "social religion" that had not yet spread to the rest of the world.[29] This meant that if Westphalian territoriality as applied to regulation led to intractable problems, the easiest solution was to relax Westphalian territoriality. Unlike harmonization, or the negotiation of an international framework governing antitrust, jurisdictional rules could be changed unilaterally.

At the time of *American Banana*, however, legal doctrine posed a major barrier to this unilateral approach. American antitrust law percolated along in the early decades of the twentieth century, with sporadic forays into cases that had some international element, such as a dispute involving a railroad that ran between the United States and Canada. (The Sherman Act was held to apply, lest the railroad escape the laws of both nations.) Without definitively declaring the existence of extraterritorial jurisdiction, various interwar decisions inched closer than the *American Banana* court had been willing to go. For example, a conspiracy to monopolize sisal, a plant grown only in Mexico, was held to be a violation of the Sherman Act in 1927. Reversing a lower court decision holding that the *American Banana* precedent decided the sisal case as well, the Supreme Court declared that the sisal case was "radically different": "here we have a contract, combination, and conspiracy entered into by parties within the United States and made effective by acts done therein."[30] The actual growing and export of sisal may have occurred abroad, the court was saying, but because the conspiracy itself was spawned at home, the Sherman Act applied.

Cases such as these moved the law bit by bit toward effects-based thinking. And as this set of disputes suggest, antitrust was the area in which this first took hold. This in part reflected the origins of the Sherman Act as one of the first American regulatory statutes. It had another unusual feature as well: a highly decentralized enforcement system. In addition to two government agencies with jurisdiction over the act, private actors could bring suit against other private actors. If successful, they won triple damages. This parallel system of privatized enforcement created very strong incentives for plaintiffs to bring creative claims. Private law enforcement also made it "more difficult for government policymakers to control developments in antitrust law through the exercise of prosecutorial discretion." And although executive branch officials were important players, this scheme meant that ultimately "it is the judiciary that has the greatest influence on antitrust policymaking, not the administrators of laws."[31] Consequently, antitrust law was structurally more likely to evolve than the average domestic statute.

Yet it was only at the very close of the Second World War that the decision generally identified with the birth of the effects theory, *United States v. Aluminum Company of America*, was handed down. Commonly referred to as *Alcoa*,[32] and decided just six weeks before the unconditional surrender of Nazi Germany in May 1945, the case's significance regarding extraterritoriality is largely unrelated to the war. Rather, *Alcoa*—"a pivotal decision" on jurisdiction—helped to foment a transformation in the way the federal courts thought about extraterritoriality.[33] It was a transformation that has shaped the course of American law ever since.

Alcoa and the Effects Test

Alcoa involved a complex set of charges. At its core, however, was the same question presented in *American Banana*: did an American statute apply to conduct that took place outside American territory? Alcoa was an unusual company in that it essentially enjoyed a complete monopoly within the United States over the production of aluminum, then a major commodity. Outside the United States aluminum production was governed by an international cartel, of which Alcoa appeared to be a quasi-member.[34] The Roosevelt administration believed that Alcoa's dominance at home was the result of illegal dealings. The regulators averred, moreover, that Alcoa relied on the international cartel to keep foreign competition out. (And in return, Alcoa did not export aluminum abroad.)[35]

The question of Alcoa's market dominance became wrapped up in the growing military mobilization occasioned by World War II, and the firm was castigated in the press for impeding the war effort. Alcoa nonetheless initially prevailed in court, and eventually the federal government contracted with the company to increase domestic aluminum production enormously. In 1945, however, the Second Circuit overturned the prior rulings and broadly upheld the Justice Department's argument that Alcoa had violated the antitrust laws.

The court began its discussion by nodding in the direction of strict territoriality. "We are not to read general words, such as those in [the Sherman Act], without regard to the limitations customarily observed by nations upon the exercise of their powers; limitations which generally correspond to those fixed by the 'Conflict of Laws.'"[36] The court was invoking international law as the source of constraint on jurisdiction, a theme familiar from the many nineteenth-century decisions discussed earlier in this book.

The court then argued that the same constraints could be found in conflicts doctrine. Judge Learned Hand, who authored the decision in *Alcoa*, was an aficionado of conflicts and a devotee of what was known as "local law" theory.[37] The theory's animating idea was that a court could apply only the law of its sovereign to a case before it, even if it were a case with many foreign elements. In such instances, however, local law theory counsels that the court ought to strain to read the local law in way that as closely as possible matched that of the foreign law implicated by the case. In other words, as a general rule judges should seek to harmonize foreign and domestic law as much as possible.

What was the implication of this theory here, in *Alcoa?* The Second Circuit noted that as an American court it had to apply American law and not foreign law. However, the court argued, "it is settled law that any state may impose liabilities, even upon persons not within its allegiance, for conduct outside its borders that has consequences within its borders which the state reprehends."[38] This was in fact not settled law, but as we have seen neither was the idea of effects-based jurisdiction entirely invented by the Second Circuit. The court then declared that because "both agreements would clearly have been unlawful, had they been made within the United States" it "follows from what we have just said that both were unlawful, though made abroad, if they were intended to affect imports and did affect them."[39] In short, foreigners who acted abroad in ways that caused harm at home, and were intended to do so, were subject to American law. The *effects* of their actions gave rise to legal liability. The liability was not derived from international law—recall there was no international law of antitrust—but instead from domestic law.

Having endorsed a significant change in thinking about territoriality, the *Alcoa* court seemed cognizant that it might have major implications for foreign relations. Hence the court quickly conceded a few important points:

> There may be agreements made beyond our borders not intended to affect imports, which do affect them, or which affect exports. Almost any limitation of the supply of goods in Europe, for example, or in South America, may have repercussions in the United States if there is trade between the two. Yet when one considers the international complications

likely to arise from an effort in this country to treat such agreements as unlawful, it is safe to assume that Congress certainly did not intend the Act to cover them.[40]

In essence the *Alcoa* court articulated a rough cost-benefit analysis of extraterritorial regulation. The analysis was based on another kind of effect—the effect of judicial rulings on foreign policy. In an interdependent marketplace, price-fixing in one place necessarily influenced prices elsewhere. Given this state of affairs, it would seem that any anticompetitive action, wherever in the world undertaken, might fall afoul of the Sherman Act under the newly launched effects standard. This would have made the effects concept very big news indeed. But the court sought to prevent that result by arguing that "it is safe to assume that Congress certainly did not intend" to reach any and all extraterritorial anticompetitive agreements.

Rather than eliminate the presumption against extraterritoriality, in other words, the court tried to recalibrate it. The higher the expected foreign policy blowback, the more clarity judges would look for from Congress. As this formula suggests, the view that the United States simply could not project its laws into the realm of another sovereign—the view articulated so strongly in *American Banana*—had quietly slipped away. In its place was a newer, more flexible vision.

The "Theory of the Long Hand"

The effects test laid out in *Alcoa* was highly significant, but it was not created out of whole cloth. As the nineteenth-century maritime cases cited in *American Banana* illustrate, courts had been thinking about overseas acts with domestic effects for some time. A case involving a man who is beaten on the high seas but dies with Massachusetts is, in essence, a case about the domestic effect of an extraterritorial act. But the high seas were a special place, and the notion of effects-based jurisdiction had not generally been accepted as a basis for jurisdiction over acts that occurred within another sovereign state. Yet just 2 years after the Supreme Court declared in *American Banana* that "the almost universal rule" regarding the geographic reach of national law was territorialism, however, Justice Holmes, the author of that opinion, handed down another opinion that described the core of what would eventually become the effects test. In a case involving a fugitive from justice, Holmes wrote that "acts done outside the jurisdiction, but intended to produce and producing detrimental effects within it, justify a state in punishing the cause of harm."[41]

These situations not infrequently arose among the sister states of the American union. Indeed, the "states" referred to by Holmes were Illinois and

Michigan. But whether a linguistic fortuity or something deeper, the concept of one state affecting another was readily transposed from the federal context to the international realm. Facts on the ground, as it were, helped. As oceanic shipping grew in the interwar period, the federal courts increasingly faced cases involving acts on the high seas and foreign ports, and, pushed along by government officials interested in policing acts abroad, they increasingly began to argue that American law extended overseas.

For example, a 1922 Supreme Court decision revisited the question of extraterritoriality and argued that some criminal statutes reached beyond the territory of the United States simply by their nature. Pointing to *American Banana*, the Supreme Court reiterated its belief that extraterritoriality was highly disfavored. Then the Court quickly noted that some criminal statutes were distinctive. Those statutes that are "not logically dependent on their locality for the government's jurisdiction, but are enacted because of the right of the government to defend itself against obstruction, or fraud" are not subject to any presumption against extraterritoriality.[42]

The case at hand involved acts in the port of Rio de Janeiro. The Supreme Court opined that applying American law to the acts of Americans in a foreign port was acceptable because "clearly it is no offense to the dignity or right of sovereignty of Brazil to hold [the defendants] for this crime against the government to which they owe allegiance." This meant that Americans abroad were subject to at least some American laws. Similarly, a 1927 case had held that American criminal law applied to conspiracies by foreigners overseas, as long as there were coconspirators within the United States.[43]

Even earlier, American courts had made reference to a concept of "constructive conduct," in which a crime, begun in one state but consummated in another, was understood to fall within the jurisdiction of the latter. This was also in some respects an early articulation of the effects test. A common hypothetical was a gun fired across a border. As a Georgia court wrote in 1893, "if a man in the State of South Carolina criminally fires a ball into the State of Georgia, the law regards him as accompanying the ball, and as being represented by it, up to the point where it strikes."[44]

The concept of constructive conduct—constructive in that the malefactor was constructively present in Georgia, even though he was shooting from South Carolina—were largely worked out among the sister states of the union. But these cases foreshadowed the sort of functional thinking about territorial jurisdiction that a more interdependent society and economy engendered. And analogues could be found abroad, as in the German "theory of the long hand," which understood the place where an instrument or device "does its work" is the place where the criminal offense occurs.[45] The hand travels across the border to do its deed. Cases and concepts like these inched toward a more encompassing extraterritorial application of domestic law. And from here it was but a small step to the full articulation of the effects test announced in 1945.

Effects Elsewhere

Extraterritoriality based on transboundary effects was consistent with another development that came from a very important source: international law. The Permanent Court of International Justice, or PCIJ, was the forerunner of today's International Court of Justice. In a famous 1927 case between France and Turkey, a very closely divided PCIJ announced something akin to the effects test. The dispute concerned a French ship, the SS *Lotus*, which had collided with a Turkish ship near Istanbul. Eight Turks died in the crash. When the French ship entered port in Istanbul for repairs, the French watch officer, Lieutenant Demons, was arrested by Turkish authorities and later found guilty of manslaughter. France protested, and France and Turkey submitted the dispute to the PCIJ.

The general rule in international law, then as now, is that the flag state has jurisdiction over its vessels at sea. In this case, the flag state was France. France's contention was that Turkey had, in essence, improperly invaded France's jurisdiction. The question before the PCIJ was whether this was true and whether as a result Turkey had violated international law by arresting and trying Demons.

The *Lotus* case is famous among international lawyers for the proposition that states can legally do what they want so long as it is not prohibited by international law.[46] But the case had a significant impact on territoriality as well. The focus in the dispute was Turkey's claim of jurisdiction over Lieutenant Demons. In its structure the *Lotus* was not so different from the nineteenth-century Massachusetts manslaughter decision that Oliver Wendell Holmes cited in *American Banana*. In both cases, events at sea caused death. The question then became whether the nearby sovereign could assert jurisdiction over the putative killer. France believed that this assertion of jurisdiction was plainly extraterritorial and therefore illegal. The PCIJ, however, held that France first had to show that Turkey's claim of jurisdiction violated some specified international rule. Because France could not do so, Turkey prevailed. In upholding Turkish jurisdiction over Demons the majority in the *Lotus* reiterated the now-familiar claim that sovereign jurisdiction was territorial. But, argued the majority, Demons's offense "was an act ... having its origins aboard the Lotus, whilst its effects made themselves felt on board [the Turkish ship]."[47] By this they meant that Turkey was basing its jurisdiction on effects that were felt within its own jurisdiction.

This interpretation creatively and dramatically expanded the concept of territoriality. Rather than being extraterritorial, a claim of jurisdiction over acts occurring beyond the state's borders was now declared to be a territorial claim, as long as there was some effect felt within those borders. Writing in 1948, the influential English jurist Hersch Lauterpacht suggested that this shift in understandings of legitimate jurisdiction was due in part to "technical developments in the field of communications and of transmission of news and sound by telegram, telephone and wireless." Because of these developments, Lauterpacht opined, "the importance of mere physical distance—and therefore, of the territorial principle—has correspondingly diminished."[48] The word *globalization* did not exist when Lauterpacht wrote, but one can see the similarities to contemporary thinking. Lauterpacht was quick to add that the effects doctrine was a very limited one. A state did not, in his view, have "unlimited jurisdiction over an alien for acts which have been committed abroad and which it considers to be prejudicial to its safety. There is no warrant in international law for a rule of such alarming comprehensiveness."[49]

The dissenters in the *Lotus*, of which there were many—the PCIJ judges were evenly divided, with the tie broken by the court's president—were even more alarmed than Lauterpacht about this new doctrine. In their view, a French ship was akin to French territory. And international law had two fundamental principles which together, the dissenters argued, determined the outcome in the dispute. These were "the principle of sovereignty and the territorial principle, according to which a nation has dominion over its territory and—on the other hand—has no authority to interfere in any way in matters taking place on the territories of other nations."[50] These principles should now be familiar, because they are precisely those invoked by Marshall, Story, Holmes, and other American judges and jurists in the decades leading up the Second World War. That the PCIJ was divided in two by the *Lotus* dispute illustrates that notions of Westphalian territoriality still had significant bite in 1927. But at the same time, the hold it had on legal thinking was clearly slipping, and the decision in the *Lotus*, coming as it did from an esteemed body of international jurists, cast any future attempts at creative jurisdictional expansion in a favorable light.

Effects and the Twentieth-Century Revolution in American Legal Thought

The postwar embrace of effects-based extraterritoriality in the United States nonetheless went beyond the principles articulated in the *Lotus*. It addressed not just the manslaughter of a nation's citizens but also what we would now think of as ordinary regulatory rules. This move to effects fit with and reinforced major developments in some other areas of American law. By the 1940s Westphalian territoriality was weakening in conflicts doctrine as well as in the law of civil procedure generally. Thus, writes one prominent commentator, "Hand's reasoning [in *Alcoa*] probably seemed quite natural in context. It was 1945, and territoriality was already giving way in other contexts."[51] Conflicts doctrine, as we have seen, had directly shaped *Alcoa*. But the influence of conflicts theory went well beyond that particular decision. Story's celebrated *Commentaries on the Conflict of Laws*, written in the 1830s, had deeply influenced the nineteenth-century vision of Westphalian territoriality. Indeed, Story's territorial approach, which drew on international law, "dominated conflict of law thinking, in the United States and elsewhere, during the nineteenth century."[52]

American Banana, for instance, had hewed closely to Story's principles. But by 1945 conflicts theory had essentially abandoned this strict understanding of territoriality. Even by the early twentieth century "the notion of territorial exclusivity had come to seem increasingly implausible."[53] In its place emerged a new theory of conflicts. This theory focused on dominant interests rather than particular places. Like the contemporaneous focus on effects, interests analysis was functional rather than formal in orientation. Where an act took place was no longer critical, and courts no longer had to bend over backward to allocate a specific location to an often complex and multipart "act." Instead, under the new approach courts would look to outcomes and interests, not to geography.

A new focus on interests rather than geographic location swept the law of personal jurisdiction as well. As discussed in chapter 2, personal jurisdiction refers to a court's power over a defendant; it asks whether a court's ruling can legitimately apply to a given defendant. Conventionally, the answer to the inquiry was simple: an American court had power solely over the people and property located within its territorial district. Its power was territorial. This was the principle reiterated in the landmark case of *Pennoyer v. Neff*. But in 1945 the Supreme Court recast this principle. In *International Shoe v. Washington*, the court rejected strict territoriality, offering instead the far more flexible and encompassing principle that mere "minimum contacts" with the forum state were both necessary and sufficient for jurisdiction over a defendant who was physically beyond state borders.[54] As a result, an individual who was outside a jurisdiction, but established commercial or other contacts within the jurisdiction, could be sued in local courts.

This shift was not a minor one. Rather, it "displaced the entire conceptual structure of the strict territorial theory" of personal jurisdiction.[55] As the Supreme Court later described the change, "the relationship among the defendant, the forum, and the litigation, rather than the mutually exclusive sovereignty of the States on which the rules of *Pennoyer* rest, became the central concern of the inquiry into personal jurisdiction."[56] The new system, in short, rejected strict territoriality in favor of something like effects.

The new minimum contacts test was not explicitly predicated on a policy judgment about what the modern world demanded. Rather, it rested on constitutional foundations; to hale an actor into court absent minimum contacts was said to be a violation of the Fourteenth Amendment's guarantee of due process. As discussed later in this book, in the late twentieth century this analysis was applied to foreign firms who lacked direct connections to the United States, but whose products nonetheless ended up in American markets. By employing the same minimum contacts test to foreigners abroad, American courts (perhaps unwittingly) gave the Fourteenth Amendment some degree of extraterritorial force.[57]

Like the development of the effects test, the transformation of the law of personal jurisdiction from territorial presence to minimum contacts was a triumph of function over form, effects over territoriality. Where an actor was located in geographic terms no longer determined the legal outcome. If the actor had sufficient contacts with the forum state, he or she was liable to be sued regardless of physical location. It was the relationship between the actor, the facts giving rise to the dispute, and the sovereign that established legal jurisdiction.

Whether labeled "effects," "interests," or "contacts," this relational approach was widely reflected in American law by the mid-twentieth century. Legal historians argue that these common themes were themselves part of a larger move afoot in legal theory. Late-nineteenth-century legal thought, whether called "formalism," "classic legal thought,"[58] or "Langdellianism" (after the influential dean of Harvard Law School, Christopher Columbus Langdell), gave way in the 1930s and 1940s to pragmatism, functionalism, legal realism, and other isms that reflected an interest in replacing a '"jurisprudence of concepts" with a "jurisprudence of interests."'[59] This evolution suggests a connection that goes beyond the simple fact that the high water mark of classical legal thought was roughly contemporaneous with the high-water mark of Westphalian territoriality, or the observation that, like the territorial reasoning in *American Banana*, classical legal thought was discredited and largely defunct by mid-century.

What was classical legal thought? It is typically described as a formal, deductive, and systematic mode of analysis. Legal rules were deduced from high-level concepts in an almost axiomatic fashion. The adherents of this approach were chiefly concerned with private law, such as contract and property. But classical legal thought also reflected international influences. Indeed, one of its leading students, Duncan Kennedy, argues that this mode of reasoning was globalized by the spread of "a single Classical system of public international law, devised by the Western Great Powers, based on the conceptual innovations of the seventeenth century natural law theorists of sovereignty as a territorial (not personal) power, absolute within its sphere."[60]

In other words, classical legal thought reflected and was built upon the same territorial principles that undergirded nineteenth-century public international law. That sovereign power was territorial and absolute, and that one sovereign could not, as a result, legitimately intrude into the territory of another, were principles central to the classical approach. These principles were not merely rhetorical devices: they determined outcomes in concrete cases. As we saw in the previous chapter, when presented with the claim that the Sixth Amendment governed the trial of John Ross by American diplomats serving in Japan, the Supreme Court had little difficulty declaring that the Constitution's protections did not and could not reach into the territory of another nation. Likewise, in cases like *Pennoyer v. Neff*, the rules of personal jurisdiction were found to flow directly from physical location, without much consideration of interests or effects.

This formal and categorical way of thinking began to decline in the early twentieth century. By the end of the First World War, balancing tests, in which judges weighed competing considerations against one another, increasingly chipped away at the earlier system of legal reasoning based on logical deduction from general premises. In his synthetic treatment of American legal thought, legal historian Morton Horwitz argues that "the triumph of the balancing test marks the demise of the late-nineteenth-century system of legal formalism."[61] Horwitz suggests that

> [n]othing captures the essential difference between the typical legal minds of nineteenth and twentieth century America quite as well as their attitude toward categories. Nineteenth century legal thought was overwhelmingly dominated by categorical thinking—by clear, bright-line classifications of legal phenomena . . . By contrast, in the twentieth century, the dominant conception of the arrangement of legal phenomena has been that of a continuum between contradictory policies and doctrines . . . Nineteenth century categorizing typically sought to demonstrate "differences of kind" among legal classifications; twentieth-century balancing tests deal only with "differences of degree."[62]

The general jurisprudential embrace of balancing and "differences of degree" certainly made the move to effects-based extraterritoriality easier. Yet assessing in any precise way the influence of general trends in legal thinking on particular doctrines is very difficult. Because the American administrative state was so limited in the late nineteenth century, there are few cases to examine for adherence to the precepts of classical legal thought. Given the great concern with Westphalian territoriality in the period, however, it seems reasonable to assume that *American Banana* would not have been an outlier. It is worth noting in this regard that *American Banana* was written by Oliver Wendell Holmes, a prominent detractor of formalism. Despite his famous impatience with formalist reasoning, even Holmes was eager to quash the notion that domestic statutes could reach foreign conduct. That he found a claim of extraterritorial scope so startling suggests that concern with the territorial basis of the law went well beyond debates over formalism or antiformalism.

It is nonetheless true that the rise of effects-based extraterritoriality coincided with the decline of classical legal thought and the rise of balancing and "interests analysis." It would be very surprising if these theoretical evolutions, in the air in the interwar years, had no effect on judges faced with hard questions about jurisdiction, or on regulators considering what sorts of claims might prevail before a judge. Certainly *Alcoa* and the extraterritorial decisions that followed exhibited a concern with interests, a focus on the functions that legislation is meant to perform, and a willingness to balance and to look past existing doctrine to the social result that flowed from judicial decision making. All of the principles reflected, or at least tracked, the major shifts underway in American legal thought. This confluence at least suggests some jurisprudential reasons why the doctrinal unbundling of territoriality, at least with regard to domestic statutes, was relatively dramatic and swift.

Regulating the World

Effects-based extraterritoriality took root rapidly in the postwar era.[63] American officials were quick to embrace it as a useful tool; litigants did the same; and courts were generally, though by no means always, responsive. Some postwar cases involving foreign elements nonetheless downplayed the effects test, and courts on occasion upheld extraterritorial jurisdiction without focusing on putative effects at home. In most cases involving extraterritorial assertions of sovereign power, however, effects within the United States played a central role. The number of areas of the law in which this approach was applied expanded over time.

In the early 1950s, for example, the Supreme Court first applied the extraterritorial approach of *Alcoa* to intellectual property law, an area that had been (and in many respects remains) resolutely territorial.[64] Watches made and sold in Mexico had been affixed with labels marked "Bulova," a well-known American watch company, and were bought by vacationing Americans and brought home. The Bulova trademark had even been registered by the defendant in Mexico. In a not-insignificant turn of events, the defendant happened to be American, though the alleged trademark violation and the sales of the watches clearly occurred abroad. The Supreme Court held that it was immaterial that the false trademark was affixed within Mexico rather than at home. As a result, American trademark law for the first time reached beyond the territory of the United States, even though the relevant statute did not specifically say it applied extraterritorially.

The Bulova case also featured an early shot across the bow of offshoring. Acting abroad in way that would not be permitted at home provides no escape from American law, the Supreme Court suggested. "We do not think that petitioner by so simple a device [as selling in Mexico] can evade the thrust of the laws of the United States in a privileged sanctuary beyond our borders."[65] Because Mexico had recently nullified the defendant's registration of the trademark, the Court felt emboldened to extend the effects principle to a new area, "Where, as here, there can be no interference with the sovereignty of another nation, the District Court . . . may command persons properly before it to cease or perform acts outside its territorial jurisdiction."[66]

The dissenters in *Bulova* were not so willing to see the new extraterritoriality expanded in this way. They harked back to the Westphalian territorialism of *American Banana*, arguing that the trademark dispute was just like the antitrust dispute. The dissenters also viewed the issue of clashing sovereignties differently. Whereas the majority perceived no interference with another sovereign because there was no directly contrary Mexican trademark law, the dissenters believed that *any* assertion of legal power beyond American borders was, by its nature, an intrusion into another sovereign's realm. In their words,

> The [trademark] Act, like the Sherman Act, should be construed to apply only to acts done within the sovereignty of the United States. While we do not condone the piratic use of trade-marks, neither do we believe that Congress intended to make such use actionable irrespective of the place it occurred. Such extensions of power bring our legislation into conflict with the laws and practices of other nations, fully capable of punishing infractions of their own laws, and should require specific words to reach acts done within the territorial limits of other sovereignties.[67]

This passage illustrates an important point, however: even the dissenters thought that Congress could regulate acts overseas if it clearly and expressly chose to do so. Echoing the foreign policy concerns about overly aggressive extraterritoriality noted in *Alcoa*, the dissenters in *Bulova* simply believed that extraterritorial assertions required clear statements; extraterritorial claims should not be read into ambiguous federal statutes lest the judiciary accidentally foment international conflict. Over the next few decades this concern with collateral foreign policy damage in international relations would dip much lower. Even in the face of substantial potential—and actual—conflict with many American allies, the embrace of effects-based extraterritoriality did not abate.

On the contrary, extraterritoriality became more frequent and generally more aggressive over the course of the postwar era (though some observers argue the high-water mark was reached in the 1970s). For example, the United States tried at times to prevent offshore firms from consummating sales that the American government believed would jeopardize national security. Some of these firms were tangentially American; they were subsidiaries of American firms, or their stock was owned by American companies. The efforts to control their offshore conduct, such as the 1964 attempt to prevent a French firm from selling tractors to China, generated considerable resistance from European allies.[68] Yet the new extraterritoriality was not applied consistently; some statutes were subject to a rigorous reading of the presumption against extraterritoriality, whereas others were not. In 1991, for instance, the Supreme Court employed a very strong version of the presumption to hold that United States labor law did not apply to a dispute between an American citizen and an American company involving employment in Saudi Arabia. (The decision was critiqued in many quarters as anachronistic, and Congress quickly acted to overturn the result.) As this illustrates, the expansion of extraterritoriality in the regulatory arena was a amalgam of judicial, legislative, and executive action. Sometimes Congress made clear its intentions, but more often it did not, leaving it to the courts to figure out.

In general, the notion that the United States could regulate extraterritorial acts became more rather than less accepted over time. This trend can certainly be discerned in court cases. But looking only at judicial decisions has a major limitation. Litigated disputes—the only sort of disputes that generate written court decisions—reflect only a small subset of potential disputes.[69] As the law gradually became more clear on questions of geographic reach, many defendants settled with regulators or were simply deterred by the threat of legal action. In many instances regulators have compelled foreign entities to comply with United States law without litigation.[70] The ability to force a settlement through the threat of suit clearly lodges great power in executive branch officials to determine when and how American law applies overseas. Yet because prosecutions are not always recorded, it is difficult to systematically measure these effects. We are instead forced to infer change from the kinds of cases brought. Consequently, any assessment of legal trends from court decisions has to be sensitive to context and nuance, and is likely to understate the prevalence of extraterritorial claims.[71]

Despite these caveats, it is clear that a raft of cases in the 1960s and 1970s elaborated and extended the effects test in the context of antitrust, securities, labor, and other regulatory areas.[72] What gave these expansive jurisdictional claims bite was usually the presence of assets within the United States. When overseas defendants had valuable assets that

American courts could reach, they were incentivized to comply with adverse judgments, lest they lose their assets or their access to the American market. But the effectiveness of judicial decisions is not limited to these situations. Judges sometimes enforce the decisions of foreign courts directly, via principles of "comity."[73] The existence of comity and the recognition of foreign judgments added some modest force to the power of American courts to seize foreign assets located within the United States. These features are not always present, but they are present sufficiently often to have made American extraterritoriality a major source of worry for foreign actors and, as a result, a font of diplomatic tension.

Pushback from other nations led some U.S. courts to try to soften the new extraterritoriality by creating malleable judge-made doctrines, such as the jurisdictional "rule of reason."[74] Likewise, postwar judges refined the degree to which American courts ought to defer to the regulatory interests of the other sovereigns—a variant of the notion of comity. Yet the overwhelming postwar trend was toward greater acceptance of the underlying principle of effects-based extraterritoriality. The strict territoriality embodied in cases such as *American Banana* had its authority "almost completely eroded" by the 1960s.[75]

The degree to which Westphalian territoriality declined over the course of the twentieth century with regard to regulation can be seen starkly in a famous antitrust decision from 1993. In *Hartford Fire v. California* the Supreme Court held that British reinsurance companies, operating in London, were liable under anticonspiracy provisions of American antitrust law. This was true, the Court said, even though the reinsurance companies were fully compliant with British law. The defendants did not even attempt to argue that the Sherman Act was inapplicable on the grounds that they acted in London rather than Los Angeles. Instead, they claimed that the United States ought to defer to British law, on the grounds that British law, despite permitting what American law did not, was a well-formed and rational regulatory system with which the defendants had complied.

The Supreme Court disagreed, finding that there was no "true conflict" between the two legal systems. Because British law was more lenient, the majority reasoned, the defendants could have readily complied with *both* American and British law. Decisions such as these exasperated other governments. In what was perhaps the apotheosis of effects-based extraterritoriality, in 2005 foreign firms sued other foreign firms in a federal court for price-fixing based solely on the economic harms the cartel caused overseas.[76]

As this brief history illustrates, the federal judiciary was a key actor in the development of effects-based extraterritoriality. In the area of antitrust, for example, Congress played only a small role. It amended American antitrust law to incorporate the effects test only in 1982, many decades after it first became entrenched in the courts.[77] Congress on occasion deliberately extended the reach of American statutes extraterritorially, as it quickly did in response to the Supreme Court ruling that American employment law did not apply to firms operating in Saudi Arabia, but this sort of action was rare.[78] But although Congress often left details to the courts, the executive branch played a more proactive role in expanding the geographic reach of American law. Administrative agencies have actively sought to wield their regulatory powers globally. In recent years the Environmental Protection Agency has applied American environmental law to a Canadian firm operating within Canada; the Department of Justice has pursued foreign cartels for price-fixing; and the Securities and Exchange Commission is currently purporting to apply the Sarbanes-Oxley Act to companies based in the United Kingdom.[79]

The expansive new conceptions of personal jurisdiction discussed earlier helped propel these legal developments by articulating a standard of "minimum contacts" with the United States rather than actual presence in American territory. As global commerce grew in the decades in the postwar era more firms sought to enter the U.S. market. As they did they established such contacts and exposed themselves to legal liability. The result, as *Hartford Fire* demonstrates, was that even when foreign actors obeyed the law in their home jurisdiction they might still be subject to U.S. law. This approach to governance, which seemed to inject American legal power into every corner of the global economy, unsurprisingly provoked strident protests from major trading partners.

Reactions Abroad

The new postwar extraterritoriality was decidedly controversial. Within a decade, the effects approach was producing enormous friction with some of the closest trading partners of the United States. Postwar extraterritoriality appeared to represent a new and often irritating form of unilateral American power.

Most of the conflict was with European allies. As Europe recovered from the devastation of the 1940s, it found the new extraterritoriality perplexing and highly troubling. Some allies, such as Germany, lacked any real equivalent to the Sherman Act, the primary vehicle for American extraterritorial claims in this era. (Germany passed an antitrust statute, based in part on the Sherman Act, in 1957.)[80] Indeed, "until the 1970s the United States was the only country with both well-developed and strictly enforced antitrust laws and a legal regime permitting broad application of those laws to foreign conduct."[81]

Many states responded to American extraterritoriality by enacting so-called blocking or clawback statutes. These were legal efforts to blunt the effect of regulatory assertions aimed at their citizens or extended within their territories. For example, the French blocking act prohibited French nationals, residents, and representatives of companies located in France from providing to foreign regulators any information that "threatens the sovereignty, the security, or the essential economic interests" of France.[82] The British act was similar. The blocking acts sought to wall off European firms from a seemingly imperialistic American legal regime.

Larger trends in the global economy exacerbated the dispute between the old and the new worlds. The United States thoroughly dominated the world economy in the aftermath of the war. Postwar American military and economic hegemony magnified fears that Europe was increasingly subservient in politics both high and low. European governments thus were pushing back on many fronts against what was widely understood as "the American challenge," the title of Jean-Jacques Servan-Schreiber's best-selling book of 1967.

The United States's increasing propensity for extraterritoriality was seen as a way to forcibly export American law and, in the process, to render the postwar economic system—a system largely designed by U.S. officials in settings such as Bretton Woods—even more favorable to American business. As a high-ranking British official declared,

> We do not dispute the right of the United States or any other nation to pass and enforce what economic laws it likes to govern business operating fully within its own country. Our objection arises only at the point when a country attempts to achieve the maximum beneficial regulation of its own economic environment by ensuring that all those having any contact with it abide by its laws and legal principles.[83]

Such skeptical views about extraterritoriality were very reminiscent of the United States a century earlier, when, as described in chapter 2, Secretary of State John Calhoun denounced British efforts to extend their criminal law into the territory of the United States.[84] Now the shoe was on the other foot, and the weaker Britain feared and resisted American incursions.

The concern was not limited to Britain. Writing in 1981, two commentators noted that "in recent years, almost every bilateral or multilateral meeting between economic officials of the United States and Western Europe has included some objection from the European side to United States antitrust enforcement."[85] Some argued that these conflicts have even "been held responsible for weakening the western alliance."[86] By the 1970s the American zeal for extraterritoriality appeared, at least in legal circles, to be a hot battlefront in the Cold War. With hindsight it is clear that these transatlantic tussles did not fracture or even particularly jar the Western alliance. Other states may have protested, and commentators may have deplored the practice, but the new extraterritoriality proved robust and resilient.

Global Trade and Global Jurisdiction

The new extraterritoriality had powerful consequences in the new world of the administrative state. The rise of extensive domestic regulation meant extensive opportunities to regulate abroad. And in an interdependent world, acts undertaken in one place frequently generated effects that spilled over into other nations around the globe. The effects test in principle encompassed any imaginable spillover. As a result, it was potentially vast in scope—vaster than the older nineteenth-century extraterritoriality, which was limited to those places that were neither so developed as to be deemed civilized, nor so undeveloped as to be colonized. In this sense, the new extraterritoriality was more neutral than the old. It treated all states as juridical equals. In practice, of course, it was other advanced industrial democracies that most often fell afoul of American jurisdictional claims.[87]

Technological and institutional changes exacerbated these effects by making actors and goods more mobile than they had ever been before. As the world economy rebounded after 1945, international trade and investment swelled. Multinational firms established beachheads around the world. What is today commonly called globalization began to take shape. Indeed, it is tempting to interpret the evolution of effects-based extraterritoriality as a simple story of legal rules tracking the deepening of globalization and its associated shrinking of economic space.[88] As the world economy grew more interdependent the Westphalian system of territorial jurisdiction simply had to give way. An increasingly unbordered economic system faced a still-bordered legal system, and the resulting tensions grew, leading to a more flexible conception of legal jurisdiction.

This view has many proponents. Gary Born, for example, has argued that nineteenth-century territorial doctrines "proved increasingly inconsistent with governmental regulatory demands as the twentieth century progressed. The expanding national and international scope of economic enterprise, together with technological advances and the development of the modern business corporation, gave rise to burgeoning pressure for broader government regulation. Inexorably, the geographic reach of national regulation confronted and eventually spilled over national territorial boundaries."[89] Likewise, another observer has claimed that "during the late nineteenth century, new factors began to threaten this neat system [of strict territoriality]. Developments in transportation and communications made it possible for persons acting in one state to quickly and effectively cause effects in other states. Moreover, the growing concentration of business and the internationalization of the world economy meant that actions taken in one state could have multiple effects far beyond that state's border."[90] Similar, too, is the claim that "the development of the U.S. doctrine on extraterritorial jurisdiction began because of the undeniable links between domestic and foreign markets."[91]

These accounts stress the connections between the territorial scope of economic and social activity and the territorial scope of the legal rules that govern such activity. As the former became increasingly global, the latter, they argue, almost inevitably followed suit. This claim of geographic mismatch and rematch has much merit in it. But it is incomplete and in some senses misleading. As economic historians often point out, in the years preceding the First World War the international system was in fact highly globalized. The notion that "the world is flat," to use *New York Times* columnist Thomas Friedman's phrase, has been challenged on many grounds, and not least among them is the claim that "flatness" is a new phenomenon.[92] It is striking just how interdependent the Victorian and Edwardian eras were.

Only recently, for instance, has the share of trade in world output reached a level that is "noticeably above its former peak" in the early twentieth century.[93] Likewise, the migration levels of the past have only recently been approached. Overseas investment, too, was robust a century ago. Inventions such as transoceanic cables linked markets at breathtaking speed, and financial movements intensified enormously. The gold standard made currency risk minimal and capital highly mobile.[94] In his recent history of global capitalism, Jeffry Frieden summarizes this position, noting that "the opening years of the twentieth century were the closest thing the world had ever seen to a free world market for goods, capital, and labor. It would be a hundred years before the world returned to that level of globalization."[95]

The First World War brought this earlier wave of globalization to an abrupt halt. Recovery from this cataclysm took a global depression, another war, and decades of institution building.[96] In the years after 1919 states increasingly looked inward, seeking to blockade themselves from competition via draconian tariffs and protectionist policies.

This history presents a puzzle for accounts that link extraterritoriality to economic interdependence. If globalization was the motive force behind the dramatic expansion of extraterritorial jurisdiction, why did the effects theory become entrenched in the 1940s, rather than much earlier? In 1909, for instance, when the Supreme Court emphatically rejected regulatory extraterritoriality as "startling" in *American Banana*, the world economy was highly interdependent. And by 1945, when *Alcoa* advanced the effects test, the world economy was in tatters. Yet *Alcoa*'s effects analysis became the template for an ever more aggressive American pursuit of extraterritorial regulation. And for much of this period the world economy, although certainly reintegrating rapidly, remained only an echo of the first great wave of globalization.

The Transformation of Territoriality

The historical pattern is made even more complex when we recall that the early twentieth century was also a time of vibrant extraterritoriality in the form of capitulations and consular jurisdiction. The United States District Court for China, for example, was created in 1906. That the same era combined strict territoriality with regard to domestic statutes, extensive extraterritoriality in the "uncivilized" world, and flourishing economic interdependence suggests that there is no simple causal relationship between globalization and extraterritoriality.

This is not to say that growing economic interdependence was an insignificant factor in the rise of the new postwar extraterritoriality. Yet what appears most significant is less the fact of interdependence—which was, after all, quite low in the years just after 1945—than the fact that postwar extraterritoriality developed against the backdrop of several significant political and economic changes. These include the rise of the regulatory state; the growth of intra-industry trade and of multinational firms; the embedding of liberal international institutions; and the general absence of military conflict among the Western industrialized powers. The decline of classical legal thought, noted above, is another area of contrast between the eras of *Alcoa* and *American Banana*.

The remarkable growth of the regulatory state has already been discussed, but it is worth probing further its role in creating a new form of extraterritoriality. An extensive administrative state was not merely or even mostly an American phenomenon; it was a development found in all the advanced industrial democracies. Starting in the late nineteenth century, but accelerating in the Depression era, these states built a panoply of domestic regulatory institutions. These growing bureaucracies and the many rules they promulgated were thus a common feature among the great powers by the 1940s.

These myriad domestic rules were, in a very obvious sense, the building blocks of effects-based extraterritoriality. One needs a regulation to apply it extraterritorially. But the growth of regulation across the industrialized world also facilitated effects-based thinking. Regulatory rules inevitably reflected national preoccupations and problems. And more domestic regulatory rules in more states created more scope for regulatory differences. As a result, despite some shared features, domestic regulatory regimes were not naturally harmonious. The uniquely American fixation on antitrust law is an excellent example of divergence. The growing regulatory disharmony among states was sometimes irrelevant to international commerce because the differences were not germane to world trade. But in other cases, differences created tangible advantages and disadvantages for firms. As the international economy reconnected, these differences in national legal landscape gradually became more visible, and increasingly were a source of international tension.

This tension was made particularly acute by another important feature of postwar globalization: the rise of intra-industry trade and the worldwide expansion of multinational firms. *Intra*-industry trade meant that American firms increasingly, and more directly, faced off against their overseas competitors in national markets. The global automotive industry is a paradigmatic example today of such competition, but there are many others. By contrast, pre-1914 globalization was characterized much more by *inter*-industry trade: that is, trade of one kind of item (steam engines) for something completely different (rubber).[97] Typically inter-industry trade featured a core-periphery pattern: the industrialized West sold steam engines and bought rubber; the developing world had the opposite portfolio.

Intra-industry trade raises the salience of domestic regulatory frameworks because regulations can directly influence the costs of production. Dovetailing with this is the rise of "geographically fragmented" production processes. As Federal Reserve Chairman Ben Bernanke has noted, a signal feature of the late twentieth-century economy (and today's) is that increasingly firms break the production process into discrete steps and perform each wherever in the world costs are lowest.[98] The postwar global economy also featured an increased role for multinational corporations. Economists have noted "a quantum leap . . . in the importance of multinationals from the pre-World War I era."[99]

The rise of multinational firms, intra-industry trade and fragmented production are intertwined; together they produced a greater political focus on "competitiveness" and the ways in which governments could work—given their newfound willingness to intervene in the national economy—to give their national firms and workers advantages and disadvantages in the increasingly global market. This confluence of factors in turn created incentives for firms to seek a more level legal playing field upon which to compete with their foreign counterparts. Cross-national regulatory differences became a problem to be solved.

The most familiar way to harmonize divergent national rules—to minimize legal difference—is the negotiation of international agreements. The Bretton Woods institutions, as well as the World Trade Organization, are famous examples: they manage and organize the processes of globalization through treaties and international organizations. A second strategy of rule harmonization has been the export of domestic models of regulation to other states via technical assistance and informal networks of regulators.[100] Unilateral assertions of extraterritorial jurisdiction are a third strategy. Rather than harmonize domestic law with relevant foreign law, states—at least powerful states—can simply impose domestic regulatory regimes on foreign competitors. This strategy has received less attention. But as this chapter has described, it was a significant part of the postwar American approach.

Thus the expansion of extraterritoriality in the postwar era is best understood as an alternative to more familiar cooperative efforts. Indeed, the legal arenas in which the United States has been most actively extraterritorial—in particular, antitrust and securities law—are also arenas in which there are no major international treaties. (These are also arenas in which networks of government officials are especially active.)[101] In antitrust, for instance, the United States has consistently rebuffed proposals for an international agreement.[102] By contrast, areas such as copyright, with an extensive array of international agreements dating back to the nineteenth century, exhibit a very different pattern. The United States has been aggressive in seeking change among other states in their copyright rules, but it has done so not via extraterritoriality but instead via the negotiation of treaties, such as the Trade-Related Intellectual Property agreement of the WTO.[103]

In short, the nature of economic interdependence was very different after 1945 than before 1914. The "embedded liberalism" of the postwar era created an environment in which one sovereign's internal law mattered to another much more than at any earlier point in history.[104] Extraterritorial claims were and remain efforts at reducing these legal differences.

Postwar Peace and the Logic of the West

Unlike the negotiation of international agreements, extraterritoriality is unilateral and often causes considerable friction with other states. For this reason, doctrines of territoriality were long justified as necessary to avoid international conflict. Having one sovereign intrude upon the domain of another was widely seen as not only wrong, but dangerous. In the postwar period something changed; the United States pursued extraterritoriality vigorously and proved quite tolerant of the resulting international conflict.

One likely source of this newfound acceptance of legal-political conflict was the dramatic change in global power relations. The political and military power wielded by the United States in the wake of the Second World War was enormous, and it allowed the nation a central role in the creation and maintenance of the postwar order. The building of a new international order paradoxically allowed the United States to absorb and sustain more legal conflict internationally. This was true even with those nations that were most closely allied with the United States. Indeed, it was *most* true with these nations.

To understand this requires an appreciation of the nature of the postwar order the United States created. After 1945 America had few rivals as leader of the West. But the United States was a not traditional hegemonic power. Rather, the order it created had a distinctive logic, what scholars in international relations have dubbed "the logic of the West." The postwar West "is not a series of states in anarchy," but rather a system "bound together by a web of complex institutional links and associations. The peace of the West does not derive simply or mainly from the fact that its polities are all democracies, but rather from the structural integration of their organs of security, economy, and society."[105]

With the United States at the core, in short, the industrialized democracies of the West created a system of institutionalized relations that was unprecedentedly peaceful and stable. Political scientists have long suggested that liberal or democratic states coexist in a striking peace. To be sure, scholars debate aspects of this peace; some argue that the effect is weaker than believed, whereas others claim it is largely a post-1945 phenomenon. The precise reasons for the lack of military conflict among liberal democracies are contested and probably quite varied. At bottom, however, it is uncontroversial that at least since the end of the Second World War liberal democracies have existed in a largely separate zone in which armed conflict among them is exceedingly rare.[106]

One underappreciated effect of this peace was its effect on legal relations. The liberal peace lowered the political barriers to the unilateral exercise of domestic legal power. (Just as in the nineteenth century the prevailing "standard of civilization" made it easy for Western states to assert extraterritorial jurisdiction in Asia and the Middle East.) American allies clearly did not hesitate to object to American extraterritoriality. Quite the contrary: the European powers complained vociferously and enacted blocking and clawback statutes in an effort to blunt American claims. But these reactions had only a small effect.

There was good reason for the United States to have remained largely unperturbed by these protests. In a world divided by the Cold War and facing a nuclear precipice, the Western allies had little option but to accept U.S. practices. The economies of the West were too closely connected, and too much was at stake in the Cold War, for arcane disputes over matters of legal jurisdiction to threaten the Western alliance. Moreover, the structural factors inherent in the "logic of the West" were bolstered by the particular nature of legal relations among Western democracies. As legal scholar Anne-Marie Slaughter has argued, the legal relationships among liberal states are distinctive and somewhat counterintuitive. The courts of liberal states "are more likely to evaluate and sometimes reject or override the laws of other liberal states than the laws of nonliberal states."[107] They are more constrained with nonliberal states; "because war remains a possibility between liberal and nonliberal states, the potential for escalation casts any hostile dispute in a different light."[108] Hostile legal disputes among liberal states are by contrast highly unlikely to spill over into military conflict.

This is not to deny that postwar U.S. courts occasionally invoked concerns about the implications of extraterritoriality for foreign relations. But by and large, these concerns were framed in terms of demands for clarity from Congress. When Congress made clear, as it often did, that it meant to regulate without geographic limitation, U.S. courts did not stand in the way. The executive branch likewise evidenced a newfound willingness to apply American law abroad, further cementing the notion that the new and frightening landscape of postwar world politics did not require unyielding deference to the wishes of foreign sovereigns. Whether the courts or the political branches recognized that the postwar world was truly distinctive is hard to say, but with hindsight it is unsurprising that a newly hegemonic United States would find extraterritoriality attractive. And the postwar environment was unusually conducive. As the United States repeatedly asserted jurisdiction over acts and actors abroad that affected American markets, and the sky did not fall, it became harder to argue that extraterritoriality was a grave and reckless violation of the traditional order of Westphalian sovereignty.

It is worth noting that the decline in interstate conflict after 1945 was concentrated in but not limited to the West. The value of territory as an economic asset also fell as globalization took hold and imperial preference schemes declined. As a result "gains through commerce have displaced gains through territorial acquisition."[109] This point sheds further light on the relationships among empire, extraterritoriality, and international agreements. Traditionally, empire was connected to what economists call site-specific investments. These investments, such as mines, are vulnerable to seizure and dispute. From this perspective colonialism is "a particular, perhaps particularly noxious, form that the 'resolution' of these quasi-contractual issues can take: the use of force by a home government to annex the host region and so eliminate the interjurisdictional nature of the dispute."[110] Empire, in other words, served to extend domestic law beyond national borders and thereby "harmonize" rules. After 1945, however, governments increasingly chose to trade rather than raid. Effects-based extraterritoriality and the use of international agreements to forge cooperation were both manifestations of this new approach to managing legal difference.

In sum, the mid-century world was quite removed from the endemic great power conflict and imperialism of the nineteenth century. In a bipolar system sustained by nuclear deterrence, war *between* the superpowers was certainly a serious threat. But war *among* the industrialized democracies increasingly came to be seen as unlikely. In this context legal conflict took on a far more benign cast. Yet at the same time the more benign international environment empowered other Western states to resist the United States through blocking and clawback statutes.[111] Disputes over jurisdiction could safely play out in parliaments and the courts without fear of spillover into more delicate areas of high politics.

Effects-based extraterritoriality was thus a rational response to an altered geopolitical context. After 1945 the costs of extraterritoriality against other sovereigns went down. The benefits, moreover, went up as the regulatory state grew in scale and scope and increasingly collided with a more interdependent global economy. The shift from old to new extraterritoriality thus masked a continuity in approach by the United States toward weaker states. Both versions of extraterritoriality applied American law to those states that lacked the power to bat back foreign intrusions. Nineteenth-century extraterritoriality preyed on the military weakness of the non-Western world in order to extract "consensual" agreements that granted Western powers extraterritorial control over their citizens. Postwar effects-based extraterritoriality preyed on the vulnerabilities and cohesiveness of the capitalist democracies of the West to impose American law unilaterally in a more diffuse, but in some senses more encompassing, manner. The result was that the United States increasingly sought to regulate the world.

The Triumph of Extraterritoriality

Although Westphalian territoriality has occasionally resurfaced in the guise of strong invocations of the judicial presumption against extraterritoriality, such cases are much more the exception than the rule.[112] What the Supreme Court in 1909 found so startling—the application of American statutory law to activities that occur within the borders of foreign sovereigns—soon became normal. Yet postwar extraterritoriality exhibited many of the features of its prewar forerunner. Like the old version, it aimed to minimize the effects of international legal differences. And like the old it was wielded by the powerful against the less powerful. Unlike traditional extraterritoriality postwar American officials did not themselves relocate abroad. Instead, the judiciary stayed home but proceeded to apply American law to actors who were abroad. These were actors who might operate, and indeed were *more* likely to operate, in a European market-based democracy than an Asian autocracy.

Because the new extraterritoriality was so catholic in its reach, it represented a more decisive break with Westphalian precepts than had the older consular courts or even empire itself. The old extraterritoriality targeted only "uncivilized" states. Indeed, it was precisely their *lack* of sovereignty that permitted it. Postwar extraterritoriality more fully upended established rules. But a sage international lawyer once said that the United States does not merely break international law; it makes precedent. Consistent with this, today effects-based extraterritoriality is no longer questioned in its fundamentals, nor is it a purely American phenomenon. Some version of the effects principle has been adopted by most major powers around the world, including Germany, Japan, Canada, and the United Kingdom.[113] By the 1980s, as Europe grew more powerful economically, the tables had begun to turn again. As one astute observer noted,

> The standard pattern in international maneuvers over extraterritoriality has been for the United States to step off by taking action that seems to project its legislative or investigative powers beyond its borders. One or more European states respond with protests, now fairly standardized, that the United States has gone too far; sometimes they go further and pass legislation designed to thwart the original move... Two recent episodes find the roles rather neatly reversed. In each the European Commission led off with proposals, voices in the United States spoke up to say that the action was extraterritorial and improper, and the consequent maneuvers are now in progress.[114]

In sum, the postwar era was a time of great change in doctrines of territoriality. These changes were driven by a combination of internal and external factors. Coupled with more general trends in American jurisprudence, what was once "startling" became normal. The central message of this story is twofold. The first is the continuity between the old and the new extraterritoriality. Despite a radical change in form, the function—to smooth out the bumps of a decidedly unflat world—remained remarkably similar. The second is the centrality of the international system, and the United States' place within that system, to our understanding of changes in legal rules.

In the next chapter we see that same smoothing function extended to another form of extraterritoriality, one that is in many ways even more reminiscent of prewar consular jurisdiction. The onset of the Cold War and the rise of American leadership in the West entailed a radical change in U.S. military practice. For the first time in its history, the nation sought to maintain an extensive network of offshore bases, one that ultimately encircled the globe. Just as nineteenth-century American officials sought to protect sojourning traders and missionaries against alien legal regimes, so, too, did postwar America seek to protect its troops overseas. In some cases, most notably Japan, only a short interregnum separated the traditional extraterritoriality for Americans from the new postwar version.

5

AMERICA ABROAD

T he single most important feature of American history after 1945 was the United States's assumption of hegemonic leadership. Europeans had noted America's enormous potential since at least the nineteenth century. After the Civil War the United States had one of the largest economies in the world, but, as noted earlier in this book, in geopolitical terms it remained a surprisingly minor player.[1] By 1900 the United States was playing a more significant political role. But it was only after 1945 that the nation's potential on the world stage was fully realized. Victory in the Second World War left the United States in an enviable position. Unlike the Soviet Union, which endured devastating fighting on its territory and lost tens of millions of citizens, the United States had experienced only one major attack on its soil. Thanks to its actions in the war America had great influence in Europe. And the national economy emerged surprisingly vibrant from the years of conflagration, easily dominant over any conceivable rival or set of rivals.

When the First World War ended the United States ultimately chose to return to its hemispheric perch. It declined to join the new League of Nations, and rather than maintaining engagement with the great powers of the day, America generally turned inward.[2] The years following the Second World War were quite different. In addition to championing—and hosting—the new United Nations, the United States quickly established a panoply of important institutions aimed at maintaining and organizing international cooperation in both economic and security affairs.[3] Rising tensions with the Soviet Union, apparent to many shortly after the war's end, led the United States to remain militarily active in both Europe and Asia. The intensifying Cold War cemented this unprecedented approach to world politics.

The prolonged occupations of Germany and Japan were straightforward examples of this newly active global role. In both cases the United States refashioned a conquered enemy into a democratic, free-market ally—a significant feat. The United States did not, however, seek a formal empire in the wake of its victory. Indeed, American leaders made clear that traditional imperialism and associated systems of colonial trading preferences were incompatible with their vision of the postwar order, and they moved quickly to grant independence to the Philippines, the major overseas American possession of the time.[4] In the wake of the war the United States also supported a "norm against conquest" that, over time, altered other states' incentives to annex the neighbors.[5] Whereas in the nineteenth century states were conquered at a rate of approximately one every 3 years, after 1945 the rate dropped tenfold, to one conquest every 30 years.[6] The result was a dramatic decline in territorial wars as well as a remarkable unraveling of empires.

But American anti-imperialism did not mean that the United States would docilely remain within its borders once the occupations ended. The war, and in particular the surprise attack on Pearl Harbor, changed the nation dramatically. The Cold War historian John Lewis Gaddis has written that Pearl Harbor was "the defining event for the American empire, because it was only at this point that the most plausible justification for the United States becoming and remaining a global power as far as the American people were concerned—an endangered national security—became an actual one."[7]

As Gaddis suggests, in response to a newfound perception of vulnerability the United States pursued a new and informal kind of empire, which some have referred to as an "empire by invitation."[8] Its signal feature was the global network of military bases established in the aftermath of the war. This network was extended and enlarged during the decades of the Cold War as the policy of Soviet containment took hold.[9] These foreign bases were "the very sinews of an American globalism that in any other age would be known as empire."[10] This worldwide projection of military power was also, in a very simple sense, extraterritorial. Many of the great bases that sourced American military power, such as Subic Bay and Ramstein, were located on foreign territory. Both Germany and Japan were major military sites for decades after their occupations ended, and remain so in the twenty-first century. This strategy of overseas basing was novel; until the Second World War overseas military bases "existed almost exclusively within the context of formal empire."[11]

To implement this novel approach, however, the United States demanded extraterritorial legal protection for its military forces stationed in foreign nations. Special immunities, carved out by treaty, have ensured that American law applies extraterritorially to U.S. troops. This form of postwar extraterritoriality had some unique features. Yet it exhibited substantial continuity with the past. As with pre-war consular jurisdiction in places such as China, the postwar United States negotiated agreements with weaker states to insulate American citizens from alien legal systems. And as in the past, exactly what law applied to these American abroad, and what constitutional protections they enjoyed, remained hazy and contested.

The postwar era thus featured two distinct forms of extraterritoriality that were nonetheless linked in a fundamental way. The effects-based, regulatory extraterritoriality discussed in the preceding chapter and the security-oriented extraterritoriality described in this chapter both shared a common root in American global dominance. Effects-based extraterritoriality permitted American statutes to reach and regulate beyond the borders of the United States. It quickly became an integral—if often irritating, to American allies—part of the new American-dominated global economic order. The extraterritorial arrangements that underpinned the vast postwar network of military bases likewise were central to the American-dominated security order. And here too a new form of extraterritoriality was closely entangled with the rise of the United States as a superpower.

United States hegemony in turn had unusual qualities that shaped American policy. The United States wielded preponderant power around the world. But rather than subjugate or annex weaker powers, the United States built a complex network of institutions and alliances that restrained American power in exchange for lasting cooperation with its allies. At the same time, however, the United States carved out a special and sometimes aggressive role for itself. Arrogating extraterritorial legal power was one such form of special behavior, and unlike the extraterritoriality of the past, postwar security arrangements aimed not only at weak states on the periphery of world events but also at America's closest allies in Europe. The strength and nature of the Western alliance and the unusual stability induced by the Cold War permitted the United States the freedom to take actions that its allies and trading partners found irritating and even repugnant, and which at times seemed to violate the ground rules of Westphalian territoriality. Yet as the preceding chapter argued, the particular mode of postwar American dominance—deep institutionalization within the West—paradoxically permitted greater legal conflict.

The newly global reach of American law had major repercussions at home, as well, as the executive, Congress, and the judiciary struggled over how to reconcile the unprecedented international assertiveness of the United States with traditional territorial legal precepts. How American law adapted to the Cold War, and the United States's new role as a superpower, is the subject of this chapter.

"Some New Problems of the
Constitution Following the Flag"

In 1947 a 19-year-old American woman named Yvette Madsen followed her husband, Air Force Lieutenant Andrew Madsen, to duty in occupied postwar Germany. In October of 1949 the two attended a party near Frankfurt, where they drank bourbon and Cokes and played parlor games. As the evening wore on, another Air Force officer belittled Yvette Madsen's Brooklyn accent. She demanded to be taken home, but her husband refused. Madsen drove home alone. Less than an hour later she fatally shot Andrew Madsen as he walked into their requisitioned German house.

Arrested by the Air Force military police, she was charged with murder and her two children sent back to New York. Madsen was tried by the United States Court of the Allied High Commission for Germany.[12] This court was composed of three American civilians appointed by the military governor of the American zone of occupied Germany. Madsen's lawyers, and her father, who had come all the way from Brooklyn for the trial, tried to argue that she was of unsound mind and did not know what she was doing when she killed her husband. Her father told reporters that she "was absolutely insane."[13] The American judges nonetheless found her guilty as charged. She was then transferred to a women's penitentiary in Alderson, West Virginia to serve her term of 15 years.

The offshore American court that convicted Yvette Madsen for murder was a product of the unusual occupation of Germany that followed the end of the Second World War. The Allied victory over the Axis powers in 1945 was total and unconditional. With both enemy nations shattered, the Allies occupied their territories, acting as the only effective government for many years. Yet the American viceroy in Japan, General Douglas MacArthur, ruled largely unfettered by concerns over Allied interests and multilateral cooperation.[14] Germany, which was occupied by several powers, presented a more complex situation. Its territory was divided among the four victorious nations (France was given an equal role as a sort of geopolitical lagniappe) with Berlin further divided among the four.[15]

The Allies made clear that they had no intention to annex Germany. The American occupation of Germany—save Berlin—ended in 1955.[16] (That of Japan ended in 1952). The Soviets never truly relinquished power in East Germany until the fall of the Berlin Wall in 1989. American forces too remained on West German soil in massive numbers throughout the Cold War, and are still in Germany today. Indeed, Lord Ismay, the first secretary general of the North Atlantic Treaty Organization, famously quipped that the purpose of NATO, ostensibly formed to counter the Soviet threat, "was to keep the Americans in, the Russians out, and the Germans down."[17]

The occupation of Germany was unusual. International law traditionally conceived of military occupation as a temporary state of affairs in which the occupier acted as a kind of trustee for the defeated power.[18] The occupying forces were in turn understood to have an extraterritorial status vis-à-vis the local legal system. As a result, they were not ordinarily subject to local law. Consistent with this approach, Allied soldiers and their families were granted immunity from the jurisdiction of local German courts. The local population under a belligerent occupation generally faced their own legal system, and this, too, was the case in postwar Germany. Then, as now, international law decreed that an occupying power was to retain as many of the local rules as practicable. The central principle was to leave as light of a legal footprint as possible.[19] The typical approach was to apply the preoccupation legal codes rather than import new rules. Here, too, this was largely the approach of the Allies in postwar Germany, though, given the nature of Nazi law, by no means fully.[20]

As a result of this legal regime, Yvette Madsen was tried by an American court. Her claim of insanity having failed, Madsen appealed her conviction by taking a new tack. Her legal challenge at the appellate level rested on a number of prongs. The most interesting was the claim that the United States Court of the Allied High Commission for Germany, as a court of the United States, had to adhere to and give effect to the protections enshrined in the Bill of Rights. Madsen argued—without any disagreement from the American government—that these constitutional protections were not in fact followed in her Berlin trial. As Madsen's lawyers claimed at one point in the proceedings, in the early days of the Allied occupation "at least lip service had been given by the tribunals in Germany to the Constitutional and statutory rights of American defendants, but these rights are now openly flouted and disregarded."[21]

Yvette Madsen's legal challenge was, in other words, highly reminiscent of John Ross's unsuccessful plea following his murder conviction by American consular officials in Japan.[22] As chapter 3 described, Ross, like Madsen, had argued that the extraterritorial U.S. court that tried him lacked the power to properly convict him. And like Madsen, Ross had claimed that his constitutional rights had been denied. Madsen argued that the occupation court in Germany lacked jurisdiction "to try anyone (especially any American citizen) because it was not established nor its judges appointed by any authority known to the American Constitution."[23] Even if the court did have jurisdiction over her, she argued, it could not deny her "any of the rights guaranteed by the Constitution of the United States to its citizens when tried in its courts."[24]

Perhaps her lawyers were unfamiliar with the Supreme Court's decision in *In re Ross*, at the time more than a half-century old. Or perhaps they were testing the legal waters, hoping that the situation faced by Yvette Madsen—the wife of an American officer on duty in a conquered nation—was distinguishable from that of John Ross, a common sailor in peacetime nineteenth-century Japan. But if they believed the situations were distinguishable, they received a rude awakening. The answer from the federal judiciary in 1949 was the same as that given to Ross 70 years earlier. In rejecting Madsen's argument, the federal district court annunciated a now-familiar position about the territoriality of American law:

> The Constitution of the United States is the supreme law of the land, in war as well as in peace. However, its guaranties have no extra-territorial scope. When an American citizen (not a member of the Armed Forces) enters a foreign country, he becomes amenable to the laws of that country, and is triable by its courts, whose procedure may or may not be in conformity with American concepts of justice and fair play... As to petitioner's complaint that she was deprived of certain rights guaranteed by the Bill of Rights of the United States Constitution, it is sufficient to say that the law has long been settled that these guaranties do not apply to citizens of the United States living or sojourning in a foreign country who are brought to trial in that country on charges of violating local laws.[25]

This reasoning perfectly reflected Westphalian territoriality. It adhered to the traditional view of the Constitution as a geographically limited set of rules, and of sovereign borders as the metes and bounds of a national legal system. At least, it did so as far as restrictions on government acts were concerned. Then, as now, constitutional *powers* were not thought to change outside the borders of the nation. The president, for example, did not cease being president when he ventured beyond the sovereign borders of the nation, nor did he suddenly gain the power to hand out titles of nobility or declare war. But it was clear that constitutional *protections* were tied to territory.

To be sure, Westphalian territoriality was under increasing pressure in American law by 1945. But the fact that in the 1940s the federal courts had begun, for example, to understand personal jurisdiction in terms of minimum contacts rather than simple geographic presence, or to regularly apply, by virtue of the effects principle, ordinary statutes in an extraterritorial fashion, did not alter the *Madsen* court's view of the extraterritorial reach of the Constitution—nor did either development seem to have come up at all in the Madsen litigation. Instead the court simply viewed the trial of Yvette Madsen as a straightforward instance of extraterritorial American justice. And it was justice of the sort that, by this point, was quite familiar to the judiciary due to the many cases that had emerged in earlier decades from overseas tribunals such as United States District Court for China.

Madsen v. Kinsella reflected another important strand of thinking about extraterritorial trials. International and foreign laws were often understood in these cases as sets of rules that were interposed between the federal government and American citizens. Americans normally enjoyed the full protection of the Constitution vis-à-vis their government. But when they entered a foreign nation, they were subject to local law, and lost those protections. The district court in *Madsen* stated this view quite directly: when an American "enters a foreign country, he becomes amenable to the laws of that country, and is triable by its courts."[26] The striking element in this logic was that this was thought true even if the *United States government* was meting out that local law. It was, of course, not a German court that convicted Yvette Madsen for murder; it was an Allied court, staffed by Americans and located in the American occupation zone.

Because the international law of occupation conceptualized the occupier as temporarily standing in for the local government, the United States could claim that it was bound to act as if it were a German court rendering a decision. It made no sense under this vision for the Bill of Rights to play a role in Yvette Madsen's trial. That would be tantamount to altering the fundamental character of the local law by importing foreign law, something generally forbidden by the international law of occupation. In short, the fact that it was the American government in *Madsen v. Kinsella* trying one of its own citizens was largely immaterial; the United States was standing in for another (now deposed) sovereign and applying that sovereign's law.

The Supreme Court in *Ross* had similarly focused on the importance of international law. The *Ross* court reasoned that under traditional Westphalian principles one state could exercise adjudicative authority within the borders of another only via consent. Consequently, the terms of that consent—in other words, the treaty that permitted American courts to exist in Japan—determined what procedures applied to the accused. To view these cases as instances in which the United States government was trying an American citizen, the court asserted, was consequently to employ the wrong frame. The right way to understand such cases was that the United States was trying a citizen under rules agreed upon via international treaty. Or, in cases such as belligerent occupation, the United States was following rules determined by what international lawyers call *customary international law*—the accreted set of rules, based on practices of longstanding, that provide a shared web of law among sovereign states. Either way, international and foreign laws, not American constitutional law, were the central determining factors in the substance and process of the trial. It is noteworthy that the significance accorded international law under this view gave substantial power to the executive branch, the lead foreign policy actor in the federal government.

In sum, despite marked changes in the jurisdiction of ordinary domestic legal rules, in the immediate postwar era constitutional constraints were still understood to be territorial. International law explained how the United States could exercise judicial power within the borders of another sovereign, and international law also helped to determine what rules and procedures applied in such situations. American law per se did not apply extraterritorially, at least as concerned the rights of defendants.

This view, as venerable as it was, collapsed less than a decade after *Madsen* was decided. But for Yvette Madsen this collapse came too late. Madsen appealed her case all the way up to the Supreme Court, where Madsen's lawyers argued inaccurately that "never before, counsel may venture to say, has it been claimed that Americans anywhere are outside the pale of the Constitution and the Laws of the United States in a case involving trial by American authority." Either Yvette Madsen was protected by the Constitution, they argued, or she was "subject to the worst form of military (in this case, State Department) dictatorship."[27] Pointed as this comparison was, the Supreme Court was not swayed. Its decision focused primarily on the more technical and narrow claim that only a U.S. court martial, and not an overseas occupation court composed of civilians, could have properly tried her for the murder of Lieutenant Madsen. In some ways Madsen's Supreme Court litigation foreshadowed current debates over the jurisdiction of military commissions, for that was how the Court conceptualized the American court that had convicted Yvette Madsen. In short, the Supreme Court upheld the jurisdiction of the military commission as proper, ending Madsen's appeal.

War and War Crimes

The end of the war led to disputes over the extraterritorial legal rights of foreigners as well. A host of cases arose concerning aliens who were detained and often tried by the United States for violations of the laws of war. In rare instances these trials occurred within the United States. But the vast majority took place overseas. Not all were related to acts of war. Many involved ordinary criminal matters that were handled by the occupation courts as part of their governance of the conquered territories. The number of such trials was quite large: there were over six hundred thousand criminal trials by the occupation courts in Germany alone between 1945 and 1953.[28]

Out of this enormous mix of extraterritorial judicial activity came a subset of appeals for what is traditionally known in Anglo-American law as habeas corpus.[29] The writ of habeas corpus is an ancient means by which the petitioner can challenge his or her detention by the executive.

The fundamental purpose is to protect the liberty of an individual by ensuring that the executive can convince a judge that a given detention is permissible.

The common question at the heart of the postwar habeas cases was whether the right of habeas was geographically limited. Location was a central element in these cases because precedent made clear that enemy aliens detained on American territory could bring habeas pleas. This was true even for unlawful enemy combatants—those individuals who violated the laws of war. The famous *Quirin* case, involving Nazi saboteurs who landed on Long Island and Florida beaches in an attempt to infiltrate the American mainland, is an excellent example. The Nazi saboteurs hid in ordinary clothing once they had entered the United States, and therefore violated the laws of war. They were captured (somewhat inadvertently; two participants turned themselves in to the FBI) and quickly tried by a military commission sitting in Washington, D.C.

Although *Quirin* achieved some fame in recent years in connection with the legality of post-9/11 military commissions, it also made clear that the federal courts could hear habeas petitions from enemy aliens held in the United States.[30] Consequently, the difficult question in the postwar period was not whether habeas applied to enemy aliens, but whether habeas protections had extraterritorial reach. Did the rights of these individuals turn on where the United States detained or tried them?

This question first arose with regard to the trial of General Yamashita of Japan. Yamashita was the Japanese military governor of the Philippines, which Japan had brutally occupied during the war. After the Philippines reverted to American control Yamashita was sentenced to death by a military tribunal for atrocities committed by his troops. He then filed a petition for a writ of habeas corpus with the Supreme Court.[31] *Yamashita* is generally studied for its teachings on the responsibility of commanding officers. But the case was important in another respect. By hearing Yamashita's plea and ruling on the merits, the Supreme Court confirmed that the federal courts did have jurisdiction over aliens convicted and detained outside the American mainland.[32] But because the Philippines were still, at this point, an American possession, *Yamashita* did not fully answer the question of habeas's extraterritorial reach.

Two years later the Supreme Court received a further set of habeas petitions from Japan. One was from a Japanese civilian sentenced to death by the International Military Tribunal for the Far East. The tribunal, commonly known as the Tokyo Tribunal, was the Pacific theater equivalent of the more famous Nuremberg Nazi trials. The plea was brought by Koki Hirota, a former prime minister of Japan. Hirota had been convicted of a range of crimes related to the war, in particular the Rape of Nanking.[33] The Supreme Court responded to these petitions with a terse, unsigned decision a mere three paragraphs long. "We are satisfied," the justices wrote, "that the tribunal sentencing these petitioners is not a tribunal of the United States."[34] The court noted that the United States and other allied countries had conquered Japan. Consequently, they reasoned, the occupation of Japan was not purely American in character, and neither was the tribunal created under its auspices. Under the foregoing circumstances, "the courts of the United States have no power or authority" to review or overrule such a multilateral tribunal.

Hirota's habeas petition was denied, in short, because it came from a foreign court, not because the court sat in Japan rather than the United States. Geography was irrelevant. This principle would later reappear in the second Iraq War, when U.S. citizens were held by American military forces in Iraq. These forces were acting, so the Bush administration argued, pursuant to United Nations Security Council authorization and multilateral agreements.[35] Because they were not U.S. forces but instead multilateral forces, the *Hirota* principle, *mutatis mutandis*, applied.[36] (As described later in this book, the Supreme Court rejected this claim in 2008.)[37]

Wartime habeas cases continued to percolate through the federal judicial system throughout the 1950s. The 1950 case of *Johnson v. Eisentrager* was the most historically significant. The petitioners were twenty-one German soldiers captured in China.[38] The D.C. Circuit Court of Appeals first concluded that although the Germans were enemy aliens held abroad, their habeas petitions could go forward. The Court of Appeals thus "gave our Constitution an extraterritorial application to embrace our enemies in arms."[39] On appeal, the Supreme Court reversed, using the case to enunciate some principles of lasting importance. Because this case lies at the heart of the George W. Bush administration's view of the rights of suspected terrorists held in Guantanamo and elsewhere, it is worth parsing in some detail.

The majority opinion was written by Justice Robert Jackson, who had recently returned to the bench from acting as chief prosecutor in the Nuremberg Tribunal trials. Jackson began by noting that under American law foreigners were typically afforded all the constitutional protections of citizens. But, the opinion stressed, "in extending constitutional protections beyond the citizenry, the Court has been at pains to point out that it was the alien's presence within its territorial jurisdiction that gave the Judiciary power to act."[40] But the prisoners at issue in *Eisentrager* were held in China and later in Germany. Because they were never "within any territory over which the United States is sovereign, and the scenes of their offense, their capture, their trial and their punishment" were all outside the borders of the nation, they lacked any right to challenge their detention before an American court.[41]

The majority then took pains to show why their decision differed so from the Court of Appeals. It was an implicit testament to the radical challenge the lower court's reasoning posed. In the Supreme Court's view, the lower court made the following argument:

> First. The Fifth Amendment, by its terms, applies to "any person." Second. Action of Government officials in violation of the Constitution is void. This is the ultimate essence of the present controversy. Third. A basic and inherent function of the judicial branch of a government built upon a constitution is to set aside void action by government officials, and so to restrict executive action to the confines of the constitution. In our jurisprudence, no Government action which is void under the Constitution is exempt from judicial power.

Why was this syllogistic approach wrong? The Supreme Court noted first that no precedent held that aliens possessed any constitutional rights abroad. Consequently, the first point in the syllogism was faulty. The Fifth Amendment might apply to "any person," but not to any person *anywhere*. Moreover, *Eisentrager* argued, the lower court's reasoning would necessarily give the enemy aliens the right to a trial by jury as well, because the Sixth Amendment likewise neither refers to citizens nor to location. Indeed, this approach would have the bizarre effect of giving enemy soldiers greater rights than American soldiers. American soldiers expressly lacked the Fifth Amendment's protections. "It would be a paradox indeed," the Court wrote, "if what the Amendment denied to Americans it guaranteed to enemies."[42]

The Supreme Court noted further that if the Court of Appeals's approach were correct, many other constitutional rights would be implicated, because few had explicit territorial limitations. "Such extraterritorial application of organic law," Jackson argued, "would have been so significant an innovation in the practice of governments that, if intended or apprehended, it could scarcely have failed to excite contemporary comment. Not one word can be cited. No decision of this Court supports such a view.... None of the learned commentators on our Constitution has even hinted at it. The practice of every modern government is opposed to it."[43] And, of course, such an approach would be decidedly impractical. Treating enemy soldiers and spies as if they were common felons would hamstring war fighting and put the United States at a major disadvantage in international affairs. Perhaps Jackson, who was both deeply embroiled in the celebrated war crime trials of leading Nazis and a former U.S. attorney general, was particularly attuned to such considerations.

Johnson v. Eisentrager turned out to be an extremely important decision. Though the case lay more or less dormant for decades, the events of 9/11 led to a renewed interest in its lessons. *Eisentrager*'s core conclusion—that wartime detainees captured and held abroad could not avail themselves of the right of habeas corpus—helped propel the strategy of offshore detention pursued in Guantanamo Bay. These events are the subject of chapter 7 in this volume. But it is worth noting here that the policy implications of *Eisentrager* were not lost on the Supreme Court of 1950. Indeed, in his dissent Justice Hugo Black (a frequent and acerbic critic of Jackson) pointed to the perverse incentives created by the majority opinion. "The Court is fashioning wholly indefensible doctrine," he wrote, "if it permits the executive branch, by deciding where its prisoners will be tried and imprisoned, to deprive all federal courts of their power to protect against a federal executive's illegal incarcerations."[44] Black's admonition proved prescient.

The Rise of the SOFA

The occupations of Germany and Japan formally ended in the 1950s, but American troops remained deployed in those countries in very large numbers. They were present as well as in many other states around the globe, as were the troops of several of the traditional imperial powers, most notably Britain and France. The Philippines, for example, were granted independence in 1946, but the United States maintained major naval and air bases there throughout the Cold War. Other nations with no colonial connection to the United States also granted basing rights, such as Korea, Taiwan, Iceland, Italy, Turkey, and Libya. American troop deployments overseas grew markedly in the early 1950s. There were some 80,000 troops stationed abroad in 1950; by 1954 that number had grown to 350,000.[45] In 1957, the year the *Sputnik* satellite launch shocked the American public by highlighting Soviet scientific and military prowess, nearly one million United States military personnel were stationed abroad in some sixty different nations.[46] Accompanying the armed forces overseas were 450,000 civilians.[47]

This massive forward deployment, keyed to the reigning doctrine of Soviet containment, was unprecedented in American history. Even contemporary troop deployments pale in comparison. Prior to the large deployment occasioned by the 2003 Iraq War, the United States had just 250,000 troops abroad—less than a third of 1957 levels. In the interim the civilian population of the nation doubled, making the disparity between the 1950s and the 2000s even more remarkable. And when compared to the United States of the late nineteenth century, with its tiny army, the Cold War's postwar extraterritorial projection of force was unprecedented in the extreme.

In peacetime, armed forces overseas are generally governed by what are known as *status of forces agreements*.[48] These agreements are in a sense rooted in the Westphalian paradigm of sovereignty; they expressly register the consent of the host state to the ongoing presence of the military forces of the "sending" state. But in another sense these arrangements subvert

Westphalian territoriality. They carve out anomalous legal regimes within the host state's territory. Although similar agreements governing foreign armed forces had existed before, the postwar pattern was distinctive and even unique.[49] First, the scale of overseas basing was unprecedented. Cold War deployments by the United States included large numbers of personnel and often permanent bases of great size. (Today the United States has some 766 bases in over forty foreign countries.)[50] Not only were the postwar bases large, they were often only in the loosest sense controlled by the host state. In particular, American armed forces in Germany and elsewhere possessed nuclear weapons, and the host state lacked control over their use. Second, the duration of the Cold War's extraterritorial projection of force was open-ended, and in some cases continues until the present day. These features challenged states to develop a new paradigm for the indefinite peaceful deployment of troops on foreign terrain.

For the Western allies, the central agreement governing this practice was the NATO Status of Forces Agreement, or SOFA, which was the model for all the member states of the North Atlantic Treaty Organization. The NATO SOFA stipulated the following:

> The military authorities of the sending State shall have the primary right to exercise jurisdiction over a member of a force or of a civilian component in relation to offences solely against the property or security of that State, or offences solely against the person or property of another member of the force or civilian component of that State or of a dependent [and] offences arising out of any act or omission done in the performance of official duty...In the case of any other offence the authorities of the receiving State shall have the primary right to exercise jurisdiction.[51]

In practice, this meant that American troops, civilian workers, and their dependents were covered by an extraterritorial legal system that allowed many crimes to be adjudicated under United States law, not local law. As noted earlier, this system bore significant resemblance to the extraterritorial jurisdiction of the past practiced in non-Western countries.

Yet there were several salient differences. Postwar SOFAs did not cover all Americans in a given state, but only those connected to the military deployment. Second, the postwar accords did not claim jurisdiction for the sending state over *all* crimes. Rather, they typically claimed primary jurisdiction only for those that were broadly "internal" in the sense that they involved other Americans or the U.S. government. So if a U.S. naval officer killed a local barkeep, in principle that officer faced local, not extraterritorial, justice. But if he killed a fellow American officer in the same bar, it would be a matter to be handled by a court-martial. Traditional extraterritorial jurisdiction was often far more sweeping. The very point was to protect

Westerners against "barbaric" and primitive legal regimes, so it was typically not germane who the victim was. The important fact was whether a Westerner was involved. Third, the host states in the nineteenth century were on the fringes of the international system, even if some, such as China, were quite large and significant in economic terms. Postwar extraterritoriality, by contrast, was aimed at "peer" states as well as weaker powers. Hence even nuclear great powers such as the United Kingdom have American troops parked on their territories. In short, SOFAs were negotiated with the weak and strong alike.

The scale of this new form of postwar extraterritoriality was remarkable, both in terms of the sheer number of individuals involved and the global scale of the network of bases the United States developed. It was not simply active duty service members who fell afoul of this legal system. The large number of civilians and dependents that followed the troops abroad ensured that many nonservice members were tried by court martial as well. The United States Army alone averaged four hundred courts-martial annually of overseas civilians during the early 1950s.[52] Extraterritorial justice was thus a regular, even common, feature of postwar America.

The Murdering Wives

Less than a decade after Yvette Madsen's unsuccessful appeal to the Supreme Court, two strikingly similar cases appeared on the Court's docket.[53] In both, the wives of American servicemen stationed in foreign nations had been convicted by military tribunals or courts-martial of murdering their husbands. Both wives sought to appeal that conviction. And both cases posed a familiar question: did the Constitution protect Americans tried overseas by the U.S. government? The wives, whom the United States argued were subject to the terms of the SOFAs with their respective host states, argued that the Constitution did have extraterritorial force. Consequently, they asserted that their constitutional rights, in particular their Sixth Amendment right to trial by jury, had been violated.

At first these arguments were batted back by familiar claims about the territorial limitations of the Bill of Rights. The Eisenhower administration harked back to *In re Ross* and argued that "settled principles" established the power of the federal government to try Americans abroad without resort to juries, bail, or grand jury indictment.[54] Thus these disputes at first unfolded much as Yvette Madsen's had. The Eisenhower administration flatly declared, with some accuracy, that the "rule of the *Ross* case has never been questioned and we think it is not seriously questioned here."[55]

The Supreme Court at first agreed, holding that strict territoriality controlled this case, just as in the many similar cases before. But then something highly unusual happened. In an abrupt about-face, the Supreme Court agreed to a rehearing of one of the overseas murder cases. The result was a landmark decision in American constitutional law, and a striking shift in how territoriality was understood in the U.S. legal system.

The first and most significant of the murder cases involved a woman named Clarice Covert. Covert was the wife of Master Sergeant Edward Covert of the U.S. Air Force, who was stationed near Upper Heyford, England. Edward Covert was deployed to England in 1951, and Clarice Covert followed several months later with their children. Clarice Covert appeared to suffer from mental illness, and on March 10, 1953 she killed Sergeant Covert in his sleep with an axe. She then "climbed into bed with his corpse and stayed there all night."[56] Tried by an Air Force court-martial and convicted of premeditated murder, Covert was sentenced to life imprisonment in May 1953. She was then sent to the same prison in Alderson, West Virginia where Yvette Madsen served out her sentence. (It is unclear if the two women ever met.)[57]

The companion case involved Dorothy Krueger Smith, the wife of Colonel Aubrey Smith of the United States Army. The Smiths and their children were based in Tokyo, Japan. A few months before Edward Covert met his demise, Dorothy Smith stabbed Aubrey Smith to death with a knife. She, too, was convicted by court-martial and was sentenced to life imprisonment. Krueger also ended up in the same the Alderson, West Virginia women's reformatory. "The murdering wives," as the justices of the Supreme Court called them, had much in common, and it was natural for the judicial system to treat their cases as a pair. Even the questions about their quality of mind were similar. Clarice Covert's lawyer asserted that she was "probably psychotic," a claim seemingly borne out by her decision to crawl into bed with her husband's bloody corpse. Dorothy Smith had been under psychiatric treatment since 1947; the Supreme Court would later state there was "considerable evidence that she was insane."[58]

Reid v. Covert became the vehicle for the Supreme Court's reconsideration of the wives' appeals. Clarice Covert had faced an American court-martial because the British had relinquished jurisdiction over American service members and their families as part of the Visiting Forces Act of 1942. The act gave exclusive jurisdiction over members of the American armed forces to the United States, and this jurisdiction included dependents.[59] Much like the SOFAs common after the war, the Visiting Forces Act functioned to insulate American troops from local law. The Uniform Code of Military Justice of the United States, in turn, provided that the military had jurisdiction over civilian dependents outside the continental limits of the United States and a few special territories where the United States was sovereign or essentially sovereign, such as Hawaii and the Panama Canal Zone.

Thus by the terms of the British-American regime for troop deployments, Edward Covert's murder was a matter for the Americans to handle, and under American law Clarice Covert was subject to the court-martial system. After her conviction she successfully appealed to the United States Court of Military Appeals, where her conviction was reversed and remanded for a new hearing. By this point she was incarcerated in the West Virginia prison. In an intriguing and probably important twist, she was then scheduled for a new court-martial at Bolling Air Force Base in Washington, D.C. In other words, she would now be court-martialed within sight of Capitol Hill. Clarice Covert never disputed that she hacked her husband to death in his sleep. Her appeal instead turned on whether the military could try a civilian outside the battlefield. Although courts-martial have an honorable tradition, they do not employ grand juries, or the impartial jury guaranteed by the Sixth Amendment. The Fifth Amendment's grand jury requirement is expressly inapplicable to the military, and the power to regulate the "land and naval forces" is granted to Congress by the Constitution. The military justice system has consequently developed as a parallel system, one tuned to the peculiar disciplinary needs of warfare. Consequently, Clarice Covert asserted, it was inappropriate for civilians.

The Eisenhower administration gave three reasons why a court martial of a civilian was proper. First, British authorities had agreed that the United States would try those troops and their families for crimes committed in England. In other words, by international agreement Britain had ceded to the United States extraterritorial jurisdiction. This argument was similar to that made in *Ross* decades earlier. (In Dorothy Krueger's case the government similarly noted that at the time of her husband's murder, Japan had again given the United States exclusive jurisdiction over all offenses committed on Japanese soil by American armed forces and their dependents.)[60] This fit with the general set of territorial principles that ruled American law for many decades. Because, as the Supreme Court declared in 1895, "no law has any effect, of its own force, beyond the limits of the sovereignty from which its authority is derived," the government argued that U.S. jurisdiction in England, or Japan, depended entirely on the terms of the agreement with the local sovereign.[61]

Yet it was not merely that the United States had agreed to a particular jurisdictional arrangement. The Eisenhower administration argued as well that the civilian dependents were in fact part of the military deployment itself. Their behavior affected the politics of the overseas bases, and even the success of the larger strategy of Soviet containment. As a result, the executive branch suggested, were the federal courts to strip the military of jurisdiction over the overseas civilians the "success of our military missions ... would be seriously impaired."[62] The American government perceived a new geopolitical reality, in which the United States' own national security required an extensive deployment that could not be readily fit into older, pre-1945 approaches to military justice. Thus the extension of military justice to overseas civilians was, as the government argued at one point, simply "a recognition of the realities of present day American military commitments."[63] As Clarice Covert's lawyer aptly summarized the government's position at one point, "well, they're overseas; they're overseas; they affect foreign relations; they affect the continued acceptability of our forces to the host government."[64] The Cold War, in short, necessitated an approach to national defense that was very different from that of the past.

The third argument of the Eisenhower administration involved the geographic reach of constitutional protections. Clarice Covert simply had no Sixth Amendment right to a jury trial; "the Constitution does not go overseas," the government flatly declared.[65] In addition to declaring that the *Ross* rule "had never been questioned," the government argued that "the principles that justify the kind of extraterritorial jurisdiction exercised in *Ross* apply perfectly here."[66] It was true, the government conceded, that the mechanisms of extraterritorial jurisdiction had changed in the twentieth century. "Now we deal with equal sovereigns upon whom we do not impose our will, but who instead recognize, all these civilized countries, the important need we have for the exercise of this American jurisdiction in their country."[67] The government was referring to the sixty or so nations with which the United States had, since the end of the war, negotiated SOFAs.

In arguing that the right to a jury trial was not applicable to trials held overseas, the Eisenhower administration perhaps could also have appealed, though it did not, to the many cases adjudicated by the United States District Court for China. It did however note the supporting role of the *Insular Cases*, claiming that they reinforced the Westphalian territoriality of *Ross*: they showed that even in places where the United States was sovereign it could, if the territory in question was unincorporated, deny certain constitutional rights to the accused. *A fortiori*, the same applied where the United States was acting on another sovereign's territory. Intraterritorial distinctions abetted extraterritorial distinctions.

The Supreme Court's initial answer came in Dorothy Krueger's case, and Clarice Covert's decision simply referenced the reasoning in *Kinsella v. Krueger. Kinsella v. Krueger* first harked back to the era of John Marshall, noting that the early nineteenth-century case *American Insurance v. Canter*, discussed in chapter 2, had established that Congress could create tribunals that lacked the usual constitutional safeguards as long as it did so outside "the territorial limits of the United States proper."[68] Picking up on the government's brief, the Court then opined that the *Insular Cases* added further weight to this conclusion, as of course did *Ross*. Thus the Supreme

Court invoked a long line of territorial precedents to support the Eisenhower administration's position. The scattered contrary precedents, such as two early 1950s cases by the United States Court of Claims holding that the Takings Clause of the Fifth Amendment applied to actions by the military against American citizens abroad, were ignored. These decisions at least opened the door to the notion that the Constitution had some extraterritorial reach.[69]

To further bolster its reasoning, the Supreme Court then cited the peculiar circumstances of the Cold War:

> In the present day, we, as a Nation, have found it necessary to the preservation of our security to maintain American forces in some sixty-three foreign countries. The practical necessity of allowing these men to be accompanied by their families [has led to] the creation of communities of mixed civilian and military population at bases throughout the world.... Congress has provided that all shall be subject to the same system of justice and that the military commander who bears full responsibility for the care and safety of those civilians attached to his command shall also have the authority to regulate their conduct.

The struggle between the superpowers thus provided a context in which Congress could reasonably choose to govern civilians via the military legal system. The Cold War required large and essentially permanent deployments abroad; "practical necessities" allowed the armed forces to bring dependents with them to these deployments; and Congress had reasonably decided to use a single judicial apparatus for all. To be sure, the Court allowed that Congress could have chosen differently: "It was conceded before this Court that Congress could have established, or might yet establish, a system of territorial or consular courts to try offenses committed by civilians abroad. While this would be within the power of Congress, In Re Ross, supra, clearly nothing in the Constitution compels it." In short, Congress had significant discretion to choose a legal system for overseas civilians. The practice of employing courts martial was not only constitutional, it was reasonable.

A "Modernist Breakthrough"

In an unusual and possibly unprecedented move, the Supreme Court reargued the appeals of the murdering wives the following year.[70] Whatever the cause, the result of the rehearing was a striking repudiation of the Eisenhower administration's position. The reversal was total. It was as if the Court suddenly realized the implications of court martialling civilians in peacetime and decided it now was simply beyond the pale. The initial approval of the convictions, wrote the Court after the rehearing, "cannot be permitted to stand."[71] The abrupt about-face in *Reid v. Covert*, which endorsed Clarice Covert's claim that her Sixth Amendment rights had been violated, made clear that the era of strictly territorial constitutionalism was over.

The Eisenhower administration seemed to sense that the terrain had shifted as the Supreme Court reheard the arguments of the murdering wives. At one point in the new deliberations the government tried to shift the burden of its position away from a reliance on traditional territoriality. "Are you arguing now that this jurisdiction [over civilians abroad] can be sustained independently of the *Ross* doctrine, that is, independently of the spring opinion of this Court, which upheld it under the *Ross* doctrine?" asked Justice Harlan. "I'm trying to argue that, yes" replied the Solicitor General.[72] Yet Clarice Covert's lawyer continued to press the issue. "What is there in the Constitution that permits all these protections to be withdrawn from these women simply because they are overseas with their husbands and rationed by the Armed Forces? That question, if the Court pleases, has not yet been answered by any source."[73]

The government lawyers struggled with the implications of this question. At one point one of the justices asked the solicitor general, was it his contention that "any American any place, with the permission of the country where he is, may be tried by an official duly appointed by the United States for that purpose?" In other words, could the federal government escape the constraints of the Constitution simply by contracting with another sovereign, and then holding trials on that sovereign's territory? This issue, slightly altered, would later feature in the Supreme Court's landmark 2008 decision in *Boumediene v Bush*, which granted the right of habeas corpus to foreigners detained in Guantanamo Bay.

The solicitor general replied that the United States government could do exactly that. "Yes, your honor. Now, I don't come down to the minimum problems of due process. Although *Ross* spoke sweepingly, I don't think you'd use tortured confessions or—," at which point he was cut off by another query.[74] This colloquy suggests the discomfort the justices had with the idea that the United States could, in effect, perform an end run around the Constitution by switching venue. It was as if by borrowing a foreign courtroom, the prosecutor gained a new and vastly more flexible set of rules. On the other hand, it appeared that even the executive branch was prepared to concede, at this point in the litigation at least, that some constitutional protections radiated outward from American borders. It nonetheless remained unclear why this was true.

That *Reid v. Covert* was understood in its time to be a landmark case was plain from the grand language of the new opinions.[75] There was no majority decision, but instead a plurality and two concurrences. The plurality decision provided a ringing passage about the repudiation of the past:

> At the beginning we reject the idea that when the United States acts against citizens abroad it can do so free of the Bill of Rights. The United States is entirely a creature of the Constitution . . . [W]hen the Government reaches out to punish a citizen who is abroad, the shield which the Bill of Rights and other parts of the Constitution provide to protect his life and liberty should not be stripped away just because he happens to be in another land.

In short, there were no longer geographic limits to the Constitution's reach, at least as far as American citizens were concerned. Of course, because the Supreme Court had previously upheld the validity of offshore trials of Americans that were clearly inconsistent with the Bill of Rights it was not enough to simply declare this. The Court had to face the legacy of *Ross*, with its territorial vision of constitutionalism, squarely.

The plurality decision chose to simply inter the nineteenth century ruling once and for all. *Ross*, wrote Justice Black, "is one of those cases that cannot be understood except in its peculiar setting; even then, it seems highly unlikely that a similar result would be reached today." It reflected "a fundamental misconception" about the law. Black had shown considerable discomfort with the result in *Johnson v. Eisentrager* a few years before, and had pointed explicitly to the incentives for offshoring trial and detention that the *Ross* doctrine created. Thus he now sought to demonstrate that *Ross* was a decision of another age, wholly inapplicable, due to its "peculiar setting," to the contemporary world. That peculiar setting was a world of unequal treaties, consular jurisdiction, and capitulations; of the United States District Court for China, foreign zones, and international cities. It was, in other words, a world far removed from the America of 1957.[76]

The Supreme Court, ever uncomfortable with constitutional reasoning based on underlying social change, then turned to the *Insular Cases* for further support. Previously, the *Insular Cases* had served to hammer home the principle of strict territoriality. They were read as reinforcing the idea that the constitutional rules varied by location, even intraterritorially. Now, by contrast, the *Insular Cases* were turned on their heads: because they held that fundamental rights applied in American overseas territories, it was clear that the Constitution *did* in fact have a worldwide reach. That the federal government since the 1920s had asserted jurisdiction over extraterritorial crimes as a general matter—in the modern sense of effects-based extraterritorial jurisdiction—only added force to the argument that the Constitution was not hemmed in by sovereign borders and lines on maps.[77] Westphalian territoriality was rapidly eroding.

Of course, there was still a Cold War going on, and in 1957 it could not be ignored, even by nine men in black robes. Much of the Eisenhower administration's argument in *Reid v. Covert* rested on the necessity of adhering to international commitments and of maintaining discipline in an enormous, far-flung military establishment. But the justices declined to read too much into current events. They rejected the government's contention that the Cold War necessitated courts-martial for civilians. No matter how grave the threat, international security considerations could not determine the contours of American constitutionalism. "If our foreign commitments become of such nature that the Government can no longer satisfactorily operate within the bounds laid down by the Constitution, that instrument can be amended by the method which it prescribes."[78] Indeed, the nature of the Cold War and the stark threat of communism to some degree reinforced the need to protect civil liberties. "We cannot close our eyes," wrote the court, "to the fact that today the peoples of many nations are ruled by the military."[79]

Nonetheless, the Supreme Court had to explain why the international agreement with Britain ceding jurisdiction to the United States didn't require that Clarice Covert face a court-martial, or at least permit it. The Court's answer was that a treaty could never violate the terms of the Constitution, for the Constitution was supreme over other forms of legislation. No treaty could empower Congress to violate the Constitution's requirements, because to do so would subvert the legal hierarchy the document mandated. In part, this was a response to a controversy of the 1920s about the nature of the treaty power.[80] At that time the Supreme Court had declared that Congress could take actions pursuant to an international treaty that ordinarily would be beyond Congress's constitutionally enumerated powers. That principle—that treaties permitted some actions not ordinarily allowed—at least suggested that a similar result here. However, the notion that international treaties expanded Congress's power like a turbocharger on an engine disturbed many Southern conservatives, who feared that the postwar push to protect individual rights via international human rights agreements might be used to desegregate schools and dismantle Jim Crow laws. Many conservatives were actively seeking a constitutional amendment that would ensure that Congress could not gain any additional legislative authority via its power to implement treaties.

It was within this broader milieu that *Reid v. Covert* was decided. In this context it was perhaps unsurprising that the Court declared that treaties could not violate the Constitution and that as a result SOFAs could not mandate that civilians be tried by court martial. The larger result soothed southern conservatives even as it deeply troubled the American military, which now faced the question of what to do with future Clarice Coverts. And it was unclear what theory of legal geography now animated the

American system of law, for the justices held divergent views on the reasoning that grounded their newfound result. That unclarity over underlying premises would cause much confusion in the decades that followed *Reid v. Covert*.

The Jurisdictional Gap

The Department of Defense at first interpreted the decision in *Reid* quite narrowly, intending to continue to try civilian dependents for noncapital crimes committed abroad and nondependents for all crimes committed abroad.[81] But by 1960 the Supreme Court made clear that the scope of their earlier decision was actually very wide. After holding that military jurisdiction over American dependents for noncapital offenses was unconstitutional, the Court then held the same for civilian employees based overseas.[82] Along the way, the extraterritorial vision of constitutional rights announced by a plurality in *Reid v. Covert* gained a majority. In short, by 1960 it was plain that the Constitution's protections had extraterritorial reach in a wide range of circumstances.

What quickly became apparent was something known as "the jurisdictional gap." The gap resulted directly from *Reid* and its progeny. After 1960 the American military could no longer try civilians. The United States had two other options: it could in principle place these civilians on trial back on American soil, or it could request that the host state try them. In some cases, the latter approach was readily available.

Host states did not always want to try Americans, however. Particularly if the crime was American on American, they often demurred. Japan, for instance, which had a very large American military presence, refused to prosecute Americans in seven serious cases brought in 1964 and three in 1965.[83] Returning the accused to the United States to stand trial was costly and difficult. Arresting the suspect abroad was not always straightforward, especially if the individual fled off base; without the host nation's consent and assistance the United States could not legally effectuate an arrest. And in some instances the relevant federal criminal statutes, ironically, lacked extraterritorial reach. If the federal statute in question did not purport to include acts undertaken overseas, the American perpetrator simply could not be tried. He, or she, fell into the jurisdictional gap.

Somewhat amazingly, the gap persisted for over 40 years. This was not for lack of trying: the military had alerted Congress on several occasions, academics and interested parties wrote about it in the law reviews, and many criminals went free. The General Accounting Office even issued a report to Congress with the title "Some Criminal Offenses Committed Overseas by DOD Civilians Are Not Being Prosecuted: Legislation Is Needed."[84]

For whatever reason, Congress remained unmoved. As the GAO report noted, the jurisdictional gap problem was not theoretical: in the late 1970s there were more than 340,000 civilians accompanying the armed forces abroad over which the United States had "virtually no criminal jurisdiction." In 1977 alone there were some 115 suspected perpetrators were released in the United States for lack of jurisdiction.[85] These cases built up year after year, irritating the Pentagon and leaving many perpetrators free to commit more crimes. Finally, an exasperated federal appellate judge, who had overturned the conviction of an American child molester due to the jurisdictional gap, instructed his clerk to forward his decision to Congress. Galvanized by the prospect of a sexual abuser running free, Congress finally passed the Military Extraterritorial Jurisdiction Act (MEJA) of 2000.[86]

MEJA applies to individuals who are "employed by or accompanying the Armed Forces outside the United States." Its aim is to reach both dependents of the armed forces overseas and military contractors who perform work for the Pentagon at offshore bases or in the field. It establishes criminal jurisdiction for extraterritorial offenses by these individuals if the offense would be punishable by imprisonment of at least 1 year if it had occurred in the United States.[87] Some complexities remain; as one analysis of MEJA noted, "absent diplomatic intervention, host nations may not routinely acquiesce in the exercise of police or magisterial functions by the Untied States on foreign soil, since such activities lie at the heart of traditional notions of sovereignty."[88] When, in the Iraq War, the United States employed large numbers of private security companies, the complexities of MEJA became even more apparent. Did MEJA apply to contractors who worked not for the military but for the Department of State, as did the controversial Blackwater USA? This issue (discussed in chapter 7) has yet to be resolved.

But MEJA nonetheless dramatically changed the legal landscape. The location of crimes committed by a person accompanying the United States armed forces no longer has much bearing on the form or substance of the justice meted out. Rather than treating extraterritorial crime distinctively, MEJA aimed to ensure that the process and standards are much like those in the ordinary American criminal justice system.

From the War in Europe to the War on Drugs

In short, by the 1960s it was clear that Americans no longer checked their constitutional rights at the jetway door. For the first time the Bill of Rights had been held to reach beyond the sovereign borders of the United States. Yet the question of what legal protections noncitizens abroad would enjoy remained uncertain—and in many respects this issue is still uncertain today. In the wake of *Reid v. Covert* courts could no longer simply cite the various canons of Westphalian territoriality, invoke the reasoning of *In re Ross*, and declare the matter easily decided. Yet American courts were unsure how to proceed in this new legal landscape. A few federal courts viewed the now-upended territorial logic of the past as a license to upend that logic in all cases, whether citizen or alien was involved. Ultimately, as the next chapter examines, the Supreme Court reined in this approach with regard to foreign nationals. But for a brief period in the 1970s and 1980s it seemed plausible that constitutional rights no longer had any territorial or citizenship restriction.

There were at least two ways to make sense of the post *Reid* legal framework, though neither theory received sustained attention from the federal courts of the time (or since). The first was the theory announced in *Reid* itself: that the Constitution applied to the United States government wherever and whenever it acted. Although this statement was dicta, it had significant appeal to those who saw the legal system of the United States as always constrained by its constitutional foundation. This approach was also simple, and it rested not on the defendant, or victim, but instead on the actions of American officials. The problem with this approach was that the Supreme Court plurality in *Reid* (and majority in the later cases extending *Reid*) referred expressly to American citizens. Going further would require some boldness.

A second approach to the legacy of *Reid* treated citizenship as the fundamental variable. In this view, American citizens are rights-bearing individuals who, by virtue of their membership in the American polity, are always protected by the Constitution's guarantees wherever they may be. This membership approach made sense of the result in *Reid*, which rested precisely on the claim that American citizens did not lose their legal rights vis-à-vis the United States government when they ventured abroad. This was the most common interpretation of *Reid*, and the one best reflected in later case law. But to be persuasive it required, or at least implied the need for, a further account of why, if citizenship was central, foreigners *within* the United States enjoyed constitutional protections as well. Some theory was necessary, in other words, to explain why spatial location mattered for some persons but not for others.

These two basic approaches of membership and government action contended for supremacy in the post-1960 world.[89] After 1960 the Supreme Court itself said little on the subject of the territorial domain of the Constitution, returning to the topic only in 1990 in the context of extraterritorial law enforcement. The executive branch, however, continued to seek a narrow interpretation of *Reid* as a means to obtain maximum leverage and flexibility over foreign suspects overseas. In the 1970s and 1980s the struggle over this issue took place in various lower courts, including one very strange court: the United States Court for Berlin.

"Sentence First, Trial Later"

The Allied division of Berlin continued until the end of the Cold War in 1989. The United States Court for Berlin, which had jurisdiction over the American sector of the occupied city, was in some respects reminiscent of the United States District Court for China. An anachronism by the 1960s, it heard its first—and only—case in 1979. The singular trial concerned an increasingly common feature of the 1970s: a hijacking of a plane. Hijacking had become a major problem in the late 1960s. From some four or five hijackings a year the figure surged, until by 1969 eighty-eight took place.[90]

The international community responded with alarm, and quickly negotiated the 1970 Hague Convention on hijacking. Parties to the treaty were obligated to punish hijackers who landed in their territory. The agreement was not well implemented, however, and in 1978 the leaders of the major industrial nations met in West Germany to discuss further steps. There they collectively declared that they would impose an aviation boycott on any state that failed to prosecute hijackers.[91] Barely 6 weeks later, a young waiter from East Berlin, seeking to flee to the West, pointed a starter's pistol at the pilot of a Polish plane. After commandeering the aircraft he directed the pilot to land it at Tempelhof Airport, in the American sector in West Berlin.[92]

The United States, seeking to follow through on the recent hijacking declaration, pressured German authorities to try the hijacker. The Germans refused. East Germans fleeing communism were heroes to many West Germans. And legally it was difficult to hold such a trial, because West German law permitted all Germans to enter West Germany. Hesitant to push their ally too hard, the United States agreed to step in and conduct the trial itself. Thus the United States Court for Berlin was stirred to life.

Presiding over the court was Herbert Stern, a federal judge flown in for the occasion from New Jersey. The defense in *United States v. Tiede* requested a jury trial, perhaps believing that the hijackers, fleeing the oppressive East, would be treated leniently by West Berliners. (Tiede was indeed greeted warmly when he landed at Tempelhof.)[93] The Carter administration opposed, arguing that the defendants, as foreigners, had no legal right to a jury in an American court. Moreover, the Carter administration said, Berlin was "an occupied city. It is not United States territory. The United States presence there grows out of conquest, not the consent of the governed."[94] Consequently, the United States need not conduct the prosecution like an ordinary American criminal trial.

The symbolism of this statement—made during the Cold War in a supposed island of the free world surrounded by a sea of communist oppression—was rich, and it clearly rankled the American judge. The Carter administration nonetheless stressed that there was a basis in international law for this assertion. Under the traditional law of occupation the occupying power does not displace the sovereignty of the occupied state; rather, it temporarily exercises governing authority. Hence the domestic laws of the occupying power do not per se have effect within the occupied territory. This was the same basic argument made in the murder trial of Yvette Madsen decades earlier. The United States was standing in for another sovereign as a result of the wartime victory; consequently normal Constitution structures did not apply to federal actions. The government lawyers further noted that a jury trial would be impractical, as there was no preexisting jury roll and no easy way to assemble a jury of the hijackers' peers.

In a book on the trial (later turned into a film, starring Martin Sheen as Stern), Judge Stern characterized the government's theory of the case as "astounding" and noted that it treated Berlin as a "territory in which the defeated inhabitants had no rights, and their conquerors no legal restraint.... This was a doctrine worthy of Adolf Hitler himself."[95] The judge's ire seemed particularly raised by the issue of who, as a result, ultimately controlled the United States Court for Berlin: the executive branch or the judiciary.

Hence at one point in the oral argument Stern asked whether he must follow the commands of the U.S. government. The State Department lawyers replied that the Berlin Court "cannot go beyond whatever restrictions the Department of State places upon the Court." Stern then asked what restraints on the power of the American authorities existed. "Is there any guarantee," he said, "that tomorrow you would not summarily arrest somebody off the street in Berlin, hold them liable for crime, and say, for example, also, I think, from Lewis Carroll, 'Sentence first, trial later?' What stops you from that?" The Carter administration lawyer replied that the "history and jurisprudence of the court" stopped them. Stern countered that the court was subservient to the State Department. Are you saying, Stern asked, that there "is no right to due process in this court?" "That is correct," replied the lawyer.[96]

Against this backdrop, it is unsurprising that the Carter administration's arguments were not well received. *Tiede* began by acknowledging the peculiarities of Berlin. What had begun as a belligerent occupation "had turned into a 'protective occupation' of a friendly and allied people." This transformation was significant, Stern suggested, because such occupations act on behalf of, and not in opposition to, the local citizenry. As a result, the occupiers' protective role "gives them no license to abuse the inhabitants."[97] The decision then stressed the centrality of the Constitution to all federal action. Never before, Stern claimed, had the United States exercised "governmental powers" in any geographic area without the Constitution applying.

In saying this, Stern was partly correct—even in the *Insular Cases* the Supreme Court had noted that fundamental rights applied in overseas possessions—but the claim ignored the governmental powers wielded by the many offshore consular courts of the past. Stern could nonetheless not avoid discussing *In re Ross*, for that was the lodestar for the government's territorial arguments. But he dismissed it as "long-discredited" and, unpersuasively, argued that the case bolstered his point because the Supreme Court "had made its decision under the Constitution—not in total disregard of it."[98] These arguments were questionable and muddled several issues. The ruling in *Tiede* was nonetheless careful to articulate its scope narrowly. The dispute was couched as one of whether aliens, tried in an American court, "under the unique circumstances of the continuing United States occupation of Berlin," have the right to a jury trial. Thus defined, the precedent value of the decision was sure to be limited. Cold War Berlin was a city governed by a unique legal regime.

Nonetheless, the United States Court for Berlin took a dramatic step and held that an alien, outside the borders of the United States, possessed a constitutional right that the American government had to respect. That ruling was certainly consistent with *Reid v. Covert*, decided some two decades earlier. But the implications were potentially far larger, for now it was not a citizen, but an offshore alien, who received the Constitution's protections.

The most immediate result was that the trial of Detlef Tiede, the chief hijacker, commenced with an all-German jury. The novelty was not unnoticed by local Berliners, and an unrelated petition was soon filed in the court concerning a housing project being built by the United States Army. Meanwhile, the German jury ultimately found Detlef Tiede guilty of hostage taking, but not of hijacking.

The State Department, now concerned not only about the hijacking problem but also about an extraterritorial American court whose jurisdiction was suddenly expanding, directed the Berlin court to ignore the new German housing petition. In doing so the Carter administration reiterated its earlier position that the court was subservient to the executive branch. Stern returned the favor by sentencing Detlef Tiede to time served. To ice the cake, he refused to rule as directed on the housing petition. The next morning Stern received a letter from the American ambassador terminating his appointment as judge.[99] The Berlin court never sat again. The thwarted German petitioners took their housing complaint unsuccessfully to the federal district court for the District of Columbia. The D.C. Circuit ruled that the Berliners had no due process right to a forum in which to adjudicate their claim, even if their claim might be valid.

The *Tiede* saga left an uncertain and confusing legacy. The United States Court for Berlin had held that constitutional rights apply extraterritorially, even to foreigners. At the same time, subsequent decisions seemed to strip away the rights of any Berliners to a jury trial. This was true even for U.S. citizens living in Berlin, because two of the petitioners in the dismissed housing complaint were, in fact, Americans based in Berlin. As one contemporaneous commentator wryly described the outcome, "Americans in Berlin still have all their rights, but have no way to win remedies."[100]

Extraterritoriality in the Cold War

The trajectory of extraterritoriality during the Cold War exhibited marked continuity even amid great world-historical change. The postwar environment was one of dramatic transformation: the onset of conflict with the Soviet Union, the buildup of an enormous and enduring global military presence by the United States, the proliferation of nuclear weapons, and the development of a deeply institutionalized and open West. Yet with regard to territoriality the era exhibited some striking similarities with the past. As with traditional extraterritoriality, after 1945 the United States used international agreements to entrench special rights for its citizens and thereby limit the disruptive and unpredictable force of foreign law. Extraterritoriality again served as a mechanism to minimize costly legal differences, differences that were grounded in the still-prevailing paradigm of Westphalian territoriality.

To be sure, there were important differences between the older and newer approaches to extraterritoriality. The postwar SOFAs of the United States and its allies were limited to members of their armed forces, whereas the pre–First World War arrangements in "uncivilized" nations were far broader in scope. The older system relied largely on consuls and diplomats, the newer on military justice. Yet the fundamental structure remained the same. Even some of the complaints of the host nations were familiar.[101] Indeed, the Non-Aligned Movement, which grew out of the postwar wave of decolonization, resolved in 1973 to oppose SOFAs as "inequitable treaties . . . maintained against the wishes of their peoples."[102] The language seemed almost lifted from Chinese protests during the Edwardian age.

Read together, the previous chapter and this chapter illustrate that there were two distinct forms of postwar extraterritoriality, both historically novel. And both were grounded in American hegemony and the increasingly-embedded liberal peace of the West. Effects-based extraterritoriality rested on U.S. economic dominance. Likewise, the extraterritoriality of the

SOFAs rested on the hegemonic nature of American political leadership. And both flourished because the "logic of the West" increasingly transformed political and military conflict into legal conflict.[103]

As the Cold War progressed, however, these new extraterritorial arrangements increasingly bumped up against the revolution in American constitutionalism that was taking place at home. The conflictual zenith came in *Reid v. Covert*, when the Supreme Court, in a striking turnabout, reversed a century of precedent to hold that the Bill of Rights did indeed apply beyond the nation's borders. The case of the murdering wives forced the United States to again square its commitment to constitutional traditions with its global ambitions, just as the *Insular Cases* had a half-century earlier. In 1957, however, the federal courts proved less pliant, less willing to accede to the executive branch's desire for maximum flexibility, than they had in the early twentieth century. And in retrospect the cost of lost flexibility to the executive was relatively low. The aftermath of *Reid* was a problematic decades-long "jurisdictional gap," but no meaningful drawdown of offshore troops and bases or change in American grand strategy.

The unique *Tiede* case provides a bridge to the next part of the story. Although it was rooted in the occupation of Germany, it spoke to larger questions in the air in postwar American legal thought: terrorism, jet travel, the geographic scope of constitutional rights, and the complex politics of alliance management. These topics remain at the core of the contemporary debate over the territoriality of American law post-9/11. In the 2 decades between *Tiede* and the September 11 attacks, the United States occasionally suffered from terrorist acts, most notably in the 1990s as al Qaeda became active. But these attacks never rose to the level of the 9/11 cataclysm, and as a result other, more conventional, concerns often loomed larger.

At the top of the list in this period was international crime. In the 1980s in particular, the global drug trade became a major focus of American law enforcement. The Reagan administration was committed to the "war on drugs" and, along with Congress, devoted substantial resources to it. Frustrated with their inability to stem the tide of drugs crossing the border, federal law enforcement agents increasingly began to take action abroad, working with their foreign counterparts to disrupt drug cartels and interdict supplies before they ever reached American territory.[104] These efforts gathered steam in the 1990s as the Cold War ended and new, more nebulous threats rose to the top of the American national security agenda.

This extensive and burgeoning offshoring of American law enforcement raised complex legal issues, especially because U.S. law increasingly provided criminal suspects with expansive legal protections. But did these protections extend extraterritorially? What rights did suspects have abroad when they were interrogated by American agents and later tried in American courts? These issues, and others, are the topic of the next chapter.

6

THE LONG ARM OF THE LAW

R ene Martin Verdugo-Urquidez was driving in San Felipe, Mexico on a winter's day in 1986 when he was stopped by several Mexican police officers. The officers arrested Verdugo-Urquidez, placed him in the back of an unmarked car, and forced him to lie down on the seat with his face covered by a jacket. A Mexican citizen, Verdugo-Urquidez was believed to be one of the leading members of a major drug cartel and was suspected of participating in the brutal murder of Enrique Camarena-Salazar, an agent of the U.S. Drug Enforcement Agency (DEA). After a two-hour drive north the Mexican officers walked Verdugo-Urquidez to the international border, where he was transferred to U.S. Border Patrol agents.[1] He was then brought to a federal detention center in San Diego. Working with the Mexican Federal Judicial Police, DEA agents based in Mexico searched Verdugo-Urquidez's residences in Mexicali and San Felipe, where they found incriminating documents relating to drug trafficking.

This seemingly smooth example of international police cooperation ran into a hurdle once Verdugo-Urquidez faced trial in the United States. His lawyers sought to suppress the evidence, arguing that it had been obtained without a warrant and in violation of the Fourth Amendment's prohibition against "unreasonable searches and seizures." The district court agreed, declaring that the Fourth Amendment applied to the search in Mexico. The court called the search a "joint venture" of the DEA and the Mexican police. Because the DEA had failed to obtain a warrant, and because the search was improperly handled, the district court held that the incriminating evidence had to be suppressed pursuant to what is usually called the "exclusionary rule."[2]

The Reagan administration immediately appealed the ruling. Drug trafficking had become a major concern of the United States in the 1980s, and the DEA overseas activities at issue in the Verdugo-Urquidez case were an important front line in what was commonly termed the war on drugs. If the Constitution regulated searches and seizures outside the United States, the DEA and other agencies would have to revamp their approach to foreign criminal investigations. The Reagan lawyers also believed the claim that constitutional rights applied to aliens abroad lacked a firm historical basis. Prior to the Supreme Court's landmark 1957 decision in *Reid v. Covert* few thought that any aspect of the Bill of Rights, let alone the Fourth Amendment's proscriptions on search and seizure, applied when federal agents were acting overseas. *Reid* and its progeny made it clear that Americans enjoyed the protections of the Constitution regardless of their geographic location. But whether the same true was true of aliens abroad was unclear. If it was not, how (and why) did American criminal procedure abroad differ from the law applied within U.S. territory?

These questions were unsettled in part for practical reasons. Prior to the 1960s policing by American officials outside the borders of the United States was relatively uncommon. As globalization gathered steam, however, international crime became as much a part of the landscape as international trade. Not content to simply patrol the border, interdict smuggled goods, and arrest traffickers within the United States, American law enforcement officers increasingly began to go on the offensive and operate directly in foreign countries and on the high seas. Offshore policing soon became commonplace.

By the early 1990s, for instance, over three hundred DEA agents were posted in 70 foreign locations.[3] Overall, more than 2000 American law enforcement agents were operating overseas by the end of the 1990s. Like their law enforcement counterparts, immigration officials also increasingly began to act overseas. This offshoring of law enforcement allowed American agents to stop drug traffickers and terrorists and intercept migrants before they reached domestic soil. These initiatives were driven by a post–Cold War security environment in which transnational crime was increasingly viewed as a national security problem, rather than merely a criminal justice problem. Offshore policing gained further vigor in the wake of the 9/11 attacks. "Pushing the border outward" quickly became a mantra of the newly created Department of Homeland Security.[4]

Here again we see the creative redrawing of territorial borders that characterized earlier episodes in American history. In many of those episodes, such as the absorption of overseas colonies in 1898, the distinctions drawn were intraterritorial. The constitutional map and the sovereign map were intentionally unaligned. This chapter explores another manifestation of this approach, in which inspections, investigations, and interrogations that normally would occur *at or within* the sovereign border increasingly occur *beyond* it. Visually, the effect is of three overlain maps, each progressively broader than the first: a constitutional map, in which all constitutional rights apply; a broader sovereign map, which delineates the international borders of the United States, and a still broader "governance" map, which extends beyond those international borders to encompass all the overseas governance and policing activities performed by U.S. officials.

In many respects, the rise of extraterritorial law enforcement was of a piece with the postwar assertion of extraterritorial jurisdiction for regulatory statutes described in chapter 4. Extending American regulatory law extraterritorially was viewed as imperative in a world in which goods and services—both licit and illicit—increasingly crossed borders but regulations did not. Though some American regulators themselves operated extraterritorially—that is, were stationed abroad or pursued investigations abroad— in general the system relied on the presence of actors and assets within U.S. territory for its bite.[5] In criminal law, by contrast, overseas deployment of American officials was more common, and the focus was on actually investigating and nabbing suspects offshore.

The belief that the constitutional rights of aliens stopped at the border helped make this form of direct overseas law enforcement attractive in the postwar era. Law enforcement agents frequently bridle under their legal fetters; moving offshore gives them more flexibility. Government officials have defended offshoring as a rational response to the transnationalization of crime. "All we are doing is following cases here in the United States to their origins abroad," said Deputy Attorney General Jamie Gorelick in 1996. "So we're performing a very traditional law enforcement function; it just takes us into foreign countries."[6] How this process of extraterritorial policing and inspection worked, and how the legal rights of suspected criminals like Rene Verdugo-Urquidez have been understood in an era of offshore policing, is the topic of this chapter.

Cops across Borders

Drug trafficking was a major impetus to the postwar rise of extraterritorial policing.[7] The 1960s and 1970s saw huge increases in the global drug trade. Indeed, by the 1990s estimates of the trade had risen into the hundreds of billions.[8] In part the growth of drug trafficking reflected the more general growth of international trade and prosperity after 1945. Wealth fed demand, and the dramatically increasing volume of licit trade in the postwar period, in combination with major infrastructural improvements such as containerization, created more hiding places for illicit trade. Traffickers sometimes smuggled drugs into the United States in speedboats on dark nights, but they also often disguised their wares amidst ordinary goods on trucks, airplanes, and cars. (Cocaine has been hidden in false-bottomed boxes, children's toys, unripe plantains, and fake soft drink bottles.)[9]

In many respects, the same logic that fed the postwar trade boom also fed the global drug trade.[10]

As a result of the intertwining of licit and illicit trade, interdiction at the border had real costs. Inspections of ships, trucks, and containers required manpower, but most importantly took time, slowed the flow of ordinary goods across the border, and were not always effective due to the sheer volume of ordinary commerce. American law enforcement agencies sought new strategies. One was to investigate and capture foreign drug traffickers and drug shipments abroad, often in the countries where the illegal drugs themselves were produced. Taking law enforcement offshore in this manner entailed a dramatic increase in extraterritorial investigations, arrests, and "joint ventures" with foreign police forces.

Yet just as transnational smuggling was not entirely new, the practice of posting law enforcement agents abroad was also not entirely new. United States customs agents had been stationed abroad in small numbers since at least the mid-nineteenth century. In the 1880s the newly created Secret Service even cooperated with Scotland Yard with regard to Irish underground groups seeking independence.[11] And in the 1930s a few agents were posted in Mexico to monitor the then-small narcotics trade.[12] Much of this activity was cooperative. The traditional rule, which still holds today, is that police officers cannot make arrests outside their jurisdiction, and so these extraterritorial agents needed to work in tandem with local officials. This rule of territorial enforcement is true even with regard to domestic police within the United States; a New York City police officer cannot generally make arrests in New Jersey. (One exception is the doctrine of "fresh" pursuit, in which a fleeing suspect is chased across state or county lines.)[13]

As Ethan Nadelmann noted over 15 years ago in *Cops Across Borders*, his landmark study of policing abroad, American extraterritorial law enforcement grew enormously from the 1970s onward.[14] Between 1979 and 1990 the U.S. central bureau of Interpol, the international crime-fighting organization, increased its staff from 6 to 110. The DEA's budget tripled in the 1980s; by the beginning of the 1990s it had hundreds of agents stationed in over sixty foreign cities.[15] By the 1980s the pursuit of traffickers and other criminals beyond the borders of the United States had become a central part of American law enforcement. A 1989 Justice Department memorandum argued that the United States

is facing increasingly serious threats to its domestic security from both international terrorist groups and narcotics traffickers ... these criminal organizations frequently operate from foreign sanctuaries. Unfortunately, some foreign governments have failed to take effective steps to protect the United States from these predations, and some foreign governments actually act in complicity with these groups. Accordingly, the extraterritorial enforcement of United States laws is becoming increasingly important to the nation's ability to protect its own vital national interests.[16]

This strategy of offshoring police work was thus deeply tied to new conceptions of security, which expanded the traditional focus on interstate war to include transnational threats from nonstate actors. The end of the Cold War accelerated the move to extraterritorial policing; with the waning of the Soviet threat, new security concerns loomed larger in comparative terms, and provided novel ways to capture budgets and attention. And with globalization the mantra of the era, transnational criminal networks of all kinds seemed to fit easily into the sense that a new paradigm in world politics was emerging. All told, there were some sixteen hundred U.S. law enforcement personnel operating abroad by 1995.[17]

The action was not merely in the executive branch. Congress played a major role by passing enabling legislation. Congress greatly expanded extraterritorial criminal jurisdiction via statutes such as the Comprehensive Crime Control Act of 1984 and the 1986 Anti-Drug Abuse Act. The 1984 act provided for, among other things, federal jurisdiction over any hostage taking overseas in which the victim or the perpetrator is an American citizen or the United States the target of the terrorist's demands.[18] The 1986 act outlawed the manufacture of and distribution of illegal drugs outside the United States if they were intended for export to the United States.

The alacrity with which the United States embraced overseas law enforcement activities after 1945 has been traced to many factors, not only the end of the Cold War and the burgeoning international drug trade. Over the course of the twentieth century the United States increasingly federalized law enforcement, and federalization in turn helped propel forward internationalization.[19] New domestic statutes on drug trafficking, money laundering, and the like provided the basis for such extraterritorial endeavors, just as twentieth-century regulatory statutes provided the basis for civil (and occasionally criminal) actions against foreign firms and actors. Important, too, was the increasing ease of foreign travel and communication. This not only fed transnational crime, such as cocaine trafficking, but also enabled government agents to increasingly communicate, coordinate, and cooperate with their foreign counterparts. But increasingly the United States relied not only on coordination with other governments; it began to place its agents and conduct its investigations outside American territory.

The New Postwar Policing

What did overseas policing look like? At first, offshore policing was largely a product of criminal investigations of Americans deployed at one of the numerous overseas military bases of the Cold War. As illustrated by the 1950s cases of Clarice Covert and Yvette Madsen discussed in the previous chapter, American military police were kept busy not only by the crimes of foreign-posted service members but also those of their dependents. The enormous number of overseas troops, dependents, and other civilians formed what were in essence large American towns transplanted to foreign locales. These bases and their satellite cities were in practice extraterritorial outposts of America, and carried with them the crime—and crime fighters—of home. The dominant policy of Soviet containment also entailed an emphasis on export controls, counterespionage, and foreign assistance. Each of these subsidiary policies encouraged extraterritorial law enforcement assistance and activities by the United States. For a long time offshore military law enforcement officials outnumbered those of even the DEA.

By the 1970s transnational crime fighting began to take precedence. Many of these efforts involved the DEA and FBI investigating transnational criminal networks. In some cases American agents teamed up on the ground with their foreign counterparts to capture suspected criminals. Other efforts were oriented around coordinated arrests, such as the 2005 initiative by the FBI and various Central American law enforcement agencies against the transnational gang Mara Salvatrucha, which involved sixty-four hundred police officers and culminated in the arrest of nearly seven hundred gang members in several different countries.[20] The United States also increasingly entered into cooperative arrangements with foreign nations to expedite both investigations and extradition requests. Coupled to this was a concerted effort to shape foreign police and prosecutorial forces and activities in the image of the U.S. criminal justice system, so as to make them more effective and more suitable for cooperation with American law enforcement agencies.[21] All of these strategies shared a similar goal: to lower crime levels *inside* the United States through more effective policing *outside* the United States.

Thus for a host of reasons the late twentieth century witnessed a wide expansion of policing activities. Agencies as diverse as the Secret Service, the Postal Inspection Service, the Securities and Exchange Commission, the Internal Revenue Service, and the Bureau of Alcohol, Tobacco, and Firearms all expanded their offshore efforts in the 1980s and 1990s.[22] But although foreign governments vigorously resisted American unilateralism in areas such as extraterritorial antitrust enforcement, transnational crime fighting efforts seemed to create somewhat less intense friction. According to Nadelmann, foreign governments "acquiesced to U.S. demands for evidence in illicit drug trafficking investigations" quite readily, and "thereby established a precedent for providing judicial assistance" in other criminal matters with a transnational dimension.[23]

The FBI often played a central role in extraterritorial policing, particularly from the 1990s onward. Between 1990 and 2000 the FBI tripled its overseas legal attaché offices.[24] The FBI's overseas work increasingly involved investigating terrorist attacks, and associated investigations often straddled the line between intelligence work and policing. Prior to the 9/11 attacks, the preferred strategy of the federal government was to prosecute terrorists in ordinary criminal court. To ensure that prosecutions could effectively move forward in American courts without compromising vital classified intelligence, the FBI investigatory teams increasingly were divided into two: a "dirty," or "dark," team and a "clean," or "light," team.

The teams were deployed abroad together, but were kept apart by an imaginary wall. The dirty team had access to classified intelligence that, although useful, might not be admissible in court or would be dangerous to reveal publicly. The clean team gathered evidence that could be used at trial back in the United States. As the *Washington Post* reported in 1999,

> Following a presidential directive issued last May, the FBI now works intimately with intelligence agencies and the military in foreign counter-terrorism operations. Under the new strategy, criminal prosecutions, guided by behind the scenes intelligence information, have become a favorite means of combating enemies overseas. Senior administration officials said that FBI agents, prepackaged into clean and dirty teams, are regularly deployed abroad in much the same manner as diplomats or aircraft carriers. [Osama] Bin Laden, for instance, has been the target of both cruise missiles and a criminal indictment.[25]

Major metropolitan police units also increasingly went international. In 1983, for instance, New York City detectives investigated activities of the Gambino crime family in Kuwait. This trend toward extraterritorial municipal policing continued and significantly accelerated after terrorism became a major national concern.[26] By 2005 the NYPD had detectives stationed in seven foreign cities, including Tel Aviv and Singapore.[27] (With a force twice as large as the FBI, and many more foreign-born and foreign-language-speaking recruits, the NYPD is in many ways the more formidable global investigatory agency.)

These varied efforts at direct extraterritorial policing built on the larger postwar trend in American law toward effects-based extraterritorial jurisdiction. Throughout most of American history criminal law was not truly extraterritorial in the sense used in this book—that is, it did not apply beyond the sovereign territory of the United States. Some cases from the nineteenth century applied state criminal law (most criminal law is state law) to acts occurring in sister states: for example, an Ohio court and an act in Kentucky. But even that practice was viewed with alarm in some quarters.[28] The idea that American criminal law reached beyond American borders altogether received a significant endorsement, however, in the 1920s from the Supreme Court.

In a case involving a conspiracy perpetrated on the high seas and in the port of Rio de Janeiro, the Court drew a distinction between crimes that were necessarily local and those that were not. Murders and the like, said the Court, are normally local, and if punishment "is to be extended to include those committed outside of the strict territorial jurisdiction, it is natural for Congress to say so in the statute." The opinion referred to the antitrust case of *American Banana*, decided a decade earlier, for support for this approach. However, the Court declared, "the same rule of interpretation should not be applied to criminal statutes which are, as a class, not logically dependent on locality for the government's jurisdiction . . . to limit their locus to the strictly territorial jurisdiction would be greatly to curtail the scope and usefulness of the statute and leave open a large immunity for frauds as easily committed by citizens on the high seas and in foreign countries as at home."[29]

This approach suggested something much like the effects test that would revolutionize U.S. regulatory law in the postwar world. And much like the effects doctrine, it was rooted in the need to ensure that American law effectively realized its aims. This evolution in legal thinking has been aptly characterized as one from a theory of "territorial commission" to a theory of "territorial security."[30] Rather than focus on the site of an act, this new approach transcended formalist thinking and focused on the ultimate purpose of criminal law, which was to ensure the safety and security of the public. The result was a further weakening of traditional Westphalian territoriality.

Though it had many roots, the postwar offshoring of American law enforcement led to common set of legal challenges at home. Many of these challenges revolved around the question of what rights applied to the foreign suspects who were interrogated or apprehended outside the United States. These questions arose just as the constitutional framework of policing at home was undergoing a dramatic revolution in the 1960s and 1970s. In its wake of this revolution suspected criminals possessed a much wider range of rights and protections, protections that were often grounded in historically expansive interpretations of constitutional provisions. Did these much more defendant-friendly rules also apply to investigations and arrests undertaken extraterritorially? Or did offshore policing operate under a different, and far more permissive, set of legal rules? Whatever the result, was this true only with regard to citizens of the United States, or did the same ground rules apply to foreigners as well?

Unlike many of the extraterritorial rights cases discussed in earlier chapters of this book, constitutional disputes implicating federal law enforcement typically did not revolve around the geographic scope of restraints on the nature of trials, such as the Sixth Amendment's right to a jury trial or the Fifth Amendment's right to a grand jury. Instead, these disputes tended to involve two other constitutional guarantees. The first was the Fourth Amendment's protection against unreasonable search and seizure and its associated warrant requirement. This was the issue in Rene Verdugo-Urquidez's appeal to the Supreme Court. The second common claim involved the Fifth Amendment's due process guarantee. Both the Fourth Amendment and the Fifth Amendment were written in broad (though differing) language that suggested wide applicability. The Fourth Amendment referred to "the right of the people" to be secure in their homes and personal effects, whereas the Fifth Amendment guaranteed that "no person" shall be deprived of life, liberty, or property without due process of law. Neither amendment distinguished citizens from aliens. Whether these terms carried with them an implicit geographic limitation was a question that increasingly rose to the fore.

The Courts Step In

In 1974 Francisco Toscanino, an Italian citizen, claimed to have been kidnapped and then tortured and interrogated in Brazil for 17 days. This torture was perpetrated, he alleged, by Brazilian agents in the presence of, and with the participation of, agents of the U.S. Bureau of Narcotics and Dangerous Drugs. Toscanino was convicted in an U.S. court of conspiracy to distribute narcotics and sentenced to 20 years in prison. He contended that his conviction was partly based on information illegally obtained via his forcible abduction and torture. The Nixon administration neither confirmed nor denied the allegations, claiming instead that they were immaterial to the drug charges Toscanino faced.[31]

In order to argue that his extraterritorial kidnapping and rendition was illegal, Toscanino had to overcome the long-standing "Ker-Frisbie" doctrine, which held that American courts had jurisdiction over a defendant regardless of how he arrived before the court. Referring to the criminal procedure revolution of the era, the Second Circuit, which heard his case, found that the Ker-Frisbie doctrine in its fullest form "cannot be reconciled with the Supreme Court's expansion of the concept of due process.... Having unlawfully seized the defendant in violation of the Fourth Amendment ... the government should as a matter of fundamental fairness be required to return him to his status quo ante."[32] The Fourth Amendment's protections did appear to have extraterritorial reach.

The Nixon administration disagreed, though it conceded that American citizens abroad could invoke the Fourth Amendment against the United

States. Prior cases had established or at least strongly suggested such a result. The First Circuit had assumed as much in a 1950 case involving treason by an American who worked for Nazi Germany during the Second World War. In *Best v. United States* the court stated that "for present purposes we assume, and we think it is probably so, that the protection of the Fourth Amendment extends to United States citizens in foreign countries under occupation by our armed forces."[33] Likewise, the 1966 case of *Powell v. Zuckert* involved U.S. Air Force investigators who joined Japanese police officials in a search of an off-base dwelling of a civilian Air Force employee.[34] Japanese officials participated only pursuant to their agreement to do so under the Status of Forces Agreement with Japan. *Powell* held that the Fourth Amendment applied despite the participation of the Japanese officials.

Had Francisco Toscanino been a citizen, in other words, he almost surely would have a valid constitutional claim.[35] But the government claimed that it was clear that the United States need not respect the Fourth Amendment with regard to aliens outside American borders. The Second Circuit thought otherwise:

> That the Bill of Rights has extraterritorial application to the conduct abroad of federal agents directed against United States citizens is well settled . . . the Fourth Amendment refers to and protects "people" rather than "areas." . . . No sound basis is offered in support of a different rule with respect to aliens who are the victims of unconstitutional action abroad, at least where the government seeks to exploit the fruits of its unlawful conduct in a criminal proceeding against the alien in the United States.[36]

In short, the court declared that the Fourth Amendment's protections had no geographic limitation; it swept all persons into its reach who were subjected to the law enforcement power of the United States. Until this point no court had been willing to state such a principle. For this reason *Toscanino* received significant attention, and was lauded by observers eager to rein in American overseas actions and subject the government to the full restrictions of the Constitution.

Toscanino can be read against a backdrop of maritime cases that dates to the 1920s. The federal courts had long upheld jurisdiction over criminals on the high seas who conspired to violate the laws of the United States, such as British rumrunners during Prohibition.[37] This jurisdiction came with a generally weak set of restraints. In the words of one famous commentator, a "different, paler" set of constitutional rules operated at sea.[38] That set of rules appeared increasingly unstable, however, as postwar courts struggled to work out the territorial limits of the Constitution.

For example, in the late 1970s the Fifth Circuit upheld the applicability of the Fourth Amendment to foreign nationals at sea in the case of *United States v. Cadena.Cadena* arose because the Coast Guard had searched a Canadian vessel off the coast of Florida. A dramatic firefight ensued; at its conclusion thirteen Colombian nationals were arrested and ultimately convicted of marijuana smuggling. On appeal the Colombians argued that the search violated the Fourth Amendment. The Fifth Circuit began its decision with a point that was once controversial, but was by now well established: "That the vessel was outside the territorial waters [of the United States] does not, of course, mean that it was beyond United States jurisdictional limits or the operation of domestic law. Jurisdictional and territorial limits are not co-terminous."[39] The court rested jurisdiction on the basis of the now-dominant effects principle. Because the Colombians were engaged in a conspiracy to import illegal drugs into the United States, their actions on the high seas were intended to have an effect on the United States, and that was sufficient to exercise extraterritorial jurisdiction.

The Colombians' more significant claim involved the extraterritorial reach of the Fourth Amendment. Here the Fifth Circuit made a relatively bold, but superficially innocuous-sounding, statement: "The Fourth Amendment prohibits unreasonable searches and seizures and the issuance of warrants but upon probable cause." However, "its applicability is not limited to domestic vessels or to our citizens; once we subject foreign vessels or aliens to criminal prosecution, they are entitled to the equal protection of all our laws, including the Fourth Amendment."[40] The Fourth Amendment consequently followed the government, not the international border.

The Fifth Circuit cited for support a series of cases of dubious applicability, among them a decision from the Second World War involving Japanese nationals located in the United States. Also cited was a case involving the applicability of the Fifth Amendment to Americans abroad and the landmark case of *Reid v. Covert*, now some 20 years old. These decisions certainly spoke to the question of whether the Constitution applied to Americans abroad. They also spoke to whether it applied to aliens within the United States. But they did not join the two factors and say whether constitutional protections were available to aliens abroad. Hence although the Fifth Circuit's notion that the Fourth Amendment followed American law enforcement power wherever it went had some plausible backing in prior American cases, and certainly had some normative appeal, it could not be called established law.[41]

The bottom line was that until the Supreme Court chose to hear the case of Rene Verdugo-Urquidez in 1990, the scope of the constitutional rights of aliens abroad remained uncertain and contested. During the 1970s and 1980s advocates and sympathetic scholars tried to discern and often encourage an emerging consensus on the applicability of the Bill of Rights abroad. For example Louis Henkin, an influential law professor, matter-of-factly wrote in 1984 that "[t]ime was when it was assumed that the U.S. Constitution, like a deity of old, ruled only its territory and did not apply outside the United States. Since 1957 we know that the Constitution applies wherever the United States exercises authority."[42] Henkin was referring to *Reid v. Covert* and its sweeping rejection of strict territoriality for the constitutional rights of American citizens. Yet nothing could decisively be said outside this context, for, as the last chapter detailed, the Supreme Court had been careful to limit its holding in *Reid* to citizens.

Many federal courts in this period chose to step back from the more extreme implications of *Toscanino*, including the Second Circuit itself. In a case just a year later, for instance, the Second Circuit narrowed the teachings of *Toscanino*, emphasizing that the decision "rests solely and exclusively on the use of torture and other cruel and inhumane treatment."[43] Another federal court, in a dispute involving allegations of illegal surveillance and harassment of Americans and an Austrian by the U.S. Army in occupied West Berlin, handed down a mixed message on the Constitution's extraterritorial reach. On the one hand, the court held that the First, Fourth, and Fifth Amendments all applied to Americans citizens living in Berlin. On the other, the court disparaged the emerging *Toscanino* "line" of cases: "Plaintiffs rely heavily on a 'trend' in the federal courts permitting non-resident aliens to sue for actions directed at them by U.S. officials which are violative of the Constitution. The 'trend' is embodied in one case, *United States v. Toscanino....*"[44] Taking stock of this welter of cases, the authoritative *Restatement of Foreign Relations*, published in 1986, tentatively stated that "at least some actions by the United States in respect of foreign nationals outside the country are also subject to constitutional limitations."[45] But, the *Restatement* noted, this has "not been authoritatively adjudicated," having been neither endorsed by the Supreme Court nor aggregated to any appreciable pattern.[46]

It is essential to pause and underscore the novelty of extraterritorial policing. Certainly some of this late-twentieth-century offshore activity on the part of American law enforcement agencies, such as the pursuit of border-crossing fugitives, would have been familiar to nineteenth-century observers. But the growth of extraterritorial policing in the late twentieth century was dramatic, and much of it reflected the new wave of postwar crime legislation focused on the transnational movement of illegal drugs, migrants, and money. It was in this context of growing transnational crime networks, rapidly globalizing policing, and increasing concern over transnational threats of all kinds that accused Mexican drug trafficker Rene Verdugo-Urquidez was arrested in Mexico, turned over the American DEA, and tried for drug trafficking in the United States. His case provided the first major opportunity since *Reid v. Covert*, some 30 years earlier, for the

Supreme Court to clarify precisely what the geographical scope of constitutional rights was.

We the People?

The Ninth Circuit, which first heard Rene Verdugo-Urquidez's appeal, began by noting that the case asked a relatively novel question. Whether the Fourth Amendment's exclusionary rule applied extraterritorially in the same way it applied on American territory had, despite the various high seas cases and extraterritorial abduction cases in recent decades, never been definitively answered. The Ninth Circuit nonetheless announced that "until this case, we have been content simply to assume that the fourth amendment constrains the manner in which the federal government may pursue its extraterritorial law enforcement objectives." In doing so the court followed many prior courts, which had generally assumed the same.[47]

The court made plain that it held this view because of the long constitutional shadow cast by *Reid v. Covert*. Indeed, the Ninth Circuit, a reliably liberal court in this period, began its consideration of the Fourth Amendment's extraterritorial reach by immediately invoking *Reid*'s statement that the United States can act only in accordance with all the limitations imposed by the Constitution. Calling this a proposition "so reasonable and unremarkable that most people would find it bizarre indeed to learn that the rule had ever been otherwise,"[48] the decision then surveyed the trajectory from *In re Ross* to the *Insular Cases* to *Reid*. It observed that individuals in Verdugo's position enjoy other constitutional rights, and reasoned that "[i]t would be odd indeed to acknowledge that Verdugo-Urquidez is entitled to due process under the fifth amendment, and to a fair trial under the sixth amendment, . . . and deny him the protection from unreasonable searches and seizures afforded under the fourth amendment."[49] The Ninth Circuit thus held the Fourth Amendment applicable to overseas aliens.

The Reagan administration was deeply unhappy with this outcome. As a practical matter the Ninth Circuit's decision made extraterritorial policing more difficult. Obtaining warrants and the like was cumbersome, and especially so in a foreign context, and comporting with the amendment's reasonableness requirement was costly. But the executive branch offered a principled reason for opposition as well. The government's theory was that the Constitution did not create or guarantee legal rights for all individuals in the world. It was instead a very particular compact between the American people and the federal government.[50] Foreigners like Verdugo-Urquidez are not part of the American community, the government contended; therefore, they are not one of "the people" referred to by the preamble of the Constitution, or by the language of the Fourth Amendment itself.

In some respects this claim harked back to much earlier debates about the geographic reach of the Constitution. Did it only apply within the states, or did the Constitution apply to the federal territories as well? Here, similar distinctions were applied to types of individuals. The goal in both cases was to define an in-group and an out-group with regard to constitutional rights. The executive branch believed that foreigners such as Verdugo-Urquidez were clearly in the out-group. To support this idea the Reagan administration looked to the 1950 decision of *Johnson v. Eisentrager*. The Reagan lawyers contended that in *Eisentrager* the Supreme Court had decisively rejected a "'universal' approach to constitutional rights.'"[51] The government acknowledged that it was true that one did not have to be a citizen to enjoy the protections of the Bill of Rights, as it had long been the case that foreigners within American borders were generally protected by the Constitution.[52] The executive branch lawyers insisted, however, that constitutional rights did not apply extraterritorially as far as foreigners were concerned.

Why, if the Constitution was a compact, and the guiding principle of constitutional applicability was membership, foreigners were protected by the Bill of Rights when *inside* American borders was necessarily left somewhat hazy. On the one hand, the Reagan administration argued that foreigners on American soil enjoy constitutional protections only because they have, whether through residency, naturalization, or something else, "maintained ongoing membership in the American community."[53] The crucial issue was identity and connection to the polity. Those who have a connection to American society enjoy a status akin to guest in the national home. As guests, they are protected much like a member of the polity would be. (The "ongoing membership" language, of course, suggested that something more permanent than a brief visit was required.)

This membership view of constitutional rights certainly was not novel, even in 1950. In 1903 the Supreme Court had queried whether the due process clause applied to an alien "who has been here for too brief a period to have become, in any real sense, a part of our population." Even the framing generation debated the question with regard to the Alien and Sedition Acts.[54]

On the other hand, the Reagan administration claimed that prior decisions establishing the rights of aliens within the borders of the United States "all involve domestic transactions." By contrast, Verdugo-Urquidez was seeking "extraterritorial protection."[55] This second claim was in some tension with the first. Its focus on domestic transactions suggested that the crucial issue was not membership in the American community but simply geographic location. Had Verdugo-Urquidez and his property been located on American soil, this argument implied, the outcome would be different. Conveniently, the government did not have to choose between theories of membership or location in *Verdugo*. Because his capture and the search of his homes both occurred in Mexico, under either theory Verdugo-Urquidez could not avail himself of the exclusionary rule. But the implications of each were quite different.

The compact/membership theory was clearly the more sweeping claim, and it had some venerable roots. Indeed, the Ninth Circuit acknowledged the various instances in which the Supreme Court had appeared to endorse it.[56] But the appellate judges were ultimately unpersuaded. The Constitution may have had compact-like elements, they conceded. But it also reflected a theory of natural rights not oriented around notions of social contract. Citing Joseph Story's *Commentaries on the Constitution of the United States*, the Ninth Circuit also noted that constitutions as a rule are not truly founded on the consent of the governed. Instead they generally rest on the consent of only some subset of the governed. For these reasons, and because constitutions are intended to be durable through time, the court asserted that the notion of social contract is only fictional and not especially meaningful.[57]

The Ninth Circuit then pointed out that prior decisions, dating back at least to the nineteenth-century case of *Yick Wo v. Hopkins*, had extended significant constitutional protection to aliens within the United States. These cases had done so "without distinguishing between those who are here legally or illegally, or between residents and visitors."[58] Taken together, these factors made the appellate judges very skeptical of the membership theory. Because Verdugo-Urquidez was in fact on American territory legally—he was, at the time of the search, detained by American law enforcement officials in San Diego—the court announced it could "discern no conceivable reason why he should be denied the protection of the fourth amendment in connection with this prosecution."[59]

The membership theory posed other problems that the Ninth Circuit did not fully probe. The Reagan lawyers had looked to *Johnson v. Eisentrager*, with its references to an "ascending scale of rights" for aliens, to explain how nonmembers became treated as members. The government thus argued that some foreigners, by virtue of the time they spent in the United States and the ties they developed, were temporary or honorary members of the American polity. Recipients of a sort of constitutional guest pass, these welcomed foreign visitors were protected as long as they stayed on U.S. soil.

This argument of an ascending scale of rights for foreigners faced at least two hurdles. First, it was (and remains) inaccurate to say that all or even most constitutional rights for aliens within U.S. territory have been treated on an ascending scale keyed to the depth of ties between the individual and the United States. For example, the ascending scale principle predicts that a first-time visitor, in the United States only briefly, would enjoy the barest minimum of protection by the Fourth Amendment. Yet that is not the result in practice; a Chinese tourist stopping over in Seattle for a couple of days en route to British Columbia would enjoy the full protections of the Fourth Amendment were she subjected to a search by local police.[60] Hence the theory put forward by the executive branch in *Verdugo* was inconsistent with established precedent and practice.

The second problem with the ascending scale concept was that this claim struggled against the facts of the case. Rene Verdugo-Urquidez was not someone wholly unconnected to the United States. He appeared to have received a green card in 1970, making him more than just a casual visitor or tourist. The executive branch disputed whether he had remained a resident alien in the years since, but Verdugo-Urquidez's lawyers claimed he was still a U.S. legal resident.[61] And of course Verdugo-Urquidez's narcotics business, although plainly illicit, had exactly the sort of market-influencing connections to the United States that had sustained decades of effects-based extraterritorial assertions of American law in areas like securities law or antitrust. Despite these problems, the ascending ties conception of alien rights, which would as a practical matter permit the government to prosecute criminals such as Verdugo-Urquidez more effectively, eventually found favor at the Supreme Court.

The Return of Territoriality

When Rene Verdugo-Urquidez's Fourth Amendment claim reached the Supreme Court it resulted in a major contemporary statement on the geographic limits of the Constitution, a statement that was in many respects a return to older understandings of territoriality. In this sense it was much like the contemporaneous *Aramco* case, in which the Supreme Court held that, despite substantial evidence about Congress's intent to do so, American labor law did not extend extraterritorially. (The *Aramco* decision, as chapter 4 described, was quickly overturned by Congress, which made plain that it did want American labor statutes to have extraterritorial reach.)[62]

The George H. W. Bush administration, now in charge of the *Verdugo* case, continued the general approach of the Reagan administration. The Bush lawyers also echoed a feature of many earlier extraterritorial cases in suggesting the importance of the foreign sovereign. They argued that even if the Bill of Rights did apply extraterritorially, the United States ought not to apply its own domestic law to what was in many respects a Mexican matter, and was a matter that had certainly transpired on Mexican territory. "The fact that this is a separate sovereignty, Mexico, indicates that it's their laws and not ours that ought to presumptively control disputes," suggested the executive branch lawyers.[63]

At the oral argument the justices pressed the government's lawyer, Lawrence Robbins, on what limitations, if any, applied to American law enforcement abroad. Would it matter with regard to the Fourth Amendment if Mexico had not given its approval for the search of the houses? Soon Justice Kennedy brought the conversation around to the larger issue:

> *Justice Kennedy*   Does the Constitution control what United States officials do when they're abroad generally? Or never? Or sometimes?
>
> *Robbins*   Well, I think the answer is sometimes, and the answer is it depends. And, of course, it's the very fact that it depends—
>
> *Justice Kennedy*   When and what does it depend on?
>
> *Robbins*   Well, if I might, Justice Kennedy, I'd like to turn to that directly because the central failing, we believe, of the [Ninth Circuit] court of appeals, is that they thought it never depends. They thought that the Constitution, as it were, provides a sort of universal declaration of rights of man. It applies whenever, wherever and against whomever government authority acts. And we don't believe that . . . in this respect it's our view that some constitutional rights do not attach to all persons by their very nature and do not apply in all settings by their very nature. And I think the Fourth Amendment in some ways is a paradigm case of a constitutional provision that makes next to no sense in most overseas settings.[64]

As this colloquy reveals, the Bush administration advanced both principled and functional arguments. The principle was that American constitutional law was not "universal." Rather, it applied in some contexts and not others. And the scope and reach of American law was functionally keyed to its utility and "sense" in particular settings. This seemed to mean that in some situations the Bill of Rights operated extraterritorially, and in some it did not; the answer would depend on context.

This explanation appeared to mollify Kennedy. In a separate concurrence, Kennedy argued that the distinction between citizens and aliens was critical when assessing the geographic reach of constitutional rights. This distinction "follows from the undoubted proposition that the Constitution does not create, nor do general principles of law create, any juridical relation between our country and some undefined, limitless class of noncitizens who are beyond our territory." Kennedy looked to the *Insular Cases* and to *Reid v. Covert* to argue that what constitutional rights applied extraterritorially depended on context. The *Insular Cases*, he asserted, "stand for the proposition that we must interpret constitutional protections in light of the undoubted power of the United States to take actions to assert its legitimate power and authority abroad."[65]

The United States was a sovereign state on the international plane, he seemed to be saying, and therefore it necessarily had the power to assert its legal authority extraterritorially. That power could only be constrained by domestic law in ways that were reasonable and practicable, lest domestic law act as a dangerous fetter on American foreign affairs. Verdugo-Urquidez's case thus required a contextual and flexible analysis that took into account the particularities of extraterritorial policing and international drug trafficking.[66] To straightforwardly apply the Fourth Amendment to a search wholly within Mexico would be "impracticable and anomalous."

The majority opinion in *Verdugo* took a different though ultimately harmonious tack. The majority began by contending that, unlike some constitutional violations, a violation of the Fourth Amendment occurred not at trial but at the time of the search or seizure in question. For this reason, whatever violation transpired occurred wholly in Mexico. The majority then argued that "the people" referred to in the Fourth Amendment had a specific meaning to the constitutional framers. The phrase "refers to a class of persons who are a part of a national community or who have otherwise developed sufficient connection with this country to be considered part of that community."[67] *Verdugo* referenced the *Insular Cases* to make the point that only the most fundamental constitutional rights applied in unincorporated federal territories such as Puerto Rico. Because these territories were clearly under the sovereignty of the United States, it followed that areas not under the sovereignty of the United States—in other words, Mexico—were even further from the core of the Constitution's zone of application.

One problem with this analysis was that Verdugo-Urquidez was not in fact overseas at the time of the search of his Mexican residences. And existing precedent made clear that aliens within the United States did have Fourth Amendment rights. The majority therefore harked back to the ascending ties principle first advanced by the Reagan administration. Verdugo-Urquidez's presence did not meet the necessary threshold:

> [t]his sort of presence—lawful but involuntary—is not of the sort to indicate any substantial connection with our country. The extent to which respondent might claim the protection of the Fourth Amendment if the duration of his stay in the United States were to be prolonged—by a prison sentence, for example—we need not decide. When the search of his house in Mexico took place, he had been present in the United States for only a matter of days.[68]

In the oral argument the Bush administration had elaborated on this idea, implying that the quantity of time spent in the United States helped to determine whether or not an alien defendant possessed constitutional rights. "It is undoubtedly the case that had [Verdugo-Urquidez] never been here our argument would be that much stronger," said the executive branch.[69] When it was pointed out that any alien defendant on trial in the

United States enjoyed the right to counsel—no matter how weak their connection to the nation—the government returned to the key theme of American power on the global stage and replied that the right to counsel was a "domestic right" and not a "restraint on the overseas application of American power."

Consequently, despite the Supreme Court's focus on the location of the defendant, it was the location of the *property* that actually seemed to matter. Had Rene Verdugo-Urquidez owned a home in San Diego that was also searched by American law enforcement agents, it seems highly doubtful that the Supreme Court would have held that an otherwise-unconstitutional search was acceptable on the grounds that the owner was present in the United States "lawfully but involuntarily." This analysis also suggested that in the reverse scenario—an individual present in the United States unlawfully but voluntarily—the Fourth Amendment might not apply either.

Indeed, this would seem to be a necessary corollary of the membership view articulated in *Verdugo*.[70] Nonetheless, an earlier case by the Supreme Court had held that in civil deportation proceedings illegal aliens were protected by the Fourth Amendment. In response, the majority in *Verdugo* hedged, claiming that the illegal aliens in that case had been in the United States voluntarily and "presumably had accepted some societal obligations."[71] This line of argument did affect later thinking about the rights of illegal aliens. In 2003 a federal court in Utah, citing *Verdugo*, held that an illegal alien in the United States "lacks entitlement to those rights which come from being a member of American society—including Fourth Amendment rights."[72]

Verdugo did not end debate over the extraterritorial rights of foreign nationals. But it provided substantial ammunition to those who thought that constitutional rights remained in large measure territorial. The decision was in many respects a return to an older and stricter Westphalian vision. But it was also a reflection of its late-twentieth-century milieu. For one, it signaled a concern on the part of conservative jurists with what some saw as a post–*Reid v. Covert* trend toward a universal or "global view" of constitutional rights. Conservative judges had never been enamored of the defendant-protective innovations of the 1960s and 1970s, and further extension to the international plane must have been unwelcome. Coupled to this was a general fear of the rising level of transnational crime and trafficking. By 1990 international crime networks were a staple of American law enforcement efforts, crime in American cities was high (the murder rate in New York City, for example, for was four times higher in 1990 than it was in 2007), and the war on drugs was hardly heading toward victory.

The decision also reflected the unique foreign policy posture of the United States. The United States was not alone in pursuing criminals extraterritorially, but it was and remains "more willing than any other [state] to intrude on the prerogatives of foreign sovereigns, to confront foreign political sensibilities, and to override foreign legal norms."[73] With the Cold War winding down, and drug trafficking and illegal immigration increasingly potent political issues, transnational threats oriented around the border and its security were rising to the forefront of American politics.

This new view was bipartisan. It could be traced to the Reagan administration, which in a 1986 security directive formally elevated drug trafficking to the status of national security threat,[74] but the Clinton administration was, if anything, even more strongly committed to viewing transnational crime through a national security lens. Testifying before the Senate, a top Clinton administration official later stated that "the end of the Cold War has changed the nature of the threats to our national security. No longer are national security risks exclusively or predominantly military in nature. Transnational phenomena such as terrorism, narcotics trafficking, alien smuggling, and the smuggling of nuclear materials all have been recognized to have profound security implications for American policy."[75]

Emphasizing these transnational threats, *Verdugo* stressed the dangerous and unpredictable nature of the contemporary world. As the Supreme Court put it, to hold that overseas foreigners possessed constitutional rights

> would have significant and deleterious consequences for the United States in conducting activities beyond its boundaries. . . . The United States frequently employs Armed Forces outside this country—over 200 times in our history—for the protection of American citizens or national security. Application of the Fourth Amendment to those circumstances could significantly disrupt the ability of the political branches to respond to foreign situations involving our national interest. . . . For better or for worse, we live in a world of nation-states in which our Government must be able to "functio[n] effectively in the company of sovereign nations." . . . Situations threatening to important American interests may arise halfway around the globe, situations which in the view of the political branches of our Government require an American response with armed force. If there are to be restrictions on searches and seizures which occur incident to such American action, they must be imposed by the political branches through diplomatic understanding, treaty, or legislation.[76]

In sum, as in so many cases from the past, the executive branch sought a free hand in governing, regulating, and punishing the harmful activities of those who fell, to varying degrees, outside the constitutional core of citizens within the states of the union. And as in the vast majority of these cases the federal courts were ultimately supportive, crafting legal doctrines that were explicitly aimed at enhancing, or at least not constraining, the extraterritorial projection of American power. The result in *Verdugo* fit well within this facilitative tradition. Legal doctrine thus served to ensure that the unusual constitutional restraints the United States government labored under were not a liability in the realm of foreign relations. The due process revolution of the mid-twentieth century and the rise of extraterritorial policing had pushed some lower courts to extend constitutional rights extraterritorially even with regard to foreign nationals. In *Verdugo*, the Supreme Court checked that tendency decisively.

The Regulatory Context

For some, *Verdugo* was a proper response to a dangerous trend toward globalizing constitutional rights. In light of the enduring international challenges faced by the United States, the nation could ill afford to carry the Constitution with it wherever national security required it to act. Others thought the decision was an anachronistic retrenchment, a repudiation of the best reading of the Bill of Rights and a return to an explicitly territorial vision of American law that had been on the wane throughout the twentieth century.

Although in this regard the opinion did run against the general tide of the postwar era, the 1980s and 1990s were certainly not consistent in terms of doctrinal change. Indeed, *Verdugo* was not the only decision by the Rehnquist Court to be dubbed a step back to older understandings of territoriality. Just 1 year after *Verdugo*, the Supreme Court held that American antidiscrimination law did not apply overseas even with regard to American firms. This decision, too, was characterized as unwittingly "slip [ping] back to the 19th century."[77] Congress moved swiftly to overrule it. Similarly, a 1972 Supreme Court decision on the geographic reach of U.S. patent law declared, "Our patent system makes no claim to extraterritorial effect." This decision was also overruled by Congress, which modified the relevant statute to make clear that one who acts "*outside* of the United States in a manner that would infringe the patent if such a combination occurred *within* the United States shall be liable as an infringer."[78]

In the main, however—and much more could be said about extraterritoriality and statutory interpretation—throughout the postwar era an ever wider range of national laws were either interpreted by U.S. courts or clearly designed by Congress to extend globally. As earlier chapters made clear, some fields of law, such as antitrust, received extensive attention for their often aggressive use of extraterritorial jurisdiction. But there were many other areas of domestic regulation that were similarly extended abroad in an effort to control acts beyond American territory. As the domestic administrative state in the United States grew in size and scope, and more and more regulatory statutes were passed and agencies created, it was only natural for litigants and the executive branch itself to seek to have these regulatory rules extended, under an effects theory, beyond American territory. In an increasingly global economy many believed that to fail to do so would weaken or even undermine the regulatory efforts taking place at home.

Labor law provides a salient example. For most of the twentieth century American labor law was treated as territorial. The presumption against extraterritoriality was first applied to labor rules in the 1920s, when American citizens working for U.S. railroads in Canada were held to be ineligible for workmen's compensation. After 1945 the presumption was again used to deny claims by Americans constructing U.S. military bases in Iran.[79] In 1975, however, the National Labor Relations Act was applied to a U.S. corporation that discriminated against an American employee at a Canadian facility. This trend continued, and by the 1990s the extraterritorial application of labor law had "expanded significantly."[80]

Similar trends unfolded in other areas of American law, following the effects-driven paradigm analyzed in this book. Legal commentators have observed that in intellectual property law, bankruptcy law, tax law, securities law, and other areas the United States continued in the 1990s to expand the geographic reach of domestic statutes.[81] To be sure, not all areas of domestic law have been treated in the same manner. Some, such as labor law, have tended to induce caution by the courts and more action from Congress. Others, such as environmental law, have produced a mosaic of somewhat contradictory judicial decisions.[82] Some of the existing variation is hard to rationalize: certain intellectual property statutes, for instance, have been held to have extraterritorial effect more readily than others, without much evidence that these differences reflect carefully considered decisions by Congress.[83]

Courts on occasion have also enhanced extraterritorial effect without necessarily applying a statute extraterritorially. For example, some decisions have looked to where federal policy decisions were *made*, rather than where they were *implemented*, to determine the relevant geographic location of the "act" in question. If an initiating decision could be traced to an agency headquarters in Washington, then the act, even if ultimately undertaken overseas, was deemed territorial rather than extraterritorial. This "headquarters" approach provided an alternative path for courts that were unwilling to straightforwardly hold that a given statute or other legal provision reached beyond U.S. borders.[84]

On the whole, however, extraterritoriality increasingly became a widely accepted notion within the United States in the latter half of the twentieth century. As a leading commentator summarized the state of affairs in 1992, "Technological, commercial and political changes have created an interdependent global economy, characterized by pervasively transnational commercial activities, in which no nation can ignore what occurs beyond its borders. Driven by these realities, national regulatory authorities and legislatures, particularly in the United States, have for the past forty years increasingly extended national laws to conduct occurring outside national borders."[85]

This same interdependent global economy also entailed a rising number of U.S. lawsuits involving foreign firms. These suits sometimes implicated firms that had little or no direct contact with the United States, though their products ended up in U.S. markets. As earlier chapters described, American courts had in the 1940s rejected older territorial rules of "personal jurisdiction" in favor of more functional tests based on "minimum contacts." (Personal jurisdiction refers to the jurisdiction of a court over the individual defendant, not jurisdiction over the act itself.) Actors who lacked minimum contacts with the forum could not be haled into court; to do so was said to violate the Fourteenth Amendment's due process clause.

In adjudicating cases involving foreign firms that lacked minimum contacts, the Supreme Court pursued a similar analysis. In various cases it held that foreign firms that never marketed or sold their products in the United States could not be sued in the United States, even if those products ended up harming someone in the United States.[86] To do otherwise, said the court, would violate the Fourteenth Amendment and the individual liberty interest it protects. These cases, in short, implicitly ruled that foreign firms had constitutional rights to due process.[87] This was true even if—*especially* if—they had never operated on American soil.

The Supreme Court's return to strict territoriality in *Verdugo* was thus rendered in a context in which the extraterritorial application of American law was increasingly common, though not always consistent. Criminal law was no exception to this broad trend, as this chapter has illustrated. Constitutional rights, which often hobbled the efforts of the executive branch to enforce and extend American law and vexed law enforcement officials, were a clearly exceptional area of the law that featured substantial resistence to extraterritorial application. But even here the pattern was by no means consistent or coherent.

The Dark Side of Globalization

The postwar rise of globalization not only entailed more international commerce; it also meant more international crime. The growing American efforts to tackle transnational crime at its source as well as at home often required close cooperation with other nations. Yet unilateral action was an attractive and sometimes irresistible option for the United States, particularly when foreign law was more lax than, or simply different from, American law. Just as in the arena of ordinary regulatory statutes, in criminal justice matters the postwar United States pursued a three-pronged strategy in the face of international legal divergence. One prong was multilateral, formal, and cooperative: the United States sought to negotiate international agreements that harmonized rules and processes in the law enforcement arena. A second was more informal, nimble, and ad hoc: American officials used global networks of law enforcement officials as a tool of flexible cooperation. The third was more extraterritorial and unilateral: federal agencies undertook extraterritorial action by deploying American agents overseas (typically with the assistance of local sovereigns) and by unilaterally extending American law to crimes and conspiracies abroad.

Thus both domestic regulatory law and domestic criminal law shared a common approach in the postwar era. Both reflected the increasingly interventionist nature of the American state. Activities that were once ungoverned (such as insider trading or opium smoking) became prohibited by Congress over the course of the twentieth century. Both areas of the law also were increasingly applied extraterritorially. And both reflected the functional logic of transboundary effects in a world of fixed sovereign borders. If actions abroad, such as a conspiracy to restrain trade or smuggle drugs, had effects on American markets or the American populace, that was enough to sustain jurisdiction over those extraterritorial acts. The conceptual evolution was one of "territorial commission" morphing into "territorial security."[88] The *act* became less important than the *effect*.

In short, extraterritorial policing and extraterritorial regulation in the postwar era both demonstrate an often overlooked face of postwar American hegemony: a marked willingness to project power and law, sometimes unilaterally, within the territorial borders of other sovereign states in an effort to better control and deter transboundary threats. As previous chapters have emphasized, this willingness reflected the tremendous power and influence of the United States. It also reflected the newly permissive international environment, which appeared, at least in comparison with the past, less likely to treat extraterritoriality as a *casus belli*. Indeed, the leading analysis of American extraterritorial policing argues that "no other government has pursued its international law enforcement agenda in as aggressive and penetrative a manner or devoted so much effort to promoting its own criminal justice norms to others."[89] Added to this was the growing propensity to view transnational crime as a national security—rather than merely a criminal—issue.

The conceptualization of international crime as a national security issue gained dramatically heightened urgency in the wake of the 9/11 attacks. The result was a blurring of military and criminal justice efforts, in which technology developed for war was increasingly deployed to fight crime.

These trends converged in the face of terrorist threats. As the *Washington Post* noted as far back as 1999, Osama bin Laden was "the target of both cruise missiles and a criminal indictment."[90]

To be sure, a law enforcement approach to terrorism dominated in the pre-9/11 era. When the Khobar Towers in Saudi Arabia were bombed killing nineteen Americans, over five hundred FBI agents were involved in the investigation.[91] Likewise, when terrorists attacked the USS *Cole* in a Yemeni harbor in 2000, the FBI sent over one hundred agents and experts to investigate.[92] These investigatory efforts did not end after 9/11. In the wake of the 2002 bombing in Bali, for example, the FBI sent agents to the scene; more recently, the FBI investigated the 2007 killing in Baghdad of seventeen Iraqi civilians by the private security firm Blackwater USA.[93] But as the next chapter will illustrate, after 2001 the approach to terrorism became far more cruise missile and far less criminal indictment.

The increasing prevalence of terrorist attacks against the United States changed many things. But it did not change the fact that hard questions still existed about what law governed American officials operating abroad. *Verdugo* certainly provided a framework for analysis, but by no means answered all queries. Did legal rights other than the Fourth Amendment kick in when investigations and interrogations of foreign nationals took place outside United States territory?

The 1998 bombings of the American embassies in Kenya and Tanzania, for example, led to a federal court challenge about the extraterritorial reach of so-called *Miranda* warnings.[94] *Miranda* warnings are the familiar statements ("You have a right to remain silent...") given to suspects in the United States when questioned by the police.[95] Questioning a suspect in the absence of a *Miranda* warning is not illegal, but the statements obtained are presumed by the courts to be coerced and cannot be used at trial. *United States v. Bin Laden* involved the interrogation by FBI agents in Kenya of al Qaeda members believed to be perpetrators of the embassy attacks. Did the self-incrimination provision of the Fifth Amendment apply to the interrogations?

The FBI had in fact offered the foreign suspects a modified *Miranda* warning. This was consistent with prior cases and U.S. practice, which tended to err in favor of *Miranda*. Indeed, in previous cases with similar facts the executive branch had not contested the application of the Fifth Amendment to overseas interrogations of foreigners.[96] Now, however, the government staked out a far less permissive stance. Relying on *Verdugo* and the 1950 case of *Johnson v. Eisentrager*, the George W. Bush administration asserted that the *Miranda* warnings were entirely discretionary. Because the suspects were aliens, and the interrogation overseas, the suspects had no Fifth Amendment rights to protect.

The district court in *Bin Laden* asserted first that the alleged extraterritoriality of the Fifth Amendment was immaterial.[97] Violations of the privilege against self-incrimination, it said, occur not at the moment law enforcement officials coerce statements, but when statements are actually used against a defendant in a criminal proceeding. (This assumes that such a criminal proceeding would occur on American territory, vitiating any extraterritorial aspect. Were trials to be held abroad, the question would be much sharper.) This argument about *where* the rights violation occurred echoed a similar claim by the majority in *Verdugo*, though in that case the "violation" was held to extraterritorial rather than domestic, and therefore, in the view of the majority, not in actuality a violation at all. *Bin Laden* presented the opposite posture: the interrogation occurred abroad, but the violation occurred at home, at the trial itself.

The *Bin Laden* court then noted the broad language of the Fifth Amendment, which refers to persons rather than to citizens. Given the general inclination of the Supreme Court to construe this right expansively, the lower court refused to read a geographic limitation into the text of the amendment.[98] It consequently held that "a defendant's statements, if extracted by U.S. agents acting abroad, should be admitted as evidence at trial only if the Government demonstrates that the defendant was first advised of his rights and that he validly waived those rights."[99]

The executive branch called this result perverse because, it argued, evidence extracted by foreign police acting abroad remained admissible in American courts. But the district court replied that it saw "nothing at all anomalous in requiring *our own* Government to abide by the strictures of *our own* Constitution whenever it seeks to convict an accused, in *our own* courts, on the basis of admissions culled via an inherently coercive interrogation conducted by *our own* law enforcement."[100] In doing so, *Bin Laden* picked up the flag of the dissenters in *Verdugo*, who believed that "the Fourth Amendment is an unavoidable correlative of the Government's power to enforce the criminal law."[101]

Whether the *Bin Laden* approach to the Fifth Amendment will stand the test of time—and the pressures of a post-9/11 world—remains to be seen.[102] In 2002 the Justice Department's Office of Legal Counsel prepared a memorandum for the Defense Department detailing how *Miranda* rules applied to the armed conflict in Afghanistan. The Office of Legal Counsel noted the decision in *Bin Laden*, but argued that it failed to fully incorporate the line of reasoning announced in *Verdugo*. "The Supreme Court," stated the memorandum, "has never squarely held that the Self-Incrimination Clause applies in the criminal attack of an alien whose only connections to the United States consists of an attack on the country followed by his arrest overseas and transportation to the United States to stand trial."[103]

The Malleable Border

The increasing projection of police power across borders is an important part of the story of late twentieth century territoriality. Running parallel to it was a trend noted at the outset of this chapter: the "forward deployment of the border."[104] This strategy was most apparent with regard to would-be migrants and goods slated for import into the United States. In the 1990s the Immigration and Naturalization Service posted an increasing number of agents abroad in an effort to detect forged documents and deter undesirable migrants earlier. At the same time Congress substantially enlarged the zone within which "expedited removal" of aliens could take place, creating a strip 100 miles deep into U.S. territory.

These and other manifestations of "interior immigration enforcement" were aimed to stanching the flow of transboundary actors by creating a more fluid and permissive legal environment for law enforcement.[105] The same trends could be discerned with regard to the shipping of goods. In the 1990s and early 2000s U.S. customs inspectors substantially increased their direct operations in foreign ports.[106] With nearly 90 percent of world trade traveling in shipping containers, inspection at the port of embarkation became increasingly attractive. To implement such a strategy, the United States created the "Container Security Initiative." The initiative relies on American agents to inspect containers at over fifty foreign ports of departure, ranging from Pakistan to Belgium, with the goal of detecting contraband before it ever enters American waters.[107]

These varied activities have worked a dramatic change in the meaning of a sovereign border. As one observer has written, with regard to migrants the federal government has redrawn and recalibrated "the once fixed and static territorial border, transforming it into something more malleable and moveable, which can be placed and replaced—by words of law—in whatever location that best suits the goal of restricting access" to the American homeland.[108]

These developments are new and significant, but in some important respects they accentuate and accelerate practices of long standing. For example, American law has often looked to formal entry into the United States rather than simple spatial location when determining what legal rights aliens enjoy.[109] In 1993, for example, the Supreme Court noted that aliens who were within U.S. territory but seeking formal admission to the United States were treated "as though they had never entered the United States at all; they were within the United States territory but not 'within the United States.'" Although the phrase "within the United States" would seem to refer to the migrant's physical presence on the sovereign territory of the United States, the court noted that in fact "it had more to do with an alien's legal status than with his location."[110] Likewise, a postwar case concerning Ellis Island held that "harborage on Ellis Island is not an entry into the United States," despite the fact that Ellis Island is incontrovertibly sovereign U.S. territory.[111] Ellis Island was thus akin to other anomalous zones that are within American territory but not legally treated as such: foreign embassies, the United Nations headquarters, runways and select parts of international airports, and so forth.[112]

More recent efforts at pushing the border outward extend this intraterritorial logic further. The move toward intraterritorial enforcement of immigration law—that is, enforcement not only at the border but throughout a wide swath of American territory—seeks to "construct virtual checkpoints throughout the country's interior" capable of controlling aliens "in a manner analogous to the control exercised at the physical border itself."[113] Rather than a *line*, the border has become a *zone*, sometimes extending into sovereign U.S. territory, other times extending outward in an extraterritorial fashion.

Intraterritoriality and Extraterritoriality in an Age of Globalization

That postwar American military power was projected extraterritorially through a dramatic expansion of overseas bases and military operations is well known. What is less commonly noted is that American police power was projected extraterritorially as well—not only during the Cold War, but increasingly after the Cold War ended. This chapter has described the increasingly global application of American criminal law in the latter decades of the twentieth century and the legal challenges that accompanied it.

Like the postwar extraterritorial extension of regulatory law described in chapter 4, the extension of American criminal law abroad was aimed at reconciling domestic law with a global marketplace. It sought to eliminate offshore legal havens—and more effectively protect American interests—by extending domestic law around the world. The desire for territorial security thus encouraged extraterritorial regulation. And as in effects-based extraterritoriality, what drove the development of legal doctrine was not simply the rise of global interdependence, but its juxtaposition with domestic legal developments. In the regulatory arena, these developments included the entrenching of the regulatory state and the demise of classical legal thought. In the criminal realm, it was largely the criminal procedure revolution of the 1960s, which created a host of legal protections for suspects that fit awkwardly with overseas policing efforts. *Reid v. Covert* had also, for the first time, established that the Bill of Rights had some global reach. In the wake of *Reid* federal courts struggled to discover the limits of global constitutionalism. If the Constitution's protections encompassed aliens abroad, their reach was wide indeed.

Put differently, the more limited and territorial the Constitution's protections were held to be, the more attractive the move to offshore law enforcement became. Concerns about unbridled offshore law enforcement drove some U.S. courts—but by no means all—to hold that the Constitution follows the flag, or at least the badge. In many respects the dangers posed by the extraterritorial evasion of constitutional precepts were a minor theme of the postwar era—prominently highlighted in Justice Black's dissent in *Johnson v. Eisentrager*, and as the next chapter will show, central to the disposition of post-9/11 legal challenges regarding Guantanamo Bay.

But as this chapter has detailed, the Supreme Court's landmark decision in *Verdugo* set a very different tone, and showed substantial deference to the executive branch's view of American national security. In the view of many justices, constitutional protections designed for the relatively placid domestic context could not be straightforwardly applied to a dangerous outside world. American power and prestige necessarily entailed the use of force around the globe, and it was clear, even by 1990, that the line between armed conflict and criminal action was at times blurry. To act effectively on the world stage, the United States could not be overly fettered by legal niceties. To do otherwise, argued the *Verdugo* court, "would have significant and deleterious consequences for the United States in conducting activities beyond its boundaries."

The result was great tension and confusion as to the underlying principles of territoriality in American law. On the one hand, extraterritoriality was by this point widely accepted in many areas of the law, and so, unlike the nineteenth century—when extraterritorial consular jurisdiction was relatively hidden from view—Westphalian territoriality was perceived to be under attack on many fronts. The dissenters in *Verdugo* leapt upon this tension, noting that "foreign nationals must now take care not to violate our drug laws, our antitrust laws, and our securities laws, and a host of other federal criminal statutes."[114] Yet, they noted, American officials need not abide by the Constitution. A doctrine more prone to stimulate the offshore use of executive power is hard to imagine.

On the other hand, it was difficult, in both conceptual and practical terms, to fully overturn the idea that the Constitution stopped at the water's edge—especially when it came to foreign nationals. What were the limits? There was no available theory of constitutionalism in a global age that judges could embrace to make sense of when and where the Bill of Rights applied abroad. Uncertain of the slippery slope they might be standing on, the judiciary was hesitant to make bold pronouncements. Hence strict territoriality remained attractive. The result was a muddle of membership and geographic assumptions, a confused mélange of doctrine that continues, in many respects, to exist today.

A year before the 9/11 attacks, for example, the D.C. Circuit heard a case that raised what it called the "difficult question" of whether "the Fifth Amendment prohibits torture of non-resident foreign nationals living abroad."[115] (The precise definition of the relevant class illustrates the difficulty that the court perceived.) The case was brought by Jennifer Harbury, the American wife of a Guatemalan who was allegedly tortured in the early 1990s by CIA affiliates working with the Guatemalan government. The D.C. Circuit contended that precedent made clear that foreign nationals abroad lack not only Fourth Amendment rights but also Fifth Amendment rights. As a result, Harbury "failed to allege a valid claim for deprivation of her husband's Fifth Amendment due process rights."[116] Opinions like these ran smack into opinions like *Bin Laden*, which the very next year found the Fifth Amendment's self-incrimination clause applicable to foreign nationals living abroad.

Although the connection between the CIA and the torture alleged in the Harbury case was at best indirect, in the aftermath of the 9/11 attacks the CIA initiated a program of calculated offshore interrogations of foreign nationals. These interrogations, often highly coercive and sometimes deadly, took place in various "black site" prisons in Europe and Asia. At first secret, this program was exposed in a series of news reports and garnered significant attention. The CIA's deliberate offshoring of interrogation and detention, as well as the use of Guantanamo Bay and other aspects of post-9/11 extraterritoriality, is the topic of the next chapter.

7

OFFSHORING THE WAR ON TERROR

---

*The Court is fashioning wholly indefensible doctrine if it permits
the executive branch, by deciding where its prisoners will be tried
and imprisoned, to deprive all federal courts of their power to
protect against a federal executive's illegal incarcerations . . .*[1]

—Justice Hugo Black, dissenting in
Johnson v. Eisentrager (1950)

A few days before New Year's Day, 2002 John Yoo and Patrick
Philbin, two lawyers in the Department of Justice, drafted a
memorandum for the Department of Defense. The memo was entitled
Possible Habeas Jurisdiction over Aliens Held in Guantanamo Bay, Cuba.[2]
Shortly after the attacks on September 11, 2001, the Bush administration
had announced plans to try suspected terrorists by military commission, a
kind of military court. As the memo was being completed, the war in
Afghanistan was still ongoing. But coalition forces had taken Kabul and
other major cities and had already captured many suspected Al Qaeda
members. The Bush administration feared detaining these individuals
within the United States and generally rejected the criminal justice model
of counterterrorism championed by previous presidents.[3]

The United States naval base at Guantanamo, the subject of the lawyers'
memo, was appealing as a long-term site for detention and trial. It was
distant from the Middle East, very secure, and, as the Justice Department
noted, probably free of the influence of American courts due to its location
outside the territory of the United States. In time the detention camp at
Guantanamo would become a source of sustained criticism around the

world and a major political liability for the United States. But in late 2001, with the World Trade Center site still a smoking ruin, Guantanamo appeared to be a very attractive option to those formulating the legal response to the 9/11 attacks.

Two years after the Guantanamo memo was written the *New York Times* reported that the CIA and the Pentagon were operating a network of offshore prisons in various foreign locations.[4] In these overseas prisons, so reported the *Times*, were some of the most high-value detainees in the war on terror. Successive stories in the *Washington Post* revealed that a number of these "black site" prisons were in Europe, and that the CIA had flown individuals there for extensive and coercive interrogation.[5] As the *Times* reported, the "suggestion that the United States might be operating secret prisons in Europe and the idea that American intelligence officers might be torturing terrorism suspects incarcerated on foreign soil have been incendiary issues across Europe in recent weeks."[6]

The CIA's program of extraordinary rendition, in which suspects were covertly flown to other nations for interrogation and detention, often in close coordination with American agents, also received significant media attention in this period. Reports of large American-run military prisons in Afghanistan and in Thailand emerged as well. Taken together, these reports depicted a major initiative on the part of the Bush administration to keep and interrogate suspected terrorists far from American territory. According to leading news reports, at the time more than nine thousand individuals were detained by the United States in overseas facilities, the vast majority by the U.S. military.

Like the decision to sequester and try suspected terrorists in Guantanamo, the revelations of clandestine renditions to a network of offshore prisons produced enormous criticism throughout the world. The decision to conduct critical interrogations beyond the territory of the United States was likewise deliberate and the subject of careful legal analysis. Each of these programs, which would become burning political issues at home as well as abroad, reflected the continuing importance of territorial assumptions about legal rights and duties.

The debate over Guantanamo and offshore interrogation touches on a plethora of issues raised throughout this book. This debate also highlights how, despite a wide range of changes in the territorial doctrines of American law, Westphalian territoriality continues to exhibit vitality. To put this claim in context, it is worth recalling what had transpired in American law in the decades before 9/11.

As the preceding chapters have described, the United States embraced a strict understanding of Westphalian territoriality for much of its history. Extraterritoriality certainly existed in the nineteenth century with regard to so-called uncivilized nations, but was not commonly applied against other sovereign states. Since 1945, however, the United States had increasingly asserted a much broader form of extraterritoriality under the new effects theory of jurisdiction. It also negotiated, and received, special extraterritorial rights for its armed forces stationed overseas. And it increasingly extended its criminal law offshore and deployed its law enforcement officials abroad.

By contrast, constitutional law exhibited a distinctive pattern. The Supreme Court had long held that constitutional protections do not extend abroad. Moreover, the *Insular Cases*, in the wake of the Spanish-American War, had drawn on a tradition of intraterritorial distinctions to hold that only fundamental legal rights applied in the newly acquired empire of the United States. Then the Cold War brought about a dramatic change. Americans for the first time were held to be protected by the Bill of Rights against federal action even when overseas. By the tail end of the twentieth century tentative steps toward a more universal conception of constitutional rights—one that encompassed aliens as well as citizens—were taken. Yet this trend was soon sharply limited by the Supreme Court's decision, in 1990, to deny the protections of the Fourth Amendment to foreign criminals searched abroad by American agents. This reinforcement of traditional territoriality was welcomed by the executive branch, which was increasingly pursuing criminals and other dangerous actors beyond U.S. borders and preferred to be unshackled from the many legal constraints present in American criminal law.

At least two messages can be distilled from this complex doctrinal evolution. One is that the rising power of the United States over the last century has coincided with a relaxation of many traditional legal doctrines. As a hegemonic power, the United States could and increasingly did extend its law unilaterally to reach and regulate actions anywhere in the world that might cause harm within the United States. Extraterritoriality was no longer limited to weak or peripheral states; it was now used against some of the most powerful states in the international system, including major American allies. Indeed, American allies were *more* likely to be the focus of postwar regulatory and military jurisdiction.

At the same time, however, an countervailing tendency can be traced: in a dangerous world with numerous transboundary threats, American courts frequently accepted the executive branch's claim that constitutional protections were largely territorial, and that the United States—which increasingly acted abroad to neutralize these transboundary threats— ought not be fettered by restrictive principles designed for a more placid domestic setting and a particular political community. In *Reid v. Covert* the Supreme Court had overturned nearly 2 centuries of strict territoriality, forcing the hand of the executive branch with regard to the constitutional rights of overseas American citizens. Yet presidents from both parties continued to seek—and in nearly all cases received—freedom from constitutional restraint when interrogating, arresting, and detaining foreign nationals offshore. Older, territorial principles supplied that freedom, and were welcomed as a result.

The shocks of September 11 only reinforced the preexisting desire for flexibility held by many in the executive branch. A welter of older precedents, some dusty and discredited, enshrined principles of Westphalian territoriality. Despite their vintage they provided a rich template for contemporary legal argument, particularly concerning Guantanamo. How these varied territorial arguments from the past were deployed to facilitate what became known as the "war on terror," and how they fared in the twenty-first century, is the topic of this chapter.

A Legal Black Hole

In November 2003 Lord Steyn, a prominent law lord of the United Kingdom, delivered a stinging lecture about U.S. detention practices in the wake of 9/11. In his speech before a London audience Steyn called Guantanamo Bay a "legal black hole."[7] This appellation quickly became a favorite of critics of the George W. Bush administration, for it captured an important element of the legal strategy of the United States. Precisely what law—domestic, international, or perhaps foreign—applied to the leased naval base at Guantanamo was the subject of considerable dispute.[8] At times the American government appeared to argue that no law whatsoever applied, at least with regard to the treatment of the foreign detainees held there. Human rights groups and foreign governments strongly contended otherwise, arguing that either U.S. constitutional law or international law applied, and that in any event no legal vacuum could be permitted to exist in a modern democratic society.

For many observers, the Bush administration's insistence that Guantanamo was beyond the reach of ordinary law became a symbol of a larger American disregard for international law. To the Bush administration, by contrast, Guantanamo was an appropriate and secure site for the detention and trial of highly dangerous terrorists who were intent on doing great harm to innocent civilians. Moreover, the executive branch believed its legal arguments were sound and historically validated in times of war.

Disputes over the reach of American law to Guantanamo are not new. Both current and past controversies have stemmed in large part from disagreement over the odd status of the base. At their core, these controversies turn on a similar question to that which animated the *Insular Cases* a century earlier: is the territory best characterized as foreign or domestic? The *Insular Cases* provided the memorable answer that the American overseas colonies were actually both. They were, the Supreme Court said enigmatically, "foreign in a domestic sense."[9]

Unlike the insular possessions at issue in the early 1900s, however, Guantanamo formally remains under Cuban rather than American sovereignty. Yet as chapter 3 detailed, the lease governing the base at Guantanamo grew directly out of victory in the Spanish-American War of 1898. Indeed, the United States has occupied Guantanamo Bay continuously since the end of that war.[10] (The Guantanamo lease was later renewed as part of a treaty with Cuba in 1934.)[11] This history, and the reality of American power and control at the base, has led many to question the significance of the distinction between sovereign offshore territory such as Puerto Rico and the ostensibly rented base at Guantanamo Bay.

The decision at the turn of the twentieth century to lease rather than annex Guantanamo reflected a general desire on the part of the American public to grant Cuba independence. The oppression of Cubans by Spain was a major issue in American politics at the time; as one commentator puts it, Cuban freedom "was what the Spanish American War was ostensibly about." Perhaps more importantly, "an acceptable resolution of Cuban status consistent with the U.S. supremacy in the hemisphere and U.S. commercial interests" did not require annexation.[12] Cuba was nonetheless strategically important, and then-president Theodore Roosevelt conditioned independence on a formal role for the United States.[13] Hence the new Cuban constitution included the notorious Platt Amendment, which permitted the United States to intervene at any time for "the preservation of Cuban independence, the maintenance of a government adequate for the protection of life, property, and individual liberty."

Guantanamo's unusual legal status is reflected in this history, and is underscored by two factors. One is the lack of any status of forces agreement for American troops at the base. As chapter 5 detailed, the hundreds of thousands of U.S. troops stationed in bases around the world are in turn the subject of dozens of status of forces agreements, or SOFAs. These SOFAs detail the rights and responsibilities of the United States Armed Forces and apportion jurisdiction over bases and associated facilities. Guantanamo is the only major American overseas base without a SOFA. The second, closely related, factor is the unique lease arrangement with Cuba. The lease that was signed by the newly independent Cuba and the United States in 1903 is effectively perpetual: it requires the assent of both parties to terminate it. Moreover, it granted the United States "complete jurisdiction and control" over Guantanamo but, in a critical phrase, left "ultimate sovereignty" in the hands of Cuba.

Sovereignty is normally treated in the Westphalian tradition as having an absolute quality (even if that absolute quality is purely a formal attribute, often violated in practice). As a result, a modifier like *ultimate* is unusual. Why *ultimate* was employed to modify sovereignty, and what significance it has, remain vexed questions. The U.S. government has in practice tended to interpret the word as superfluous text. In other words, had the lease been drafted using the unadorned term *sovereignty*, the executive branch's theory of the legal rights and powers applicable in Guantanamo would remain exactly the same. The phrase *ultimate sovereignty* can alternatively be interpreted to refer to residual sovereignty, an existing concept in international law.[14] Under this view the United States is a temporary sovereign for the duration of the lease, and at the end of the lease term Cuba reverts to full, "ordinary" sovereignty over the base.

Together, the indefinite nature of the lease, and its division between jurisdiction and sovereignty, give the United States an unusual degree of flexibility and control. The result is untrammeled *de facto* governance by the United States without any necessary claim or pretense of *de jure* sovereignty. As a 1929 memorandum from the Justice Department explained, the naval base is "a mere governmental outpost beyond our borders," a place "subject to the use, occupation and control" of the United States, which is nonetheless not part of the United States.[15]

The formal division between sovereignty and jurisdiction in Guantanamo is in many respects a remarkable vestige of nineteenth-century-style extraterritorial jurisdiction. Like the United States District Court for China, Guantanamo is a treaty-based regime of legal control in which a great power asserts complete jurisdiction within a bounded parcel of territory in a foreign nation. That territory nonetheless remains, as a formal matter, under the aegis of the (much weaker) foreign sovereign. This arrangement has proved extremely convenient for the United States, which has on several occasions employed the base as an offshore detention center for unwanted or dangerous individuals. And because Guantanamo is completely controlled by the United States but not possessed by it, the base arguably represents the apotheosis of the intraterritorial distinctions described throughout this book. Like tribal lands or insular possessions, the international community generally recognizes the territory of the Guantanamo base as American territory. Yet for domestic legal purposes the base remains in many important respects foreign terrain. The position of the executive branch in this regard has been consistent: as far as the rights of foreigners are concerned, the naval base is Cuban, not American, territory.

The U.S. position on Guantanamo is not shared by Cuba, which considers the base an illegitimate vestige of Cuba's former colonial status. Castro called it "a base thrust upon us by force, in a territory that is unmistakably ours...imposed by force and a constant threat and a constant source for concern."[16] In the early 1960s Cuban hostility toward Guantanamo was so high that some feared that the Cuban army might invade the base. International lawyers of the era queried whether the United Nations Charter, which guaranteed the right of a member state to self-defense in the event of an invasion, would apply to an invasion of an American base by the putative host nation. The threatened invasion never occurred, though Cuba did shut off all water supplies and took other hostile actions. As a result, the border between the base and Cuba (or, if the position of the United States is correct, between Cuba and Cuba) was long lined with land mines.[17]

Despite the evident hostility between Washington and Havana, the United States continues to adhere to the letter of the century-old accord, claiming that because it does not seek termination of the lease agreement, Cuba cannot unilaterally repatriate Guantanamo Bay. Indeed, the State Department issues an annual rent check to Cuba, which the Castro government refuses to cash.[18] Today, the 45-square mile naval base, in which several thousand Americans reside, is fully self-sufficient, with a movie theater, several fast food outlets, and a shop where visitors can purchase souvenirs emblazoned with phrases like "It don't GTMO better than this."[19]

Haitians and Cubans

This strange arrangement was largely dormant as a legal matter for most of the twentieth century. To be sure, a variety of low-profile domestic legal disputes raised questions about the legal status of Guantanamo. *Bird v. United States*, for example, was a suit for medical malpractice involving a diagnosis by a Navy physician at the base. Because the Federal Tort Claims Act bars claims arising within a "foreign country," the case raised the issue of whether Guantanamo was foreign or domestic territory. Referring to the lease of 1903, *Bird* held that Guantanamo was indeed part of a foreign country.[20] Other cases from the 1970s and 1980s nonetheless upheld American jurisdiction over the base with regard to most matters.[21]

Guantanamo's status became more pointed in the aftermath of a coup against Haitian president Jean Bertrand Aristide in 1991. Many Aristide supporters took to the seas in a desperate attempt to flee to the United States. The Coast Guard intercepted many off shore, and the George H. W. Bush administration initiated a policy of summarily returning them to Haiti. After a federal court prohibited this practice, the United States began to hold the Haitians on ships in Guantanamo Bay. Eventually the number of refugees outstripped the ships' capacity. By December 1991 there were nearly 1,500 Haitians detained at Guantanamo and another 1,000 in the harbor. All told, more than 20,000 Haitians would eventually pass through the Guantanamo base; nearly all were eventually returned to Haiti.[22]

The enormous refugee camps constituted the first American use of the base for the detention of unwanted foreigners.[23] And the subsequent litigation foreshadowed several of the debates that would arise in the aftermath of the 9/11 attacks. For example, the Haitian Refugee Center, a U.S.-based organization, argued to the Eleventh Circuit that it had a First Amendment right of access to the Haitians detained in Guantanamo. The Eleventh Circuit rejected this argument. Most significantly, however, the court declared that the Haitians themselves had "no recognized substantive rights under the laws or the Constitution of the United States."[24] Like the Supreme Court a century earlier in the case of John Ross, the Eleventh Circuit conceived of the sovereign borders of the United States as sharp lines delimiting the reach of domestic protections. That a local government—in this case Cuba, and in Ross's case Japan—had consented to extraterritorial American jurisdiction via an international treaty only strengthened this view, for it reinforced the notion that not only was the United States *not* sovereign, but some other government *was* sovereign.

Nonetheless, the effects of a century of legal change are hard to repress, and in the same year the Second Circuit came down in precisely the opposite direction. Holding that detained Haitians did have constitutional rights despite their extraterritorial status, the court argued that

> the language of the fifth and fourteenth amendments does not suggest that they apply only to areas fitting a circumscribed definition of the United States. Guantanamo Bay is a military installation that is subject to the *exclusive* control and jurisdiction of the United States. The Supreme Court has recently reaffirmed that fundamental constitutional rights are guaranteed to inhabitants of territory where the United States has sovereign power [citing *United States v. Verdugo-Urquidez's* invocation of the *Insular Cases*]...It does not appear to us to be incongruous or overreaching to conclude that the United States Constitution limits the conduct of United States personnel with respect to officially authorized interactions with aliens brought to detained by such personnel on a land mass exclusively controlled by the United States.[25]

Here again we see the flexibility of the *Insular Cases*, which have been tweaked to support a wide variety of conclusions. Some courts, including the Supreme Court in *Verdugo*, used them to bolster the claim that outside the constitutional core of the United States some constitutional rights *did not apply*. Others, such as the Second Circuit here, cited them for the proposition that even on distant island possessions, parts of the Bill of Rights *did apply*. The Second Circuit then elided the difference between sovereignty and jurisdiction; because the United States had complete jurisdiction, the court contended, the situation in Guantanamo was just like that in Puerto Rico. The nature of the relationship between sovereignty and jurisdiction would arise again after 9/11.

The story of the Haitians at Guantanamo reflected assumptions about territoriality in other ways as well. The United States was a party to the

Convention Relating to the Status of Refugees, which required signatories to refrain from returning asylum seekers to the country from which they fled. The assumption in the treaty was that refugees would appear at international borders. By intercepting the Haitians at sea, however, the executive branch sought to skirt this no-return rule. The government claimed that the treaty did not have extraterritorial reach, and therefore the United States was not bound by it when it acted on the high seas. The Supreme Court agreed that the Refugee Convention did not extend extraterritorially.[26]

By intercepting the Haitians outside American borders, U.S. officials successfully shifted the relevant place of contact away from American territory. And by so doing, U.S. officials escaped important legal constraints and gained greater freedom of action. (Interdiction at sea was consistent with the more general shift, noted in the previous chapter, toward "offshoring the border.") Events in Haiti continued to boil over, however, and the United States eventually intervened militarily in 1994 under UN Security Council auspices. This intervention itself raised questions about whether other human rights treaties to which the United States was a party applied to American action in Haiti.[27] Then a mid-1990s wave of Cuban refugees produced similar, if less protracted, litigation as the original Haitian crisis. In *Cuban American Bar Association v. Christopher*, the Eleventh Circuit revisited the question of the extraterritorial constitutional rights of aliens. The court again flatly decreed that "these migrants are without legal rights that are cognizable in the courts of the United States."[28]

By April 1996, after 5 years of turmoil in the Caribbean, the detention of all foreigners at Guantanamo Bay came to end. Guantanamo slipped from the courts and the public consciousness until the arrival of handcuffed, orange jumpsuited terrorist suspects nearly 8 years later.

Offshoring the War on Terror

The 2001 invasion of Afghanistan was aimed at both ending a terrorist sanctuary and capturing those who participated in or supported the 9/11 attacks. In a relatively short amount of time the United States detained a large number of suspected Al Qaeda and Taliban fighters. Unlike traditional prisoners of war, many wore no uniforms and did not have an obvious chain of command. They often resisted their detention vigorously and violently. Tommy Franks, the American general in charge of the Afghan invasion, told Pentagon officials he couldn't maintain adequate security for their detention, and wanted them moved elsewhere fast.[29]

The Bush administration, intent on trying many of the detainees by military commission for crimes of war, considered several options. These included military bases within the United States and on the island of Guam, one of the insular possessions remaining from the Spanish-American War. Each of these options was rejected in favor of Guantanamo Bay. As one former Bush administration official later wrote, military bases within the United States

> were relatively easy targets for terrorists to attack. They would frighten and possibly endanger U.S. civilians. And detentions there were more likely to be subject to legal challenges since they were on U.S. soil. GTMO, by contrast, was isolated and well defended. And because it was technically not a part of U.S. sovereign soil, it seemed like a good bet to minimize judicial scrutiny.[30]

The first post-9/11 detainees arrived at the base in January 2002, and were housed in a simple, spartan detention facility. Reactions to the detention camp from abroad soon grew quite negative, with many criticizing not only the conditions the detainees lived under, but the unwillingness of the United States to commit to applying international human rights and humanitarian law in Guantanamo. And the Bush administration did resist the reach of international law to Guantanamo. Even the International Red Cross, which has a special role in policing the laws of war, was at times barred from visiting the detainees.[31]

These actions fed the perception that Guantanamo Bay was indeed a legal black hole, and that the United States had deliberately sought to place suspected terrorists beyond the reach of any legal system. That many detainees were citizens of allies, including the United Kingdom and Australia, only served to ratchet up the criticism even higher. By 2007 Guantanamo had become a commonplace theme in books, films, and plays, often portrayed as a contemporary gulag and a stain on American honor.

Nonetheless, the legal issues at stake with regard to the Al Qaeda and Taliban detainees were complex. At the core of many of the legal disputes over the Guantanamo detainees was the availability of what the Anglo-American legal tradition calls the "writ of habeas corpus." As described in earlier chapters, habeas corpus is aimed at ensuring that the government does not deprive a person of liberty without providing an adequate basis to a court of law.[32] The habeas process consequently presupposes a separation between the courts and the executive, and injects the judiciary into the fray in order to ensure that detentions by the executive are supported as a matter of domestic law.

Because it is grounded in the common law, debates over the scope of habeas often turn on ancient precedents, and the Guantanamo litigation was no different. In the post-9/11 era American courts and lawyers frequently sparred over the meaning of obscure and musty decisions involving imperial India and the Cinque Ports. Despite its common law roots, habeas is protected in the United States both by statute and the Constitution. To underscore its significance, the Constitution singles out the writ and provides that it cannot be suspended absent a situation of invasion or rebellion, and even then only by Congress.

Habeas quickly became central to the legal debates over offshore detention of suspected terrorists because many of the detainees argued that in fact they were not Al Qaeda or Taliban fighters. Instead, they had been accidentally swept up by American forces in the chaotic battles that ensued in the rough terrain of Afghanistan. Because the purpose of habeas is to constrain unjust executive power, advocates for the detainees argued that habeas review ought to be available wherever the executive engages in detention. Indeed, some observers feared that the idea that there are geographic no-habeas zones would foster the creation of other offshore detention camps.

This incentive-based fear was one source of resistance to the Bush administration's claim that habeas did not apply to foreigners held overseas. Another was moral, or principled: The United States government, proponents suggested, ought not to possess unfettered power over any individual. Autocratic power of that sort was inconsistent with American traditions and ideals. A third source of resistance to the executive branch's claim was historical. Many scholars contended that English law had long held that the right of habeas does not turn on the petitioners' location, but simply on the exercise of state power.[33] These varied issues were at the core of a series of cases before the Supreme Court in the first decade of the twenty-first century.

Fighting the Last War

Part of the complexity raised by the question of what rights the Guantanamo detainees possessed stemmed from the claim that the United States was in a state of war. On September 18, 2001, Congress authorized the use of military force by the United States, triggering a series of legal consequences involving the law of armed conflict. This authorization did not mean that enemy aliens were wholly barred from using the habeas process. That even enemy aliens in wartime can protest their detention before a judge is a principle of long standing in American law, and was the central message of the famous 1942 decision in *Ex parte Quirin. Quirin* involved German saboteurs who, under cover of night and emerging from offshore submarines, landed on beaches in Florida and Long Island, changed into civilian clothes, and proceeded to infiltrate American cities. At least one of the would-be saboteurs was actually an American citizen.[34] After one of the participants had a change of heart and alerted the FBI, the saboteurs were imprisoned in Washington D.C. and tried by military commission. The saboteurs then appealed to the Supreme Court using the writ of habeas corpus.

The Roosevelt administration argued vociferously that the Nazi saboteurs lacked any access to American courts. As the Supreme Court put it (referring to a executive proclamation issued by Roosevelt) the president "insists that petitioners must be denied access to the courts, both because they are enemy aliens or have entered our territory as enemy belligerents, and because the President's Proclamation undertakes in terms to deny such access to the class of persons defined by the Proclamation." The Supreme Court rejected this contention. "Neither the Proclamation nor the fact that they are enemy aliens forecloses consideration by the courts of petitioners' contentions that the Constitution and the laws of the U.S. constitutionally enacted forbid their trial by military commission."[35] Both *Quirin* and the contemporaneous case of General Yamashita of Japan established that enemy aliens had a right to habeas jurisdiction, at least if they were held on American territory.[36] Whether the same was true for enemy aliens (or any aliens) held beyond American territory, however, was unclear. Add in the unusual status of Guantanamo Bay, and the legal questions become very hard indeed.[37]

As a result, when the Justice Department endeavored in December 2001 to draft a memo assessing the legal rights of enemy aliens held in Guantanamo, it faced a challenging task. The memo was the first major analysis of the issue in the wake of 9/11, and it looked back at a wide range of precedents. The early 1990s litigation over Guantanamo's Cuban and Haitian refugees clearly influenced the authors, both because it directly addressed the unusual status of the naval base and because it was somewhat ambiguous in its ultimate message. The executive branch lawyers nonetheless concluded that although the question was not free from doubt, "the great weight" of legal authority indicated that federal courts could not entertain habeas petitions from enemy alien detainees held in Guantanamo. This conclusion reflected one major difference between *Quirin* and the post 9/11 situation: in *Quirin* the trial took place on U.S. territory. And it reflected one major difference between the Clinton-era cases concerning Guantanamo and the post-9/11 situation: the former did not implicate war, and federal courts are generally more deferential to the executive branch in wartime.

The Justice Department lawyers noted that in an ordinary war prisoners are governed by the international law of war. They were not traditionally afforded the right to petition domestic courts for relief. The war against Al Qaeda certainly differed from prior wars in that there was no state or organized army as the adversary. Rather, there were shadowy actors loosely affiliated in a network, and these actors were often, if not typically, nationals of friendly states. But the Bush administration consistently argued that this was nonetheless a war. The Justice Department lawyers consequently rested much of their conclusion on another case from the Second World War, *Johnson v. Eisentrager*. As noted in chapter 5, *Eisentrager* involved the habeas pleas of several German soldiers captured by American forces in China after the end of the Second World War. The Germans were tried by an U.S. military commission for war crimes and then detained in a U.S. prison in occupied Germany.

In hearing the claims of the German soldiers, the *Eisentrager* court acknowledged that the "privilege of litigation" had historically been granted to enemy aliens in the past. But, the court said, this privilege had been extended only "because permitting their presence in the country implied protection." The opinion then distinguished *Quirin* and *Yamashita*. The petitioners in those cases were plainly captured, imprisoned, or tried within U.S. territory. The petitioners in *Eisentrager*, by contrast, were never "within any territory over which the United States is sovereign, and the scenes of their offense, their capture, their trial, and their punishment were all beyond the territorial jurisdiction of any court of the United States."[38] Consequently, said the Supreme Court, they lacked any right to habeas jurisdiction. But precisely why this was true, and which factual elements were essential, was never made plain in this somewhat opaque decision.[39]

Though more than 50 years old at the time of the 9/11 attacks, *Eisentrager* suggested an appealing approach for addressing captured Al Qaeda members. If the suspected terrorists were captured abroad and kept away from American territory at all times, they, too, could be kept out of the federal court system. From 2002 onward the case was used repeatedly to bolster executive branch arguments that the legal rights of foreign detainees were sharply delimited by their geographic location. The Bush administration lawyers who drafted the Guantanamo memo in late December of 2001 nonetheless were careful to point to a potential pitfall in this approach. In *Eisentrager* the Supreme Court seemed to have used the concepts of sovereignty and jurisdiction interchangeably, even carelessly. At one point the opinion refers to the importance of sovereignty, but a few sentences later the opinion switches to "territorial jurisdiction."

Traditionally, as this book has made clear, territorial jurisdiction and sovereign control were understood to go in hand in hand. That is the core of the Westphalian model of territorial sovereignty. Yet practice and precedent have made clear that sovereignty and jurisdiction are not in fact coterminous, and thus the Westphalian model has long been understood to be an ideal type—a formal and abstract conception of sovereign statehood that reality often deviates from. The United States District Court for China had exercised jurisdiction over Americans in China, for example, but the United

States was never sovereign over China or parts of China. The same was true for all the consular courts that had operated in "uncivilized" places around the world. Even the law governing the Panama Canal Zone did not technically rest on American sovereignty over the Canal Zone, though American territorial jurisdiction there was total. And of course the many status of forces agreements negotiated in the postwar era granted jurisdiction to the United States over important aspects of military bases and deployed troops. The United States was not sovereign over these offshore bases either.

This complex history threw a wrench into the (perhaps inadvertent) locution of the Supreme Court in *Eisentrager*. The Justice Department memo alluded to this history obliquely, stating that "a nation . . . can retain its sovereignty over its territory, yet at the same time allow another nation to exercise limited jurisdiction within it."[40] This was precisely the scenario in Guantanamo, at least according to the executive branch's own theory of the lease. And it troubled the Justice Department lawyers. Moreover, at least one case from the earlier wave of Haitian litigation had held that because Guantanamo was subject to the complete jurisdiction and control of the United States, some constitutional rights applied to the Haitians detained there.[41]

The Justice Department lawyers consequently feared that a similar logic might drive a federal court to decide that Guantanamo was not in fact like the German prison in *Eisentrager*. A judge might be persuaded that Guantanamo was actually more like the Panama Canal Zone or even Puerto Rico. At the same time, the Bush administration lawyers took solace in the fact that the Haitian cases had not directly addressed habeas jurisdiction. Indeed, no decision of the federal courts had, at that time, ever upheld habeas rights for foreigners in Guantanamo.

Litigating Guantanamo

A great contrast between the Second World War cases such as *Quirin* and *Eisentrager* that were suddenly dusted off after 9/11 and the world of the twenty-first century was the degree to which legal considerations and arguments loomed large in debates, both public and within the government, over the treatment of enemy aliens.[42] Thus it was unsurprising that the federal courts did not simply take the Bush administration's word about the extraterritorial rights of enemy aliens. Indeed, several courts were quick to address the question of precisely what rights were possessed by detainees held offshore. For their part, the Bush administration consistently argued that aliens held outside the sovereign territory of the United States "have no basis to challenge the constitutionality of their detentions." To make things perfectly clear, the administration added that even if they could challenge their detention, the detainees "have no cognizable constitutional rights."[43]

The federal courts were at times quite uneasy with these expansive claims, which not only defined a class of persons without apparent rights, but also sidelined the judiciary from playing any supervisory role. Several courts nonetheless accepted this position. The 2003 decision of the D.C. Circuit in *Al Odah v. United States*, for example, noted that there were some differences between the Guantanamo detainees and those 50 years earlier in *Eisentrager*. The postwar German detainees were acknowledged enemy soldiers, whereas the Guantanamo detainees were challenging that status. Indeed, many of the Guantanamo detainees were nationals of friendly states.

But these distinctions were deemed insufficient to alter the result. The D.C. Circuit reasoned that despite these differences, "the Guantanamo detainees have much in common with the German prisoners in *Eisentrager*. They, too, are aliens, they too were captured during military operations, they were in a foreign country when captured, they are now abroad, they are in the custody of the American military, and they have never had any presence in the United States."[44] It followed that the detainees similarly lacked the right of habeas corpus. Undergirding this was a relatively simple idea that went back much further than the Second World War: "We cannot see why, or how, the writ may be made available to aliens abroad when basic constitutional protections are not."[45]

Similar views were expressed in other cases at the time. But the federal courts were hardly undivided on this issue. In 2003 a brother of a Guantanamo detainee, Belaid Gherebi, filed a habeas petition before the Ninth Circuit Court of Appeals. Unlike *Al Odah*, the court in *United States v. Gherebi* rejected the government's territorial approach. The Ninth Circuit held that that Guantanamo was American territory for the purposes of habeas jurisdiction and, in the alternative, that the base was American sovereign territory as well.[46] Relying on the ambiguity in *Eisentrager* between sovereignty and jurisdiction, the court agreed with the fundamental premise of the government that the rights possessed by the detainees turned on the nature of their location. But the majority argued that the *Eisentrager* did not in fact rest on sovereignty: "The [Supreme] Court nowhere suggested that 'sovereignty,' as opposed to 'territorial jurisdiction,' was a necessary factor." Consequently, "we do not believe that [Eisentrager] may properly be read to require 'sovereignty' as an essential prerequisite of habeas jurisdiction."[47] Territorial jurisdiction, in short, was all that was needed. And as the lease for Guantanamo made clear, the United States possessed complete territorial jurisdiction.

More sweepingly, the reliably liberal Ninth Circuit rejected the Bush administration's contention on grounds of deep principle, and in a manner that seemed on some level to reflect the widely voiced charge that Guantanamo constituted a legal black hole:

We simply cannot accept the government's position that the Executive Branch possesses the unchecked authority to imprison indefinitely any persons, foreign citizens included, on territory under the sole jurisdiction and control of the United States, without permitting such prisoners recourse of any kind to any judicial forum . . . We hold that no lawful policy or precedent supports such a counter-intuitive and undemocratic procedure, and that, contrary to the government's contention, *Johnson* [v. *Eisentrager*] neither requires nor authorizes it. In our view, the government's position is inconsistent with fundamental tenets of American jurisprudence and raises most serious concerns under international law.[48]

It was a surprise to no one that the struggle over what rights foreigners held in Guantanamo eventually reached the Supreme Court. In the 2004 case of *Rasul v. Bush* the Supreme Court was able—temporarily at least—to square the circle by finding a very narrow basis for decision. In doing so, the court sidestepped the thorny constitutional questions. *Rasul* did so by distinguishing between the constitutional right to appeal to a judge for release and the similar statutory right. Congress had previously granted federal courts the ability to hear applications for habeas corpus by any person who claims to be in violation of U.S. law. The majority in *Rasul* argued that prior decisions about the Guantanamo detainees did not actually address this statutory right. Whether the habeas statute was meant to apply to foreign nationals held in Guantanamo was a new question.

The interpretation of a statute with regard to its geographic reach would ordinarily be thought to raise questions of extraterritoriality, and therefore would be subject to the judicial "presumption against extraterritoriality." As chapter 4 described, this presumption, a judge-made interpretive principle, has a long history. But the Supreme Court stressed that the presumption did not apply in these circumstances. Because the lease with Cuba established that Guantanamo was under the complete U.S. jurisdiction and control, Guantanamo was within the territorial jurisdiction of the United States.

Consequently, the court reasoned, there was no issue of extraterritoriality. And because the Bush administration itself conceded that an American citizen held in Guantanamo would be able to appeal to a federal judge for release, so, too, could an alien. "Considering that the statute draws no distinction between Americans and aliens held in federal custody," wrote the majority, "there is little reason to think that Congress intended the geographical coverage of the statute to vary depending on the detainee's citizenship." As a result, Rasul was entitled to bring a claim under the habeas statute.[49] The statute was intended to apply wherever the United States possessed jurisdiction, and to apply equally to citizens and aliens. *Ipso facto*, it applied to the Guantanamo detainees.

The deeper constitutional question of whether aliens in Guantanamo possess any constitutional rights was carefully avoided. The only hint was a short footnote, which contended that the detainee's allegations "unquestionably describe 'custody in violation of the Constitution or laws or treaties of the United States.' "[50] Advocates and legal scholars lit upon this footnote as a guidepost to the future, should the judicial branch again be asked to weigh in on the constitutional rights of the Guantanamo detainees. (The court indeed chose to do so in 2008, in the case of *Boumediene v. Bush*, discussed below.) In a separate concurrence, Justice Kennedy, the now-critical swing vote on the Supreme Court, stepped out of the lawyerly mode of the majority and more pointedly noted the unusual attributes of Guantanamo. The base, he wrote, "is in every practical respect a United States territory...from a practical perspective, the indefinite lease of Guantanamo Bay has produced a place that belongs to the United States, extending the 'implied protection' of the United States to it."[51] Kennedy's focus on assessing practicalities in extraterritorial cases would later prove very significant.

This moment of realism aside, the decision in *Rasul* did not actually appear to rest on any unique qualities of Guantanamo, as the dissenters heatedly pointed out. Declaring that the majority's decision "boldly extends the scope of the habeas statute to the four corners of the earth," a move of "breathtaking" consequence, the dissenters contended that the court's decision would inject the judiciary into the conduct of an ongoing war and overturn a venerable line of precedent.[52] More powerfully, the dissenters rejected the majority's reasoning concerning the presumption against extraterritoriality. If a lease granting jurisdiction and control is sufficient to render the naval base American territory for purposes of domestic statutes, then why stop at Guantanamo?

> The Court does not explain how "complete jurisdiction and control" without sovereignty causes an enclave to be part of the United States for purposes of its domestic laws. Since "jurisdiction and control" obtained through a lease is no different in effect from "jurisdiction and control" acquired by lawful force of arms, parts of Afghanistan and Iraq should logically be regarded as subject to our domestic laws.[53]

This riposte underscored the appeal of a simple territorial rule keyed to sovereignty. Who was sovereign over a particular spot on earth was rarely difficult to determine. Sovereignty was a formal attribute. And for American courts it was even easier to determine sovereignty than one might imagine, because existing precedent established that the determination is for the political branches to decide.[54] If legal rights flowed only to the sovereign borders of the nation, disputes such as that in *Rasul* were easy to resolve.

The majority's approach, by contrast, offered no similar limiting principle. Jurisdictions could overlap; control was hard to assess. Once jurisdiction was unbundled from claims of sovereignty, the determination of legal rights and duties grew much more complicated. To be sure, the United States had in some respects crossed this particular Rubicon long ago. The United States had exercised power extraterritorially throughout its history without any concomitant claim of sovereignty. Consular courts of the kind that tried John Ross in 1880s Japan were one example. The phenomenon appeared again with the rise of postwar effects-based extraterritoriality, the extensive use of status of forces agreements, and the dramatic increase in extraterritorial law enforcement. But because many older decisions grounded in strict territoriality had never been directly overruled, and because only a few cases in the 1970s and 1980s had ever held that constitutional rights applied extraterritorialy with regard to aliens, it was still possible to trace a line back to the Westphalian territoriality of the past—as the executive branch consistently urged and as the Supreme Court had done in 1990 in *United States v. Verdugo*. Territoriality remained a powerful and appealing default assumption.

Given this history, it was no surprise that in the aftermath of the *Rasul* decision the Bush administration argued that sovereignty provided "an administrable bright-line rule" for the application of constitutional rights. Moreover, it was a line that was "deeply entrenched" in U.S. precedent. By contrast, to make decisions about the reach of constitutional rights turn on concepts of jurisdiction or control "would involve the courts in sensitive foreign affairs questions . . . and implicate a variety of sensitive foreign policy and military considerations."[55] In short, for the executive branch Westphalian territoriality was attractively straightforward, even if it seemed to many increasingly anachronistic. Most significantly, it gave the executive branch the powers and freedom it desired in a complex and dangerous world.

The Black-Site Prisons

An important consequence of jurisdictional bright lines is that variations in rules across jurisdictions create conflict, or the potential for conflict, as actors seek to arbitrage those differences for competitive advantage. This is one reason that effects-based extraterritoriality was so appealing to the postwar United States. In a world of increasing regulatory complexity, extraterritorial jurisdiction provided a means by which the American government could create some semblance of a level legal playing field for its increasingly active multinational firms. Extraterritoriality, as well, served to protect American markets from unwanted foreign influence; it allowed regulators, for instance, to target firms that price-fixed abroad in ways that harmed American consumers. In a world of global markets but strictly territorial jurisdiction, foreign firms could take advantage of legal difference by colluding in some offshore locale where such collusion was lawful. Extraterritorial jurisdiction curbs that tendency.

But the same incentive to seek advantage by shifting jurisdiction—to "jurisdiction shop"—exists for governments as well. Hugo Black's admonition in *Johnson v. Eisentrager,* which opened this chapter, proved quite prescient in this regard. Black asked whether "a prisoner's right to test the legality of a sentence [rests] on where the Government chooses to imprison him." He declared that the court was "fashioning wholly indefensible doctrine if it permits the executive branch, by deciding where its prisoners will be tried and imprisoned, to deprive all federal courts of their power to protect against a federal executive's illegal incarcerations."[56] In saying this, Black anticipated many of the issues at stake in the post-9/11 offshore prison program. The *Washington Post* noted when breaking the story that "it is illegal for the government to hold prisoners in such isolation in secret prisons in the United States." This existence of this domestic legal constraint, said the *Post,* "is why the CIA placed them overseas, according to several former and current intelligence officials and other U.S. government officials."[57]

The exact details of the CIA program remain unclear even now because so much of the program is classified. Some reports claim that the use of offshore prisons began in 2002, though in its 2007 report on the matter the Council of Europe suggested that the program dates back to the weeks immediately after 9/11.[58] Either way, the existence of the CIA-run overseas prisons, sometimes called "black sites," was first revealed by a series of stories in prominent American newspapers. According to these reports the CIA established secret prisons in Afghanistan (known by unusual monikers such as the "Salt Pit" and the "Dark Prison") and Thailand before shifting to undisclosed locations in Eastern Europe, most likely Poland and Romania.[59] The Eastern European facilities apparently were shut down in 2005 after the prisons received media coverage throughout the world.[60] Prisoners were typically flown to the detention sites in a series of unmarked planes owned by shell companies.[61]

President Bush acknowledged the existence of the offshore prisons for the first time in 2006, but declared that the secret sites had closed. At the time, U.S. officials suggested that fewer than 100 individuals had ever been held in these foreign locations.[62] In late 2006, the few remaining prisoners, 14 in total, were transferred to Guantanamo to await trial. Among them was Khalid Shaikh Mohammed, a purported mastermind of the 9/11 attacks. Whether the offshore prisons are really closed remains unclear, however. In July 2007, the *New York Times* reported that officials speaking on background claimed that the CIA again was holding prisoners in black sites overseas.[63]

Some of the critical media coverage about the prisons dovetailed with coverage of the CIA extraordinary rendition program. *Rendition* refers to the practice of flying suspected terrorists covertly to foreign governments for interrogation, presumably in some cases by means, or with intensities, that would be illegal if pursued by agents of the United States. Rendition by the United States dates back well before 2001. But it grew much more common after the terrorist attacks. Like the eventually acknowledged offshore prisons, the extraordinary rendition program was described by executive branch officials as a necessary response to a very dangerous enemy. Vice President Cheney suggested on *Meet the Press* shortly after the attacks that the U.S. government needed to "work through, sort of, the dark side. . . . [A] lot of what needs to be done here will have to be done quietly, without any discussion, using sources and methods that are available to our intelligence agencies, if we are going to be successful."[64] Rendition, as well as offshore prisons, was a part of this dark side.

The offshore prisons and the extraordinary rendition program were distinct, though they were sometimes muddled in the public debate. Rendition was, as *New Yorker* writer Jane Mayer provocatively put it, a strategy of "outsourcing torture."[65] The black-site prisons were instead a strategy of offshoring, in which the interrogators remained American but the interrogation (and perhaps torture) occurred within another jurisdiction. But both the offshore prisons and the extraordinary rendition program reflected a common aversion: the reach of American courts and American law to acts of interrogation and to the interrogators themselves. Both were also highly classified and politically volatile programs. Only in 2008, for example, did the British government concede that its earlier repeated denials about the use of British territory for "rendition flights" were incorrect, and that the CIA had in fact used the British-controlled Indian Ocean island of Diego Garcia for refueling—a result for which Foreign Secretary David Miliband characterized himself as "very sorry indeed."[66]

The offshore prisons program illustrates at least two important points. One is central to the argument of this book: the persistence of doctrines of territoriality in the twenty-first century. Just as Guantanamo was not chosen as a detention site simply for its security, the CIA did not choose interrogation facilities in Eastern Europe or Afghanistan for convenience. By operating offshore, the CIA believed it was insulating its operatives from the risk of prosecution within the United States. As in the past, the U.S. government strategically deployed arguments about the territorial nature of the law to further its perceived vision of the national interest.

The second, related point is the importance of law for American officials. Although the Bush administration was widely branded as lawless, in fact the executive branch's actions can be seen as highly motivated by and solicitous of legal rules. Why create a complex program thousands of miles away in unfamiliar terrain, which requires the creation of a network of front companies to fly suspects halfway around the world under false pretenses? The U.S. government did so because it was motivated by concerns over the legal impact of its actions, yet also under intense political pressure to act aggressively against terrorists. At the same time, the tremendous expansion of lawyers throughout the national security apparatus, as well as the existence of federal statutes such as the War Crimes Act of 1996, created powerful incentives to seek legal means by which to take action.[67]

The result was a significant effort to keep what was perceived as critical intelligence gathering and detention outside the reach of American law. The favorable precedents under U.S. law with regard to the extraterritorial rights of aliens provided a strong inducement to move as much counter-terrorism as possible offshore.

In short, Justice Black was right to be worried in *Johnson v. Eisentrager*. The incentives to relocate detention and interrogation to a more favorable legal climate ultimately proved irresistible to the executive branch. To be sure, the idea of offshoring detention did not begin on September 11, 2001. Imperial Britain maintained a distant prison system in the Antipodes as far back as the late eighteenth century.[68] But the journey to Australia took months and was fraught with peril. As the CIA's creation of an offshore prison program demonstrated, modern jet travel has made offshore prison locations far more accessible and useful. Globalization's "death of distance" was surely declared prematurely, but it is impossible to ignore the advances in transportation and infrastructure that now allow governments (and others) to easily reach distant shores. This effective shrinking of space creates deep tensions with jurisdictional principles that still rest on geographic borders. And it strengthens incentives to seek legal advantage by shifting location to some other jurisdiction. Thus in the more globalized world of the twenty-first century this sort of reverse forum shopping by governments is much easier than it would have been in the past.

The offshoring of detention and interrogation by the United States has also been facilitated by other, less obvious factors. The Cold War bequeathed the United States a vast network of overseas military bases, many of which are large, secure, and suitable for offshore detention sites. And the Cold War gave the United States some very indebted friends in distant places. These nations proved willing to buck the highly negative views that prevailed elsewhere of the Bush administration's war on terror, and provide the U.S. government with hidden sites for the most valuable suspected terrorists.

The Constitution in Iraq

The controversial invasion of Iraq in 2003 was one important source of these negative views. Shortly after the defeat of Saddam Hussein's forces the United States, in conjunction with other coalition states, created the

Coalition Provisional Authority. The CPA's role was to govern Iraq until a viable Iraqi government could be formed. It did so until the formal restoration of Iraqi sovereignty in June 2004.

Under the leadership of L. Paul Bremer, the CPA quickly took a series of controversial actions, including disbanding the Iraqi Army and engaging in "de-Baathification." Although the CPA was nominally a coalition entity, it was overwhelmingly funded and supported by the U.S. government. Indeed, Bremer was a government employee with the title of presidential envoy. He was, according to the Justice Department, "under the supervision of the President and Secretary of Defense" and his salary was paid by the United States Army.[69] Nine out of ten CPA staffers were U.S. citizens.[70] For all intents and purposes, then, the CPA was an American operation. Did this mean American law governed the CPA's actions in Iraq?

Iraq was hardly the first belligerent occupation undertaken by the United States. The nation had occupied considerable foreign territory before, most notably Germany and Japan but also Haiti, Cuba, and even parts of Mexico. Whether the Constitution followed the flag in military occupations was a question upon which there were few precedents, however. Most suggested that there were few if any domestic legal restraints on an American occupation. As described in chapter 2, whether the occupied Mexican city of Tampico fell within the tariff rules of the Constitution had arisen in *Fleming v. Page*. (The answer was no.) *Neely v. Henkel* in 1901 had similarly held that laws enforced by the United States in occupied Cuba were not subject to the Constitution. And during the Civil War even the occupation of New Orleans was held to be governed by international law, not constitutional law.

These precedents were both more than a century old, however, and much had changed in constitutional law. More recently, the unusual 1979 *Tiede* decision, stemming from the dramatic landing of East German hijackers in the American sector of postwar occupied Berlin, had come down in the opposite direction, granting constitutional rights to the foreign defendants tried by U.S. officials. *Tiede* was of course anomalous in many respects, not least that, unlike the relatively fleeting Cuban or Mexican occupations, the occupation of Berlin lasted decades.

Perhaps the most striking discussion of the constitutional restraints on occupation can be found in *Eisentrager*. In his remarkable dissent in that case, Justice Black queried whether American military occupation was controlled by the Constitution. If the United States occupies another nation, it assumes responsibility for governing, Black thought. This responsibility "immediately raises questions concerning the extent to which our domestic laws, constitutional or statutory, are transplanted abroad." He continued:

> Probably no one would suggest, and certainly I would not, that this nation either must or should attempt to apply every constitutional provision of

the Bill of Rights in controlling temporarily occupied countries. But that does not mean that Constitution is wholly inapplicable in foreign territories that we occupy and govern ... Our constitutional principles are such that their mandate of equal justice under law should be applied as well when we occupy lands across the sea as when our flag flew only over thirteen colonies.[71]

Here again, we see the constitutional tradition of the United States squared off against its global ambitions. To Black's way of thinking, constitutional rights were always applicable to actions of the American government—even to foreign military adventures—even if they did not necessarily apply in the precise way they did at home. To take decisive action and topple a foreign regime was plainly within the power of the United States. But whether the United States faced special restraints when exercising its awesome military power, restraints that were grounded in its fundamental legal and political commitments, as Black believed, was far less clear.

Black's view was that ordinary constitutional fetters did not fall away when the United States acted abroad; the Bill of Rights always and everywhere constrained the government. Conquest by the United States, "unlike conquest by many other nations, does not mean tyranny," he opined.[72] When the United States governed, it necessarily did so subject to its fundamental law. In stating this view, he echoed a long line of American elites who had feared the effects of international power politics on the United States, and who had urged that the federal government could not necessarily act as other sovereign states did. This restrained view of American power even predated the Civil War. The "peculiar character of the Government of the United States," the Supreme Court had declared in the antebellum case of *Dred Scott*, "is that although it is sovereign and supreme in its appropriate sphere of action, yet it does not possess all the powers which usually belong to the sovereignty of a nation." Most pertinently, it cannot ever assume "despotic powers," even in an overseas colony.[73]

The restrained view was hardly universal, however, as previous chapters have made clear. Many presidential administrations have understood the federal government to be unfettered by the Constitution when it acts beyond American borders. The executive branch has steadfastly adhered to the view that no constitutional rights apply to foreign nationals abroad—and many courts have agreed. This approach implies that the only legal constraints the United States faces when it acts outside American borders, or occupies a foreign nation, are international legal constraints.

What did this backdrop mean for American action in Iraq? International law provided some limits on the occupying power, but these limits were not particularly tight. Did U.S. law provide further limits? Consider the question of whether the CPA could have engaged in religious discrimination in

Iraq—favoring Shiites over Sunnis, for instance. Only a few cases have ever considered the extraterritorial reach of the First Amendment, and none involved the Supreme Court. Certainly none involved belligerent occupation.

A 1989 case asked whether the federal government could restrict aid to private family planning organizations overseas if those groups did not renounce abortion as an option. The district court held that the government could do so—that the "interests in free speech and freedom of association of foreign nationals acting outside the borders, jurisdiction, and control of the United States do not fall within the interests protected by the First Amendment."[74] A later case came to the opposite conclusion. The Second Circuit employed the "headquarters" rationale to hold that when the U.S. government funds overseas religious activities, any First Amendment harm occurs inside American territory, where the funding decision is actually made.[75] That decision took place in an office in Washington. Whatever the merits of this latter approach, because the CPA sat not in Washington but in Baghdad, it has little purchase.

In any event, the constitutionality of the CPA's actions in Iraq appears to have remained an academic question. And although earlier precedents such as *Neely v. Henkel* provide an easy answer to such a question, the geographic limits of the Constitution were far less sharp in the opening years of the twenty-first century then they had been in the opening years of the twentieth century. *Reid v. Covert* had in the 1950s overturned the idea that constitutional protections were strictly territorial; later courts had divided over what this new rule really entailed. The resulting confusion has perplexed many knowledgeable observers. Faced with a direct question about the geographic scope of the Constitution, American judges have tended to deny its extraterritorial reach. Yet they sometimes hedge and suggest that perhaps, in some circumstance not precisely before them at the moment, an overseas alien might have constitutional protection. The full implications of the blanket view—that there is simply no constitutional restraint whatsoever when the government acts abroad against noncitizens—seem hard to swallow.

The executive branch has on occasion conceded as much, though usually under duress. At one point in oral argument in *Verdugo*, for example, Justice Kennedy pressed the government's lawyer to explain what constitutional limits did in fact exist: "Does the Constitution control what United States officials do when they're abroad generally? Or never? Or sometimes?" The executive branch lawyer replied, "I think the answer is sometimes, and the answer is it depends."[76] Similarly statements had slipped from the lips of lawyers representing the executive branch before when they faced skeptical questioning from the bench.[77] But this was never a position reliably put forward by the United States in those disputes.

Instead, the executive branch persistently argued that the Constitution simply does not reach aliens abroad at all.

Whose Flag?

Whether the Constitution followed the flag to Iraq was further complicated by the multilateral character of the CPA and the occupying forces. Were the coalition forces American forces, or some kind of international force that happened to comprise a vast number of Americans? In litigation stemming from the Iraq War, the Bush administration has referred to the multilateral nature of the military forces to claim that U.S. troops are acting not simply as Americans, but as part of a larger international entity. The significance of this claim turns largely on its implications for the role of federal courts. If U.S. forces are in some sense operating as part of a multilateral effort, they are less likely to be subject to supervision by American judges.

The idea that multilateralism can serve as a domestic law-blocking (or court-blocking) device is drawn from an old dispute over the war crimes trials held in Japan. In a terse 1948 opinion (only two sentences long, and unsigned), the Supreme Court in *Hirota v. MacArthur* denied to review the detention of a defeated Japanese general on the grounds that the International Military Tribunal for the Far East that tried the general was not an American court.[78] The tribunal was therefore outside the Supreme Court's purview. *Hirota*'s legacy became central to two important cases in Iraq. In each, U.S. forces detained American citizens within Iraqi territory.[79] The detained Americans then sued in U.S. courts for release. The question before the Supreme Court was whether they indeed possessed the right to bring a habeas plea before a U.S. court, and whether the military had to release them if the plea was successful.

The Bush administration followed the logic of *Hirota*. It argued that the U.S. troops were in Iraq under United Nations auspices and consequently were part of a multilateral force. (The executive branch conceded, however, that the troops remained subject to U.S. command.) As a result, the federal courts could not hear their habeas petitions. Moreover, said the Bush administration, the exigencies of foreign affairs made deference to the executive by the courts essential. Granting habeas rights to the imprisoned Americans would interfere "with the Executive Branch's solemn international commitments and its ability to carry out its foreign policy and military objectives. Other nations would inevitably take offense if American courts were to assume the authority to review the determinations of international bodies in which United States forces or personnel may participate abroad..."[80] This argument also had roots in the Second World War. In an influential survey of post–1945 extraterritorial cases, eminent constitutional lawyer Charles Fairman had argued that to have American courts supervise allied occupations abroad would impede collaborative efforts. "Ours is not the only nation that might insist upon the extraterritorial application of its national legal conceptions," noted Fairman in 1949.[81]

Lawyers for the American detainees in Iraq challenged both positions of the Bush administration, asserting that the right of a U.S. citizen to habeas review could not be eliminated by the nominal creation of a multilateral military force. To do so would vest the power to deny habeas review in the executive's hands, because the executive had the ability to enter into international agreements single-handedly. (Although some international agreements require congressional action, many accords are the product of presidential action alone.)

The detainees echoed a critique of the *Hirota* principle put forward by Justice William Douglas, who some months after *Hirota* issued a concurring opinion featuring markedly different reasoning. Douglas saw a distinction between reviewing the actions of a multilateral body and reviewing the actions of American officials participating in that body. "If an American General holds a prisoner," wrote Douglas, "our process can reach him wherever he is. To that extent at least, the Constitution follows the flag. It is no defense for him to say that he acts for the Allied Powers."[82] Douglas's approach is familiar: it is the same view later held by the dissenters in *Verdugo*, by Justice Black in *Eisentrager* (whose dissent Douglas joined), and by a host of lower courts: when U.S. officials act, they are always governed by and subject to the Constitution. Where they act, and with whom, cannot change this fundamental fact.

To underscore the importance of this position, lawyers for the American detainees in Iraq stressed that there was no territorial limitation to the Bush administration's *Hirota*-based argument. In other words, the insulating effects of multilateralism did not, in the *Hirota* paradigm, seem to turn on foreign location. The same could be true for actions *within* the United States.

For instance, the Bush administration had in 2001 captured suspected terrorist Jose Padilla in O'Hare Airport, declaring that the war on terror did not have a traditional front line safely resting overseas. After much courtroom maneuvering Padilla eventually received habeas review. The government's multilateralism argument, said the detainees, would give even more flexibility to the executive, for it "brooks no geographic limit: Invoking 'international authority,' Executive officials could seize and detain citizens in the United States without judicial review."[83] To permit Americans to be held on U.S. soil without any judicial review, simply because other states were involved in the war effort, would eviscerate the very point of habeas corpus.

The Supreme Court ultimately rejected the Bush administration's reliance on *Hirota* and embraced Douglas's minority view. In a unanimous decision, the court held that habeas "extends to American citizens held overseas by American forces operating subject to an American chain of command." However, the Court also held that the detainees could not be released from captivity. Harking back to the many earlier cases in which the ordinary legal restrictions applicable to the U.S. government were held to have changed because the United States was acting in place of, or at the behest of, another sovereign, the Supreme Court looked to the relationship between the now-sovereign Iraq and the United States. Because the American detainees were held at the behest of Iraq for crimes committed within Iraqi territory, their release, said the court, "would interfere with the sovereign authority" of Iraq.[84] Like the Americans in occupied Berlin after the *Tiede* decision, they had rights but no remedies.

The Jurisdictional Gap, Part II

The Iraq War is striking for its use of private military contractors. Although the turn to contractors is not entirely new, the levels seen in Iraq are unprecedented. Military contractors fall into an ambiguous legal zone overseas. An early act of the CPA in Iraq, "Order 17," immunized contractors from Iraqi law. The order was in many respects akin to other extraterritoriality arrangements discussed in this book. These arrangements, ranging from consular courts to status of forces agreements, share the common goal of insulating American citizens from what the United States considered primitive, corrupt or unreliable legal systems. Yet the CPA order was far more sweeping than typical American status of forces agreements. Order 17 states that coalition forces, the CPA staff, and consultants are generally immune from Iraqi law. Specifically, contractors "are immune from Iraqi legal process with respect to acts performed by them pursuant to" their contracts.[85]

The legal status of contractors in Iraq became headline news around the world in the wake of an incident in Baghdad in 2007 that left seventeen civilians dead. A convoy of Blackwater USA guards shot an Iraqi man behind the wheel of the car in Nisour Square. The car's continued movement apparently triggered a barrage of gunfire and mayhem in the streets.[86] In the aftermath, many questions emerged about the use of private contractors as well as the legal liability they might face for killing Iraqi civilians. The Iraqi government, facing a domestic uproar, threatened to prosecute the shooters, but was stymied by the still-extant CPA order.

Strikingly, the United States government faced prosecutorial hurdles of its own. After *Reid v. Covert* it was clear that American civilians overseas could no longer be tried by court-martial. The resulting "jurisdictional gap," as chapter 5 described, lasted until the passage in 2000 of the Military

Extraterritorial Jurisdiction Act (MEJA). MEJA was aimed at ensuring that civilians working for the American military could not escape punishment for crimes that occurred overseas, as had frequently happened in the decades after *Reid*. However, MEJA's extraterritorial reach was limited to those who worked for the Department of Defense. Many of the private military contractors in Iraq, including Blackwater, instead worked for the State Department or the CIA.[87]

This structure of employment created a second jurisdictional gap, one that protected many contractors from legal liability for extraterritorial crimes. A proposed statutory fix, titled the "MEJA Expansion and Enforcement Act," passed the House of Representatives but remains stalled in the Senate.[88] As of 2008 this issue was still unresolved, though the removal of immunity for contractors was a central demand of the Iraqi government in the negotiations over a future status of forces agreement. This agreement, just negotiated at the time of this writing, is set to take force in 2009 when the existing United Nations Security Council authority lapses.

As the Blackwater story suggests, there are many extraterritorial questions raised by the Iraq War beyond the question of whether the Constitution constrains the U.S. government when it occupies foreign territory. The incremental evolution of territoriality has left some holes, and these holes are not easy to fix. It took Congress over 40 years to fix the jurisdictional gap created by *Reid v. Covert*. And as the Blackwater story shows, that fix was not perfect.

The Constitution in Guantanamo

The territorial questions raised by the Iraq War are interesting, but they have rarely grabbed the attention of the larger world. The central front in the battle over the geographic scope of constitutional rights has remained Guantanamo. As the first decade of the twenty-first century unfolded, the drumbeat of criticism over Guantanamo grew rather than abated. The position of the United States—that the base was simply leased foreign land, free of the Constitution's reach—absorbed increasing attacks.

As noted earlier in this chapter, the Supreme Court avoided consideration of Guantanamo's constitutional status for several years after the first suspected terrorists arrived in 2001. When the Court ruled in *Rasul v. Bush* that the federal habeas statute permitted foreign detainees to contest their detention before an American judge, Congress and the executive quickly amended the statute. The issue continued to bubble up from the lower courts, however. Many of the Guantanamo detainees claimed to be innocent men, accidentally swept up in a raid or turned in maliciously for a bounty. Eventually the question of their constitutional rights returned to the Supreme Court.

In *Boumediene v. Bush*, the Court for the first time endorsed the principle that the detainees had a constitutionally protected right to challenge their detention before a federal court. The decision was hailed on the left as a constitutional landmark. But it caused a firestorm of criticism from the right, inspiring an unusually bitter dissent from Justice Scalia, who predicted that it would "almost certainly cause more Americans to be killed."[89]

The case arose when Lakhdar Boumediene, a Bosnian seized in Bosnia by American forces and transferred to Guantanamo, sought to challenge his status as an enemy combatant. The question before the Supreme Court was whether Boumediene could bring such a claim despite the aforementioned change in the habeas statute. The Supreme Court began by noting the central importance of the writ of habeas corpus and reviewing the complex history of its geographic scope. Unlike the Bill of Rights, which was the product of amendments, the significance of the right to habeas review is signaled by its inclusion in the original 1789 Constitution. Surveying what was known about ancient British practice in places such as India and the Channel Islands, the Court found the history of habeas murky and inconclusive on the question of extraterritoriality.

The justices then considered whether the lack of American sovereignty over Guantanamo decided the question. Reviewing obscure cases from the nineteenth-century American occupation of Mexico, as well as many other early decisions, the majority declared that sovereignty was not a clear-cut status, nor was it dispositive for purposes of judicial review of detention. Territory could be under the formal sovereignty of one state and the "practical sovereignty" of another. Moreover, the history of the United States illustrated that constitutional rights are not, in any event, coterminous with sovereign borders.

So what did determine the geographic scope of habeas rights? The opinion stressed the central importance of functional and practical considerations when evaluating the reach of the Constitution. In a brief history, the majority argued that practicality and reasonableness had influenced a welter of prior territorial decisions, ranging from the *In re Ross*, the late nineteenth-century case involving a consular American trial in Japan, to the *Insular Cases*, involving the new American empire gained in 1898, to the postwar cases of *Reid v. Covert* and *Johnson v. Eisentrager*, granting constitutional rights to American dependents at overseas military bases and denying habeas to German soldiers captured in China, respectively. In each of these landmark decisions, said the Court, "practical considerations weighed heavily." There was "a common thread" uniting them: "the idea that questions of extraterritoriality turn on objective factors and practical concerns, not formalism."[90]

This focus on practicality rather formalism can directly be traced back to the case of Rene Verdugo-Urquidez, in which Justice Anthony Kennedy, the author of *Boumediene*, penned a concurring opinion holding the extraterritorial application of the Fourth Amendment to be "impracticable." Kennedy's concurrence foreshadowed his approach to Lakhdar Boumediene's habeas plea, with its focus not on abstract categories but instead on practicalities and function.

With regard to Guantanamo, however, the practicality calculus swung the opposite direction. Kennedy noted the unbroken control of the United States over the base, which dated to Spain's repudiation of sovereignty over a century ago. As a result, Guantanamo was "in every practical sense . . . not abroad." Nor was it in an active war zone. In such a situation it was hardly impractical to adhere to normal constitutional rules. If sovereignty rather than practicality were dispositive, moreover, the government could easily evade the Constitution by ceding land to another sovereign and then leasing it back. Such expediency would make a mockery of the separation of powers. To allow a situation in which the executive could "switch the Constitution on or off at will" was unacceptable. "Our basic charter cannot be contracted away like this."[91]

In reality, there was little in *Boumediene* that truly stopped the executive branch from switching the Constitution on or off at will. The Bush administration could have held the same detainees in Iraq, or Afghanistan, or a military base elsewhere in the world. (Though unlike in Guantanamo, permission from the host nation would likely be needed.) Indeed, the detainees could be moved to such places now. In these situations the practicality calculus would be very different; few would consider Bagram Air Base to be essentially American territory. On the other hand, there was nothing in the Supreme Court's decision that necessarily precluded the reach of habeas corpus to offshore bases such as these. But in its careful attention to practicality, and to function rather than form, it suggested that there was something quite special, even unique, about Guantanamo. No other American base could be said to be formally within another sovereign state but "in every practical sense . . . not abroad."

That said, the focus on practicality in *Boumediene* also suggested that the constitutional test for habeas rights was not written in stone. It was instead subject to change given technological and political developments. What was impractical one day might become practical in a future day. During the Cold War it seemed very impractical to fly Americans back to the United States to stand trial. Few probably imagined that, several decades later, the United States would readily fly detainees outside the United States to stand trial. Practicality was a moving target, and one whose measure was in the eye of beholder.

Although practicality was a touchstone of the majority, it is clear that for at least some justices the duration of the detention at issue in *Boumediene* was significant as well. Some of the prisoners in the case had been locked up in Guantanamo for 6 years. Yet at the time of the decision no trial had been held for any prisoner at the base. (Later that summer Salim Hamdan, Osama bin Laden's driver, was convicted of several counts by a military commission and sentenced to time served plus a few extra few months.)[92] In this context, Guantanamo seemed like an almost permanent purgatory.

The dissenters on the court had a very hostile reaction to this analysis. Justice Scalia pithily summarized their most fundamental objection: "The writ of habeas corpus does not, and never has, run in favor of aliens abroad; the Suspension Clause thus has no application, and the Court's intervention in this military matter is entirely *ultra vires*."[93] Taking a different page from *Verdugo* than had Justice Kennedy, Scalia went on to stress the dire national security implications of the majority's decision. "America," he wrote, "is at war with radical Islamists." The principles laid out in *Boumediene* would yield more deaths for the United States and "make the war harder on us." On its own, he claimed, the sheer fact that bad outcomes might flow from the decision would not be dispositive; if they were necessary to preserve a time-honored constitutional principle they would be tolerable. But here, Scalia declared, the Supreme Court was instead *abandoning* a time-honored principle. The "Nation will live to regret what the Court has done today."[94]

Quoting directly from the Justice Department memo that opened this chapter, Scalia argued that the Court had perpetrated a bait and switch on the Bush administration. Had the executive branch known that the Supreme Court would extend habeas rights extraterritorially, they surely would not have transported prisoners halfway around the world to Guantanamo. Instead, they "would have kept them in Afghanistan, transferred them to another of our foreign military bases, or turned them over to allies for detention."[95] Hence although the majority decision was "devastating" to the United States in the short run, in the long run it would accomplish little. The executive branch would simply scour the globe to find a new offshore detention site—one that was more distant, where the United States had fewer formal measures of control, where constitutional rights were more "impractical."

Boumediene generally received a rapturous reception from the left. A spokesman for Senator Edward Kennedy declared that the Supreme Court had thankfully rejected the Bush administration's "blatant attempt to create a legal black hole beyond the reach of the rule of law." Liberal commentators cast the decision as a "nail in Guantanamo's coffin" and a victory for individual rights and the rule of law.[96] On the right, *Boumediene* was blasted as "a blatant power grab" by an "imperial court" eager to micromanage the war on terror and hamstring the president while "inventing rights for foreign jihadists."[97]

As another landmark in the history of extraterritoriality, however, the decision was significant less for its wartime context and more for its willingness to further extend a functional approach to the geographic reach of American law. Although the opinion was somewhat tendentious in its reading of history—as this book has detailed, there were major shifts in ideas about territoriality that occurred over the past 150 years, not merely an evolving calculus of practicality—it was the first time that the Supreme Court itself had held that a constitutional right applied to an alien held outside the United States. And as Justice Scalia noted, probably correctly, the functional/practical test employed in *Boumediene* would, in time, likely be applied to other constitutional protections as well.

Executive Power Overseas

The end of the Cold War transformed world politics, but it did not bring about a dramatic retreat of American forces from around the globe. New security threats quickly rose to the fore, or at least were perceived as such, and old threats, such as conflict on the Korean peninsula, kept many troops in forward positions. The new threats included transnational criminal networks, resource scarcity, failed states, and, increasingly, terrorism. The 1960s and 1970s were certainly plagued by hijackings and acts of terror in Italy, Ireland, and elsewhere. But at the time terrorism was generally not viewed by the United States as a leading security threat. By the 1990s, however, President Clinton had begun noting terrorism in his State of the Union addresses, and by 1998 terrorism was placed in the top tier of threats in executive branch reports to Congress.[98]

That the *existence* of external threats to the United States has not changed, even if the *source* of these threats has, is reflected in the continued deployment of law enforcement agents overseas as well as the reactions of the courts and the executive branch alike to disputes over the extraterritorial reach of American law. The ratio of overseas cops to soldiers certainly shifted markedly from the 1950s to the 1990s. Yet the general approach to dealing with security threats—to extend American power abroad in an effort to protect the American homeland—was consistent from the Cold War through today. The recent efforts at "offshoring the border" described in the preceding chapter are only the latest instance of this strategy.

Consistency can also be discerned in terms of legal doctrine. One of the persistent themes in post-9/11 judicial decisions and government briefs alike is the executive branch's need to retain flexibility in the face of external threats and to preserve the ability to act, as much as possible, without the slow and often intrusive supervision of the judiciary. The extraterritorial application of basic legal rights to aliens has long been seen as impeding that flexibility. Cumbersome but essential protections designed for peacetime use at home, many have argued, ought not to be blindly applied to the far more complex and dangerous arena beyond our borders.

This is not simply a post-9/11 mindset, however. Even in 1990, in the case of Rene Verdugo-Urquidez, the Supreme Court pointed to the perils that the extraterritorial extension of constitutional rights would pose. To extend legal rights abroad to aliens "would have significant and deleterious consequences for the United States in conducting activities beyond its boundaries . . . For better or for worse, we live in a world of nation-states in which our Government must be able to 'functio[n] effectively in the company of sovereign nations.'"[99] The United States was not going to retreat from external threats; hence the executive branch must retain the ability to cooperate with other sovereigns to maintain the security of the United States. And to do so, it must not be unduly fettered by restraints designed for the internal, domestic protection of civil liberties. This view still has a powerful sway.

And the Supreme Court was not alone in thinking that traditional legal rules could not be safely exported from the domestic realm to the international realm. Many in Washington believed these liberties, although valuable and time honored at home, exacted a real cost in a world in which groups like Al Qaeda could target American cities and civilians with planes or dirty bombs. Doctrines of territoriality were helpful in this context, for they markedly limited the impact of these valuable rights and liberties.

Yet in some instances traditional territorial assumptions had the reverse effect, hampering—in the view of many executive branch officials—their ability to defend the United States against future attack. Part of the problem stemmed from the fact that the forces of interdependence that have so transformed the world over the last few decades have, on occasion, also served to render the line between domestic and international invisible, or at least convoluted. As a result, courts have sometimes applied domestic rules to what might be characterized as international behavior.

The Foreign Intelligence Surveillance Act, for example, was passed in 1978 to rein in government eavesdropping on American citizens. After 9/11 the Bush administration found the FISA law constraining as it tried to spy on suspected terrorists abroad. A 2008 *New Yorker* profile of Director of National Intelligence Mike McConnell tellingly described the challenge from the perspective of the executive branch. During a lunch interview with the author, McConnell

put down his sandwich and walked over to a world map on his wall. "Terrorist on a cell phone, right here"—he pointed at Iraq—"talking to a tower, happens all the time, no warrant. Goes up to a satellite, back to the ground station, no warrant. Now, let us suppose that it goes up to a satellite, and in the process it does this"—his finger darted to the U.S. before angling back to Pakistan. "Gotta have a warrant! So it was crazy."[100]

Because the hypothetical phone call was routed through a node in the United States, McConnell was saying, U.S. judges believed that it "touched" American territory and was consequently subject to the strict rules of FISA. A call between two international actors had effectively become domestic because the signal crossed the U.S. border. Had the call instead been routed through France, no such problem would exist and no warrant would be required. These kinds of geographic quandaries highlight the enduring appeal, but also the frequent anachronism, of territorial legal reasoning. A rigid divide between the rules of international spying and domestic spying seemed to make decreasing sense in a world in which so many forms of communication crisscrossed the globe, and sovereign borders, at the speed of light.

The FISA example also shows how U.S. officials chafed at certain territorial assumptions (and the laws that were built upon them) while freely availing themselves of other, more helpful assumptions, such as the belief that constitutional rights lacked extraterritorial effect. Like the interpretation of FISA, the use of Guantanamo and the CIA black-site prisons reflected the persistence of territoriality in the contemporary world. But in these instances, unlike in FISA, traditional territoriality proved very useful. Restrained at home by a skein of legal doctrines, the Bush administration sought to slip those legal bounds by operating as much as possible overseas. The *Insular Cases,* with their holding that fundamental rights apply to unincorporated American territories, made the remaining American colonies less than ideal for this purpose. The use of foreign territory required the permission of the host government. In some cases, this was obtainable, as the CIA overseas prison program demonstrates. Yet it was not always easy to obtain, given the passionate opposition to U.S. foreign policy in so many other nations. Consequently, the sole major U.S. overseas military base without a status of forces agreement—Guantanamo Bay—appeared to be the most attractive choice for a large-scale detention center.

Guantanamo had been used for foreign detentions before. With surprising ease, the twenty-first-century executive branch could move detainees around the globe in an effort to find the most secure and legally friendly location available. And from the vantage point of 2001 there was substantial support from the federal courts for the position that the base was not American territory. As a result, although executive branch lawyers never said so directly, they plainly believed that Guantanamo was indeed, in Lord Steyn's words, a kind of legal black hole. The geographic premises of American law encouraged this decision. Territoriality, as Justice Black warned in 1950 in *Johnson v. Eisentrager*, incentivized the executive to seek offshore locations for actions that might run afoul of the Bill of Rights.

Efforts by the U.S. judiciary to restrain executive branch power within the United States, however laudable, may only exacerbate this tendency to go off shore. As noted conservative judge J. Harvie Wilkinson argued in another recent decision,

> [T]he difference between the elaborate procedural protections required [by some decisions] in the United States and those required elsewhere will give the executive branch the incentive to pursue more extraterritorial detentions and more acts of rendition—not because these actions are necessarily dictated by the struggle against terror but because of the disparities between refined procedural regimes at home and more rudimentary ones abroad.[101]

The same basic point was made by Justice Scalia in *Boumediene*. Whatever the defined territorial scope of the Constitution, the executive will seek to move just beyond it. Yet as *Boumediene* suggests, the federal judiciary may have an increasingly difficult time swallowing a legal argument that, in so many ways, seems formalistic and drawn from ancient notions of Westphalian territoriality. In a world in which suspects, soldiers, and special agents can be flown around the world in a matter of hours, the idea that legal rights would still be tethered to territory is likely to strike at least some members of the federal judiciary as highly problematic.

If nothing else, this approach would seem to disturb the balance of power between the branches of the U.S. government. The supple and footloose executive branch would surely gain in such a world, and the more rooted judiciary would lose. The essence of the more conventional offshoring debate—footloose multinational firms versus slow, territorial states— seems replicated, in short, in the emerging struggle between the executive and judicial branches over the role of the Constitution in the so-called war on terror.

Indeed, just 2 years after *Eisentrager* was decided the Supreme Court had recognized the dangerous incentives created by strictly territorial conceptions of legal rules. In a case involving the comparatively very mild threat of extraterritorial trademark infringement, the Court declared, "[W]e do not think that petitioner by so simple a device [as selling in Mexico] can evade the thrust of the laws of the United States in a privileged sanctuary beyond our borders."[102] Yet the same Court laid the groundwork for precisely such a "privileged sanctuary beyond our borders" when it had held, 2 years earlier, that the German soldiers captured by American forces abroad had no right to habeas corpus. The offshore sanctuary of Guantanamo ultimately proved irresistible to an executive desperate to halt the next attack.

8

TERRITORIALITY'S EVOLUTION

At the turn of the last century Americans heatedly debated whether their constitution followed the flag. Did the United States possess a "home-stayin' constitution," as the satirist Finley Peter Dunne suggested at the time, or did its foundational rules extend wherever and whenever the federal government governed? Perhaps the newly muscular nature of American power in an overtly imperial age had changed the answer; perhaps the flag was now, in Dunne's clever words, "so lively that no constitution could follow it and survive."[1] In the century that followed, of course, the flag became livelier than anyone at the time could have imagined.

With the presidential election of 1900 couched as a referendum on the Constitution and the flag, the victory of William McKinley over the anticolonial William Jennings Bryan signaled a new American willingness to embrace empire in places like the Philippines. McKinley's campaign had declaimed that the flag "has not been planted in foreign soil to acquire more territory, but for humanity's sake." McKinley nonetheless did not disappoint the substantial interests that favored more territory. The subsequent ratification by the Supreme Court of a peculiarly American form of imperialism facilitated this expansion. Yet by holding that only some rights applied in the new island possessions, whereas others lost their strength at the water's edge, the early-twentieth-century *Insular Cases* cobbled together an odd and unstable marriage of imperialism and constitutionalism.

Although it deeply polarized the United States at the time, this debate over the Constitution and the flag is now largely forgotten. Yet as the previous chapter detailed, a very similar debate emerged almost exactly a century later. Whether Guantanamo Bay was a "legal black hole" or a legitimate detention center for dangerous enemy combatants became a topic of often passionate argument the world over. Despite a very different political and legal context, the dispute over Guantanamo focused attention on the geographic reach of American law with an intensity not seen since the early 1900s. And despite a century of often radical constitutional evolution, and the contemporaneous and remarkable rise of international human rights law, the United States still lacks a firm answer to the question of whether the Constitution follows the flag, the government, the individual, or the directive of the president.

The election of 1900 and the American response to the attacks of 2001 are consequently connected by more than just the historical curiosity that Guantanamo Bay was a fruit of the same war that placed the Philippines and other islands into American hands. Many of the same issues about territoriality, extraterritoriality, and intraterritoriality arose in each episode. Both episodes illustrate the geopolitical benefits of offshore islands. And both illustrate the desire to control territory that is somehow insulated from the full protections of American law. Unlike the sovereign borders of the United States, which are precisely delineated on a map, constitutional and jurisdictional borders remain complex, messy, and contingent.

Indeed, the zone between what sovereignty empowers and constitutionalism permits has long been contested in American history. As the story of the Louisiana Purchase demonstrates, even the question of whether the United States could legally expand beyond the eastern seaboard of North America was, for a brief moment, in some doubt. The United States nonetheless grew from a minor power on the edge of the civilized world to a hyperpower with unprecedented global influence and reach. This dramatic growth engendered a wide range of territorial questions and challenged traditional assumptions. In a host of historical instances, the same central issue—the nature of the connection between law and land—led to profound disagreement.

In this book I have endeavored to advance two broad arguments about these disagreements, and in doing so to chart the ebb and flow of territoriality in American law. The first is that the evolution of *extraterritoriality* can and ought to be understood as a cohesive phenomenon. Seemingly discrete episodes in American history—such as the creation of the U.S. District Court for China, or the offshoring of federal law enforcement—share common roots. By viewing them as a connected set, we can begin to trace significant patterns and practices. A primary connection is the motivating role of legal difference, a difference that is grounded in the nature of the Westphalian order. Extraterritoriality can mitigate (and sometimes capitalize on) this difference. The assertions of extraterritorial jurisdiction described in this book have largely done so in the service of enhancing American power and interests on the world stage.

The second major argument is that many of the debates over the geographic scope of American law feature not only extraterritoriality, but *intraterritoriality*. Westphalian territoriality was aimed at preserving autonomy within each sovereign's territory, and extraterritoriality at minimizing the effects of legal variance among these territories. By contrast, intraterritoriality draws distinctions between a legal core and a legal periphery *within* a single territory. The resulting "borders" are internal, not international. The persistence of intraterritoriality stems not from Westphalian notions of territorial sovereignty, but instead from the challenges of liberal constitutionalism in a global context.

In making both these arguments I have paid close attention to the role of world politics. The international system has deeply shaped ideas and doctrines of territoriality. As both American power and interests changed, and as the nature of the international order itself changed, the relationship between law and land has also changed. The rise of the United States as a great power, the demise of formal imperialism, the intensifying pace of postwar interdependence—these and other features of world politics have helped to alter the assumptions as well as the rules of territoriality.

In this concluding chapter I elaborate these arguments. Each is dependent on a more foundational claim: that territoriality merits substantial analysis. The study of sovereignty is deep and rich. By comparison, outside of the academic field of geography the topic of territoriality, sovereignty's Westphalian twin, has received only glancing attention.[2] Yet territoriality is a central phenomenon in international law and politics. If anything, it is becoming more central in the twenty-first century, and the increasing tendency in a globalizing world to move critical activities offshore invites far greater attention to how territoriality has been manipulated to strategic advantage. Much of this offshoring activity has been economic and private, and most analyses have focused on the impacts for employment, regulation, and competition. The aftermath of the 9/11 attacks has wrought many changes; one of them is an intensifying extension of the logic of offshoring to core security functions of the state. These trends all counsel much greater attention to the past, present, and future of territoriality.

Territoriality Over Time

Many books and articles have been written on America's late-nineteenth-century rush to empire and the resulting debate over constitutional rights in the new colonies. Likewise, there is a substantial literature, largely legal and doctrinal, on postwar extraterritorial jurisdiction in narrow and technical areas such as antitrust law, securities regulation, and labor law. Many pages are devoted to the constitutional relationship between native tribes and the U.S. government and the resulting patchwork of law in "Indian country." There are also studies of consular courts and capitulations, the law and politics of citizenship, the global network of American military bases, and the dramatic postwar rise of overseas law enforcement. And in the last few years, a flourishing literature has examined the Bush administration's strategy of offshore detention, military occupation, and extraordinary rendition.

To date, scholars have largely treated these as separate phenomena. Each is a rich and complex topic, and writers from many disciplines have successfully explored their nuances and consequences. Yet the linkages among them are compelling. Consequently, I have argued that territoriality in the law of the United States ought to be understood as a cohesive, though complex, phenomenon. There are varying strands, to be sure, and both continuity and change across time. By analyzing these episodes together we necessarily lose detail and texture. But we gain from this synthesis an understanding of the surprisingly broad and underappreciated themes that link them.

As noted above, extraterritoriality reflects an effort to manage or mitigate difference. It is a response to heterogeneity in the international system—and to the incentives, in terms of wealth, power, and security—to reduce (or occasionally capitalize on) that heterogeneity. Even in the supposedly "flat" world of today, heterogeneity in law across the globe is readily apparent. These differences among domestic political and legal systems are deeply rooted, protected and reinforced by the Westphalian conception of territorial sovereignty that has reigned supreme for centuries. Indeed, the very point of territorial sovereignty was to enable each government to establish and defend a unique domestic order within his or her demarcated zone of control. The Westphalian system emerged in response to violent conflict, and aimed to preserve peace by walling off the domain of one sovereign from that of another.

The resulting heterogeneity across territories is unproblematic and even salutary in many areas of law and policy. But it also engenders high costs. Reducing those costs often entails international agreements and organizations. Although this form of "difference management" has received extensive attention, far less attention has been paid to the option of extraterritoriality. Just as the rise of the ambassador and of diplomatic immunity in the Renaissance was an accommodation between nascent sovereign control of territorial city-states on the one hand, and the need for rulers to cooperate on the other, the episodes explored in this book all reflect the idea of a territorial sovereign facing and attempting to manage the challenges of a global world by manipulating rules of territoriality. Extraterritoriality minimized the costs, to key American constituencies, of the legal differences inherent in territorial sovereignty.

Comparing postwar effects-based extraterritoriality to prewar consular courts in Asia and the Islamic world illustrates this common dynamic.

Nineteenth-century capitulations functioned as a sort of halfway house between full sovereign respect and imperial control. Formal imperialism reached its peak at the start of the twentieth century, and although impressive—Britain at one point ruled over a quarter of the globe—not all the non-Western world was colonized by the great powers. As chapter 3 detailed, in many instances Western powers instead sought a lesser or at least less formal mode of control: control over the legal apparatus, and substantive rules, that their nationals would fall under while residing in alien societies.

China is a paradigmatic example. The vast Chinese market was viewed then as now with some awe, and extraterritorial jurisdiction permitted the many Western traders and missionaries to safely reside in China without fear of its allegedly uncivilized legal system. This extraterritorial regime humiliated China. But China was powerless to end it for a very long time. Indeed, the U.S. District Court for China formally disbanded only in 1943. Extraterritoriality in China reflected many concerns, not only the imperative of increasing commerce between East and West. But commerce was central, and extraterritorial jurisdiction made it easier for the United States to engage China economically. Faced with enormous legal heterogeneity, and unable or unwilling to conquer China, the United States instead followed the lead of other great powers in demanding extraterritorial rights. The result was that American traders resided in a sort of legal bubble—one that, by protecting them from unfamiliar Chinese law, facilitated their sojourns in a strange land.

After the Second World War this system of capitulations entered a deep and terminal decline. Self-determination and sovereign equality were the new watchwords of the international order. With the backing of the United States, and of the new United Nations Charter, these principles were entrenched across the globe. The postwar era nonetheless ushered in new forms of extraterritoriality. Prominent among these was the effects-based theory of jurisdiction. Effects-based extraterritoriality entered the American legal system just 2 years after the demise of the U.S. District Court for China. The animating purpose behind this new form of extraterritoriality was the control of transboundary effects. Rather than projecting American law into a foreign zone, the new extraterritoriality focused on policing actors overseas who created significant impacts on American markets and territory.

Effects-based jurisdiction was certainly at odds with the traditional focus in U.S. law on respect for sovereignty and adherence to strict notions of territoriality. The United States in the nineteenth century frequently paid homage to Westphalian principles. As the Supreme Court announced in the 1824 case of *The Apollon*, "the laws of no nation can justly extend beyond its own territory, except so far as regards its own citizens. They can have no force to control the sovereignty or rights of any other nation, within its jurisdiction."[3] Statements such as this, of which there are many, embodied the essence of Westphalian territoriality.

As a weak state, the early United States was unsurprisingly drawn to such principles. It was particularly concerned by the prospect of incursions into its territorial sovereignty by the major hegemonic power of the day, Great Britain. Secretary of State John Calhoun's statement to the British government in 1844 was typical of the time:

> We hold that the criminal jurisdiction of a nation is limited to its own dominions and to vessels under its flag on the high seas, and that it cannot extend it to acts committed within the dominion of another without violating its sovereignty and independence. Standing on this well-established and unquestioned principle, we cannot permit Great Britain or any other nation ... to infringe our sovereignty and independence by extending its criminal jurisdiction to acts committed within the limits of the United States.[4]

The postwar innovation of effects-based jurisdiction pioneered in cases like *Alcoa v. U.S.* thus signaled a distinctive vision of jurisdiction. It was a vision, moreover, that many believe was necessitated by the burgeoning globalization of the postwar era, which increasingly created regional and global markets that challenged national regulatory systems.[5] Yet pairing it with the capitulation system shows that it was not a wholly novel development, nor a bolt from the blue.

Like its nineteenth-century predecessor, effects-based extraterritoriality served to harmonize law across heterogeneous jurisdictions. It "flattened" the legal landscape in order to further the interests of the United States. Here, however, the impetus was not perceived barbarism or corruption but concern over unequal burdens in the context of a newly invigorated regulatory state. The aim was to subject foreigners to U.S. law, rather than protect Americans from foreign law. In both cases, however, the result was more commercial opportunity for Americans.

Effects-based extraterritoriality also bolstered the powerful regulatory state then emerging in the United States. By projecting U.S. law overseas when courts inferred that Congress intended to, extraterritoriality expanded the effective geographic scope of regulation enormously. American firms competing in an increasingly international market benefited from this extension; although incumbents might have preferred a different (and weaker) set of rules altogether in areas like antitrust, better that foreign competitors faced the same rules they did than operate within a more favorable legal climate. U.S. consumers benefited, as well, to the degree the relevant laws reflected shared social and political values. American officials, tasked with enforcing the law at home, also wanted to ensure that their efforts at regulation and prosecution were not thwarted by actors taking advantage of the expedience of acting just over the border. In short, assertions of extraterritoriality were a way to level the legal playing field across jurisdictions.

To be sure, effects-based extraterritoriality was not the only way to level the playing field. A more familiar alternative was to entrench U.S. domestic law in international law. In the wake of new domestic regulatory statutes, affected actors within the United States often pressed the executive branch to negotiate multilateral treaties that bound foreigners to similar rules. More informal, network-based alliances of national regulators were another approach to rule harmonization.[6] In the past, empire provided yet another way to minimize differences in rules. Each of these choices—to conquer and control a foreign territory; to negotiate new international rules; to harmonize informally; and to assert domestic law extraterritoriality—reduced the impact of the legal differences inherent in Westphalian sovereignty.

Postwar extraterritoriality did so, however, in a distinctive fashion. Rather than multilateral or bilateral negotiation, it was unilateral. Rather than applying to only some states, as was the case with capitulations, it was applicable everywhere. Rather than targeting the weak and the peripheral, it primarily targeted the rich and the strong (though from the vantage point of the even greater wealth and power of the United States). Rather than being explicitly unequal—Americans in China faced American law, but Chinese in the United States did not face Chinese law—it was a tool that in theory could be used by any state against actors in any other state.

To work, however, effects-based jurisdiction required that the relevant actors have some valuable asset or stake in the jurisdiction-asserting state that made them vulnerable to suit.[7] For an enormous market like the United States this was often true. And although it took some time for other large markets to do the same, in recent years European states have also adopted the effects-based approach. Other major powers have ceased fighting the United States about its penchant for unilateral extraterritoriality and instead have joined it.

Extraterritoriality in the postwar era was of course not limited to regulation. As chapter 5 described, the onset of the Cold War fostered a striking change in U.S. security policy. Rather than retreating back to its Western hemispheric redoubt after victory in 1945, American forces remained overseas in large numbers. Containment, the reigning political strategy of the Cold War, entailed the projection of power across the globe. To do so, the United States developed large offshore bases, and by the 1950s it possessed an unrivaled and unprecedented network of military installations. These bases were occasionally sited on soil controlled by the United States, such as occupied Berlin or Guantanamo Bay. But the vast majority was within the territories of allied states. This structure was historically anomalous; great powers in the past had overseas bases in their colonies, but only very rarely on the territory of allied or peer states.[8]

To ensure that legal differences in the states that hosted American bases did not serve as an impediment to U.S. base policy, the United States established dozens of status of forces agreements. These agreements sought to keep overseas GIs under American law as much as possible. In some states, such as Britain, the differences between local and American law were minimal. More significant in these cases were the political implications of foreign control over American troops. But in other cases the legal differences were notable. Either way, extraterritoriality permitted the United States to extend its military power overseas while insulating itself from many of the implications of presence in another sovereign's domain.

Again, a sort of extraterritorial bubble was created for Americans. This system certainly did not go as far as the nineteenth-century capitulations in creating an offshore legal order. But by minimizing the control of local governments over U.S. troops and dependents, postwar status of forces agreements addressed a very large group of individuals and ensured that the complex relationships among the Western allies were as smooth as possible.

In short, the legal differences inherent in the Westphalian system of territorial sovereignty create strong incentives for extraterritoriality. Hegemonic powers in the past reacted to these incentives by creating empires and negotiating unequal treaties; in the twentieth century these reactions took the form of effects-based extraterritoriality, status of forces agreements, and extraterritorial law enforcement. Extraterritoriality should consequently be understood as an important yet underappreciated alternative to more familiar forms of managing difference across jurisdictions, whether more consensual, such as the negotiation of treaties, or more coercive, such as colonization. With imperialism and international law, it shares a common root in the fundamental tension between sovereignty and interdependence.

Core and Periphery

American law has long distinguished between a legal core and a legal periphery. This divide has been marked out within the borders of the United States, not outside those borders. This intraterritorial distinction is in a sense a mirror of the harmonizing impulse just discussed. Extraterritoriality in its varied forms served to *reduce* difference by extending U.S. law outward into the realms of other sovereigns or near-sovereigns. Here, by contrast, we see the federal government seeking to *establish* difference by withdrawing American law inward toward an internally defined core.

In the constitutional periphery—such as federal territory, overseas colonies, and Indian country—the government has, to varying degrees, sought to deny inhabitants the full measure of legal protections. The result is that the Constitution does not necessarily reign where the United States rules.

Intraterritoriality is grounded in domestic law, not international law. Yet it reflects the long-prevailing practice of empire, which rested on the idea that imperial powers could rule colonies distinctively. As a recent history of empires notes, "whereas states ... integrate their populations equally— above all, grant them equal rights whether they live at the core of the state or in its border regions—this is not the case with empires: there is almost always a scale of integration descending from centre to periphery."[9] For the United States intraterritorial differentiation was particularly fraught, because the American political system was based on the idea of a limited government that both rested on the consent of the governed and was respectful of equality (however imperfectly defined for most of American history). To many, to carve out distinctive geographic areas for differentiated rule flew in the face of the American political tradition.

Constitutionalism has consequently long stood in tension with imperial-ism. The great nineteenth-century theorist of sea power Alfred Thayer Mahan once proclaimed that "any project of extending the sphere of the United States is met by the constitutional lion in the path."[10] Yet history shows that the "constitutional lion" may well have roared, but it rarely lunged. Despite Mahan's fears, constitutional concerns have rarely stood in the way of expansion; geographic expansion has been an enduring and central feature of American history. The embrace of intraterritoriality by the United States made colonial expansion far easier, by minimizing the governance costs associated with controlling territory populated by alien peoples with differing cultures and languages.

A striking example of intraterritoriality is the concept of "Indian coun-try." In the early nineteenth century the Supreme Court noted that "[t]he Indian territory is admitted to compose a part of the United States ... In all our intercourse with foreign nations ... [Indians] are considered as within the jurisdictional limits of the United States."[11] Nonetheless, the judiciary emphasized time and again that Indian country was distinct from the rest of the United States and often subject to different rules. Because the tribes were "domestic dependent nations," in some domains tribal law applied, whereas in others federal power took precedence. In Indian country the federal government acted with a breadth and depth of power it never possessed within the states. Yet as far as the larger world was concerned, Indian lands were as much American territory as the city of Philadelphia.

The intraterritorial distinction between core and periphery arose with regard to federal territories as well. The antebellum debate between Daniel Webster and John Calhoun is illustrative. Webster asserted that the

Constitution was made for the states alone, and did not extend automatically to the territories. Calhoun countered that the Constitution always followed the flag. Obviously, he pointed out, Congress could not do as it pleased in the federal territories: "Can you establish titles of nobility in California?" he asked rhetorically. "If not, if all the negative provisions extend to the territories, why not the positive?"[12]

Calhoun's clever question was telling. Why was it that only those rights that the federal government found inconvenient or cumbersome failed to apply in peripheral American territories? As a political matter the answer was obvious: intraterritorial distinctions made governance easier by reducing restraints on executive power. Yet it was difficult to convincingly distinguish between those constitutional provisions that bound the federal government everywhere—like the prohibition on noble titles—and those that did not.

As chapter 2 described, the essence of the Calhoun-Webster debate eventually reached the Supreme Court in the infamous case of *Dred Scott*. The Court followed Calhoun's lead, holding that the government "cannot, when it enters a Territory of the United States, put off its character and assume discretionary or despotic powers which the Constitution has denied to it."[13] In a passage reminiscent of the Supreme Court's extension of habeas rights to Guantanamo some 150 years later, the Court also emphasized that imperialism was not a way out of this constraint on "despotism." "There is certainly no power," said the justices, "... to establish or maintain colonies ... to be ruled and governed at its own pleasure, nor to enlarge its territorial limits in any way except by the admission of new States."[14] In short, *Dred Scott* seemed to declare some forms of intraterritoriality dead. The United States government could not rule "despotically" within particular zones of its established territory, nor could it acquire new territory to rule despotically.

Although the outcome of the Civil War and the repudiation of slavery appeared to inter *Dred Scott* forever, the American embrace of empire at the dawn of the twentieth century brought back to life its debate over the geographic reach of constitutional rights. Could the United States govern with the islands with fewer constitutional restrictions—or, in the Supreme Court's more pejorative words—with despotic powers? Could it draw constitutional distinctions between the mainland and offshore possessions? The answer had major economic, legal, and political implications. It determined whether goods from the islands could enter duty free at mainland ports (and therefore more effectively compete with goods from the homeland); whether the United States needed to respect the full, and costly, panoply of constitutional protections when governing the local populace; and, as a result of both of these, whether the new imperial project was politically viable.

The desire to retain the new colonies was palpable. Americans at the time understood they were on the cusp of great power, and many sought to follow the lead of Great Britain in using island colonies as a strategy of geopolitical control.[15] Some of the justices on the Court acknowledged that the principles enunciated in *Dred Scott*, if taken at face value, were inconsistent with empire. None thought it possible that these islands, with their alien and non-English speaking populations, could as a political matter be treated as part of the core of the United States. Some form of distinction was essential. Given this, *Dred Scott's* tainted reputation was very welcome; it made it easier to ignore the implications of the decision for the new century.

With *Dred Scott* shunted aside, the Supreme Court could more easily endorse intraterritorial distinctions. The legal key became the theory of "incorporation." The animating idea was that international law gave sovereign states a range of options with regard to a newly acquired territory. The United States had the power, derived from its status as a sovereign state, to decide whether these territories were "incorporated" into the constitutional core.[16] Those not incorporated did not enjoy the full protections of the Constitution.

The implications of the theory for American foreign policy were obvious. By allowing the United States to remove some sovereign territory from the reach of the Constitution, incorporation greatly facilitated the move toward empire.[17] Here again we see international law and perceived political realities used to grant flexibility, strengthen executive power, and weaken constitutional constraints. The Supreme Court was remarkably explicit about this. Without this discretionary power of incorporation, said the Court, the United States would be left "helpless in the family of nations."[18] The triumph of the theory of incorporation meant that United States became, as a colonizer, more like other great powers that were generally unfettered by complex (and costly) bills of rights and restrictive constitutional principles. Intraterritoriality, in short, cabined the costs of American constitutionalism, providing a way to reconcile the nation's constitutional past with its great power future.

Intraterritoriality also abetted extraterritoriality. The principle that *some* constitutional rights could be denied *within* American borders made it easier to maintain that *no* constitutional rights applied *outside* those borders. The late-nineteenth-century precedent of *In re Ross* had established that constitutional rights did not restrict the United States when, for example, it tried a U.S. citizen in another sovereign's domain. The result was a remarkably free hand for the United States when it acted offshore—freer even than in its imperial domains. As American constitutional law was transformed in the twentieth century however, this doctrine, grounded in the nineteenth-century system of capitulations, seemed increasingly difficult to defend. But the executive branch found frequently found solace in the *Insular Cases*, which helpfully bolstered the contention that the Constitution had no extraterritorial power.

Just as intraterritorial distinctions made the acquisition of American empire far easier, extraterritorial distinctions made the postwar global projection of American power far easier. Major offshore military bases, to be sustainable, required the presence of families and other civilians. The number of such dependents was surprisingly large; during the Cold War the United States essentially created a vast network of large American towns around the world. Here, too, the executive branch believed that it was impractical and costly to govern these offshore cities consistent with constitutional precepts. It was much easier to use the existing court-martial system to try civilians as well as service members. This system survived until the 1957 decision in *Reid v. Covert*, in which the Supreme Court suddenly and dramatically reversed itself, declaring that the Bill of Rights did indeed extend to citizens overseas.

Whether the new constitutional extraterritorialism announced in that case applies only to citizens of the United States—whether the transformation worked was one of recalibrated principles of territoriality or revived principles of personality—is an issue that continues to be debated in courtrooms today. That the rights of citizens no longer evaporated at the U.S. border did not necessarily mean the same was true of aliens. The *Reid* court several times invoked citizenship. And before the 1960s, instances in which the United States asserted jurisdiction over aliens outside American territory were relatively few and far between. As a result, there were few direct precedents addressing the offshore rights of aliens. But as the United States began to deploy an ever larger array of law enforcement agents abroad to combat growing transnational trafficking, the issue grew in importance. Seizures on the high seas and joint ventures with foreign police became more common, and consequently the federal courts increasingly had to determine whether the normal array of legal fetters on law enforcement applied extraterritorially. The executive branch here again argued that legal protections were different, and weaker, outside American borders.

Changing ideas about constitutional rights, however, increasingly rubbed up against this position in the postwar era. Cases from the 1970s and 1980s such as *Toscanino v. United States*, the *Tiede* decision in the U.S. Berlin Court, and the Ninth Circuit in the case of drug trafficker Rene Verdugo embraced an expansive reading of the grand principles announced in *Reid*. For a time it looked as if the Constitution followed the federal government, rather than simply the flag. Proponents saw an emerging norm of equal treatment that applied anywhere the U.S. government acted and was grounded in the human rights of all persons. Opponents saw a dangerous and unfounded global constitutionalism propounded by idealist and unelected judges. This brief era turned out to be a high watermark of the extraterritorial Constitution. In 1990 the Supreme Court declared that the Fourth Amendment did not apply to a search of drug trafficker Rene Verdugo-Urquidez's Mexican homes. The opinion was fractured in its reasoning, but the result was clear. The Fourth Amendment—and perhaps many other amendments—did not extend beyond the borders of the United States.

The connections between intraterritoriality and extraterritoriality are perhaps most striking in the unusual saga of Guantanamo Bay. The George W. Bush administration carefully considered its options as the Afghan war unfolded, and, with some justification, came to the conclusion that Guantanamo was outside the reach of the federal courts. The base was one step removed from the "normal" offshore possessions of the United States; though under the complete and indefinite control of the United States, it retained a flimsy veneer of foreign sovereignty sufficient (it was hoped) to deny any constitutional restrictions whatsoever. Guantanamo came to exemplify the effort to draw distinctions between different geographic zones under American control in order to maximize the flexibility and power of the executive branch.

This particular episode is still unfolding. But it is clear that many in the U.S. judiciary are quite uncomfortable with the idea that the government can slip its constitutional fetters by choosing the location of detention or, as in Guantanamo, by using international agreements of a dubious nature to allocate sovereignty (and thus rights) elsewhere. The landmark 2008 decision in *Boumediene v. Bush* made this distaste plain when it held that at least some constitutional rights apply to the aliens held at Guantanamo.

Yet nothing in the decision necessarily repudiated the *Insular Cases*, for the right to contest detention has long been seen as the sort of fundamental right that exists even in American colonies. In other words, even if Guantanamo is ultimately treated as identical in all respects to its Caribbean neighbor Puerto Rico, it remains unclear if the full panoply of constitutional rights applies there. Guantanamo can easily be normalized into the prevailing, if dusty, intraterritorial framework of law. Nonetheless, in *Boumediene* we see the contemporary Supreme Court chastising the government for trying to evade the Constitution by moving actors and activities around in space—a practice built on territorial distinctions. Equally important, the Supreme Court stressed in *Boumediene* that considerations of practicality and control—not sovereignty—determine the effective scope of constitutional protections. Functional considerations of effects and relationships, in short, seem now to trump formal considerations of sovereignty—just as occurred many decades ago in a wide range of non-constitutional legal doctrines.

How far this principle really extends will determine much about the legal framework of American power in the twenty-first century. Already the vast majority of detainees held by the United States are not in Guantanamo but in Bagram Air Base in Afghanistan, Iraqi facilities of various kinds, and other offshore sites located on the soil of friendly nations. Easy analogies between Guantanamo and "ordinary" federal territory do not readily apply to these sites. Indeed, in one of its earliest litigation decisions, the Obama administration rejected such an analogy and pointedly affirmed the territorialist stance of the Bush administration. The Obama administration contended that despite the decision in *Boumediene*, habeas corpus did not extend to Bagram Air Base because Bagram lacked the "exceptional circumstances that led the Supreme Court to extend the writ to detainees at Guantanamo Bay."[19] But there is little doubt that the United States possesses a significant, if not overwhelming, measure of jurisdiction and control at these facilities.

Drug war analysts commonly use the metaphor of a balloon to explain their inability to stanch the flow of narcotics into the United States: squeeze one part and the balloon pops out in another. The struggle between the courts and the executive branch over the rights of foreign detainees may share similar characteristics. As the CIA's use of black-site prisons illustrates, in a globalizing world of rapid transportation, offshore "jurisdiction shopping" by the government is surprisingly easy. As Guantanamo is squeezed, Bagram becomes more attractive.

Indeed, in some respects the interesting question is why the United States has not moved more activities off shore, where constitutional rights are at least hazy, if not often unavailable. A sizable fraction of the inmates in federal prisons, for instance, are aliens. Prisons for these ordinary criminals could be located off shore in Mexico or Colombia; not only would detention costs be lower, legal rights would be even further diminished. Such ideas have already been floated.[20] In sum whether future U.S. courts will embrace the functional, practicality-oriented path signaled by *Boumediene*, or retreat to the welter of older territorial precedents, has important implications that extend well beyond the current crisis.

From the Outside In

In a classic article some 30 years ago Peter Gourevitch explored the ways in which international politics shape domestic politics.[21] Gourevitch contrasted this perspective with the more common "inside-out" or "second-image" approach, which looks to how domestic forces and trends shape world politics. He canvassed a perspective that looks in the opposite direction: "from the outside in."[22]

This viewpoint proved influential in the study of international relations and in comparative politics. Yet as chapter 1 of this book noted, it has had far less impact on the study of American politics. As one authoritative survey notes, it is still true today that "the degree and character of influence exercised by international factors on American political development remains remarkably unprobed."[23] For the most part, research into the political development of the United States has, outside of a few obvious areas such as trade politics, failed to explore the significance of the global context.

This myopia is even more acute in the study of American law. At a certain level few would disagree that the international context has shaped domestic law; the U.S. Constitution, for instance, reflects the ideals of a "Tudor polity" on a distant continent far removed from the endemic war of eighteenth-century Europe.[24] Yet it is the rare work that directly considers how international forces have shaped American law. Nonetheless, like domestic politics, domestic law is often subject to powerful pressures from abroad. Even areas of the law that seem wrapped up in domestic struggles, such as the pursuit of racial equality, can be better understood through an international lens. For example, Mary Dudziak has shown how the Cold War, and the powerful contest it spawned for the allegiance of the emerging states of the Third World, had a dramatic impact on the struggle for civil rights in the United States. Landmark decisions such as *Brown v. Board of Education* were deeply influenced by the concern that coercive segregation was harming American foreign relations and costing the nation allies in its battle against communism.[25] This sort of analysis is exceptional; it is unusual for legal scholars to think systematically about the influence of international relations on legal change.

This book has deliberately embraced an international orientation. To be sure, the study of territoriality lends itself to this approach; it is not surprising that international factors are significant in the evolution of legal rules that themselves draw deeply from international law. But existing studies of discrete aspects of territoriality have failed to move much beyond this linkage, nor have they connected the larger themes of territoriality to major trends and events in American foreign policy and in the international system. The evolution of territoriality, intraterritoriality, and extraterritoriality in the United States cannot be understood absent a global context.

The most significant such connection relates to the rise of American power and the shifting place of the United States within the international order. As a young state with few resources, the United States of the eighteenth and early nineteenth centuries was naturally drawn to principles of Westphalian territoriality. British and French forces were still formidable, and the early United States found solace in rules of international law that denied one sovereign influence or control in another. Extraterritoriality was then seen as "incompatible with the principle of sovereign equality, since sovereignty is characterized specifically by the exclusivity of a sovereign state's normative powers in its own territory."[26]

Thus when Secretary of State John Calhoun insisted in the nineteenth century that the United States "cannot permit Great Britain or any other nation ... to infringe our sovereignty and independence by extending its criminal jurisdiction to acts committed within the limits of the United States," he was invoking Westphalian territoriality as a shield against Britain. Invoking territoriality was of course not itself a powerful bulwark against aggression by more powerful enemies. Violations of such rules are plentiful in world history. Rather, because the international legal system is suffused with principles of reciprocity and consistency, the federal government and the courts were keen to adhere to those rules that appeared to best serve American interests of the time. Persistent invocation of strict territorial principles helped to at least reduce provocation. From this point of view, it was no surprise that the Supreme Court would regularly announce, as it did in 1812, that "the jurisdiction of the nation within its own territory is necessarily exclusive and absolute."[27] Similar statements abound throughout the nineteenth century.

As the United States finally began to translate its considerable economic power into military and political power, these doctrines began to chafe. The United States increasingly sought to shape actors and events around the world. Already in the nineteenth century the United States had embraced traditional incursions into the domain of other nations in the form of foreign capitulations and consular jurisdiction. What changed was its willingness to move past these traditional limits by claiming jurisdiction over acts occurring within the territorial domain of other great powers. The rise of effects-based jurisdiction, extraterritorial protections for overseas troops, and offshore law enforcement were all related to this newfound American power and assertiveness.

Here again we can observe the parallels between extraterritoriality and international institutions. The dramatic wave of institution building that took place after 1945 has been closely analyzed by many students of international affairs. Less widely noticed is that the United States also pioneered new conceptions of territoriality in this era. The Second World War ended in two major settlements.[28] One was military and took the form of Cold War bipolarity. The other was economic and political and took the form of a dense network of institutions among the United States and the other major industrialized democracies. Each settlement also corresponded to a major new form of extraterritoriality. The widespread use of status of forces agreements in the Cold War employed extraterritorial jurisdiction to facilitate containment and the forward deployment of U.S. forces. And the rise of the effects-based theory employed extraterritorial jurisdiction to reinforce American competitiveness and maintain a level economic playing field for American firms in world markets.

That the United States grew from a weak to a strong state is thus central to the transformation of legal doctrines of territoriality, but it is not the entire story. The international system itself has changed dramatically over the last two centuries. These changes largely decreased the barriers to extraterritoriality while increasing the incentives for it. For example, the combination of rising economic interdependence and a more expansive regulatory and criminal law apparatus at home helped to propel American law outward. As I have argued throughout this book, however, contemporary forms of extraterritoriality were not foreordained by growing globalization. High levels of interdependence before World War I coincided with the high point of strict territoriality. And the birth of the effects-based extraterritoriality actually coincided with a relative low point in economic interdependence.

Instead, as chapter 4 described, it was the juxtaposition of several factors—such as the postwar expansion of competition between national firms (intra-industry trade), the entrenchment of the post–New Deal regulatory state, and the demise of classical legal thought—that conspired to make extraterritorial regulation far more attractive to the United States. The cheaper movement of goods and services in a world of territorially differentiated states was certainly influential. But only in conjunction with national regulatory rules and global competition did globalization meaningfully raise the costs of legal difference. In short, globalization was a driver of legal change, but it had many passengers that helped guide the way.

Although these factors help explain demand for extraterritorial regulation, a different set of international factors promoted its supply. In the nineteenth century, to extend national law into another sovereign's domain was widely seen as a dangerous repudiation of Westphalian principles. What made the postwar era different, at least for the United States?

The dramatic decline of territorial warfare, the stability of bipolarity, and the intricate institutional enmeshing of the Western powers after 1945— what has been arrestingly called the "logic of the West"—stand in stark contrast to the endemic great power conflict of the nineteenth century.[29] These developments created a novel and permissive political climate, one in which the advanced industrial democracies essentially renounced war amongst themselves and pursued disputes through legal and diplomatic means. In this context conflict over jurisdiction took on a far more benign cast. Europe and Japan certainly complained vociferously about U.S. violations of established doctrines of territoriality. Yet they did not rattle sabers in response. The American experiment with effects-based extraterritoriality was thus in many respects an entirely rational, and even overdetermined, response to an altered geopolitical context.

Likewise, the Cold War and its high-stakes nuclear stalemate permitted and encouraged a massive offshore troop presence on friendly soil. Some measure of jurisdictional immunity for American forces was a small price for allied nations to pay for protection against the perceived Soviet threat. In a bipolar world nations aligned with one or the other pole; for the Western powers the choice was clear. Extraterritorial protections for American troops were thus a building block in the larger security settlement that scholars like John Ikenberry have described.[30] In short, both in economic and in security terms the postwar international system enabled the flourishing of new forms of extraterritoriality.

My focus on the influence of international system highlights an important limitation of this book: the very uniqueness of the United States—its huge economy, its federal structure, its comparatively ancient constitution, its tremendous territorial expansion, and its dramatic rise to global leadership—may make it difficult to draw out plausible lessons for other states. Some aspects of the story told here are certainly uniquely American. Only the United States has a vast network of military bases encircling the globe, for instance, and thus only the United States has faced so many issues of extraterritoriality with regard to foreign-deployed troops. (Other states, such as Britain, have remnants of imperial systems, but those systems relied far more on colonization than on bases arranged via international agreements with friendly powers.) The United States is also one of the few great powers with a wide array of indigenous peoples within its borders, a situation that has prompted some of the most unusual aspects of intraterritoriality.

Yet these contrasts should not be overdrawn. Much of the early doctrine of the United States with regard to territoriality was drawn straightfor-wardly from international and English law. Likewise, the embrace of empire by the United States in 1899 followed decades (and centuries) of rampant imperialism by European powers. Indeed, Kipling's famous poem about "the white man's burden," which introduced this book, was directly aimed at the United States, imploring Americans to act like other great powers. The burst of American imperialism after 1898 was anomalous only from an internal, domestic perspective. Externally, what was anomalous was instead Amer-ica's long period of "imperial understretch."[31] Likewise, capitulations in Asia and elsewhere were not uniquely American; many great powers had asserted extraterritorial jurisdiction outside the West. The U.S. District Court for China was even modeled on the British Supreme Court for China.

The parallels between the United States and other great powers continued into the twentieth century, even as the United States grew into a superpower. By the end of the twentieth century, for example, many other industrialized democracies had begun both to engage in overseas policing and to claim effects-based jurisdiction over offshore actors. European nations fought the American effects theory for decades, yet once the European Community grew in size and wealth it chose to switch rather than fight. As a result, today "a number of European states have begun to apply selected national regulatory statutes extraterritorially ... arousing complaints from both the United States and international businesses."[32]

By the 1990s Canada, Denmark, France, Germany, Japan, Norway, Spain, and Switzerland, among others, had adopted something akin to the effects doctrine. The European Commission has become an active exponent of extraterritorial jurisdiction.

In short, the United States is certainly a special case with exceptional features. But much about the career of territoriality in American law can be discerned in the experiences of other major powers. This is reflective of a larger point: the evolution of territoriality, intraterritoriality, and extraterritoriality in the United States cannot be understood absent a global context. International politics has deeply shaped not only domestic politics, but also domestic law.

Territoriality and Extraterritoriality in the Twenty-First Century

It is tempting to trace out an arc across American history from the strict territoriality of the past to the extraterritoriality of today: from a time when sovereign borders were thought sacrosanct to a more fluid and interdependent world of overlapping jurisdictions. Many believe the Internet extends this deterritorializing trend even further: cyberspace yields the ultimate borderless world.[33] As this book has emphasized, however, the reality is more complex.

It is true that traditional Westphalian territoriality—visible in the nineteenth century in a range of legal areas, from the law of personal jurisdiction to statutory interpretation to constitutional doctrine—has eroded over time. In some respects the legal changes are marked. From the 1890 decision of *In re Ross*, holding that the Constitution does not apply to American officials acting within other nations, to the 1957 decision in *Reid v. Covert*, interring *Ross* as a "relic from another era," the spatial ambit of the Bill of Rights underwent a transformation. Likewise, postwar effects-based jurisdiction, largely unremarkable by the 1980s, would have been almost unimaginable in the 1880s, when the Supreme Court declared that it was an "axiom of international jurisprudence" that "the laws of a country have no extra-territorial force."[34] Even as late as 1909 Oliver Wendell Holmes pointedly rejected the idea that American law could reach within another sovereign's domain, calling it a startling proposition.[35]

Although these changes are undeniable and significant, there is no simple path from older, territorial concepts of jurisdiction to a contemporary globalized world of extraterritoriality. Extraterritoriality was common prior to the Second World War, albeit in a different form than today. And the dawn of the twentieth century was actually a highly interdependent era, one that coincided with the acknowledged zenith of Westphalian territoriality in U.S. law. A territorial age did not simply give way to an extraterritorial age; extraterritoriality was instead transformed, expanded, and reconfigured over history to meet the challenges of a new great power in a new international order.

This surprising degree of continuity is hard to discern absent the kind of synoptic vision offered by this book. The extraterritoriality of the many postwar status of forces agreements is a direct descendent of the extraterritoriality of capitulations and consular courts. Likewise, the postwar effects theory, though novel, served a similar rule-harmonizing purpose as consular jurisdiction in the nineteenth century. Intraterritorial distinctions drawn in the age of American empire have their roots in much older concepts and practices, such as Indian country, and yet retain vitality even in the twenty-first century. Other examples abound; because these continuities are more a matter of function than form, however, they tend to be overlooked. They go to the *reasons why* the United States has asserted extraterritoriality or reinforced territoriality, rather than the precise manner in which these claims have been made.

Still, it is undeniable that in some areas territorial rules have retained their form as well as their function. Consider the rights of aliens in domestic law. Gerald Neuman and others have ably pointed out the complex history of the constitutional rights of aliens.[36] Aliens on U.S. territory have long been treated much like citizens. Courts have generally held, however, that when abroad they lack any constitutional rights against the United States. Their geographic location decisively determines the bundle of rights they enjoy.

In this context, territoriality has been used to entrench rather than elide legal differences. From the nineteenth century right up to the present day the executive branch has looked to traditional Westphalian principles to justify weaker protections for overseas citizens and aliens alike, on the grounds that constitutional protections were intrinsically territorial. Moreover, by acting on foreign soil the U.S. government was, in essence, acting at the discretion and at times in the stead of the foreign sovereign. In this manner constitutional rights, seen as costly trumps that interfered with the freedom of action the executive branch desired, could be sidestepped. What made *Reid v. Covert* so noteworthy is that it rejected the long-standing view that treaties with foreign sovereigns (such as status of forces agreements) determined not only the powers the United States wielded in those foreign lands, but also the rights the United States was bound to respect.

The transformation *Reid* worked in this regard was expressly limited to American citizens, however. In justifying its ruling that the Bill of Rights now protected Americans extraterritorially, the Supreme Court pointed to the ancient lineage of personal jurisdiction, a much older principle than territorial jurisdiction. This approach certainly left aliens untouched. Yet aspects of the opinion—that the "United States is entirely a creature of the Constitution...[that can] only act in accordance with all the limitations imposed by the Constitution"—at least suggested that the same principles applied to all persons. This chain of reasoning nodded toward a global conception of constitutional rights. Justice, in short, might be independent of geography and citizenship.

As chapters 5 and 6 described, a few courts in the 1970s and 1980s picked up this flag, but ran only a short way. Soon thereafter the Supreme Court announced in *Verdugo* that "the people" referred to in the Fourth Amendment meant only American citizens, plus those foreigners who were on American soil and had some connection to the nation.[37] The decision cast considerable doubt on whether any other constitutional protections had extraterritorial effect.

The result today is a somewhat tangled skein of doctrine. Constitutional rights generally apply extraterritorially to Americans. Yet only "fundamental" constitutional rights apply in Puerto Rico and some other insular possessions of the United States. (The bizarre result is that the rights of Americans are, as a matter of legal doctrine, more secure when the government acts in Japan than in Puerto Rico.)[38] Aliens abroad can be and often are subject to American statutes and regulations, even if they fully comply with their local law. Yet these aliens "have no cognizable constitutional rights."[39]

It is against this backdrop that the many post-9/11 Guantanamo cases have forced the courts, Congress, and the executive to again grapple with the geographic reach of American law. The most notable example is the striking decision in *Boumediene v. Bush*, upholding the right of alien detainees in Guantanamo to challenge their detention in federal court. *Boumediene* underscored the unique attributes of Guantanamo, and hence its impact beyond that unusual location is uncertain. Nonetheless, the approach outlined in that decision—with its focus on practicality and context, rather than formalities—at least suggests that in other places subject to extensive and stable American control, though not American sovereignty, aliens may also fall within the Constitution's reach.[40]

The Geography of the Constitution

The courts of the United States rarely give a big answer when a smaller one will suffice. Hence the basic question at the heart of many of the disputes described in this book—why, in a liberal polity of limited powers, should constitutional rights vary on one side of a geographic line but not another?—has never been adequately answered. But it has occasionally arisen. At the oral argument in the *Verdugo* litigation Justice Anthony

Kennedy asked the government whether the Constitution ever constrains the executive abroad. "It depends," responded the executive branch lawyer. The "central failing" of the lower court's decision, he continued, "is that they thought it never depends. They thought that the Constitution, as it were, provides a sort of universal declaration of rights of man. It applies whenever, wherever and against whomever government authority acts."[41]

Many legal scholars have contended that, contrary to the claims of the executive branch, the lower court (in this case, the Ninth Circuit) was correct. Looking to the Constitution's animating theory of limited government, expansive conception of rights, and lack of explicit reference to citizenship, some have argued that the most persuasive reading of the Constitution is one that rejects territorial distinctions and reaches all persons everywhere.[42] As the influential champion of human rights Louis Henkin has framed this argument,

> The Constitution does not state its geographic reach or, more specifically, whether it applies solely within the United States . . . Our federal government must not invade the individual rights of any human being. The choice in the Bill of Rights of the word "person" rather than "citizen" was not fortuitous; nor was the absence of a geographical limitation. Both reflect a commitment to respect the individual rights of all human beings.[43]

This perspective is interesting in light of the view of framers such as James Madison that enumerated rights were unnecessary. The move to amend the Constitution to include discrete rights obviously prevailed, and this decision may shed light on the structure of current legal doctrine about the territorial reach of constitutional rights. Because the enumerated rights pertain to individuals, it is perhaps natural that later U.S. courts thought their scope ought to turn on the traits of individuals, such as citizenship.[44] Structural provisions, such as bans on title of nobility, are arguably different. Because they determine the scope of federal power, they apply everywhere the federal government acts. The geographic implications of this distinction between structural and individual rights provisions, noticed as early as the antebellum debates of Calhoun and Webster, undergirded the Supreme Court's reasoning in the *Insular Cases*, and can be traced through many later judicial decisions.

For example, en route to ratifying the new American imperialism, the Supreme Court in the *Insular Cases* asserted a "clear distinction between such prohibitions as go to the very root of the power of Congress to act at all, irrespective of time or place, and such as are operative only 'throughout the United States' or among the several States." Prohibitions on bills of attainder, titles of nobility, and the like go "to the competency of Congress" to pass such a bill, said the court. Whether the same was true for individual rights was left undecided. "We do not wish," said the Court, "to be understood as expressing an opinion how far the bill of rights contained in the first eight amendments is of general and how far of local application."[45]

Yet some constitutional scholars reject the notion that the Bill of Rights lacks structural features. For example, Akhil Amar has argued that the right to a jury trial is best understood not as a right possessed by individual defendants but as a structural constraint on government action, akin to the command of bicameralism and presentment.[46] Under this view the extraterritorial location of a trial is immaterial: just as the Senate could not bypass bicameralism and pass laws on its own by the expedient of convening overseas, so, too, could an American court not, simply by virtue of sitting abroad, convict a criminal absent adherence to the ordinary constitutional rules. By this logic the First Amendment and the Eighth Amendment, for example, certainly appear to have structural features— Congress shall make no law; cruel and unusual punishments shall not be inflicted—-that apply wherever and whenever the federal government acts. But so, too, do other parts of the Bill of Rights.

The structural approach broadly parallels the various judicial decisions that, when considering whether an ordinary domestic statute applies extra-territorially, have focused on where the relevant policy decision is *made* rather than where it is *implemented*. From this perspective an act of the United States government that has extraterritorial effect, but is initiated in a government office somewhere in Washington, is not properly considered an extraterritorial act. The relevant act (or decision) occurs on American soil and is therefore governed by American law. These "headquarters" cases, such as one holding that the National Environmental Policy Act applies to U.S. research facilities in Antarctica, have in practice had the effect of extending domestic legal controls beyond American borders, even though they are not technically couched as "extraterritorial" cases.[47] The result is that certain acts remain forbidden regardless of the fact that their effects are solely felt outside American borders.

These cases thus exhibit a kind of reversed effects principle. Under the standard effects principle, it is the *presence* of transboundary effects that permits American law to govern foreign acts. Here the claim is that the *absence* of national effects is not sufficient to deny that American law governs the act. As long as the act has its origin in, or some connection to, U.S. territory, U.S. law applies. This gives extraterritorial force to Ameri-can law without actually claiming that the law applies extraterritorially.

Similar in structure as well is the usual approach to the Fourteenth Amendment's due process clause in civil litigation. Many judicial decisions have upheld the right of foreign corporations not to be sued in U.S. courts absent "minimum contacts" with the United States.[48] These cases have the effect of granting an alien outside U.S. territory a constitutional right to due process. They thus would seem to grant the foreign defendant an extraterritorial right. This odd outcome is typically rationalized not as extraterritoriality, but instead as relating to a local act; namely, it is litigation in a U.S. court that makes the right to due process applicable.[49] Were the litigation to go forward the defendant would appear before the court, and therefore the right would no longer be extraterritorial. The same basic approach grounded the application of *Miranda* to foreign suspects interrogated abroad in the Bin Laden litigation, discussed in chapter 6. It was their trial within the United States that created a right to a *Miranda* warning, even if the relevant interrogation occurred extraterritorially.[50]

These conceptual niceties aside, the more straightforward way to tackle the question of whether the Constitution has extraterritorial force is to argue, as Henkin does, that geographic or citizenship distinctions simply have no real place in the interpretation of constitutional rights. Proponents of this sweeping view have generally been disappointed, however. As Supreme Court Justice Ruth Bader Ginsburg has succinctly summarized the state of the law, "The Bill of Rights, few would disagree, is our nation's hallmark and pride. One might assume, therefore, that it guides and controls U.S. officialdom wherever in the world they carry our flag or their credentials." But, as Ginsburg notes with some understatement, "that is not our current jurisprudence."[51]

That the persistence of territorial limits on constitutional rights has come under attack from law professors and liberal judges is hardly surprising. What is more noteworthy is that, in the twenty-first century, the detention and trial of suspected terrorists at Guantanamo Bay has become such a potent symbol of unfettered offshore American power. Complaints about the camp's perceived lawlessness came quickly, but the criticisms soon moved beyond civil libertarians, Democrats, and foreign diplomats. Guantanamo became a *cause célèbre* around the world. Plays about the camps have debuted in major cities around the world, and novels have used "the gulag of our times" as a setting for "hopeless imprisonment."[52] Signs of protest have even appeared on fashion runways, with the British designer Vivienne Westwood offering up models in orange underwear strategically emblazoned with "Fair Trial My Arse."[53] The 2008 comedy *Harold and Kumar Go to Guantanamo* amply illustrates just how far Guantanamo's reputation has transcended the chattering classes.

Much of the popular criticism is broad-gauged and not legally sophisticated. But often at the core is the concern—an accurate one—that Guantanamo is a deliberate refuge from the reach of American law, chosen precisely because it is legally distinctive, and subject to nothing other than the whim of the U.S. government. This concern has special resonance abroad in an era of hyperpower, in which there is no credible challenger to American primacy. The response to the attacks of 9/11 caused undeniable consternation even among close allies. The vehemence exhibited against the Bush administration may well largely rest on a fundamental gap in worldviews between the United States and Europe—between, in Robert Kagan's famous phrase, Americans who are from Mars and Europeans who are from Venus.[54] But it may also reflect the fear that a United States that can evade its own constitution will have no difficulty evading international law.

Of course, as fervid as the Guantanamo debate is, this is not the first time the public and elites have disputed the territoriality of American law and imbued the question of the Constitution's geographic scope with political meaning. When the *Insular Cases* were handed down in the 1900s massive crowds formed to hear the news. Newspapers throughout the nation focused on little else. The *New York Daily Tribune* reported "an anxious throng" assembled outside the Supreme Court chambers, waiting to hear the ruling "in a frenzy of excitement."[55] The confusing decision that emerged—that the Constitution only partly followed the flag—was both welcomed and derided. But all saw it as a legal ruling of the utmost importance for the future of both American power and American constitutionalism.

The furor over Guantanamo Bay is thus deeply connected to earlier debates in American history. Today's debate, however, suggests two significant things. First, it reaffirms that questions of territoriality are not simply narrow issues for lawyers to debate. Nor are they simply domestic issues. The human rights revolution of the postwar era has rested on the principle that all individuals possess rights, rights that transcend whatever domestic law or national sovereignty might dictate. Human rights law is in this sense eroding or at least recasting traditional notions of sovereignty. This trend is exemplified by the recent rise of the doctrine of a "responsibility to protect" within the United Nations system, normally a bastion of Westphalian principles of noninterference in domestic affairs.[56] This new conception of sovereignty puts the rights of individuals above state sovereignty; hence for the United States to attempt to use the *absence* of sovereignty to gain greater leeway to detain and punish has raised particular alarm.

The Guantanamo debate has also underscored a powerful disjuncture between the Westphalian doctrines of the past that were revived to bolster the Bush administration's policies in the war on terror and the common understanding of American constitutionalism that the twentieth century has forged. Over the last half-century many Americans have come to see the Constitution as a far-reaching document whose roving powers can rein in almost any malfeasance. To argue that the Constitution does not apply as long as the executive is careful to act only in particular offshore places strikes them—and many others around the world—as a proposition just as startling as Oliver Wendell Holmes, back in 1909, found the now-unexceptional claim that a U.S. statute could govern acts beyond American borders.

NOTES

Preface

1. John Gerard Ruggie, "Territoriality and Beyond: Problematizing Modernity in International Relations," International Organization 47, no. 1 (1993): 174.

Chapter One

1. "Political Party Platforms," *The American Presidency Project*, available at http://www.presidency.ucsb.edu/ws/index.php?pid=29587.

2. Memorandum to William J. Haynes II from Patrick Philpin and John Yoo, December 28, 2001, reprinted in Karen Greenberg and Joshua L. Dratel, eds., *The Torture Papers: The Road to Abu Ghraib* (Cambridge: Cambridge University Press, 2005). As this book will describe, the question of whether constitutional rights follow the flag and whether U.S. courts have jurisdiction over places like Guantanamo are separate but closely linked issues.

3. Dana Priest and Joe Stephens, "Secret World of U.S. Interrogation: Long History of Tactics in Overseas Prisons is Coming to Light," *Washington Post*, May 11, 2004, A1.

4. Richard Stevenson and Joel Brinkley, "More Questions as Rice Asserts Detainee Policy," *New York Times*, December 8, 2005.

5. Johan Steyn, "Guantanamo Bay: A Legal Black Hole," *International and Comparative Law Quarterly* 53, no. 1 (2004); Phillippe Sands, *Lawless World: America and the Making and Breaking of Global Rules—From FDR's Atlantic Charter to George W. Bush's Illegal War* (New York: Viking, 2005).

6. John Agnew, "Territoriality," in Geraldine Pratt et al. (eds.). *The Dictionary of Human Geography*, 5th Edition (Oxford: Blackwell, forthcoming).

7. Lawyers distinguish various forms of jurisdiction. On the permissible bases of jurisdiction see American Law Institute, *Restatement (Third) of the*

Foreign Relations Law of the United States (St. Paul, Minn.: American Law Institute 1987), 1: part 4.

8. Hartford Fire Insurance Co. v. California, 113 Sup. Ct. 2891 (1993).

9. In some cases these statutes police actions that occur and cause harm to Americans abroad, as in laws aimed at terrorist acts outside U.S. borders. This is known as "passive personality" jurisdiction.

10. The question of extraterritoriality does arise vis-à-vis the American states, and there are various cases about whether the law of Georgia can extend into South Carolina and vice versa. Structurally, these cases raise many of the same issues, and involve many of the same principles, as extraterritorial disputes involving international sovereigns.

11. There is a vast literature on sovereign statehood. See, in particular, Stephen D. Krasner, *Sovereignty: Organized Hypocrisy* (Princeton, N.J.: Princeton University Press, 1999); Daniel Philpott, *Revolutions in Sovereignty* (Princeton, N.J.: Princeton University Press, 2001); Saskia Sassen, *Losing Control? Sovereignty in an Age of Globalization* (New York: Columbia University Press, 1996); Robert O. Keohane, "Sovereignty, Interdependence and International Institutions," in *Ideas and Ideals: Essays on Politics in Honor of Stanley Hoffmann*, ed. Linda B. Miller and Michael Smith (Boulder, Colo.: Westview, 1993); Christopher Schreur, "The Waning of the Sovereign State: Towards a New Paradigm for International Law?," *European Journal of International Law* 4, no. 1 (1993); F. H. Hinsley, *Sovereignty*, 2nd ed. (Cambridge: Cambridge University Press, 1986).

12. These views are often critiqued by geographers: e.g., John Agnew, "The Territorial Trap: The Geographical Assumptions of International Relations Theory," *Review of International Political Economy* 1 (1994); John Agnew and Stuart Corbridge, *Mastering Space: Hegemony, Territory, and International Political Economy* (New York: Routledge, 1995).

13. Kenichi Ohmae, *The Borderless World: Power and Strategy in the Interlinked Economy* (New York: HarperCollins, 1999); Thomas Friedman, *The World Is Flat: A Brief History of the 21st Century* (New York: Farrar, Straus and Giroux, 2005).

14. David R. Johnson and David Post, "Law and Borders—The Rise of Law in Cyberspace," *Stanford Law Review* 48, no. 5 (1996): 1370. Numerous examples of cyber conflict are given in Paul Schiff Berman, "The Globalization of Jurisdiction," *University of Pennsylvania Law Review* 151, no. 2 (2002).

15. On globalization see Miles Kahler and David A. Lake, eds., *Governance in a Global Economy: Political Authority in Transition* (Princeton, N.J.: Princeton University Press, 2003); on the Internet see Jack Goldsmith and Tim Wu, *Who Controls the Internet?: Illusions of a Borderless World* (New York: Oxford University Press, 2005); Jack L. Goldsmith, "Against Cyberanarchy," *University of Chicago Law Review* 65, no. 4 (1998); Oliver August, "The Great Firewall: China's Misguided (and Futile) Attempt to Control What Happens Online," *Wired Magazine* 15, no. 11 (October 2007).

16. Friedrich Kratochwil, "Of Systems and Boundaries," *World Politics* 39 (1987): 27.

17. See, e.g., Kratochwil, ibid.; John G. Ruggie, "Territoriality and Beyond: Problematizing Modernity in International Relations," *International Organization* 47, no. 2 (1993) for examples. Some are territorial but do not feature exclusive territoriality; various groups shared a territory or a migration range.

18. Ruggie, "Territoriality and Beyond"; Hendrik Spruyt, *The Sovereign State and Its Competitors* (Princeton, N.J.: Princeton University Press, 1995); Hedley Bull and Adam Watson, eds., *The Expansion of International Society* (New York: Oxford University Press, 1984).

19. Ruggie, "Territoriality and Beyond," 150.

20. E. R. Adair, *The Exterritoriality of Ambassadors in the 16th and 17th Centuries* (London: Longmans, 1929), 11.

21. Johnson v. Eisentrager, 339 U.S. 263, 269 (1950). In fact, Paul was in a Roman territory when he made this plea, so Jackson's interpretation is not entirely apt.

22. J. L. Brierly, "The Lotus Case," *Law Quarterly Review* 44 (1928): 156.

23. F. A. Mann, "The Doctrine of Jurisdiction in International Law," *Recueil des Cours de l'Académie de Droit International* 111, no. 1 (1964): 24.

24. Cedric Ryngaert, "Jurisdiction in International Law, Volume 1" (PhD thesis, Katholieke Universiteit Leuven, 2006), 53. On Westphalia generally, see Leo Gross, "The Peace of Westphalia, 1648–1948," *American Journal of International Law* 42, no. 1 (1948).

25. Ryngaert, "Jurisdiction," 53.

26. The Schooner Exchange v. M'Faddon, 11 U.S. (7 Cranch) 116, 136 (1812). Wheaton argued similarly to the Court in United States v. Bevans, 16 U.S. (3 Wheat.) 336 (1818) at 348, that "[t]he exemption of the territory of every sovereign from any foreign jurisdiction, is a fundamental principle of public law."

27. Krasner, *Sovereignty*; Andreas Osiander, "Sovereignty, International Relations, and the Westphalian Myth," *International Organization* 55 (2001); James Caporaso, "Changes in the Westphalian Order: Territory, Public Authority, and Sovereignty," *International Studies Review* 2, no. 2 (2000); Janice Thomson, *Mercenaries, Pirates, and Sovereigns: State Building and Extraterritorial Violence in Early Modern Europe* (Princeton, N.J.: Princeton University Press, 1994); Spruyt, *Sovereign State*. Similar claims about territoriality are made by Agnew, "The Territorial Trap"; and Agnew and Corbridge, *Mastering Space*.

28. Alexander Murphy, "The Sovereign State as a Political-Territorial Ideal," in *State Sovereignty as a Social Construct*, ed. Thomas Biersteker and Cynthia Weber (Cambridge: Cambridge University Press, 1996).

29. John H. Herz, "Rise and Demise of the Territorial State," *World Politics* 9, no. 4 (1957): 480–81. See also Kratochwil, "Of Systems and Boundaries."

30. That clarity is not always perfect; border disputes are the bread and butter of the International Court of Justice (see, e.g., *The Temple of Preah Vihear* [Cambodia v. Thailand], Judgment of June 15, 1962). More unusual,

Neal Ascherson catalogs a few examples of alleged dead space in the international system, including the probably apocryphal "Akwizgran Discrepency," an unallocated piece of land between nineteenth-century Belgium, Germany, and the Netherlands (Ascherson, "Reflections on International Space," *London Review of Books* 23, 1996). The high seas were the subject of a separate set of rules (later codified by treaty). With regard to piracy, for instance, states employed "universal jurisdiction," which granted any state in the system the right to pursue pirates and other particularly disfavored criminals.

31. Robert Sack, *Human Territoriality: Its Theory and History* (New York: Cambridge University Press, 1986), 5.

32. The classic work is Benedict Anderson, *Imagined Communities: Reflections on the Origin and Spread of Nationalism* (London: Verso, 1983).

33. Eric Hobsbawm, *Nations and Nationalism since 1790* (Cambridge: Cambridge University Press, 1990), 19. See also J. Samuel Barkin and Bruce Cronin, "The State and the Nation: Changing Norms of Sovereignty in International Relations," *International Organization* 48, no. 1 (1994): 107–30.

34. This was especially argued by Vattel.

35. Hinsley, *Sovereignty*, 158.

36. Michael R. Fowler and Julie M. Bunck, *Law, Power, and the Sovereign State* (University Park, Pa.: Penn State Press, 1995), 12.

37. Some aspects of territorial sovereignty are currently under attack by the rise of international human rights law and increasing demands that states intervene in other states to protect vulnerable populations. The recent efforts to entrench a "responsibility to protect" norm in the international system are part of this evolution of sovereignty. See the Secretary-General's High Level Panel on Threats, Challenges, and Change, *A More Secure World: Our Shared Responsibility*, U.N. Doc. A/59/565 (2004); J. L. Holzgrefe and Robert O. Keohane, eds., *Humanitarian Intervention: Ethical, Legal, and Political Dilemmas* (Cambridge: Cambridge University Press, 2003); International Commission on Intervention and State Sovereignty, *The Responsibility to Protect: Report of the International Commission on Intervention and State Sovereignty* (Ottawa: International Development Research Centre, 2001).

38. Adair, *Exterritoriality of Ambassadors*, 9. This is closely intertwined with the rise of principles of comity and general notions of sovereign immunity.

39. Ibid., 7. Adair uses the phrase *exterritoriality*, but the meaning is the same; another common phrase from the nineteenth century is *extrality*. Adair states that by the beginning of the seventeenth century ambassadors "were one of the normal methods of diplomatic intercourse."

40. Garrett Mattingly, *Renaissance Diplomacy* (New York: Dover, 1988), 236. An influential nineteenth-century international lawyer, James Lorimer, wrote that "[a]n English ambassador, with his family and his suite, whilst abroad in the public service, is domiciled in England, and his house in English ground." James Lorimer, *The Institutes of the Law of Nations:*

A Treatise of the Jural Relations of Separate Political Communities (London: William Blackwood and Sons, 1883–84), 1: 248.

41. Ibid., 244.

42. Schooner Exchange v. M'Faddon, 137.

43. Henry Wheaton, *Elements of International Law*, 8th ed. (Philadelphia: Carey, Lea & Blanchard, 1866), sec. 78. Similar statements abound in judicial decisions of the era. See, e.g., *Hilton v. Guyot*, 159 U.S. 113 (1895) at 163: "No law has any effect, of its own force, beyond the limits of the sovereignty from which its authority is derived."

44. Gerald Neuman, *Strangers to the Constitution: Immigrants, Borders, and Fundamental Law* (Princeton, N.J.: Princeton University Press, 1996), 7.

45. On the advantages of the European powers see Jared Diamond, *Guns, Germs, and Steel: The Fates of Human Societies* (New York: Norton, 1996). In recent years there has been a marked revival of the study of empire; see, e.g., Herfried Munkler, *Empires: The Logic of World Domination from Ancient Rome to the United States* (Malden, Mass.: Polity Press, 2007); John Darwin, *After Tamerlane: The Global History of Empire since 1405* (London: Bloomsbury Press, 2007); Harold James, *The Roman Predicament: How the Rules of International Order Create the Politics of Empire* (Princeton, N.J.: Princeton University Press, 2006); Hendrik Spruyt, *Ending Empire: Contested Sovereignty and Territorial Partition* (Ithaca, N.Y.: Cornell University Press, 2005); Niall Ferguson, *Empire: The Rise and Fall of the British World Order and the Lessons for Global Power* (New York: Basic Books, 2003); Anthony Pagden, *Peoples and Empires* (Random House, 2003); Alexander Motyl, *Imperial Ends: The Decay, Collapse, and Revival of Empires* (New York: Columbia University Press, 2001). An older treatment is Michael W. Doyle, *Empires* (Ithaca, N.Y.: Cornell University Press, 1986).

46. David Strang, "Contested Sovereignty: The Social Construction of Colonial Imperialism," in Biersteker and Weber, *State Sovereignty*, 27.

47. Diamond, *Guns, Germs, and Steel*. See also the discussion in Darwin, *After Tamerlane*.

48. Antony Anghie, *Imperialism, Sovereignty, and the Making of International Law* (Cambridge: Cambridge University Press, 2005).

49. Cited in Anghie, ibid., 23. See also James Lorimer, *The Institutes of the Law of Nations: A Treatise of the Jural Relations of Separate Political Communities*, 2 vols. (Edinburgh and London: Blackwood and Sons, 1883, 1884), 101–2. Some dispute the European character of international law in the past, though unpersuasively in my view. See, e.g., Alexander Orakhelashvili, "The Idea of European International Law," *European Journal of International Law* 17, no. 2 (2006).

50. Whether the United States constitutes an empire today is a topic of great controversy. On the parallels see Munkler, *Empires*; Harold James, *Roman Predicament*; Charles Maier, *Among Empires: American Ascendancy and Its Predecessors* (Cambridge, Mass.: Harvard University Press, 2006); Chalmers Johnson, *The Sorrows of Empire: Militarism, Secrecy, and the End of the Republic* (New York: Metropolitan Books, 2004); Andrew Bacevich, *American Empire: The Realities and Consequences of U.S. Diplomacy* (Cambridge,

Mass.: Harvard University Press, 2004); Michael Mann, *Incoherent Empire* (New York: Verso, 2003).

51. Darwin, *After Tamerlane*, 244.

52. Maier, *Among Empires*, 23. Munkler says similarly that "whereas states ... integrate their populations equally—above all, grant them equal rights whether they live at the core of the state or in its border regions—this is not the case with empires: there is almost always a scale of integration descending from centre to periphery ..." Munkler, *Empires*, 5.

53. Steyn, "Guantanamo Bay."

54. Anthony Pagden, *Worlds at War: The 2500 Year Struggle Between East and West* (Random House, 2008) provides extensive treatment. Alternatives to empire included spheres of influence and "preponderance"; see Kratochwil, "Of Systems and Boundaries," 37–41.

55. The practice was not limited to Europe, and some argue it dates back over a millennium. Arab traders may have enjoyed similar extraterritorial legal rights as far back as eighth- and ninth-century China. See Eileen Scully, *Bargaining with the State from Afar* (New York: Columbia University Press, 2001), 23. See also Shalom Kassan, "Extraterritorial Jurisdiction in the Ancient World," *American Journal of International Law* 29, no. 1 (1935); Orakhelashvili, "Idea," 332: "... It was common practice in different parts of the world and in different stages of history for local sovereigns to allow foreigners to reside in their territories and be governed by their own laws. This took place in the inter-European and inter-Asian contexts, as well as between Europeans and Asians. From the 8th century, Muslim merchants enjoyed jurisdictional privileges in Hindu states, as did Chinese merchants in Siam and Indonesia."

56. Ingrid Detter, "The Problem of Unequal Treaties," *The International and Comparative Law Quarterly* 15 (1966): 1069–1089.

57. Shinya Murase, "The Most-Favored-Nation Treatment in Japan's Treaty Practice during the Period 1854–1905," The American Journal of International Law 70, no. 2 (1976): 273–97.

58. A vestige of this approach is the 1963 Vienna Convention on Consular Relations, which grants nationals of the parties the right to notify their consulate when they are arrested in the territory of another party.

59. For example, Shih Shun Liu describes the sixth-century B.C. practice of permitting Greeks to live in Egypt under their own laws and religion, as well as many more recent examples from Roman times. Shih Shun Liu, *Extraterritoriality: Its Rise and Decline* (New York: AMS Press, 1969 [1925]), 24. But Liu notes that in many parts of the world it was only the rise of coercive and unequal treaties in the late nineteenth century that led to full extraterritoriality for Westerners: "With the exception of Japan, the Powers of Eastern Asia, prior to the middle of the 19th century, assumed their territorial jurisdiction and were not in the habit of granting to foreigners extraterritorial privileges," 83.

60. Kurt Nadelmann, "American Consular Jurisdiction in Morocco and the Tangier International Jurisdiction," *American Journal of International*

Law 49 (1955). The United Nations headquarters in New York City is a sort of contemporary international zone. "Agreement between the United Nations and the United States Regarding the Headquarters of the United Nations," signed June 25, 1947, available at http://www.yale.edu/lawweb/avalon/decade/decad036.htm.

61. The court operated formally until 1942 and appeals flowed to the Ninth Circuit. Scully, *Bargaining*, 15.

62. Scully, *Bargaining*, 106; see also Teemu Ruskola, "Canton Is Not Boston: The Invention of American Imperial Sovereignty," in "Legal Borderlands: Law and the Construction of American Borders," ed. Mary L. Dudziak and Leti Volpp, special issue, *American Quarterly* 57, no. 3 (2005): 867–68; David Bederman, "Extraterritorial Domicile and the Constitution," *Virginia Journal of International Law* 28, no. 2 (1988).

63. Spruyt, *Ending Empire*, 4.

64. Darwin, *After Tamerlane*, 441–42.

65. Quoted in Liu, *Extraterritoriality*, 90.

66. Ibid. 100–114.

67. See, generally, G. John Ikenberry, *After Victory: Institutions, Strategic Restraint, and the Rebuilding of Order after Major Wars* (Princeton, N.J.: Princeton University Press, 2000); Jose E. Alvarez, *International Organizations as Law-Makers* (Oxford: Oxford University Press, 2006).

68. On the latter see Anne-Marie Slaughter, *A New World Order* (Princeton, N.J.: Princeton University Press, 2004); Kal Raustiala, "The Architecture of International Cooperation: Transgovernmental Networks and the Future of International Law," *Virginia Journal of International Law*, 43, 1 (2002).

69. Karen DeYoung, "Lacking an Accord on Troops, U.S. and Iraq Seek a Plan B," *Washington Post*, October 14, 2008.

70. Federalism of course entailed an internal division that had no meaning under international law. The key here is instead the role of federal territory and anomalous areas such as tribal lands. Did the Bill of Rights reach into these territories fully, or was it fully applicable only in the states of the Union?

71. As Alex Aleinikoff notes, "[T]he antiexpansionist constitutional argument that 'the Constitution follows the flag' was pressed more in order to prevent empire building (since the inapplicability of the Constitution to the 'savages' of the Philippines seemed apparent) than to ensure that all residents on U.S. soil would be guaranteed basic civil rights." T. Alexander Aleinikoff, *Semblances of Sovereignty: The Constitution, the State, and American Citizenship* (Cambridge, Mass.: Harvard University Press, 2002), 25.

72. As a matter of statutory law, the Bill of Rights applies in unincorporated territories such as Puerto Rico; it is unclear whether it applies as a matter of constitutional law.

73. So-called *Miranda* warnings are familiar to viewers of American crime shows; pursuant to a Supreme Court decision from the 1960s police must read certain rights to a suspect before beginning an interrogation. The extraterritoriality of *Miranda* is discussed in chapter 6.

74. Robert O. Keohane and Joseph S. Nye, *Power and Interdependence* (Boston: Little, Brown, 1977), ch. 2.

75. Peter Gourevitch, "The Second Image Reversed: The International Sources of Domestic Politics," *International Organization* 32, no. 4 (1978); Ira Katznelson and Martin Shefter, eds., *Shaped by War and Trade: International Influences on American Political Development* (Princeton, N.J.: Princeton University Press, 2002).

76. The "second image" concept is drawn from Kenneth Waltz, *Man, the State, and War* (New York: Columbia University Press, 1959).

77. Ira Katznelson, "Rewriting the Epic of America," in Katznelson and Shefter, eds., *Shaped by War and Trade*, 4.

78. On this process see Fareed Zakaria, *From Wealth to Power: The Unusual Origins of America's World Role* (Princeton, N.J.: Princeton University Press, 1998).

79. Ruggie, "Territoriality and Beyond"; see also Christopher Ansell and Giuseppe Di Palma, eds., *Restructuring Territoriality: Europe and the United States Compared* (Cambridge: Cambridge University Press, 2004), noting that "[i]n many respects, Ruggie's argument is simply one of the more subtle and provocative examples of an emerging genre arguing that the modern state and the modern state system are being challenged, and perhaps eroded, by a variety of forces ranging from domestic privatization to economic and cultural globalization."

80. As just noted, this is not Ruggie's much more nuanced and complex view, but shares with his a sense that traditional territoriality is facing new challenges. Ohmae, *Borderless World*; Friedman, *World Is Flat*.

81. The links between globalization and jurisdiction are extensively discussed in Berman, "Globalization."

82. The phrase is John Ikenberry's. See G. John Ikenberry, "The Liberal Leviathan," *Prospect* (October 2004); Anne-Marie Slaughter, "Security, Solidarity, and Sovereignty: The Grand Themes of UN Reform," *American Journal of International Law* 99, 3 (July 2005).

83. Maier, *Among Empires*, 101.

Chapter Two

1. Bartholomew Sparrow, *The Insular Cases and the Emergence of American Empire* (Lawrence: University of Kansas Press, 2006), 1–2.

2. Gary Lawson and Guy Seidman, *The Constitution of Empire: Territorial Expansion and American Legal History* (New Haven, Conn.: Yale University Press, 2004), 2.

3. I borrow this term from Miles Kahler, "Territoriality and Conflict in an Era of Globalization," in *Territoriality and Conflict in an Era of Globalization*, ed. Miles Kahler and Barbara Walter (Cambridge: Cambridge University Press, 2006).

4. *The Declaration of Independence* (U.S. 1776).

5. Peter Onuf and Nicholas Onuf, *Federal Union, Modern World: the Law of Nations in an Age of Revolutions, 1776–1814* (Madison: University of

Wisconsin Press, 1993); David C. Hendrickson, *Peace Pact: The Lost World of the American Founding* (Lawrence: University of Kansas Press, 2003); Sarah Cleveland, "Our International Constitution," *Yale Journal of International Law* 31, no. 1 (2006). Throughout American history the courts have assumed that the United States possesses powers inherent in sovereignty, whether or not the Constitution explicitly discusses them. See, e.g., Blackmer v. United States, 284 U.S. 421 (1932) at 437: "Nor can it be doubted that the United States possesses the power inherent in sovereignty to require the return to this country of a citizen, resident elsewhere, whenever the public interest requires it, and to penalize him in case of refusal."

6. *The Definitive Treaty of Peace between the United States of America and His Britannic Majesty*, 80 Stat. 80, U.S.–Gr. Brit. (September 3, 1783). Some in the early United States were nonetheless eager to prove that it belonged in the charmed circle of sovereign states. Chancellor Kent, in his influential commentaries on American law, was highly interested that "the United States be perceived by other countries as a qualified sovereign partner in the European Christian community of nations." Mark W. Janis, *The American Tradition of International Law* (New York: Oxford University Press, 2004), 37.

7. For an argument that the constitution was in essence a preemptive peace pact among putative sovereigns, see Hendrickson, *Peace Pact*. The role of the Supreme Court in a peacekeeping framework is addressed in Thomas H. Lee, "The Supreme Court of the United States as Quasi-International Tribunal," *Columbia Law Review* 104 (2004). That the resulting system represents a hybrid between international anarchy and state hierarchy is argued in Daniel Deudney, "The Philadelphian System: Sovereignty, Arms Control, and Balance of Power in the American States-Union Circa 1787–1861," *International Organization* 49, no. 2 (1995).

8. Federalist 13, in Clinton Rossiter, ed., *The Federalist Papers* (New York: New American Library, 1961).

9. Ibid., Federalist 7. See also Hendrickson, *Peace Pact*, chs. 1–3.

10. Lawson and Seidman, *Constitution of Empire*, 2.

11. See e.g. Luc Reydams, *Universal Jurisdiction: International and Municipal Legal Perspectives* (Oxford: Oxford University Press, 2004); *The Princeton Principles on Universal Jurisdiction* (2001), available at http://lapa.princeton.edu/hosteddocs/unive_jur.pdf.

12. Schooner Exchange v. M'Faddon, 11 U.S. (7 Cranch) 116 (1812) at 136. Marshall wrote that "the world being composed of distinct sovereignties, possessing equal rights and equal independence, whose mutual benefit is promoted by intercourse with each other . . . all sovereigns have consented to a relaxation in practice, in cases under certain peculiar circumstances, of that absolute and complete jurisdiction within their respective territories which sovereignty confers" (136).

13. Letter from Calhoun to Everett, August 7, 1844, quoted in Lawrence Preuss, "American Conception of Jurisdiction with Respect to Conflicts of Law on Crime," *Transactions of the Grotius Society* 30 (1944): 187.

14. Robert Kagan, *Dangerous Nation: America's Place in the World from Its Earliest Days to the Dawn of the 20th Century* (New York: Knopf, 2006), 76. Kagan notes in this regard that the Northwest Ordinance of 1787, guaranteed settlers of the western lands "equal rights of self-government and with it the political clout to further their expansionist interests . . . [I]t was a consciously designed 'machine' of expansion."

15. Quoted in Fareed Zakaria, *From Wealth to Power: The Unusual Origins of America's World Role* (Princeton, N.J.: Princeton University Press, 1998), 56.

16. Johnson v. M'Intosh, 21 U.S. (8 Wheat.) 543 (1823).

17. Ibid., 573. Indeed, in the oral argument the defendants argued that Indians were incapable of sovereignty, invoking in the process leading international theorists such as Emmerich de Vattel, Grotious, and Samuel Pufendorf. See Sarah Cleveland, "Powers Inherent in Sovereignty: Indians, Aliens, Territories, and the Nineteenth-Century Origins of Plenary Power over Foreign Affairs," Texas Law Review 81 (2002): 23.

18. Johnson v. M'Intosh, 21 U.S. 543 (1823) at 587.

19. Kagan, *Dangerous Nation*, 130.

20. This was truer of Jefferson than Madison. Madison believed that large size was sometimes beneficial. See especially Federalist 10 and Federalist 63, in Clinton Rossiter, ed., *Federalist Papers;* Robert Dahl and Edward Tufte, *Size and Democracy* (Palo Alto, Calif.: Stanford University Press, 1973).

21. Letter to John Dickinson, cited in Lawson and Seidman, *Constitution of Empire*, 21; Lawson and Seidman exhaustively analyze the issue and come to the conclusion that "even under the assumptions least generous to the powers of Congress, the Louisiana Purchase was easily a constitutional exercise of the treaty power," 85. See also Henry Wolf Bikle, "The Constitutional Power of Congress over the Territory of the United States," *American Law Register* 49 (January–December 1901): 14.

22. Quoted in Sanford Levinson, "Installing the Insular Cases into the Canon," in *Foreign in a Domestic Sense: Puerto Rico, American Expansion, and the Constitution*, ed. Christina Burnett and Burke Marshall (Durham, N.C.: Duke University Press, 2001), 129.

23. Quoted in Sparrow, *Insular Cases*, 22.

24. American Insurance Co. v. Canter, 26 U.S. (1 Peters) 511 (1828) at 542.

25. Christina Duffy Burnett, "The Edges of Empire and the Limits of Sovereignty: American Guano Islands," in "Legal Borderlands: Law and the Construction of American Borders," ed. Mary Dudziak and Leti Volpp, special issue, *American Quarterly* 57, no. 3 (2005).

26. Gerald Neuman, "Constitutionalism and Individual Rights," in *Foreign in a Domestic Sense* (see note 23), at 186–87.

27. Loughborough v. Blake, 18 U.S. (5 Wheat.) 317 (1820). Later cases also viewed the Constitution as operative within the district in the same manner as within the states; see, e.g., Callan v. Wilson, 127 U.S. 540 (1888).

28. Antony Anghie, *Imperialism, Sovereignty, and the Making of International Law* (Cambridge: Cambridge University Press, 2005).

29. Ibid., 37.

30. Stuart Banner, *How the Indians Lost Their Land* (Cambridge, Mass.: Harvard University Press, 2005). The questions of territorial sovereignty and of who possessed property rights over land were separate inquiries that are frequently conflated. The Indians might, as a polity, lack sovereign territorial control in the Western sense. Yet individual parcels of land were still bought and sold and property rights in them generally respected.

31. Ibid., 113.

32. Cherokee Nation v. Georgia, 30 U.S. 1 (1831) at 16.

33. As a later writer put it, tribal powers are thus extra- or preconstitutional: not powers delegated by Congress but instead "inherent powers of a limited sovereignty which has never been extinguished." Felix Cohen, *Handbook of Federal Indian Law* (Washington, D.C.: U.S. Dept. of the Interior, 1942), 122.

34. Cherokee Nation, 16–17.

35. Ibid., Justice Johnson, 24.

36. Ibid., Thompson and Story, dissenting, 53–54.

37. Worcester v. Georgia, 31 U.S. 515 (1832) at 542.

38. Ibid., 557. Allison Dussias, "Geographically-Based and Membership-Based Views of Indian Tribal Sovereignty: The Supreme Court's Changing Vision," *University of Pittsburgh Law Review* 55, no. 1 (1993).

39. Philip P. Frickey, "(Native) American Exceptionalism in Federal Public Law," *Harvard Law Review* 119, no. 2 (2005); T. Alexander Aleinikoff, *Semblances of Sovereignty: The Constitution, the State, and American Citizenship* (Cambridge, Mass.: Harvard University Press, 2002); Nell Jessup Newton, "Federal Power over Indians: Its Sources, Scope, and Limitations," *University of Pennsylvania Law Review* 132 (1984).

40. United States v. Kagama, 118 U.S. 375 (1886); Tee-Hit-Ton Indians v. United States, 348 U.S. 272 (1955).

41. Cherokee Nation v. Georgia, 7.

42. Elk v. Wilkins, 112 U.S. 94 (1884).

43. The Slaughter-House Cases, 83 U.S. (16 Wall.) 36 (1872) at 73.

44. Elk v. Wilkins, 99.

45. Quoted in David P. Currie, "Indian Treaties," *The Greenbag* 10, no. 4 (2007): 447.

46. United States v. Wheeler, 435 U.S. 313 (1978).

47. Kagan, *Dangerous Nation*, 226. In the 1840s "Americans in both the north and the south insisted on viewing all questions of expansion and foreign policy as part of the great struggle over the future of slavery."

48. Fleming v. Page, 50 U.S. (9 How.) 603 (1850) at 614–15.

49. United States v. Rice, 17 U.S. 246 (1819).

50. American Insurance v. Canter.

51. Ibid., 515.

52. Halleck, discussed in this volume in ch. 3.

53. Worcester v. Georgia, 561.

54. Robert McCloskey, *The American Supreme Court* (Chicago: Chicago University Press, 1960), discussing Scott v. Sanford, 60 U.S. (19 How.) 393 (1857).

55. Jack Balkin and Sanford Levinson, "13 Ways of Looking at Dred Scott," *Chicago Kent Law Review* 82 (2007).

56. Kagan, *Dangerous Nation*, 252.

57. Quoted in Donald E. Fehrenbacher, *The Dred Scott Case* (New York: Oxford University Press, 1978), 156. In addition to issues of territoriality, the case implicated many other aspects of international law. See the extensive discussion in Janis, *The American Tradition*, 76–94.

58. Dred Scott v. Sanford, 452.

59. Ibid., 446.

60. See, e.g., Henry W. Bikle, *The Constitutional Power of Congress over the Territory of the United States* (Philadelphia: University of Pennsylvania Press, 1901), 83–84.

61. Ibid., 80.

62. Late Corporation of the Church of Jesus Christ of Latter-day Saints v. United States, 136 U.S. 1 (1890) at 44. See, generally, Sarah Barringer Gordon, *The Mormon Question: Polygamy and Constitutional Conflict in Nineteenth Century America* (Chapel Hill: University of North Carolina Press, 2002).

63. *Ex parte* Milligan, 27 U.S. 2 (1866) at 20.

64. *Ex parte* Quirin, 317 U.S. 1 (1942), which involved the trial of captured Nazi saboteurs, is discussed further in ch. 5 in this volume.

65. Detlev F. Vagts, "Military Commissions: The Forgotten Reconstruction Chapter," *American University International Law Review* 23 (2008): 241.

66. Ibid.

67. In the 1979 case of United States v. Tiede, 86 F.R.D. 227 (U.S. Ct. Berlin, 1979). See the discussion in ch. 5 in this volume.

68. Pennoyer v. Neff, 95 U.S. 714 (1877).

69. Ibid., 720.

70. Ibid., 722–23.

71. Larry Kramer, "Vestiges of Beale: Extraterritorial Application of American Law," *Supreme Court Review* (1991): 189 (quoting Ulrich Huber, *De Conflictu Legum*). See also Kermit Roosevelt III, "Guantanamo and the Conflict of Laws: Rasul and Beyond," *University of Pennsylvania Law Review* 153, no. 6 (2005).

72. Ibid.

73. Paul Dubinsky, "Human Rights Meets Private Law Harmonization: The Coming Conflict," *Yale Journal of International Law* 30, no. 1 (2005): 255, 260.

74. This history is extensively discussed in Gerald Neuman, *Strangers to the Constitution: Immigrants, Borders, and Fundamental Law* (Princeton, N.J.: Princeton University Press, 1996), ch. 4.

75. Ibid., 58.

76. United States v. Verdugo-Urquidez, 494 U.S. 259 (1990) discussed at length in ch. 6 in this volume.

77. Neuman, *Strangers to the Constitution*, 60–61.

78. Yick Wo v. Hopkins, 118 U.S. 356 (1886).

79. Ibid., 369.

80. Wong Wing v. United States, 163 U.S. 228 (1896) at 238. Neuman, *Strangers to the Constitution*, provides a comprehensive discussion of these issues.

81. See, e.g., Hiroshi Motomura, "Immigration Law after a Century of Plenary Power: Phantom Constitutional Norms and Statutory Interpretation," *Yale Law Journal* 100, no. 2 (1990); T. Alexander Alienikoff, "Federal Regulation of Aliens and the Constitution," *American Journal of International Law* 83 (1989).

82. Gisbert v. Attorney General, 988 F. 2d 1437 (5th Cir. 1993). Some courts have questioned the notion that even excludable aliens lack constitutional rights. In Rosales-Garcia v. Holland, 322 F. 3d 386 (6th Cir. 2003) at 409, the court declared that "[e]xcludable aliens—like all aliens—are clearly protected by the Due Process Clauses of the Fifth and Fourteenth Amendments . . . while we respect the historical tradition of the 'entry fiction' we do not believe it applies to deprive aliens living in the United States of their status as 'persons' for the purposes of constitutional due process."

83. Zadvydas v. Davis, 533 U.S. 678 (2001) at 693. T. Alexander Aleinikoff, "Detaining Plenary Power: The Meaning and Impact of Zadvydas v. Davis," *Georgetown Immigration Law Journal* 16, no. 2 (2002); Linda Bosniak, "A Basic Territorial Distinction," *Georgetown Immigration Law Journal* 16, no. 2 (2002).

84. Ayelet Shachar, "The Shifting Border of Immigration Regulation," *Stanford Journal of Civil Rights & Civil Liberties* 3 (2007), 167.

85. Preuss, "American Conception of Jurisdiction," 193.

Chapter Three

1. Philip C. Jessup, *Elihu Root*, vol. 1, *1845–1909* (New York: Dodd Mead, 1938), 348.

2. *In re* Ross, 140 U.S. 453 (1890).

3. The first such arrangement by the United States was with Morocco; Shih Shun Liu, *Extraterritoriality: Its Rise and Decline* (New York: AMS Press, 1929) (originally presented in Columbia University Studies in History, Economics, and Public Law), 69.

4. Fareed Zakaria, *From Wealth to Power: The Unusual Origins of America's World Role* (Princeton, N.J.: Princeton University Press, 1998), especially ch. 3. Zakaria dubs this "imperial understretch." He argues that "American influence abroad was so minimal in the second half of the nineteenth century that many historians have skipped over the period in their accounts, beginning their discussion of American expansionism with the 1890s."

5. Albert Beveridge, quoted in Gary Lawson and Guy Seidman, *The Constitution of Empire: Territorial Expansion and American Legal History* (New Haven, Conn.: Yale University Press, 2004) at 109.

6. See, generally, Marius Jansen, ed., *The Cambridge History of Japan*, vol. 5, *The Nineteenth Century* (Cambridge: Cambridge University Press, 1989). The longer-term effects are discussed in Hidemi Suganami, "Japan's Entry into International Society," in *The Expansion of International Society*, ed. Hedley Bull and Adam Watson (New York: Oxford University Press, 1984).

7. Liu, *Extraterritoriality*, 69–71.

8. Michael W. Doyle, *Empires* (Ithaca, N.Y.: Cornell University Press, 1986), 45. See also the discussion of imperialism in Chapter 1. The classic treatment of informal empire is John Gallagher and Ronald Robinson, "The Imperialism of Free Trade," *Economic History Review* 6, no. 1 (1953).

9. Martti Koskenniemi, *The Gentle Civilizer of Nations: The Rise and Fall of International Law 1870–1960* (Cambridge: Cambridge University Press, 2001), 151.

10. Gallagher and Robinson, "The Imperialism of Free Trade."

11. *In re* Ross, 465.

12. Editorial comment, "Extraterritoriality and the U.S. Court for China," *American Journal of International Law* 1, no. 2 (1907): 469.

13. *In re* Ross, 462.

14. Cited in "Extraterritoriality and the U.S. Court for China," 475.

15. *In re* Ross, 463.

16. Ibid., 464, emphasis added.

17. Ibid., 465.

18. Suganami, "Japan's Entry into International Society."

19. Garrett Mattingly, *Renaissance Diplomacy* (New York: Dover Publications, 1955; reprinted 1988).

20. See Liu, *Extraterritoriality*, ch. 4.

21. Akhil Reed Amar, "The Bill of Rights as a Constitution," *Yale Law Journal* 100 (1991): 1196.

22. Gerald Neuman, *Strangers to the Constitution: Immigrants, Borders, and Fundamental Law* (Princeton, N.J.: Princeton University Press, 1996), 4, cites *Ross* as "the classic holding" for the proposition that government action outside the borders of the United States was not constrained by anyone's constitutional rights. See also T. Alexander Aleinikoff, *Semblances of Sovereignty* (Cambridge, Mass.: Harvard University Press, 2002).

23. W. P. Ker, "Treaty Revision in Japan: A Survey of the Steps by Which the Abolition of Foreign Privilege Was Accomplished in the Island Empire," *Pacific Affairs* 1, no. 6 (1928): 6. Japan did not regain its tariff autonomy, however, until 1911. Suganami, "Japan's Entry into International Society," 192.

24. Reid v. Covert, 354 U.S. 1 (1957) at 12. This case is discussed at length in ch. 5 in this volume.

25. The story is recounted in Gerrit Gong, "China's Entry into International Society," in Bull and Watson, *Expansion of International Society*, 174–75 and in Teemu Ruskola, "Canton Is Not Boston: The Invention of American Imperial Sovereignty," in "Introduction: Legal Borderlands: Law and the Construction of American Borders," ed. Mary L. Dudziak and Leti

Volpp, special issue, *American Quarterly* 57, no. 3 (2005): 867–68. Gong claims that Macartney was able to bow on one knee in lieu of the required kowtow.

26. Cited in Crawford Bishop, "American Extraterritorial Jurisdiction in China," *American Journal of International Law* 20 (1926).

27. Eileen Scully, *Bargaining with the State from Afar: American Citizenship in Treaty Port China, 1844–1942* (New York: Columbia University Press, 2001). See also Ruskola, "Canton Is Not Boston"; Gong, "China's Entry"; Tahirih Lee, "The United States Court for China: A Triumph of Local Law," *Buffalo Law Review* 52, no. 4 (Fall 2004); David J. Bederman, "Extraterritorial Domicile and the Constitution," *Virginia Journal of International Law* 28 (1988). The classic account, written by a participant, is Frank Hinckley, *American Consular Jurisdiction in the Orient* (Washington, D.C.: W. H. Lowdermilk, 1906). The longest serving judge on the court recounted his views in Charles Sumner Lobinger, "A Quarter Century of Our Extraterritorial Court," *Georgetown Law Journal* 20 (1931–32).

28. Figures from Scully, *Bargaining with the State from Afar*, 192.

29. *In re* Allen's Will, 1 Extraterritorial Cases 92 (1907) at 98.

30. "The Docket," *American Law Review* 57 (1923): 136.

31. United States v. Furbush, 2 Extraterritorial Cases 81 (1921).

32. "Rules Governing Admission of Attorneys," *Millard's Review of the Far East* (March 19, 1918): 68.

33. Liu, *Extraterritoriality*, gives an overview of the unraveling of extraterritorial jurisdiction in ch. 5.

34. Kurt H. Nadelmann, "American Consular Jurisdiction in Morocco and the Tangier International Jurisdiction," *American Journal of International Law* 49, no. 4 (1955).

35. Doyle, *Empires*, 254. For an extensive history see John Darwin, *After Tamerlane: The Global History of Empire since 1405* (London: Bloomsbury Press, 2008).

36. Doyle, *Empires*, 340. The Belgians were hardly a powerhouse in Europe, yet King Leopold held one of the largest colonies, the Congo, as practically a personal fiefdom. Adam Hochschild, *King Leopold's Ghost: A Story of Greed, Terror, and Heroism in Colonial Africa* (New York: Houghton Mifflin, 1998); Koskenniemi, *Gentle Civilizer of Nations*, 155–66.

37. Peter Liberman, *Does Conquest Pay?: The Exploitation of Industrial Societies* (Princeton, N.J.: Princeton University Press, 1998), 6–7. Many realists question this, of course. In the influential *War and Change in World Politics* (New York: Cambridge University Press, 1981), Robert Gilpin argued that economic power was a function of geographic size for most of human history.

38. Harold James, *The End of Globalization* (Cambridge, Mass.: Harvard University Press, 2001); Doyle, *Empires*.

39. Quoted in Niall Ferguson, *Empire: The Rise and Demise of the British Empire and the Lessons for World Order* (New York: Basic Books, 2002), xix.

40. Jennifer Pitts, *A Turn to Empire* (Princeton, N.J.: Princeton University Press, 2006).

41. French journalist Gabriel Charmes, quoted in Alice Conklin, *A Mission to Civilize* (Palo Alto, Calif.: Stanford University Press, 1997), 13.

42. Quoted in Ferguson, *Empire*, xx.

43. See, generally, Owen Fiss, "The American Empire?," ch. 8 in *Troubled Beginnings of the Modern State, 1888–1910* (Cambridge: Cambridge University Press, 2006).

44. Zakaria, *From Wealth to Power*, 46.

45. Christina Duffy Burnett, "The Edges of Empire and the Limits of Sovereignty: American Guano Islands," in "Introduction: Legal Border-lands: Law and the Construction of American Borders," ed. Mary L. Dudziak and Leti Volpp, special issue, *American Quarterly* 57, no. 3 (2005); Lawson and Seidman, *Constitution of Empire*, 98–102.

46. Burnett, "The Edges of Empire," 779–80.

47. Ibid., 786.

48. Jones v. United States, 137 U.S. 202 (1890) at 216.

49. Walter LaFeber, *The New Empire: An Interpretation of American Expansion, 1860–1898* (Ithaca, N.Y.: Cornell University Press, 1963), 5.

50. On the century anniversary of the overthrow of the Kingdom of Hawaii, President Clinton signed the "Apology Bill," in which the Congress "apologizes to Native Hawai'ians on behalf of the people of the United States for the overthrow of the Kingdom of Hawai'i on January 17, 1893 . . . and the deprivation of the rights of Native Hawai'ians to self-determination." Joint Resolution, Public Law 103–150, 107 Stat. 1510 (1993). See generally Stephen Kinzer, *Overthrow: America's Century of Regime Change from Hawaii to Iraq* (New York: Times Books, 2006).

51. Zakaria, *From Wealth to Power*, 155.

52. William Forbath, "Politics, State Building, and the Courts," in *Cambridge History of Law in America*, vol. 2, *The Long Nineteenth Century*, ed. Michael Grossberg and Christopher Tomlins (Cambridge: Cambridge University Press, 2008).

53. Ernest R. May, *American Imperialism: A Speculative Essay* (Chicago: Imprint Publications, 1991), ix. See also Ernest R. May, *Imperial Democracy: The Emergence of America as a Great Power* (New York: Harcourt, Brace and World, 1961). For a view that the empire-building aspect of the period had long roots see LaFeber, who writes that "two conclusion [are] implicit in this work. First, the United States did not set out on an expansionist path in the late 1890's in a sudden, spur-of-the-moment fashion. The overseas empire that Americans controlled in 1900 was not a break in their history, but a natural culmination." LaFeber, *New Empire*, vii. Contemporary mani-festations are detailed in Andrew J. Bacevich, *American Empire: The Realities and Consequences of U.S. Diplomacy* (Cambridge, Mass.: Harvard University Press, 2002).

54. On Britain's decline see Aaron Friedberg, *The Weary Titan: Britain and the Experience of Relative Decline, 1895–1905* (Princeton, N.J.: Princeton University Press, 1988).

55. James C. Fernald, *Imperial Republic* (New York: Funk and Wagnalls, 1899); Robert Beisner, *Twelve against Empire: The Anti-Imperialists, 1898–1900* (Chicago: Imprint, 1992).

56. Loughborough v. Blake, 18 U.S. (5 Wheat.) 317 (1818).

57. Dred Scott v. Sanford, 60 U.S. (19 How.) 393 (1857).

58. The racial dimensions of American empire, and of the *Insular Cases*, are extensively discussed in Aleinikoff, *Semblances of Sovereignty*.

59. Robert Kagan, *Dangerous Nation* (New York: Knopf, 2006).

60. The Platt Amendment (1903), available at http://www.ourdocuments.gov/doc.php?flash=old&doc=55.

61. Joseph Lazar, "International Legal Status of Guantanamo Bay," *American Journal of International Law* 62 (1968): 734: "Thus, the agreement for the lease, by its own terms as well as by admission of the Cuban executive, was anchored in the legal relationships evidenced by the Platt Amendment incorporated into the Cuban fundamental law." See also Lazar, "'Cession in Lease' of the Guantanamo Bay Naval Station and Cuba's 'Ultimate Sovereignty,'" *American Journal of International Law* 63 (1969); Gary Mavis, "Guantanamo: No Rights of Occupancy," *American Journal of International* 63 (1969).

62. Letter to Root, reprinted in Bartholomew Sparrow, *The Insular Cases and the Emergence of American Empire* (Lawrence: University Press of Kansas, 2006).

63. John T. Woolley and Gerhard Peters, *The American Presidency Project*, available at http://www.presidency.ucsb.edu/ws/?pid=29587.

64. Richard Hofstadter, "Manifest Destiny and the Philippines," in *Problems in American Civilization: American Imperialism in 1898*, ed. Theodore Green (Lexington, Mass.: D.C. Heath, 1955).

65. See May, *American Imperialism*, 4. A focused treatment of the Philippine-United States relationship can be found in H. W. Brands, *Bound to Empire: The United States and the Philippines* (New York: Oxford University Press, 1992).

66. Sumner, quoted in Fred H. Harrington, "Literary Aspects of American Anti-Imperialism," *New England Quarterly* 10, no. 4 (1937): 663–64; Beisner, *Twelve against Empire*, 57.

67. Fiss, *Troubled Beginnings*, 234.

68. Sparrow, *Insular Cases*, 63.

69. Congress, however, did not accept the cession of the Samoan territory until 1929. See United States General Accounting Office, "U.S. Insular Areas: Application of the U.S. Constitution," GAO/OGC-98-5 (November 1997), 8, and the discussion in Lawson and Seidman, *Constitution of Empire*, 116. The Canal Zone was held by the United States until the 1970s.

70. Frederick Coudert, "The Evolution of the Doctrine of Territorial Incorporation," *Columbia Law Review* 26 (1926): 823.

71. Harrington, "Literary Aspects," 664.

72. Edward Stanwood and Charles Knowles Bolton, *A History of the Presidency* (New York: Houghton Mifflin, 1916), 58.

73. "Status of New Possessions: House Committee Named to Ascertain If They Are in Fact Parts of the United States," *New York Times*, January 11, 1900.

74. For a comprehensive overview with special attention to Puerto Rico see Christina Burnett and Burke Marshall, eds., *Foreign in a Domestic Sense: Puerto Rico, American Expansion, and the Constitution* (Durham, N.C.: Duke University Press, 2001). See also Aleinikoff, *Semblances of Sovereignty;* Neuman, *Strangers to the Constitution;* Coudert, "The Evolution of the Doctrine."

75. Downes v. Bidwell, 182 U.S. 244 (1901).

76. Ibid. (Chief Justice Fuller dissenting), at 374.

77. Quoted in Sparrow, *Insular Cases*, 86.

78. Aleinikoff, *Semblances of Sovereignty*, 81.

79. Fiss, *Troubled Beginnings*, 228–29.

80. Donald E. Fehrenbacher, *The Dred Scott Case* (Oxford: Oxford University Press, 1978), 585.

81. Quoted in Fehrenbacher, ibid., 586.

82. Downes v. Bidwell.

83. DeLima v. Bidwell, 182 U.S. 1 (1901).

84. White drew inspiration for this notion from Abbott Lowell's article entitled "The Status of Our New Possessions—A Third View," *Harvard Law Review* 13 (1899).

85. Ibid.

86. Downes v. Bidwell, at 302–3.

87. See the discussion in Chapter 2.

88. As the GAO report put it in 1997, "The question whether particular rights are fundamental has been answered only as specific cases come before the Supreme Court." The Fifth Amendment privilege against self-incrimination has been deemed fundamental; the Sixth Amendment right to trial by jury has been found to be nonfundamental. GAO, "U.S. Insular Areas," 24.

89. The islands of Hawaii, for example, were incorporated into the United States in 1900. Within the brief period after the American annexation and before incorporation, however, the Supreme Court held that the right to trial by jury did not to apply to Hawaii. Most of the bill of rights was intended to apply to the new American territory, the court asserted in *Hawaii v. Mankichi*. But the right to jury trial, as "merely a method of procedure," was neither intended to apply nor fundamental enough to apply of its own force. Hawaii v. Mankichi, 190 U.S. 197 (1902).

90. For a different view see Christina Duffy Burnett and Burke Marshall, "Between the Foreign and the Domestic: The Doctrine of Territorial Incorporation, Invented and Reinvented," in Burnett and Marshall, *Foreign in a Domestic Sense*, 11.

91. Henry W. Bikle, "The Constitutional Power of Congress over the Territory of the United States," *American Law Register* 49, no. 8 (1901): 94.

See also Sedgwick Green, "The Applicability of American Law to Overseas Areas Controlled by the United States," *Harvard Law Review* 68 (1955).

92. Sparrow, *Insular Cases*, 51. Vest was no fan of the local inhabitants of the insular possessions; he referred to them as the "half-civilized, piratical, muck-raking inhabitants of 2000 islands." Ibid., 63.

93. Downes v. Bidwell, 341–42.

94. Neely v. Henkel, 180 U.S. 109 (1901) at 122.

95. Hawaii v. Mankichi, 236.

96. Quoted in Jessup, *Elihu Root*, 384.

97. Finley Peter Dunne's Mr. Dooley, quoted in Harrington, "Literary Aspects," 664.

98. Both quotes are drawn from Robert Kagan, "Neocon Nation: Neoconservatism, c. 1776," *World Affairs* (Spring 2008).

99. In this regard, the fictional Mr. Dooley recounted a representative conversation between two others about the *Insular Cases*. Dooley begins by noting that the Supreme Court decided "th' constitution don't follow th' flag." When asked who said it did, he replies that he wasn't sure, but that some fellow said that "ivrywhere th' constitution wint, th' flag was sure to go." Another then replied that he didn't believe this because "It's too old. It's a home-stayin' Constitution with a blue coat with brass buttons onto it, an' it walks with a gold-headed cane . . ." Finley Peter Dunne's Mr. Dooley, quoted in Sparrow, *Insular Cases*, 79.

100. *Chicago Record-Herald*, quoted in Sparrow, *Insular Cases*, 100.

101. Downes v. Bidwell, 286.

102. Dorr v. United States, 195 U.S. 138 (1904) at 278.

103. Christina Duffy Burnett, "United States: American Expansion and Territorial Deannexation," *University of Chicago Law Review* 72 (2005).

104. Hay-Bunau Varilla Treaty, Convention for the Construction of a Ship Canal to Connect the Waters of the Atlantic and Pacific Oceans, U.S.–Pan., 33 Stat. 2234, November 18, 1903, available at http://www.yale.edu/lawweb/avalon/diplomacy/panama/pan001.htm.

105. For some insightful comparisons see Gerald L. Neuman, "Closing the Guantanamo Loophole," *Loyola Law Review* 50, no. 1 (2004).

106. Jessup, *Elihu Root*, 404–5. Jessup admits that the story may be apocryphal, but tells it anyway because "it is so characteristic of Root that it may well be true."

107. Lawrence Ealy, "The Development of an Anglo-American System of Law in the Panama Canal Zone," *American Journal of Legal History* 2, no. 4 (1958) at 300–301.

108. Wilson v. Shaw, 204 U.S. 24 (1907) at 33. Others have argued, somewhat technically, that the Panamanian government never ceded the territory in perpetuity—only its use, occupation, and control. Norman Padelford, "American Rights in the Panama Canal," *American Journal of International Law* 34, no. 3 (1940).

109. Ealy, "Development of an Anglo-American System," 284.

110. Ibid., 285–86.

111. Neuman, "Closing the Guantanamo Loophole," 19. "As the era of colonialism waned, however, three decisions in the 1940s foreshadowed a deeper reception of the Constitution in the Canal Zone."

112. Ibid., 20.

113. Government of the Canal Zone v. Scott, 502 F. 2d 566 (CA Canal Zone, 1974) at 1.

114. Ibid.

115. Ibid.

116. See the discussion in ch. 5 in this volume.

117. Charles Gordon, "Who Can Be President of the United States?," *Maryland Law Review* 28, no. 1 (1968). Gordon was general counsel of the Immigration and Naturalization Service.

118. Michael Mandelbaum, "The Truth about the Panama Canal," *New York Times Book Review*, February 19, 1978. On the reaction of the Zonians see "No More Tomorrows: An Era Ends, as the U.S. Quits the Canal Zone," *Time*, October 15, 1979.

119. That vision was realized after 1945; see G. John Ikenberry, *After Victory* (Princeton, N.J.: Princeton University Press, 2000).

120. On the importance of naval bases to the nineteenth-century rush to empire see Sparrow, *Insular Cases*, 64–71; for a critical look at American overseas bases see Chalmers Johnson, *The Sorrows of Empire: Militarism, Secrecy, and the End of the Republic* (New York: Metropolitan, 2004).

121. John Lewis Gaddis, *We Now Know: Rethinking Cold War History* (Oxford: Oxford University Press, 1997), 27. That the colonized welcomed the colonizers is argued in Geir Lundestad, "Empire by Invitation? The United States and Western Europe, 1945–1952," *Journal of Peace Research* 23 (1986). The literature on American empire has blossomed in recent years; see, e.g., Bacevich, *American Empire;* Niall Ferguson, *Colossus: The Price of America's Empire* (New York: Penguin Press, 2004); Charles S. Maier, *Among Empires: American Ascendancy and Its Predecessors* (Cambridge, Mass.: Harvard University Press, 2006); Chalmers Johnson, *Blowback: The Costs and Consequences of American Empire* (New York: Henry Holt, 2000).

Chapter Four

1. Aaron Friedberg, *The Weary Titan: Britain and the Experience of Relative Decline, 1895–1905* (Princeton, N.J.: Princeton University Press, 1989); see also Fareed Zakaria, *From Wealth to Power: The Unusual Origins of America's World Role* (Princeton, N.J.: Princeton University Press, 1999).

2. Edward H. Carr, *The Twenty Years' Crisis, 1919–1939* (London: Macmillan, 1940).

3. The classic account is Stephen Skowronek, *Building a New American State: The Expansion of National Administrative Capacities, 1877–1920* (New York: Cambridge University Press, 1982). See also Thomas McCraw, *Prophets of Regulation* (Cambridge, Mass.: Belknap Press of Harvard University Press, 1984); Daniel Carpenter, *The Forging of Bureaucratic Autonomy:*

Networks, Reputations, and Policy Innovations (Princeton, N.J.: Princeton University Press, 2001); Edward Glaeser and Andrei Shleifer, "The Rise of the Regulatory State," *Journal of Economic Literature* 41, no. 1 (June 2003). For an account stressing earlier origins, see William Novak, *The People's Welfare: Law and Regulation in Nineteenth-Century America* (Chapel Hill: University of North Carolina Press, 1996).

4. Steve Fraser and Gary Gerstle, eds., *The Rise and Fall of the New Deal Order* (Princeton, N.J.: Princeton University Press, 1989); Cass Sunstein, "Constitutionalism After the New Deal," *Harvard Law Review* 101 (1987).

5. Act of July 2, 1890 (Sherman Anti-Trust Act), ch. 647, 26 Stat. 209, as amended.

6. Paul Kennedy, *The Rise and Fall of the Great Powers: Economic Change and Military Conflict from 1500 to 2000* (New York: Random House, 1987), 368–69.

7. G. John Ikenberry, *After Victory: Institutions, Strategic Restraint, and the Rebuilding of Order After Major Wars* (Princeton, N.J.: Princeton University Press, 2001); Robert Keohane, *After Hegemony: Cooperation and Discord in the World Economy* (Princeton, N.J.: Princeton University Press, 1984); Stephen D. Krasner, ed., *International Regimes* (Ithaca, N.Y.: Cornell University Press, 1983).

8. For a recent discussion of American exceptionalism in state building see Eric Rauchway, *Blessed Among Nations: How the World Made America* (New York: Farrar, Straus, and Giroux, 2006).

9. Wyatt Wells, *Antitrust and the Formation of the Postwar World* (New York: Columbia University Press, 2002), 1.

10. United States v. E.C. Knight Co., 156 U.S. 1 (1895).

11. American Banana Co. v. United Fruit Co., 213 U.S. 347 (1909).

12. Ibid., 355.

13. Hilton v. Guyot, 159 U.S. 113 (1895) at 163.

14. Canadian State Railway v. Gebhard, 109 U.S. 527, 536 (1883)

15. American Banana, 356.

16. Ibid.

17. Commonwealth v. Macloon, 101 Mass. 1 (1869). In his *Report on Extraterritorial Crime*, written in 1887, John Bassett Moore wrote that "the principle that a man who outside of a country willfully puts in motion a force to take effect in it is answerable at the place where the evil is done, is recognized in the criminal jurisprudence of all countries." John Bassett Moore, *Report on Extraterritorial Crime* (Washington, D.C.: Government Printing Office, 1887), 251.

18. Commonwealth v. Macloon, 8.

19. Lassa Oppenheim with Ronald T. Roxburgh, ed., *International Law: A Treatise*, 3rd ed. (New York: Longmans, Green, 1920), 240.

20. That Congress has the power to violate international law has been well-established since the 19th century. However, prudential doctrines of statutory construction exist that guide courts to avoid violations where possible by interpreting domestic statutes in line with international rules.

See respectively Whitney v. Robertson, 124 US 190 (1888) and Murray v. The Charming Betsy, 6 US (2 Cranch) 64 (1804).

21. At 357, citing *Ex parte* Blain, L. R. 12 Ch. Div. 522, 528. *American Banana* is generally viewed as the first articulation of the "presumption against extraterritoriality." See, e.g., Currie et al., *Conflicts of Laws*, 6th ed. (St. Paul: West, 2001), 744: "The 'presumption against extraterritoriality made its first formal appearance in American Banana Co. v. United Fruit Co."; Larry Kramer, "Vestiges of Beale: Extraterritorial Application of American Law," *Supreme Court Review* (1991): 184.

22. The Zollverein, 166 Engl. Reports Swab. 97 (1856) 1038, at 1040.

23. William Dodge, "Understanding the Presumption Against Territoriality," *Berkeley Journal of International Law* 16, no. 1 (1998): 86. Examples of recent cases in which the Supreme Court invoked the presumption include Smith v. United States, 507 U.S. 197 (1993), which involved Antarctica, a stateless region, and Sale v. Haitian Centers Council, Inc., 509 U.S. 155 (1993), involving immigrants on the high seas, another stateless area. In neither case was it plausible that the application of American law would intrude upon the domain of another sovereign. Perhaps the best-known recent invocation of the presumption is EEOC v. Aramco, 499 U.S. 244 (1991).

24. Dodge, "Understanding the Presumption"; Curtis A. Bradley, "Territorial Intellectual Property Rights in an Age of Globalization," *Virginia Journal of International Law* 37 (1997); Gary Born, "A Reappraisal of the Extraterritorial Reach of U.S. Law," *Law and Policy for International Business* 24, no. 1(1992).

25. Walton v. Arabian American Oil Co., 233 F. 2d 541 (2d Cir. 1956); D'Agostino v. Johnson & Johnson, Inc., 133 N.J. 516 (Supreme Court of N.J., 1993).

26. E.g., Currie et al., *Conflicts of Laws*, 744–45; discussion in Brilmayer, *Conflict of Laws: Introduction to Law Series* (New York: Aspen Law and Business, 1995), section 5.4.2.

27. Joseph Story, *Commentaries on Conflicts of Laws* (Boston: Hilliard, Gray, 1934), cited in Kramer, "Vestiges of Beale," 186. See also Pennoyer v. Neff, 95 U.S. 714 (1877), reiterating these principles.

28. Born, "Reappraisal," 9.

29. Wells, *Antitrust*, 1, quoting Supreme Court Justice Abe Fortas. Many major economic actors, such as Germany, were supportive of cartels. Hannah Buxbaum, "German Legal Culture and the Globalization of Competition Law," *Berkeley Journal of International Law* 23, no. 2 (2005).

30. United States v. Sisal Sales Corp., 274 U.S. 268 (1927); also United States v. American Tobacco, 221 U.S. 106 (1911).

31. Diane P. Wood, "United States Antitrust Law in the Global Market: Implications for Domestic Law Reform," *Indiana Journal of Global Legal Studies* 1 (1994): 415.

32. United States v. Aluminum Co. of America (Alcoa), 148 F. 2d 416 (2d Cir. 1945).

33. Jean Gabriel Castel, "The Extraterritorial Effects of Antitrust Laws," *Recueil des cours* 179, no. 1 (1983): 40. The case in full was closely related to the war, even if the extraterritorial aspects of interest here were generally not. As Wells recounts, Alcoa's effective monopoly over aluminum production drew considerable political attention as demand for the metal rose precipitously in the wake of Pearl Harbor. Wells, *Antitrust*, 59–63.

34. Wells, *Antitrust*, 59–60.

35. Ibid.

36. United States v. Aluminum Co. of America (Alcoa), 30.

37. William S. Dodge, "Extraterritoriality and Conflict-of-Laws Theory: An Argument for Judicial Unilateralism," *Harvard International Law Journal* 39 (1998). See also Kermit Roosevelt III, "Guantanamo and the Conflict of Laws: Rasul and Beyond," *University of Pennsylvania Law Review* 153, 6 (2005).

38. United States v. Aluminum Co of America (Alcoa), 443. Hand cited Holmes's decision in Strassheim v. Daily, discussed above for this proposition.

39. Ibid., 444.

40. Ibid., 443.

41. Strassheim v. Daily, 221 U.S. 280, 284 (1911). Alcoa was also preceded by some antitrust cases that hinted at a rejection of strict territoriality. See, e.g., United States v. Pacific and Arctic Railway & Navigation Co., 228 U.S. 87 (1913); United States v. Sisal Sales Corp., 274 U.S. 268 (1927).

42. Bowman v. United States, 260 U.S. 94 (1922). Contrast this view with the English case of Regina v. Keyn, 2 Ex. D 63 (1876), which held that "there was even no jurisdiction in respect of offenses committed by aliens in British territorial waters." Hersch Lauterpacht and Elihu Lauterpacht, ed., *International Law*, vol. 3, *The Law of Peace* (London: Cambridge University Press, 1970), 235.

43. Ford v. United States, 273 U.S. 593 (1927).

44. Simpson v. State (1893), cited in Cedric Ryngaert, "Jurisdiction in International Law" (unpublished PhD thesis, Katholieke Universiteit Leuven, 2006), 87.

45. Ibid.

46. Ole Spiermann, *International Legal Argument in the Permanent Court of International Justice: The Rise of the International Judiciary* (Cambridge: Cambridge University Press, 2005); J. L. Brierly, "The 'Lotus' Case," *Law Quarterly Review* 44 (1928): 155. For more on the role of the *Lotus* in American antitrust doctrine see Joseph Jude Norton, "Extraterritorial Jurisdiction of U.S. Antitrust and Securities Laws," *International and Comparative Law Quarterly* 28 (October 1979).

47. The Case of the S.S. *Lotus*, PCIJ, Ser. A., No. 10 (1927), available online at http://www.worldcourts.com/pcij/eng/decisions/1927.09.07_lotus/, 30.

48. Lauterpacht and Lauterpacht, *International Law*, 237.

49. Ibid., 241. Other commentators, such as Brierly, disputed the historical underpinnings of the decision, because international law was

traditionally based on personal notions of jurisdiction, not territorial ideas. J. L. Brierly, "The 'Lotus' Case," 44.

50. The Case of the S.S. *Lotus*, 59 (Nyholm, M., dissenting). The specific holding of the *Lotus* was effectively overruled by the 1958 Geneva Convention on the High Seas art. 11, Apr. 29, 1958, 13 U.S.T. 2312, 450 U.N.T.S. 82.

51. Kramer, "Vestiges of Beale," 192; Dodge, "Extraterritoriality," 35.

52. Born, "Reappraisal," 17. See also Gary Born and Peter Rutledge, *International Civil Litigation in United States Courts*, 4th ed. (New York: Aspen Publishers, 2007), 563–67.

53. Kramer, "Vestiges of Beale," 208. See also Jack L. Goldsmith, "Against Cyberanarchy," *University of Chicago Law Review* 65, no. 4 (1998): 1205–07, referring to the "hermetic territorialism" of the nineteenth century and the subsequent "overthrow" of this approach in the twentieth century.

54. International Shoe v. Washington, 326 U.S. 310 (1945); George Rutherglen, "International Shoe and the Legacy of Legal Realism," *Supreme Court Review* (2001): 347.

55. Ibid.

56. Shaffer v. Heitner, 433 U.S. 186, 204 (1977).

57. One might argue that the foreign defendant has a right to be free of the court's jurisdiction because it is arguing before the court itself, and therefore (constructively) is within American territory. In other words, were a U.S. court sitting abroad (e.g., the District Court for China) to hear a case under the same facts, the defendant would lack a Fourteenth Amendment right to be free of jurisdiction. "It is local litigation that triggers the constitutional protection." Lea Brilmayer, "The Extraterritorial Application of American Law," *Law and Contemporary Problems* 50, no. 3 (1987): 33.

58. The phrase is usually attributed to Duncan Kennedy; see Duncan Kennedy, "Two Globalizations of Law and Legal Thought," 1850–1968, *Suffolk Law Review* 36, no. 3 (2003); Duncan Kennedy, "The Rise and Fall of Classical Thought" (an unpublished manuscript).

59. Thomas C. Grey, "The New Formalism," Stanford Law School, Public Law and Legal Series, Working Paper No. 4. (1999), available at http://ssrn.com/abstract=200732, 9. See also Morton J. Horwitz, *The Transformation of American Law, 1870–1960: The Crisis of Legal Orthodoxy* (New York: Oxford University Press, 1992); Neil Duxbury, *Patterns of American Jurisprudence* (Oxford: Oxford University Press, 1995).

60. Kennedy, "Two Globalizations," 640.

61. Horwitz, *Transformation*, 131.

62. Ibid., 17.

63. I borrow the phrase "regulating the world" from Anne-Marie Burley (Slaughter), "Regulating the World: Multilateralism, International Law, the Projection of the New Deal Regulatory State," in John G. Ruggie, ed., *Multilateralism Matters* (New York: Columbia University Press, 1993).

64. Steele v. Bulova Watch, 344 U.S. 280 (1952); Graeme B. Dinwoodie, "Trademarks and Territory: Detaching Trademark Law From the Nation-State," *Houston Law Review* 41 (2004).

65. Steele v. Bulova Watch, 287.

66. Ibid., 289.

67. Ibid., 292.

68. On this and other incidents see Detlev F. Vagts, "Extraterritoriality and the Corporate Governance Law," *American Journal of International Law* 97, no. 2 (April 2003).

69. This problem of selection bias in actual litigated disputes reflects what lawyers call the "Priest-Klein hypothesis." George L. Priest and Benjamin Klein, "The Selection of Disputes for Litigation," *Journal of Legal Studies* 13, no. 1 (1984).

70. Robert Litan and Carl Shapiro write, for instance, that "it is our experience from serving in the DOJ during the Clinton years that most serious antitrust investigations are settled without formal trial; this is one reason that we believe so much enforcement power is actually lodged in the prosecutors." Robert Litan and Carl Shapiro, "Antitrust Policy during the Clinton Administration," UC Berkeley Competition Policy Center Working Paper No. CPC01–22 (2001); interview, Department of Justice, May 2006.

71. For a systematic study of court decisions, see Tonya Putnam, Courts Without Borders: Domestic Sources of U.S. Extraterritoriality in the Regulatory Sphere, forthcoming, *International Organization*.

72. E.g., Schoenbaum v. First-Brook, 403 F. 2d 200 (2d Cir. 1967).

73. Hilton v. Guyot, 159 U.S. 113 (1895). Though the United States is not party to any of the international agreements mandating recognition of foreign judgments, domestic law abroad sometimes mandates such judicial cooperation. Canadian law, for instance, directs judges to enforce foreign decisions if the foreign court has properly and appropriately exercised jurisdiction over the matter in question. American law lacks a similar statute, though federal courts liberally enforce foreign judgments. Comity is "the recognition which one nation allows within its territory to the legislative, executive, or judicial acts of another ... " Hilton v. Guyot.

74. Introduced in the *Timberlane* case, 549 F. 2d 597 (9th Cir. 1976), the "rule" was invented by Kingman Brewster.

75. Castel, "Extraterritorial Effects," argues *American Banana* has never been overruled. Born, "Reappraisal," argues that the case was overruled in Continental Ore in 1962. Regardless, the *American Banana* approach is effectively moribund.

76. In Empagran v. Hoffman La Roche Ltd., 542 U.S. 155 (2004). The suit was denied, but the principle of effects-based extraterritoriality upheld. Christopher Sprigman, "Fix Prices Globally, Get Sued Locally? U.S. Jurisdiction Over International Cartels," *University of Chicago Law Review* 72 (2005).

77. Foreign Trade Antitrust Improvements Act of 1982, 15 U.S.C. Section 6a (2000).

78. EEOC v. Aramco.

79. On the E.P.A. see Pakootas v. Teck Cominco Metals. Ltd., 452 F.3d 1066 (E.D. Washington, 2004). The first set of Antitrust Enforcement

Guidelines for International Operations were promulgated by the Justice Department in 1977. Since 1990 the percentage of enforcement matters with some international aspects went from less than 5 percent to nearly 40 percent. *International Competition Policy Advisory Committee Report* (2000), available at http://www.usdoj.gov/atr/icpac/finalreport.htm.

80. David Gerber, "The Extraterritorial Application of the German Antitrust Laws," *American Journal of International Law* 77 (1983): 757.

81. Ibid., 756.

82. David Gerber, "Beyond Balancing: International Law Restraints on the Reach of National Laws," *Yale Journal of International Law* 10 (1984–85): 220.

83. Cited in Jeffrey Dunoff et. al., *International Law, Norms, Actors, Process: A Problem-Oriented Approach*, 2nd ed. (New York: Aspen, 2006), 365–66.

84. Letter from Calhoun to Everett, August 7, 1844, quoted in Lawrence Preuss, "American Conception of Jurisdiction with Respect to Conflicts of Law on Crime," *Transactions of the Grotius Society* 30 (1944): 187.

85. J. Atwood and Kingman Brewster, *Antitrust and American Business Abroad* (Colorado Springs: Shepard's/McGraw Hill, 1981), 101. Though the protests were largely directed at the executive branch, the American courts were not unaware of them, not least because other nations often filed amicus briefs in relevant federal court disputes. The Ninth Circuit, for instance, wrote in 1976 that "[e]xtraterritorial application is understandably a matter of concern for the other countries involved. Those nations have sometimes resented and protested, as excessive intrusions into their own spheres, broad assertions of authority by American courts." Timberlane Lumber Co. v. Bank of America, 549 F. 2d 597 (9th Cir. 1976).

86. Gerber, "Beyond Balancing," 187.

87. This is a similar pattern, though for different reasons, to that noted by Anne-Marie Slaughter in the context of the American act of state doctrine. Slaughter (Burley), "Law among Liberal States: Liberal Internationalism and the Act of State Doctrine," *Columbia Law Review* 92 (1992).

88. See also Paul Schiff Berman, "The Globalization of Jurisdiction," *University of Pennsylvania Law Review* 151, no. 2 (2002).

89. Born, "Reappraisal," 21.

90. E.g., Gerber, "Beyond Balancing," 194, 195.

91. Diane P. Wood, "United States Antitrust Law in the Global Market," *Global Legal Studies Journal* 1 (1994): 409.

92. Thomas Friedman, *The World Is Flat: A Brief History of the Twenty-First Century* (New York: Farrar, Straus and Giroux, 2005).

93. Paul Krugman, "Growing World Trade: Causes and Consequences," *Brookings Papers on Economic Activity* 1 (1995): 331. See also and Michael D. Bordo, Barry Eichengreen, and Douglas A. Irwin, "Is Globalization Today Really Different than Globalization a Hundred Years Ago?," *NBER Working Paper* 7195 (June 1999).

94. Richard E. Baldwin and Philippe Martin, "Two Waves of Globalization: Superficial Similarities, Fundamental Differences," *NBER Working Paper* 6904 (January 1999), 23.

95. Jeffry Frieden, *The Fall and Rise of Global Capitalism* (New York: Norton and Co., 2006), 16. With regard to financial liberalization and capital mobility—two central aspects of globalization—it has been said that "the only real debate among informed observers is whether we have returned to 1914-levels of financial integration." Baldwin and Martin, "Two Waves," 7–8.

96. Frieden, *The Fall and Rise*. Niall Ferguson, "Sinking Globalization," *Foreign Affairs* 84, no. 2 (March–April 2005); Harold James, *The End of Globalization: Lessons from the Great Depression* (Cambridge, Mass.: Harvard University Press, 2001).

97. Bordo et. al., "Globalization Today," 45; Baldwin and Martin, "Two Waves"; Ben Bernanke, "Global Economic Integration: What's New and What's Not?," http://www.federalreserve.gov/newsevents/speech/Bernanke20060825a.htm.

98. Bernanke, "Global Economic Integration."

99. Bordo et al., "Globalization Today," 11. Krugman, "Growing World Trade," characterizes the rise of intra-industry trade as one of four new aspects of modern international trade. Bordo et al. note a large increase in intra-industry trade in the postwar era, but find it less distinctive than does Krugman.

100. Kal Raustiala, "The Architecture of International Cooperation," *Virginia Journal of International Law* 43 (2002); Anne-Marie Slaughter, *A New World Order* (Princeton, N.J.: Princeton University Press, 2004).

101. Raustiala, "Architecture." For other arguments on the use of alternative measures by hegemonic powers, see Nico Krisch, "International Law in Times of Hegemony: Unequal Power and the Shaping of the International Legal Order," *European Journal of International Law* 16, no. 3 (2005).

102. Andrew Guzman, "Is International Antitrust Possible?," *NYU Law Review* 73, no. 5 (1998); Diane Wood, "The Impossible Dream: Real International Antitrust," *University of Chicago Legal Forum* (1992).

103. Subafilms, Ltd. v. MGM-Pathe Communications Co., 24 F. 3d 1088 (9th Cir. 1994).

104. John Gerard Ruggie "International Regimes, Transactions, and Change: Embedded Liberalism in the Postwar Economic Order," *International Organization* 36, no. 2 (1982).

105. Deudney and Ikenberry, "The Logic of the West." *World Policy Journal* (Winter 1993/1994).

106. Paul K. Huth et al., *The Democratic Peace and Territorial Conflict in the Twentieth Century* (New York: Columbia University Press, 2003); John O'Neal and Bruce Russett, "The Kantian Peace: The Pacific Benefits of Democracy, Interdependence, and International Organizations 1885–1992," *World Politics* 52, no. 1 (1999); C.f. Joanne Gowa, *Ballots and Bullets: the Elusive Democratic Peace* (Princeton, N.J.: Princeton University Press, 1999).

107. Slaughter, "Law among Liberal States," 1910.

108. Ibid., 1921.

109. Hendrik Spruyt, *Ending Empire: Contested Sovereignty and Territorial Partition* (Ithaca, N.Y.: Cornell University Press, 2005), 4. See also Tanisha Fazal, *State Death: The Politics and Geography of Conquest, Occupation, and Annexation* (Princeton, N.J.: Princeton University Press, 2007); Mark W. Zacher, "The Territorial Integrity Norm: International Boundaries and the Use of Force," *International Organization* 55, no. 2 (2001).

110. Jeffry Frieden, "International Investment and Colonial Control: A New Interpretation," *International Organization* 48, no. 4 (1994): 559.

111. I thank Detlev Vagts for this point.

112. In its 1991 *Aramco* decision, for example, the Supreme Court "slipped back to the 19th century, seemingly unaware that it was doing so." Kramer, "Vestiges of Beale," 204.

113. See, generally, Jurgen Basedow, ed., *Limits and Control of Competition with a View to International Harmonization* (New York: Aspen Publishers, 2002).

114. Detlev F. Vagts, "A Turnabout in Extraterritoriality," *American Journal of International Law* 76, no. 3 (1982): 591.

Chapter Five

1. Fareed Zakaria, *From Wealth to Power: The Unusual Origins of America's World Role* (Princeton, N.J.: Princeton University Press, 1998); Eric Rauchway, *Blessed among Nations: How the World Made America* (New York: Farrar, Straus, Giroux, 2006); Robert Kagan, *Dangerous Nation: America's Place in the World from Its Earliest Days to the Dawn of the Twentieth Century* (New York: Knopf, 2006).

2. The major exception was within the Western Hemisphere. Stephen Kinzer, *Overthrow: America's Century of Regime Change from Hawaii to Iraq* (New York: Times Books, 2006).

3. G. John Ikenberry, *After Victory: Institutions, Strategic Restraint, and the Rebuilding of Order after Major Wars* (Princeton, N.J.: Princeton University Press, 2000). Melvin Leffler, *A Preponderance of Power: National Security, the Truman Administration, and the Cold War* (Palo Alto, Calif.: Stanford University Press, 1993), provides discussion of the historical context within which this institutional strategy developed.

4. This position caused significant tensions with the British government. In 1944 Churchill wrote to Anthony Eden that "if the Americans want to take Japanese islands which they have conquered, let them do so with our blessing . . . but 'hands off the British Empire' is our maxim and it must not be weakened or smirched to please sob-stuff merchants at home or foreigners of any hue." Quoted in Tony Smith, *The Pattern of Imperialism: The United States, Great Britain, and the Late-Industrializing World since 1815* (Cambridge: Cambridge University Press, 1981), 161.

5. Tanisha M. Fazal, *State Death: The Politics and Geography of Conquest, Occupation, and Annexation* (Princeton, N.J.: Princeton University Press,

2007), 7; Mark W. Zacher, "The Territorial Integrity Norm: International Boundaries and the Use of Force," *International Organization* 55, no. 2 (2001).

6. Data in Fazal, *State Death*, 178.

7. John Lewis Gaddis, *We Now Know: Rethinking Cold War History* (New York: Oxford University Press, 1997), 35–36.

8. Geir Lundestad, *The United States and Western Europe since 1945: From "Empire" by Invitation to Transatlantic Drift* (New York: Oxford University Press, 2005).

9. George Kennan, "The Sources of Soviet Conduct," *Foreign Affairs* 25 (July 1947); Wilson D. Miscamble, *George F. Kennan and the Making of American Foreign Policy, 1947–1950* (Princeton, N.J.: Princeton University Press, 1992).

10. Kent E. Calder, *Embattled Garrisons: Comparative Base Politics and American Globalism* (Princeton, N.J.: Princeton University Press, 2007), 1.

11. Ibid., 8; John Woodliffe, *The Peacetime Use of Foreign Military Installations under Modern International Law* (London: Martinus Nijhoff, 1992), ch. 5.

12. Charles Fairman, "Some New Problems of the Constitution Following the Flag," *Stanford Law Review* 1, no. 4 (1949).

13. Further details on the Madsen trial can be found in "The Dialect of the People," *Time*, March 27, 1950.

14. John W. Dower, *Embracing Defeat: Japan in the Wake of World War II* (New York: Norton, 1999).

15. Protocol on Zones of Occupation in Germany and Administration of "Greater Berlin," September 12, 1944, U.S.-U.K.-U.S.S.R., 5 U.S.T. 2078, T.I.A.S. No. 3071, 227 U.N.T.S. 279.

16. U.S. control over Okinawa, where a large number of U.S. installations were sited, is a more complex issue. Some argue that the U.S. effectively governed Okinawa for decades pursuant to the 1951 Peace Treaty with Japan. Indeed, it was the view of Secretary of State John Foster Dulles that under the Peace Treaty Japan only retained "residual sovereignty" in Okinawa. See Secretary John Foster Dulles, Statements at the Second Plenary Session, at San Francisco Peace Conference, Sept. 5, 1951, in Dep't St. Bull.

17. On the history of NATO see Marc Trachtenberg, *A Constructed Peace: The Making of European Settlement, 1945–1963* (Princeton, N.J.: Princeton University Press, 1999).

18. Eyal Benvenisti, *The International Law of Occupation* (Princeton, N.J.: Princeton University Press, 1993), 6. Stalin knew better: "This war is not as in the past. Whoever occupies a territory also imposes his own social system . . . it cannot be otherwise," he told the Yugoslav communist Milovan Djilas in 1945. Gaddis, *We Now Know*, 14.

19. This principle has increasingly come under stress. See, generally, Adam Roberts, "Transformative Military Occupation: Applying the Laws of War and Human Rights," *American Journal of International Law* 100, no. 3 (July 2006); Benvenisti, *The International Law*.

20. The question of whether the German and Japanese occupations were in fact consistent with what international lawyers refer to as "Hague law" was debated at the time. On Germany compare Kurt von Laun, "The Legal Status of Germany," *American Journal of International Law* 45 (1951), with Pitman Potter, "The Legal Bases and Character of Military Occupation in Germany and Japan," *American Journal of International Law* 43 (1949), Charles Fahy, "Legal Problems of German Occupation," *Michigan Law Review* 47 (1948), and Josef L. Kunz, "The Status of Occupied Germany under International Law: A Legal Dilemma," *Western Political Quarterly* 3 (1950). Benvenisti argues that "the Allies never treated the law of occupation as the source of their authority in Germany and Japan, nor did they consider their administrations bound by the Hague Regulations, which they saw as inapplicable in Germany and Japan." Benvenisti, *International Law*, 91.

21. Supplemental Brief for Petitioner, Madsen v. Kinsella, 343 U.S. 341 (1952), 1851 WL 7498 (October 8, 1951).

22. Ross v. McIntyre, 140 U.S. 453 (1891).

23. Madsen v. Kinsella, 93 F. Supp. 319 (D.C. W.Va. 1950) at 322–23.

24. Ibid., 323.

25. Ibid., 324–25.

26. Ibid., 323.

27. Petitioner's Reply Brief in Madsen v. Kinsella, 343 U.S. 341 (1952), 1952 WL 82037 (1952) at 12, 14.

28. McCauley, "American Courts in Germany: 600,000 Cases Later," *ABA Journal* 40 (1954).

29. Many of these cases are discussed in Fairman, "Some New Problems," 13.

30. Louis Fisher, *Nazi Saboteurs on Trial: A Military Tribunal and American Law* (Lawrence: University of Kansas Press, 2003); David J. Danelski, "The Saboteurs' Case," *Journal of Supreme Court History* 61 (1996).

31. Yamashita v. Styer, 327 U.S. 1 (1946). The story is told in Richard L. Lael, *The Yamashita Precedent: War Crimes and Command Responsibility* (Wilmington, Del.: S. R. Books, 1982).

32. Stephen I. Vladeck, "Deconstructing Hirota: Habeas Corpus, Citizenship, and Article III," *Georgetown Law Journal* 95 (2007).

33. Ibid., 1507–8.

34. Hirota v. MacArthur, 338 U.S. 197 (1948) at 198.

35. Omar v. Harvey, 416 F. Supp. 2d (D.D.C. 2006).

36. A parallel can also be discerned in the law enforcement cooperation discussed in chapter 6 in this volume, as well in the renditions and interrogations discussed in chapter 7. In both cases cooperation with foreign officials working overseas has permitted American agents to achieve aims that otherwise would remain elusive, and in the process to skirt legal restrains that might apply if the actions were solely undertaken by American officials.

37. Munaf v. Geren, 553 U.S. (2008).

38. Some may have been civilians working for the German forces—their exact status was in dispute.

39. Johnson v. Eisentrager, 339 U.S. 763 (1950) at 781.

40. Ibid., 771.

41. Ibid., 778.

42. Ibid.

43. Ibid., 784–85.

44. Ibid., 795–96.

45. Simon Duke and Wolfgang Krieger, eds., introduction to *U.S. Military Forces in Europe: The Early Years, 1945–1970* (New York: Westview Press, 1993), 3.

46. These numbers are drawn from the oral argument in Reid v. Covert; see Philip B. Kurland and Gerhard Casper, eds., *Landmark Briefs and Arguments of the Supreme Court of the United States: Constitutional Law* (Arlington, Va.: University Publications of America, 1975), 52: 825.

47. This is the U.S. government's figure at the time of the Reid v. Covert litigation; see ibid.

48. As of 2001 the United States was party to 107 status of forces agreements; Mark J. Yost and Douglas S. Anderson, "The Military Extraterritorial Jurisdiction Act of 2000: Closing the Gap," *American Journal of International Law* 95, no. 2 (2001): 451. These agreements are not unique the United States, though the United States appears to have many more of them than any other state. See, e.g., Woodliffe, *Peacetime Use*; Aurel Sari, "Status of Forces and Status of Mission Agreements under the ESDP: The EU's Evolving Practice," *European Journal of International Law* 19, no. 1 (2008); Jost Delbruck, "International Law and Military Forces Abroad: U.S. Military Presence in Europe, 1945–1965," in Duke and Krieger, *U.S. Military Forces*; Joseph Rouse and Gordon Baldwin, "The Exercise of Criminal Jurisdiction under the NATO Status of Forces Agreement," *American Journal of International Law* 51 (1957).

49. Woodliffe, *Peacetime Use*, 15, notes several ways in which the practice was unprecedented.

50. Fareed Zakaria, *The Post-American World* (New York: Norton, 2008), 238.

51. Agreement between the Parties to the North Atlantic Treaty Regarding the Status of Their Forces, signed June 19, 1951, U.N.T.S. 199, Article VII at 67.

52. Government's Reply Brief in Reid v. Covert, 354 U.S. 1 (1957), 1956 WL 89113 (1956) at 4: "Figures obtained from the Army alone show that in the six fiscal years from July 1, 1949 to June 30, 1955, a total of 2280 civilians were tried by court martial, or an average of just under 400 per year."

53. Indeed, the Eisenhower administration would characterize the cases as "strikingly similar" to Madsen v. Kinsella. Brief for Appellant, Reid v. Covert, 354 U.S. 1 (1957), 1956 WL 89112 (October 8, 1951), at 19. Murder-by-wife was apparently not uncommon; Fairman, "Some New Problems,"

626–28, discusses the 1949 *Ybarbo* case before the district court of the military government in Germany.

54. Kurland and Casper, *Landmark Briefs*, 778.

55. Ibid., 780.

56. Petition for Writ of Habeas Corpus, Reid v. Covert, Habeas Corpus No. 87–55 (November 17, 1955) at 1.

57. There Clarice Covert gave birth to a child, approximately 9 months after the murder of her husband. Habeas Petition, Reid v. Covert, 2.

58. Clarice Covert received extensive psychiatric care before the murder; see Exhibit C in the Petition for Habeas Corpus, Reid v. Covert. Quote from Reid v. Covert, 354 U.S. 1 (1957), opinion of Justice Black at 4.

59. The act is described in Norman Bentwich, "The U.S.A. Visiting Forces Act, 1942," *The Modern Law Review* 6, no. 1 (December 1942).

60. Ibid.

61. Hilton v. Guyot, 159 U.S. 113 (1895) at 163.

62. Government Reply Brief, Reid v. Covert, 354 U.S. 1 (1957), 1956 WL 89113 (1956), at 5.

63. Government Reply Brief, Reid v. Covert, 21.

64. Oral argument 1956 in Kurland and Casper, *Landmark Briefs*, 797.

65. Oral argument 1956, in Kurland and Casper, *Landmark Briefs*, 779.

66. Ibid., 780.

67. Ibid., 783.

68. Kinsella v. Krueger, 475.

69. Seery v. United States, 127 F. Supp. 601 (Ct. Cl. 1955) and Turney v. United States, 115 F. Supp. 457 (Ct. Cl. 1953). Arguably this door was opened a tiny bit in the nineteenth century by *Mitchell v. Harmony*, which involved property taken from an American in Mexico by U.S. forces. The majority noted that the trespass had taken place "out of the limits of the United States," but maintained that an "action for it in the Circuit Court for any district in which the defendant might be found . . . " Mitchell v. Harmony, 54 U.S. 115 (1851) at 137. The case has almost entirely been read as one about military necessity, rather than extraterritoriality. A major exception to this reading is *Reid v. Covert* itself, in which the plurality cited *Mitchell*, along with the *Insular Cases* and several others, as evidence that the Constitution was not strictly limited by the sovereign borders of the United States.

70. Frederick Bernays Wiener, "Persuading the Supreme Court to Reverse Itself: Reid v. Covert," *Litigation* 14, no. 4 (Summer 1988). Frederick Wiener was counsel for Clarice Covert, and argues it was unique. What motivated the rehearing is unclear. Justice Harlan, the sole individual to change his vote, suggested that there had been insufficient time in the first round to properly consider the issues. "The petitions for rehearing which were filed last summer afforded an opportunity for a greater degree of reflection upon the difficult issues involved in these cases than, at least for me, was possible in the short interval between the argument and decision of the cases in the closing days of last Term." Reid v. Covert, Harlan concurrence.

71. Reid v. Covert, Black opinion, 5.

72. Reid 2, oral argument, in Kurland and Casper, *Landmark Briefs*, 822.

73. Ibid., 855.

74. Kurland and Casper, *Landmark Briefs*, 785.

75. Gerry Neuman termed this decision a "modernist breakthrough." Gerald Neuman, *Strangers to the Constitution: Immigrants, Borders, and Fundamental Law* (Princeton, N.J.: Princeton University Press, 1996), 89 (referring to Reid v. Covert).

76. Though, in point of fact, not that far removed: *Reid* was handed down in the very same year the United States ended its last system of traditional extraterritorial jurisdiction, in Morocco. This was duly noted in *Reid*.

77. Reid v. Covert, 12. The Court's invocation of cases like *Bowman* shows that it recognized that the jurisdictional concepts at play in the contemporary world were different from those of the past. And of course by 1957 the United States was routinely applying regulatory statutes abroad, something that could not escape the attention of the nation's highest judicial officials.

78. Ibid., 14.

79. Ibid., 40.

80. Louis Henkin, *Foreign Affairs and the United States Constitution*, 2nd ed. (New York: Oxford University Press, 1996); David Golove, "Treatymaking and the Nation: The Historical Foundations of the Nationalist Conception of the Treaty Power," *Michigan Law Review* 98, no. 3 (2000).

81. Robinson O. Everett, "Military Jurisdiction over Civilians," *Duke Law Journal* 9 (1960); Note, "Criminal Jurisdiction over Civilians Accompanying American Armed Forces Overseas," *Harvard Law Review* 71 (1958).

82. Kinsella v. United States *ex rel.* Singleton, 361 U.S. 234 (1960); Grisham v. Hagan, 361 U.S. 278 (1960); McElroy v. United States *ex rel.* Guagliardo, 361 U.S. 281 (1960).

83. United States General Accounting Office, Comptroller General Report to Congress, *Some Criminal Offenses Committed Overseas by DOD Civilians Are Not Being Prosecuted: Legislation Is Needed* (September 11, 1979).

84. GAO Report, ibid.

85. Ibid. The GAO numbers were technically for the 12-month period preceding November 30, 1977.

86. 18 U.S.C. Section 3267. The case that spurred the act was United States v. Gatlin, 216 F.3d 207 (2d Cir. 2000). Mark J. Yost and Douglas S. Anderson, "The Military Extraterritorial Jurisdiction Act of 2000: Closing the Gap," *American Journal of International Law* 95, no. 2 (2001).

87. Technically, the act refers to the "special maritime and territorial jurisdiction" of the United States, which in turn means "lands reserved or acquired for the use of the United States, and under the exclusive and concurrent jurisdiction thereof."

88. Ibid., 453. In 2007 MEJA became the subject of significant public comment after the shootings of seventeen Iraqi civilians by members of an American private military firm, Blackwater USA. As the subsequent furor

illustrated, MEJA had not in fact fully closed the jurisdictional gap; because Blackwater employees worked for the State Department rather than the Defense Department, their lawyers argued they were not subject to MEJA. This issue is discussed further in chapter 7.

89. See, in particular, Neuman, *Strangers to the Constitution*, and Gerald Neuman, "Whose Constitution?," *Yale Law Journal* 100 (1990), which provides four approaches.

90. Henry J. Steiner, Detlev F. Vagts, and Harold Hongju Koh, *Transnational Legal Problems: Materials and Text*, 4th ed. (New York: Foundation Press, 1994), 861.

91. Andreas F. Lowenfeld, "Hijacking, Freedom, and the 'American Way,'" *Michigan Law Review* 83, no. 4 (1985).

92. Details can be found in Herbert Stern, *Judgment in Berlin* (New York: Universe Books, 1984). There were in fact several hijackers, but Tiede was the main figure.

93. Ibid., 4.

94. United States v. Tiede, 30.

95. Stern, *Judgment*, 95–96.

96. Ibid., 109.

97. United States v. Tiede, 93.

98. Ibid., 35.

99. Dostal v. Haig, 652 F.2d 173 (1981).

100. David Bederman, "Extraterritorial Domicile and the Constitution," *Virginia Journal of International Law* 28, no. 1 (1988): 492.

101. Though more commonly voiced against Britain and France than the United States. Woodliffe, *Peacetime Use*, 69–73.

102. Ibid., 70.

103. Not all SOFAs were with other Western powers; many were with weak states such as the Philippines. But many of the major bases of the United States were sited in nations that were part of the advanced industrial world—Germany, Italy, Iceland, Japan, and so forth.

104. Peter Andreas and Ethan Nadelmann, *Policing the Globe: Criminalization and Crime Control in International Relations* (New York: Oxford University Press, 2006).

Chapter Six

1. United States v. Verdugo-Urquidez, 856 F.2d 1214 (9th Cir. 1988). The connection to the Camarena murder is noted in United States v. Verdugo-Urquidez, 1994 U.S. App. LEXIS 16083 (9th Cir. 1994) (unpublished opinion, dissent by Judge Reinhardt).

2. The exclusionary rule is a judge-made doctrine that holds that evidence obtained in violation of the Fourth Amendment must be excluded from trial. Weeks v. United States, 232 U.S. 383 (1914), is generally credited with setting forth the rule. See also Boyd v. United States, 116 U.S. 616, 6 S. Ct. 524 (1886).

3. Peter Andreas and Ethan Nadelmann, *Policing the Globe: Criminalization and Crime Control in International Relations* (New York: Oxford University Press, 2006), 129; Maria Celia Toro, "The Internationalization of Police: The DEA in Mexico," *Journal of American History* 86, no. 2 (September 1999).

4. Gregory Bowman, "Thinking Outside the Border: Homeland Security and the Forward Deployment of the U.S. Border," *Houston Law Review* 44, no. 2 (2007); Ayelet Shachar, "The Shifting Border of Immigration Regulation," *Stanford Journal of Civil Rights & Civil Liberties* 3 (2007): 175.

5. Kal Raustiala, "The Architecture of International Cooperation: Transgovernmental Networks and the Future of International Law," *Virginia Journal of International Law* 43, no. 1 (2002).

6. Andreas and Nadelmann, *Policing the Globe*, 169.

7. I have borrowed the title of this section from the excellent study by Ethan A. Nadelmann, *Cops across Borders: The Internationalization of U.S. Criminal Law Enforcement* (University Park, Pa.: Penn State Press, 1993).

8. Paul B. Stares, *Global Habit: The Drug Problem in a Borderless World* (Washington, D.C.: Brookings Institution, 1996), 2. Some high numbers, such as the $500 billion given by Stares, have now been seriously challenged.

9. See, e.g., "Smugglers Try New Recipe: Hiding Drugs in Food," *U.S. Customs and Border Protection Today*, July–August 2005, available at www.cbp.gov/xp/customstoday/2005/Jul_Aug/other/drugs_food.xml; Moises Naim, *Illicit: How Smugglers, Traffickers, and Copycats are Hijacking the Global Economy* (New York: Doubleday, 2005); Peter Andreas and Richard Friman, eds., *The Illicit Global Economy* (Lanham, Md.: Rowman and Littlefield, 1999).

10. Kal Raustiala, "Law, Liberalization, and International Narcotics Trafficking," *New York University Journal of International Law & Politics* 32, no. 1 (1999).

11. Nadelmann, *Cops across Borders*, 50. Andreas and Nadelmann note that by 1900 U.S. Treasury agents were active in five European cities: Paris, London, Berlin, Cologne, and St. Gall, Switzerland. Andreas and Nadelmann, *Policing the Globe*, 112.

12. Toro, "Internationalization of Police," 627.

13. The common law doctrine was codified in the United States by the Uniform Fresh Pursuit Act of 1937. See, generally, "Recent Statutes: Interstate Rendition—Uniform Act on Fresh Pursuit," *Columbia Law Review* 38, no. 4 (1938).

14. I have borrowed this title from the excellent study by Ethan A. Nadelmann, *Cops across Borders: The Internationalization of U.S. Criminal Law Enforcement* (University Park, Pa.: Penn State Press, 1993).

15. U.S. Government Accountability Office, *Drug Control: International Narcotics Activities of the United States* (Washington, D.C.: GAO, 1987); Toro, "Internationalization of Police," 625.

16. Department of Justice, Office of Legal Counsel, *Authority of the Federal Bureau of Investigation to Override International Law in Extraterritorial Law Enforcement Activities*, 3 Op. Off. Legal Counsel 163 (1989).

17. Peter Andreas, "Redrawing the Line: Borders and Security in the Twenty-First Century," *International Security* 28, no. 2 (2003): 87.

18. See the Comprehensive Crime Control Act of 1984, Pub. L. No. 98–473, 98 Stat. 2068, and the 1986 Anti-Drug Abuse Act, Pub. L. No. 99–570, 100 Stat. 3207. Congress's power to extend U.S. criminal law extraterritorially is generally grounded in the power of Congress to "define and punish . . . offenses against the Law of Nations" and to regulate foreign commerce.

19. Andreas and Nadelmann, *Policing the Globe*.

20. FBI, "Cracking Down on Violent Gangs," September 9, 2005, available at http://www.fbi.gov/page2/sept05/ngtf090905.htm.

21. This practice became common in the 1980s and since as a means of enhancing what are known as transgovernmental networks. Raustiala, "Architecture of International Cooperation"; Anne-Marie Slaughter, *A New World Order* (Princeton, N.J.: Princeton University Press, 2004); Maximo Langer, "Revolution in Latin American Criminal Procedure: Diffusion of Legal Ideas from the Periphery," *American Journal of Comparative Law* 55 (2007): 617.

22. Nadelmann, *Cops across Borders*, chapter 3.

23. Nadelmann, *Cops across Borders*, 395.

24. Andreas and Nadelmann, *Policing the Globe*, 170.

25. Roberto Suro, "FBI's 'Clean' Team Follows 'Dirty' Work of Intelligence; Units Pool Facts on Sensitive Foreign Cases but Work Apart," *Washington Post*, August 16, 1999.

26. Nadelmann, *Cops across Borders*, 177.

27. Judy Miller, "A New York Detective's Tricky Beat in Israel," *New York Times*, May 14, 2005.

28. See, e.g., People v. Merrill, 2 Parker's Crim. 590 (N.Y. 1855) at 596, cited in Gary B. Born, "A Reappraisal of the Extraterritorial Reach of U.S. Law," *Law and Policy in International Business* 24, no. 1 (1992), in which a New York court wrote that "[i]t cannot be pretended or assumed that a state has jurisdiction over crimes committed beyond its territorial limits" and declined jurisdiction over a non–New Yorker who lured a black man from New York and then sold him as a slave.

29. United States v. Bowman, 260 U.S. 94 (1922).

30. Lawrence Preuss, "American Conception of Jurisdiction with Respect to Conflicts of Law on Crime," *Transactions of the Grotius Society* 30 (1944): 198.

31. Andreas Lowenfeld, "U.S. Law Enforcement Abroad: The Constitution and International Law," *American Journal of International Law* 84 (1990): 467–68.

32. United States v. Toscanino, 500 F.2d 267 (1974) at 274–75.

33. Best v. United States, 184 F.2d 131 (1st Cir. 1950) at 138. This was before *Reid v. Covert* overturned the long-standing rule against extraterritorial

application of constitutional rights, and thus the fact of American occupation seemed to be critical.

34. Powell v. Zuckert, 366 F.2d 634 (D.C. Cir. 1966).

35. A much later case in the Second Circuit held that American citizens abroad have a Fourth Amendment right to be free of unreasonable searches, but those searches need not be pursuant to a warrant. This holding flowed in part from the Verdugo decision's emphasis on the alleged impracticality of warrants for offshore searches. In re Terrorist Bombings of U.S. Embassies in East Africa (Fourth Amendment Challenges), F.3d, (2d. Cir. 2008), 2008 WL 4967686.

36. United States v. Toscanino, 280.

37. See, e.g., United States v. Lee, 274 U.S. 559 (1927) and Ford v. United States, 273 U.S. 593 (1926), upholding jurisdiction over persons aboard a British ship in international waters attempting to smuggle alcohol into the United States.

38. Louis Henkin, "The Constitution at Sea," *Maine Law Review* 36 (1984): 201.

39. United States v. Cadena, 585 F.2d 1252 (5th Cir. 1978) at 1257. Compare, however, United States v. Warren, 578 F.2d 1058 (5th Cir. 1978).

40. *Cadena*, 1262.

41. Although the court was bold in making this pronouncement about the extraterritoriality of the Fourth Amendment, it tempered its impact. It ruled that although the search of the Canadian vessel was indeed warrantless, it was nonetheless reasonable. Exigent circumstances—the need for alacrity on the high seas, and the belief that a felony was ongoing—made the search constitutional.

42. Henkin, "Constitution at Sea," 201.

43. United States *ex rel.* Lujan v. Gengler, 510 F.2d (2d Cir. 1975) at 69 (Judge Anderson, concurring). See also United States v. Lira, 515 F.2d 68 (2d Cir. 1975).

44. Berlin Democratic Club v. Rumsfeld, 410 F. Supp. 144 (D.C.D.C., 1976) at 152.

45. *Restatement of Law Third of the Foreign Relations Law of the United States*, section 722, comment M. The chief reporter was Louis Henkin, who has long championed this idea. See, e.g., Louis Henkin, "The Constitution as Compact and as Conscience: Individual Rights Abroad and at Our Gates," *William & Mary Law Review* 27 (1985).

46. As one commentator noted at that time, these decisions "form a curious mosaic." R. D. Hunter, "The Extraterritorial Application of the Constitution—Unalienable Rights?," *Virginia Law Review* 72 (1986): 649. For a critical take see Paul B. Stephan, "Constitutional Limits on the Struggle against International Terrorism: Revisiting the Rights of Overseas Aliens," *Connecticut Law Review* 19 (1987). See also Paul B. Stephan, "Constitutional Limits on International Rendition of Criminal Suspects," *Virginia Journal of International Law* 20, no. 3 (1980).

47. United States v. Verdugo-Urquidez, 1217. Earlier examples with similar assumptions about the Fourth Amendment include United States v. Montez-Hernandez, 291 F. Supp. 712 (E.D. Cal. 1968); Au Yi Lau v. INS, 445 F.2d 217 (D.C. Cir. 1971); Babula v. INS, 665 F.2d 293 (3d Cir. 1981). See also James G. Connell III and René L. Valladares, "Search and Seizure Protections for Undocumented Aliens: The Territoriality and Voluntary Presence Principle in Fourth Amendment Law," *American Criminal Law Review* 34 (1997): 1307, noting, "Before *Verdugo*, courts repeatedly stated that both legal and undocumented aliens in the United States are protected by the Fourth Amendment."

48. United States v. Verdugo-Urquidez.

49. Ibid., 1224.

50. For pre-*Verdugo* discussions of social contract theory as applied to extraterritoriality, see Louis Henkin, "The United States Constitution as Social Compact," *Proceedings of the American Philosophical Society* 131, no. 3 (1987); Hunter, "Extraterritorial Application"; Stephan, "Constitutional Limits."

51. Brief of the Government (Petitioner) at 9, United States v. Verdugo-Urquidez, 494 U.S. 259 (1990).

52. Whether illegal aliens were protected in the same manner as legal aliens has never been entirely clear, but the majority of courts have assumed that illegal aliens did fall within the protections of the Fourth Amendment. Connell and Valladares, "Search and Seizure Protections." Since *Verdugo* at least one federal court has denied the Fourth Amendment to illegal aliens. United States v. Esparza-Mendoza, 265 F. Supp. 2d 1254 (D. Utah 2003).

53. Brief of the Government (Petitioner) at 7, United States v. Verdugo-Urquidez.

54. Quote is from Yamataya v. Fisher, 189 U.S. 86 (1903); on the early debates in the eighteenth century see Gerald Neuman, *Strangers to the Constitution: Immigrants, Borders, and Fundamental Law* (Princeton, N.J.: Princeton University Press, 1996), chapter 4.

55. Brief of the Government (Petitioner) at 6, United States v. Verdugo-Urquidez.

56. Leading scholars have also endorsed versions of it. For a recent example see Richard Fallon and Daniel Meltzer, "Habeas Corpus Jurisdiction, Substantive Rights, and the War on Terror," *Harvard Law Review* 120, no. 8 (2007): 2083. With regard to the lesser rights of aliens, they write "our acceptance reflects an assumption that the Constitution is a continuing compact among the American people, established and accepted principally for the benefit of Americans . . . aliens are by definition outsiders to the fair scheme of social cooperation and mutual advantage that the Constitution aims to establish among the American people."

57. United States v. Verdugo-Urquidez, 1220.

58. Ibid., 1222. Alexander Bickel famously noted that "remarkably enough . . . the concept of citizenship plays only the most minimal role in

the American constitutional scheme." Alexander Bickel, *The Morality of Consent* (New Haven, Conn.: Yale University Press, 1974), 33; David Cole, "Enemy Aliens," *Stanford Law Review* 54 (2002): 978. For areas in which differences exist see *Hampton v. Mow Sun Wong*, 426 U.S. 88 (1976); Mathews v. Diaz, 426 U.S. 67 (1976).

59. United States v. Verdugo-Urquidez, 1223.

60. Unless she was at the border or its functional equivalent, where a general "border exception" to aspects of the Fourth Amendment is well established. Almeida Sanchez v. United States, 413 U.S. 266 (1973).

61. See Respondent's Brief at 3, Note 2, United States v. Verdugo-Urquidez.

62. See the discussion in chapter 4 in this volume.

63. Oral Argument Transcript at 16, United States v. Verdugo-Urquidez.

64. Ibid., 9–10.

65. United States v. Verdugo-Urquidez, 277.

66. Neuman had dubbed this a "global due process" approach. Neuman, *Strangers to the Constitution*, 92–93.

67. United States v. Verdugo-Urquidez, 265.

68. Ibid., 271–72.

69. Oral Argument Transcript at 20, United States v. Verdugo-Urquidez.

70. For a complete discussion of the membership conception of the United States constitution see Neuman, *Strangers to the Constitution*.

71. United States v. Verdugo-Urquidez, 273.

72. United States v. Esparza-Mendoza, 265 F. Supp. 2d 1254 (D. Utah 2003).

73. Andreas and Nadelmann, *Policing the Globe*, 241.

74. Andreas, "Redrawing the Line," 87.

75. Cited in Andreas and Nadelmann, *Policing the Globe*, 158. See also Naim, *Illicit*.

76. United States v. Verdugo-Urquidez, 273–74.

77. Larry Kramer, "Vestiges of Beale: Extraterritorial Application of American Law," *Supreme Court Review* (1991): 202: "[in *EEOC v. Aramco*] the Court slipped back to the nineteenth century, seemingly unaware that it was doing so."

78. Deepsouth Packing v. Laitram, 406 U.S. 518 (1972) at 531. The quoted statute is 35 U.S.C. Section 2271(f) (1984) (emphasis added). Congressional overruling of extraterritoriality decisions is analyzed in Einar Elhauge, *Statutory Default Rules* (Cambridge, Mass.: Harvard University Press, 2008), chapter 11.

79. Foley Bros. v. Filardo, 336 U.S. 281 (1949).

80. Katherine Van Wezel Stone, "Labor and the Global Economy: Four Approaches to Transnational Labor Regulation," *Michigan Journal of International Law* 16, no. 4 (1995): 1016. Courts continue to read the labor statutes narrowly, however; see e.g. *Shekoyan v. Sibley International,*. 409 F.3d 414 (D.C. Cir. 2005).

81. See, e.g., Jane Ginsburg, "Extraterritoriality and Multiterritoriality in Copyright Infringement," *Virginia Journal of International Law* 37 (1997);

Reuben S. Avi-Yonah, "National Regulation of Multinational Enterprises: An Essay on Comity, Extraterritoriality, and Harmonization," *Columbia Journal of Transnational Law* 42, no. 2 (2003).

82. Amlon Metal, Inc. v. FMC Corp., 775 F. Supp. 668 (SDNY 1991); EDF v. Massey, 986 F.2d 528 (D.C. Cir. 1993).

83. Curtis A. Bradley, Territorial Intellectual Property Rights in an Age of Globalism, *Virginia Journal of International Law* 37 (1997): 508: "Trademark is therefore 'extraterritorial' in a way that patent and copyright law is not. The reason for this differential treatment of trademark law is far from clear."

84. For example, EDF v. Massey, 986 F 2d 528 (D.C. Cir. 1993).

85. Born, "A Reappraisal," 99–100.

86. Asahi Metal Industry Co. v. Superior Court, 480 U.S. 102 (1987).

87. As the Seventh Circuit put it, "Countless cases have assumed that foreign companies have all the rights of U.S. citizens to object to extraterritorial assertions of personal jurisdiction." Afram Export Corp. v. Metallurgiki Halyps, S.A. 772 F.2d 1358, 1362 (7th Cir. 1985), *abrogated on other grounds by* Salve Regina Coll. v. Russell, 499 U.S. 225 (1991).

88. Preuss, "American Conception of Jurisdiction," 198.

89. Nadelmann, *Cops across Borders*, 12.

90. Suro, "FBI's 'Clean' Team."

91. Ibid.; see also Andreas and Nadelmann, *Policing the Globe*, 170.

92. Andreas and Nadelmann, *Policing the Globe*.

93. Department of Justice, Federal Bureau of Investigation, Counterterrorism Unit, *Terrorism 2002–2005* (2006): 5, available at http://www.fbi.gov/publications/terror/terrorism2002_2005.pdf. On the investigation of Blackwater see David Johnston and John M. Broder, "FBI Says Guards Killed 14 Iraqis without Cause," *New York Times*, November 13, 2007.

94. A 2008 decision by the Second Circuit, stemming from the same litigation, held that the Fourth Amendment's Warrant Clause did not apply to a search of an American citizen abroad, though its requirement of reasonableness did apply. In re Terrorist Bombings of U.S. Embassies in East Africa (Fourth Amendment Challenges), ____F.3d ___, (2d. Cir. 2008), 2008 WL 4967686.

95. Miranda v. Arizona, 384 U.S. 436 (1966).

96. E.g., United States v. Yunis, 859 F.2d 953 (D.C. Cir. 1988) at 957. See also United States v. Yousef, 327 F.3d (2d Circ., 2003) and United States v. Davis, 905 F.2d 245 (9th Cir. 1990) at 248–49, employing the Fifth Amendment's due process standard: "In order to apply extraterritorially a federal criminal statute to a defendant consistently with due process, there must be a sufficient nexus between the defendant and the United States, so that such application would not be arbitrary or fundamentally unfair."

97. United States v. Bin Laden, 132 F. Supp. 2d 168 (S.D.N.Y. 2001) at 181–82.

98. Ibid.

99. Ibid., 187.

100. Ibid. Emphasis in original.

101. Brennan and Marshall, dissenting, in *Verdugo* at 282.

102. Subsequent cases have not overturned *Bin Laden*, and even the Bush administration has conceded the vitality of its holding in a recent case. United States v. Karake, 443 F. Supp. 2d 8 (D.D.C. 2006). United States v. Yousef, 327 F.3d 56, 145–46 (2d Cir. 2003), held that "statements taken by foreign police in the absence of Miranda warnings are admissible if voluntary."

103. "Potential Legal Constraints Applicable to Interrogations of Persons Captured by U.S. Armed Forces in Afghanistan," memorandum from Jay S. Bybee to William J. Haynes II (Feb. 26, 2002), reprinted in Karen Greenberg and Joshua L. Dratel, eds., *The Torture Papers: The Road to Abu Ghraib* (Cambridge: Cambridge University Press, 2005), 149.

104. Bowman, "Thinking Outside the Border."

105. Anil Kalhan, "The Fourth Amendment and Privacy Implications of Interior Immigration Enforcement," *UC Davis Law Review* 41 (2008).

106. Philip Shenon, "U.S. Widens Checks at Foreign Ports," *New York Times*, June 12, 2003, 1A.

107. U.S. Customs and Border Protection, "Container Security Initiative," available at http://www.cbp.gov/xp/cgov/trade/cargo_security/csi/.

108. Ayelet Shachar, "Shifting Border," 167; Peter Andreas refers to this as "a 'thickening' of borders and the creation of buffer zones." Andreas, "Redrawing the Line," 79.

109. Leng May Ma v. Barber, 357 U.S. 185 (1958).

110. Sale v. Haitian Centers Council, 509 U.S. 155 (1993) at 175.

111. Shaughnessy v. United States *ex rel.* Mezei, 345 U.S. 206 (1953) at 213.

112. Gerald Neuman, "Anomalous Zones," *Stanford Law Review* 48 (1996).

113. Kalhan, "Fourth Amendment," 27.

114. Brennan and Marshall, dissenting, at 494 (footnotes omitted).

115. Harbury v. Deutsch, 233 F.3d 596 (2000) at 602.

116. Ibid., 604.

Chapter Seven

1. Justice Black dissenting in Johnson v. Eisentrager, 339 U.S. 763 (1950) at 795–96.

2. Memorandum to William J. Haynes II from Patrick Philpin and John Yoo, December 28, 2001, reprinted in Karen Greenberg and Joshua L. Dratel, eds., *The Torture Papers: The Road to Abu Ghraib* (Cambridge: Cambridge University Press, 2005), 29.

3. John Yoo, *War by Other Means: An Insider's Account of the War on Terror* (New York: Atlantic Monthly Press, 2006). See also Jack Goldsmith, *The Terror Presidency: Law and Judgment Inside the Bush Administration* (New York: Norton, 2006); James Goldgeier and Derek Chollet, *America Between the Wars: From 11/9 to 9/11* (PublicAffairs, 2008).

4. James Risen and Thom Shanker, "Hussein Enters Post-9/11 Web of U.S. Prisons," *New York Times*, December 18, 2003, A1.

5. Dana Priest and Joe Stephens, "Secret World of U.S. Interrogation: Long History of Tactics in Overseas Prisons is Coming to Light," *Washington Post*, May 11, 2004, A1. See also Jane Mayer, *The Dark Side: The Inside Story of How the War on Terror Turned into a War on American Ideals* (Random House, 2008).

6. Richard Stevenson and Joel Brinkley, "More Questions as Rice Asserts Detainee Policy," *New York Times*, December 8, 2005.

7. Johan Steyn, "Guantanamo Bay: A Legal Black Hole," *International and Comparative Law Quarterly* 53, no. 1 (2004).

8. Whether Cuban law might apply in Guantanamo was expressly raised, for example, by Chief Justice John Roberts in the oral argument in Boumediene v. Bush, No. 06–1195 (2008).

9. Downes v. Bidwell, 182 U.S. 244 (1901) at 341.

10. Joseph Lazar, "International Legal Status of Guantanamo Bay," *American Journal of International Law* 62 (1968): 739.

11. The Treaty of 1934 "preserved U.S. rights regarding the naval base at Guantanamo Bay and reasserted the validity of the acts of the 1899–1902 occupation government." Jules Robert Benjamin, *The United States and Cuba: Hegemony and Dependent Development, 1880–1934* (Pittsburgh: University of Pittsburgh Press, 1977), 182.

12. Arnold H. Leibowitz, *Defining Status: A Comprehensive Analysis of United States Territorial Relations* (The Netherlands: Martinus Nijhoff, 1989), 19. Robert Kagan, *Dangerous Nation: America's Place in the World from Its Earliest Days to the Dawn of the Twentieth Century* (New York: Knopf, 2006), chapter 12; Ernest May, *Imperial Democracy: The Emergence of America as a Great Power* (New York: Harcourt, Brace and World, 1961).

13. Robert Montague, "A Brief Study of Some of the International Legal and Political Aspects of the Guantanamo Bay Problem," *Kentucky Law Journal* 50 (1962): 459; "Customs Duties—Goods Brought into United States Naval Station at Guantanamo Bay, Cuba," Op. Atty. Gen. 35 (1929) at 537.

14. See, e.g., Ian Brownlie, *Principles of International Law*, 5th ed. (New York: Oxford University Press, 2003), 110–11. Residual sovereignty was also the principle underlying the United States's control over the Okinawan islands in the wake of the Japanese surrender in 1945, at least according to John Foster Dulles. United States v. Ushi Shiroma, 123 F. Supp. 145 (9th Cir. 1954). A reversionary reading of the Guantanamo lease is consistent with both the plain meaning of the text and with the realities of the subsequent behavior of the parties—two central considerations when interpreting the texts of international agreements. See also Joseph Lazar, " 'Cession in Lease' of the Guantanamo Bay Naval Station and Cuba's 'Ultimate Sovereignty,' " *American Journal of International Law* 63 (1969): 116, and Gherebi v. Bush, 352 F.3d 1278 (9th Cir. 2003) at 1291.

15. "Customs Duties," Op. Atty. Gen. 35 (1929) at 537.

16. Montague, "Brief Study," 472.

17. The United States removed the minefield in 1999, when it ratified the Amended Mines Protocol to the Convention on Certain Conventional Weapons. Speech by Assistant Secretary of State Lincoln P. Bloomfield Jr., "U.S. Humanitarian Mine Action: Make the World Safer," available at http://usinfo.state.gov/journals/itps/0104/ijpe/bloomfield.htm.

18. The annual rent is $4,085. Jeffrey Toobin, "Inside the Wire," *New Yorker*, February 9, 2004.

19. David Rose, "Guantanamo Bay on Trial," *Vanity Fair*, January 2004, 91. The usual figure given is 45 square miles, but some sources cite a smaller size, e.g., Michael Ratner, "How We Closed the Guantanamo HIV Camp: The Intersection of Politics and Litigation," *Harvard Human Rights Journal* 11 (1998).

20. Bird v. United States, 923 F. Supp. 338 (D. Conn. 1996).

21. United States v. Rogers, 388 F. Supp. 298 (D.C. Va. 1975); United States v. Lee, 906 F.2d 117 (4th Cir. 1990).

22. Elaine Sciolino, "U.S. Tells Haitians Held at Guantanamo They Must Go Home," *New York Times*, December 30, 1994. Harold H. Koh, "America's Offshore Refugee Camps," *University of Richmond Law Review* 29 (1994); Harold H. Koh, "The Haitian Centers Council Case: Reflections on Refoulement and Haitian Centers Council," *Harvard International Law Journal* 35, NO. 1 (1994).

23. A brief episode in the 1970s involved some detentions at the camp.

24. Haitian Refugee Center v. Baker, 953 F.2d 1498 (11th Cir. 1992) at 1512.

25. Haitians Centers Council Inc. v. McNary, 969 F.2d 1326 (2d Cir. 1992), emphasis in original. The Second Circuit cited *United States v. Tiede* for this last proposition, and the language of the opinion echoes, *mutatis mutandis*, that of Judge Stern in *Tiede*.

26. Sale v. Haitians Centers Council, Inc., 113 S. Ct. 2549 (1993) at 2565.

27. See, e.g., Theodor Meron, "Extraterritoriality of Human Rights Treaties," *American Journal of International Law* 89, no. 1 (1995).

28. Cuban American Bar Ass'n, Inc. v. Christopher, 43 F.3d 1412, 1430 (1995).

29. Goldsmith, *Terror Presidency*, 107–8.

30. Ibid.

31. William Glaberson, "Red Cross Monitors Barred from Guantanamo," *New York Times*, Nov. 16, 2007. Glaberson references a confidential manual from 2003 describing this policy of exclusion. The ICRC at one point accused the United States of engaging in inhumane treatment at Guantanamo. Josh White and John Mintz, "Red Cross Cites Inhumane Treatment at Guantanamo," *Washington Post*, December 1, 2004, A10.

32. For a comprehensive review see Richard Fallon and Daniel J. Meltzer, "Habeas Corpus Jurisdiction, Substantive Rights, and the War on Terror," *Harvard Law Review* 120, no. 8 (2007).

33. The various amicus briefs in *Rasul* and *Boumediene* raised these issues extensively. See also Paul Halliday and Edward G. White, "The

Suspension Clause," *Virginia Law Review* 94, no. 2 (2008); Fallon and Meltzer, "Habeas Corpus Jurisdiction."

34. David Danelski, "The Saboteurs' Case," *Journal of Supreme Court History* 1 (1996); Louis Fisher, *Nazi Saboteurs on Trial: A Military Tribunal and American Law* (Lawrence: University Press of Kansas, 2003).

35. *Ex parte* Quirin, 317 U.S. 1 (1942) at 24–25.

36. In *Yamashita v. Styer* the Supreme Court reviewed a habeas petition brought by a Japanese general sentenced to death in the Philippines, at the time still an American colony. The Court declared that Congress "has not withdrawn, and the Executive branch of the Government could not, unless there was suspension of the writ, withdraw from the courts the duty and power to make such inquiry into the authority of the commission as may be made by habeas corpus." Application of Yamashita, 327 U.S. 1 (1946) at 9.

37. The law with regard to citizens abroad was more straightforward, but less so than one might imagine. As two eminent legal scholars argued in 2007, there is little doubt that federal courts have statutory jurisdiction to review the detention of citizens held abroad. Yet the precedents supporting this claim of extraterritorial jurisdiction "are far clearer than the reasons underlying them." Fallon and Meltzer, "Habeas Corpus Jurisdiction," 2053. Burns v. Wilson, 346 U.S. 137 (1953) and U.S. *ex rel.* Toth v. Quarles, 350 U.S. 11 (1955) both upheld habeas jurisdiction for American service members held abroad.

38. Johnson v. Eisentrager, 777–78.

39. See the discussion in Fallon and Meltzer, "Habeas Corpus Jurisdiction," 2055–56.

40. Memorandum from Philbin and Yoo in *The Torture Papers*, 34.

41. Haitian Centers Council, Inc. v. McNary, 969 F.2d 1326 (2d Cir. 1992).

42. This point is made at length in Goldsmith, *Terror Presidency*. See also Jack Goldsmith and Cass R. Sunstein, "Military Tribunals and Legal Culture: What a Difference Sixty Years Makes," *Constitutional Commentary* 19 (2002).

43. Motion to dismiss in Hicks v. Bush, Civil Action No 02-CV-0299 (CKK) (D.C. District Court 2005) at 19.

44. Al Odah v. United States, 321 F.3d 1134 (2003) at 1140.

45. Ibid. See also Pauling v. McElroy, 278 F.2d 252 (D.C. Cir. 1960) at 254 ("non-resident aliens ... plainly cannot appeal to the protection of the Constitution or laws of the United States."); People's Mojahedin Org. v. Dept of State, 182 F.3d 17 (D.C. Cir. 1999) at 22 ("a foreign entity without property or presence in this country has no constitutional rights, under the due process clause or otherwise").

46. Gherebi v. Bush, 1291. *In re Guantanamo Detainees* likewise held that "in light of the Supreme Court's decision in Rasul, it is clear that Guantanamo Bay must be considered the equivalent of a U.S. territory in which fundamental rights apply " *In re* Guantanamo Detainees, 355 F.Supp. 2d 443 (2005) at 464.

47. Gherebi v. Bush, 1288.

48. Ibid., 1283.

49. Rasul v. Bush, 542 U.S. 466 (2004) at 468. See also Kermit Roosevelt III, "Guantanamo and the Conflict of Laws: Rasul and Beyond," *University of Pennsylvania Law Review*, 153, no. 6 (2005), fitting this decision into modern conflicts analysis.

50. Footnote 15, at 15, citing United States v. Verdugo-Urquidez, 494 U.S. 259 (1990), Kennedy concurrence.

51. Rasul v. Bush, 487, quoting *Eisentrager*.

52. Rasul v. Bush dissent, 498.

53. Ibid., 501.

54. Connell v. Vermilya-Brown Co., 335 U.S. 377 (1948) at 380. Jones v. United States, 137 U.S. 202 (1890).

55. Brief for Respondent in *Boumediene* (2007), 25.

56. Black dissent in *Eisentrager*, 795–96.

57. Dana Priest, "CIA Holds Terror Suspects in Secret Prisons; Debate Is Growing Within Agency about Legality and Morality of Overseas System Set Up After 9/11," *Washington Post*, November 2, 2005.

58. "The framework for such assistance" by European states, said the council report, "was developed around NATO authorisations agreed on 4 October 2001." Council of Europe Committee on Legal Affairs and Human Rights, *Secret Detentions and Illegal Transfers of Detainees Involving Council of Europe Member States: Second Report* (June 7, 2007), 4.

59. Priest, "CIA Holds Terror Suspects"; Council of Europe Report, *Secret Detentions*, 17. Similar reports aired on *ABC News* in late 2005. Brian Ross and Richard Esposito, "Sources Tell ABC News Top Al Qaeda Figures Held in Secret CIA Prisons," *ABC News*, Dec. 5, 2005.

60. Council of Europe Report, *Secret Detentions*; Jan Silva, "EU Official: No Evidence of Illegal CIA Action," *Boston Globe*, April 21, 2006.

61. One such company was sued in 2007 for "enabling the clandestine and forcible transportation of terrorism suspects to secret overseas detention facilities where they are placed beyond the reach of the law..." Binyam Mohamed v. Jeppesen Dataplan, Inc., 539 F. Supp. 2d 1128 (2008). See Amnesty International, *Below the Radar: Secret Flights to Torture and Disappearance* (April 2006); Stephen Grey, *Ghost Plane: The True Story of the CIA Torture Program* (New York: St. Martin's Press, 2006).

62. Mark Silva, "Bush Confirms Use of CIA Secret Prisons," *Chicago Tribune*, September 7, 2006. Whether all the CIA detainees remaining were transferred to Guantanamo is in some doubt; Human Rights Watch, *Ghost Prisoner: Two Years in Secret CIA Detention* (February 2007).

63. Scott Shane, David Johnston, and James Risen, "Secret U.S. Endorsement of Severe Interrogations," *New York Times*, October 4, 2007.

64. Quoted in Jane Mayer, "Outsourcing Torture: The Secret History of America's 'Extraordinary Rendition' Program," *New Yorker*, February 14, 2005.

65. Ibid.

66. Adrian Croft, "U.K. says U.S. Rendition Flights Used Its Territory," *Washington Post*, February 21, 2008. Some media reports allege that rendition and torture took place at Diego Garcia itself. Adam Zagorin, "Source: US Used UK Isle for Interrogations," *Time Magazine*, July 31, 2008.

67. Goldsmith, *Terror Presidency*. The War Crimes Act, 18 U.S.C. Section 2441, defines a war crime as a grave breach of the Geneva Conventions, and applies regardless of whether the perpetrator or victim is a U.S. citizen or member of the U.S. Armed Forces.

68. Robert Hughes, *The Fatal Shore* (London: Harvill Press, 1987).

69. Bremer was named presidential envoy to Iraq on May 6, 2003. See White House, Office of the Press Secretary, "President Names Envoy to Iraq," May 6, 2003, available at http://www.whitehouse.gov/news/releases/2003/05/20030506-5.html. See also Donald Rumsfeld, Secretary of Defense, "Designation as Administrator of the Coalition Provisional Authority," memorandum, May 13, 2003, cited in U.S. General Accounting Office, *Rebuilding Iraq: Resource, Security, Governance, Essential Services, and Oversight Issues*, Doc. No. GAO-04–902R, (June 2004), 3. The Justice Department quote is from Supplemental Brief of the United States, United States *ex rel*. DRC, Inc. v. Custer Battles, LLC, 376 F. Supp. 2d 617 (E.D. Va. April 22, 2005) (No. 1:04cv199). The original brief is not available, but the relevant portion is quoted in L. Elaine Halchin, *Congressional Research Service, The Coalition Provisional Authority (CPA): Origin, Characteristics, and Institutional Authorities*, CRS Doc. No. RL32370, 37–39 (June 6, 2005).

70. GAO Report, *Rebuilding Iraq*.

71. Eisentrager, 796–98 (Black dissenting).

72. Eisentrager, 798 (Black dissenting).

73. Scott v. Sanford, 60 U.S. (19 How.) 393 (1857) at 446. Aspects of this view are apparent in the debate over whether the foreign affairs power of the United States is somehow "extra-constitutional." See, e.g., United States v. Curtiss-Wright Export Corp, 299 U.S. 304 (1936).

74. DKT Memorial Fund LTD v. AID, 887 F.2d 275 (D.C. Cir. 1989) at 55. Some scholars argue that the Establishment Clause of the First Amendment should apply extraterritorially, on the theory that the purpose of the clause is to deny government endorsement of a particular religion. See, e.g., Roosevelt, "Guantanamo and the Conflict of Laws, 2067.

75. Lamont v. Woods, 948 F.2d 825 (1991) at 834–35.

76. Transcript of Oral Argument, United States v. Verdugo-Urquidez, 494 U.S. 259 (1990) (No. 88–1353).

77. In *Reid v. Covert*, for example. See the discussion in ch. 5.

78. Hirota v. MacArthur 338 US 197 (1949).

79. Omar v. Harvey, 479 F.3d 1 (D.C. Cir. 2007), cert. granted sub nom., Geren v. Omar, 128 S. Ct. 741 (2007) (No. 06–1666) and Munaf v. Geren, 482 F.3d 582 (D.C. Cir. 2007), cert. granted, 128 S. Ct. 741 (2007) (07–394).

80. Brief for the Federal Parties at 13, Munaf v. Geren and Omar v. Geren, Nos. 06–1666 and 07–394 (January 22, 2008).

81. Charles Fairman, "Some New Problems of the Constitution Following the Flag," *Stanford Law Review* 1, no. 4 (1949): 645. He stressed in particular the likely negative view of Great Britain. In an ironic twist, however, the House of Lords, faced with a very similar set of facts—a British citizen, detained in Iraq by British troops—held in 2007 that the British troops in Iraq were not acting for the UN but for the United Kingdom. See R (Al Jedda) v. Secretary of State for Defence, U.K. House of Lords 58 (2007).

82. Hirota, supra, Douglas concurring) at 204.

83. Brief for the Habeas Petitioners at 16, Munaf v. Geren and Omar v. Geren, Nos. 06–1666 and 07–394 (February 21, 2008).

84. Munaf v. Geren et al. (Slip opinion, June 12, 2008).

85. CPA Order 17, as amended, available at http://www.cpa-iraq.org/regulations/20040627_CPAORD_17_Status_of_Coalition__Rev__with_Annex_A.pdf.

86. James Glanz and Alissa J. Rubin, "From Errand to Fatal Shot to Hail of Fire to 17 Deaths," *New York Times*, October 3, 2007.

87. Though not all private military contractors were American, most were. Blackwater, the firm involved in the Nisour Square incident, had a workforce that was at the time about 75 percent American. See figures given in http://news.bbc.co.uk/2/hi/middle_east/7024370.stm. As of late 2008 no Blackwater employees had been indicted by the United States. Jeremy Scahill, "Blackwater Busted?," *The Nation*, November 14 2008.

88. HR 2740, MEJA Expansion and Enforcement Act of 2007, at http://www.govtrack.us/congress/billtext.xpd?bill=h110-2740.

89. Boumediene et al. v. Bush (Slip op. June 12, 2008) at 2 (Scalia dissenting).

90. Boumediene, 32, 34.

91. Ibid., 36.

92. Hamdan was acquitted on some charges. See Jess Bravin, "Hamdan Jury Felt Evidence Didn't Back U.S. Claim," *Wall Street Journal*, August 11, 2008.

93. Boumediene (Scalia dissenting), 1.

94. Ibid., 25.

95. Ibid., 2–3.

96. David Stout, "Justices Rule Terror Suspects Can Appeal in Civilian Courts," *New York Times*, June 13, 2008; Joanne Mariner, "What *Boumediene* Means," Findlaw.com, at http://writ.news.findlaw.com/mariner/20080616.html.

97. John Yoo, "The Supreme Court Goes to War," *Wall Street Journal* (June 17, 2008) (power grab); "Combating the Combatants Decision," *National Review*, June 13, 2008 (editorial) (imperial court; foreign jihadists).

98. National Commission Terrorist Attacks, *The 9/11 Commission Report: Final Report of the National Commission on Terrorist Attacks Against the United States* (New York: Norton, 2004); Amy Zegart, *Spying Blind: The CIA, the FBI, and the Origins of 9/11* (Princeton, N.J.: Princeton University Press, 2007); Richard A. Clarke, *Against All Enemies: Inside America's War on Terror*

(New York: Free Press, 2004); Goldgeier and Chollet, *America Between the Wars*.

99. United States v. Verdugo-Urquidez, 273–74.

100. Lawrence Wright, "The Spymaster: Can Mike McConnell Fix America's Intelligence Community?," *New Yorker*, January 21, 2008, 46.

101. Al-Marri v. Pucciarelli (4th Cir. 2008, en banc) (Wilkinson concurring in part and dissenting in part), at 153.

102. Steele v. Bulova Watch Co., 344 U.S. 280 (1952) at 287. Black took no part in the decision in *Steele*.

Chapter Eight

1. Finley Peter Dunne, *Mr. Dooley's Opinions* (Whitefish, Mont.: Kessinger, 2004) at 22–23.

2. A recent exception is Saskia Sassen, *Territory, Authority, Rights: From Medieval to Global Assemblages* (Princeton, N.J.: Princeton University Press, 2006).

3. The Apollon, 22 U.S. 362 (1824) at 370.

4. Letter from Calhoun to Everett, August 7, 1844, quoted in Lawrence Preuss, "American Conceptions of Jurisdiction with Respect to Conflicts of Law on Crime," *Transactions of the Grotius Society* 30 (1944): 187.

5. Whether this is true is discussed in chapter 4.

6. Elizabeth Desombre, *Domestic Sources of International Environmental Policy* (Cambridge, Mass.: MIT Press, 2000); Anne-Marie Slaughter, *A New World Order* (Princeton, N.J.: Princeton University Press, 2004); Kal Raustiala, "The Architecture of International Cooperation," *Virginia Journal of International Law* 43 (2002).

7. U.S. doctrines of personal jurisdiction make this easy. Kevin Clermont and John Palmer, "Exorbitant Jurisdiction," *Maine Law Rev* 58 (2006): 5: "[C]ourts in the U.S. shock the world by asserting jurisdiction over a defendant based merely on the defendant's transient physical presence."

8. John Woodliffe, The Peacetime Use of Foreign Military Installations Under Modern International Law, (Martinus Nijhoff, 1992).

9. Herfried Munkler, *Empires: The Logic of World Domination from Ancient Rome to the United States* (Malden, Mass.: Polity Press, 2007); 5; Charles Maier, *Among Empires: American Ascendancy and Its Predecessors* (Cambridge, Mass.: Harvard University Press, 2006).

10. Bartholomew H. Sparrow, *The* Insular Cases *and the Emergence of American Empire* (Lawrence: University Press of Kansas, 2006), 1.

11. Cherokee Nation v. Georgia, 30 U.S. 1 (1831) at 16–17.

12. Quoted in Don E. Fehrenbacher, *The Dred Scott Case* (New York: Oxford University Press, 1978), 156.

13. Scott v. Sanford, 60 U.S. 393 (1857) at 449–50.

14. Ibid., 446.

15. Walter Russell Mead, *God and Gold: Britain, America, and the Making of the Modern World* (New York: Knopf, 2007) describes the many similarities.

See also Ira Katznelson, "Flexible Capacity: The Military and Early American Statebuilding," in Ira Katznelson and Martin Shefter, eds., *Shaped by War and Trade: International Influences on American Political Development* (Princeton, N.J.: Princeton University Press, 2002).

16. Justice White, who championed incorporation in *Downes*, believed that the United States possessed all the powers "of sovereign nations recognized under international law," and that included the right to govern colonies differently from the metropole. Sarah H. Cleveland, "Powers Inherent in Sovereignty: Indians, Aliens, and the Nineteenth Century Origins of Plenary Power over Foreign Affairs," *Texas Law Review* 81, no. 1 (2002): 165.

17. Christina Burnett suggests that at the root of these decisions was also the desire to be free to discard territory at a later time; Burnett, "*Untied States*: American Expansion and Territorial Deannexation," *University of Chicago Law Review* 72, no. 3 (2005).

18. Downes v. Bidwell, 182 U.S. 244 (1901), at 306 (White, J., concurring).

19. Al Maqaleh v. Gates, No. 06-01669 (D.D.C. filed Sept. 28, 2006), Government Motion to Dismiss at pg 1 (Oct 3, 2008). After the inauguration of Barack Obama, the District Court for the DC Circuit requested that the Obama administration uphold or refine the position of the Bush administration that habeas did not apply to Bagram. Shortly thereafter Michael F. Hertz, Acting Assistant Attorney General, replied that "[h]aving considered the matter, the Government adheres to its previously articulated position."

20. For example, by a county commissioner in Florida. See "Commissioner: Send Sex Offenders to Mexico," available at http://www.local6.com/news/4614328/detail.html.

21. Peter Gourevitch, "The Second Image Reversed: The International Sources of Domestic Politics," *International Organization* 32, no. 4 (1978).

22. Bartholomew H. Sparrow, *From the Outside In: World War II and the American State* (Princeton, N.J.: Princeton University Press, 1996).

23. Ira Katznelson, "Rewriting the Epic of America," in Katznelson and Shefter, *Shaped by War and Trade*, 7.

24. Samuel Huntington, *Political Order in Changing Societies* (New Haven, Conn.: Yale University Press, 1968).

25. Mary Dudziak, "*Brown* as a Cold War Case," *Journal of American History* 91, no. 1 (2004); Mary Dudziak, *Cold War Civil Rights: Race and the Image of American Democracy* (Princeton, N.J.: Princeton University Press, 2000).

26. Pierre Marie Dupuy, Comments on chapters 4 and 5, in *United States Hegemony and the Foundations of International Law*, ed. Michael Byers and Georg Nolte, 180–81 (Cambridge: Cambridge University Press, 2003).

27. Schooner Exchange v. M'Faddon, 11 U.S. (7 Cranch) 116, 136 (1812).

28. G. John Ikenberry, *After Victory: Institutions, Strategic Restraint, and the Rebuilding of Order After Major Wars* (Princeton, N.J.: Princeton University Press, 2001), ch. 6.

29. Daniel Deudney and G. John Ikenberry, "The Logic of the West," *World Policy Journal*, 10, no. 4 (1993).

30. Ikenberry, "After Victory."

31. Fareed Zakaria, *From Wealth to Power* (Princeton, N.J.: Princeton University Press, 1999).

32. Gary B. Born and Peter B. Rutledge, *International Civil Litigation in United States Courts*, 4th ed. (New York: Aspen, 2007), 569.

33. E.g., David Johnson and David Post, "Law and Borders—The Rise of Law in Cyberspace," *Stanford Law Review* 48, no. 3 (1996). For alternative views see Jack Goldsmith and Tim Wu, *Who Controls the Internet? Illusions of a Borderless World* (New York: Oxford University Press, 2006); Paul Berman, "The Globalization of Jurisdiction," *University of Pennsylvania Law Review* 151, no. 2 (2002).

34. Canada Southern Railway Co. v. Gebhard, 109 U.S. 527 (1883) at 536.

35. American Banana v. United Fruit Co., 213 U.S. 347 (1909).

36. Gerald Neuman, *Strangers to the Constitution: Immigrants, Borders, and Fundamental Law* (Princeton, N.J.: Princeton University Press, 1996); Alexander Aleinikoff, *Semblances of Sovereignty: The Constitution, the State, and American History* (Cambridge, Mass.: Harvard University Press, 2002); Hiroshi Motomura, *Americans in Waiting: The Lost Story of Immigration and Citizenship in the United States* (New York: Oxford University Press, 2006.

37. Only a plurality followed this reasoning; the crucial fifth vote, Justice Kennedy's, concurred in the result but followed the kind of practical reasoning at the heart of Kennedy's later decision in *Boumediene v. Bush* (2008).

38. Neuman, *Strangers to the Constitution*, 101.

39. E.g., Motion to Dismiss in Hicks v. Bush, Civil Action No. 02-CV-0299 (CKK) (D.C. District Court, 2005) at 19.

40. Advocates for detainees there immediately began seeking habeas review in the wake of *Boumediene*; see Del Quentin Wilber, "In Courts, Afghan Air Base May Become Next Guantanamo," *Washington Post*, June 29, 2008.

41. Oral Argument Transcript at 9–10. 1989 U.S. Trans. LEXIS 98.

42. The competing schools of interpretation are legion, and I do not engage them here. For more extensive treatment see Neuman, *Strangers to the Constitution*; Kermit Roosevelt III, "Guantanamo and the Conflict of Laws: Rasul and Beyond," *University of Pennsylvania Law Review* 153, no. 6 (2005).

43. Louis Henkin, "The Constitution as Compact and as Conscience: Individual Rights Abroad and at Our Gates," *William and Mary Law Review* 27, no. 1 (1985), 18, 32. Similar views are expressed in Neuman, *Strangers to the Constitution*; Roosevelt, "Guantanamo"; Aleinikoff, *Semblances of Sovereignty*; David Cole, *Enemy Aliens: Double Standards and Constitutional Freedoms in the War on Terror* (New York: New Press, 2003); John A. Ragosta, "Aliens Abroad: Principles for the Application of Constitutional Limitations to Federal Actions," *NYU Journal of International Law & Policy*, 17 (1985).

For critiques of this view see Andrew Kent, "A Textual and Historical Case Against a Global Constitution," *Georgetown Law Journal*, 95, no. 2 (2007); Paul B. Stephan III, "Constitutional Limits on the Struggle against Terrorism: Revisiting the Overseas Rights of Overseas Aliens," *Connecticut Law Review* 19, no. 3 (1987).

44. My colleague Ken Karst famously identified "equal citizenship" as a central theme in the Warren Court's jurisprudence. Karst, "Foreword: Equal Citizenship under the Fourteenth Amendment," *Harvard Law Review* 91 (1977).

45. Downes v. Bidwell, 277.

46. Akhil Reed Amar, "The Bill of Rights as a Constitution," *Yale Law Journal* 100, 1131 (1991): 1196.

47. EDF v. Massey, 986 F.2d 528 (D.C. Cir. 1993).

48. See, e.g., Asahi Metal Industry v. Superior Court, 480 U.S. 102 (1987).

49. Lea Brilmayer, "The Extraterritorial Application of American Law: A Methodological and Constitutional Appraisal," *Law and Contemporary Problems* 50, no. 3 (1987): 33. This rationale suggests, however, that were the United States to convene a federal court outside American borders, as was done with the U.S. District Court for China, the due process clause would not apply to defendants like Asahi.

50. United States v. Bin Laden, 132 F. Supp. 2d 168 (S.D.N.Y. 2001).

51. Ruth Bader Ginsburg, "Looking Beyond Our Borders: The Value of a Comparative Perspective in Constitutional Adjudication," *Yale Law and Policy Review* 22 (Spring 2004): 334.

52. William Glaberson, "Guantanamo, Evil and Zany in Pop Culture," *New York Times*, February 18, 2008.

53. "London Fashion Week: Vivienne Westwood," *The Telegraph*, available at http://www.telegraph.co.uk/fashion/main.jhtml?xml=/fashion/2008/02/14/efwestwood114.xml.

54. Robert Kagan, *Of Paradise and Power: American and Europe in the New World Order* (New York: Random House, 2003).

55. Sparrow, *Insular Cases*, 85–86.

56. Secretary-General's High Level Panel on Threats, Challenges, and Change, *A More Secure World: Our Shared Responsibility* (2004); Report of the Secretary General, *In Larger Freedom: Toward Development, Security and Human Rights For All*, A/59/2005 (March 2005).

INDEX

Adams, John Quincy, 36
Al Odah v. United States, 201
al Qaeda detainees
    description of, 195
    Eisentrager application to, 199
    habeas corpus and, 196–197
Alcoa case, 102–104, 108, 111, 118–119
Aliens
    Bill of Rights applicability to, 54–56
    constitutional rights of, 170–171,
        174, 200, 219
    extraterritorial rights of, 55–56,
        135–138, 152–154, 165–177,
        200, 214–218, 244–246
    formal admission vs. spatial location,
        183–184
    Fourth Amendment protection for,
        174–175, 286n52
Amar, Akhil, 67, 245
Ambassadors, 13–14, 17, 66
American Banana Company case,
        96–100, 110, 112, 114, 118, 164
American Insurance Co. v. Canter, 45, 83
American Revolution, 31–32
Antidiscrimination law, 177
Anti-Drug Abuse Act, 161
Antitrust law
    cases involving, 101
    effects test in, 113–114

European objection to, 116
    origins of, 94, 96–101
    Sherman Anti-Trust Act of 1890, 94,
        100–101, 115
Apollon, 227
"Apology Bill," 264n50
Appertaining, 74–75
Aramco case, 172
Aristide, Jean Bertrand, 193
Article I of Constitution, 34
Article IV of Constitution, 34
Articles of Confederation, 33
Ascending scale principle, 171–172
Asia, 17, 66, 90
Australia, 207

Balancing tests, 110–111
Bentham, Jeremy, 73
Berlin Court, 151–153, 234
Bernanke, Ben, 120
Best v. United States, 166
Bicameralism, 67
Bikle, Henry W., 84
Bill of Rights
    applicability to aliens, 54–55
    description of, 49–50
    extraterritorial application of,
        166–177, 181–182, 189, 255n72
    Ginsburg's views on, 246

Europe
   American territoriality objected
       to by, 122
   empire building in, 15
   late-twentieth century growth of, 125
   military power of, 15
   territorial conquest in, 15
   U.S. antitrust laws objected to by, 116
Ex parte Milligan, 50–51
Ex parte Quirin, 51, 197–198
Exclusionary rule, 157, 171, 282n2
Exclusive jurisdiction, 53, 75, 141
Executive power, 218–221
Extrality, 17–18, 252n39
Extraordinary rendition, 188, 205–206,
   221
Extraterritorial consular courts
   in China, 69
   description of, 21, 97
   in Japan, 63–65
Extraterritorial jurisdiction
   American Banana case, 101
   of Americans in foreign lands, 62,
       64–65
   in China, 69
   description of, 21
   in Japan, 62, 64–65, 68
   in nineteenth century, 60, 62
   sovereign consent to, 66
Extraterritorial policing, 159–161, 163,
   168–169, 180
Extraterritoriality
   Bill of Rights application, 166–177,
       181–182, 189, 255n72
   in China, 14, 17, 57, 65, 69, 113, 136,
       140, 199, 215, 224, 227, 229. *See
       also* U.S. District Court for China
   in Cold War, 154–155
   conflicts caused by, 121
   of Constitution, 61, 132
   of criminal statutes, 105
   definition of, 5
   economic interdependence effects
       on, 119
   effects-based, 23, 27, 101, 107, 111
   empires and, 19
   evolution of, 223–247

examples of, 5–6
forms of, 6–7
Insular Cases and, 189
international institutions and, 238
intraterritoriality and, 233–235
in Japan, 63–64, 66, 68
legal differences minimized through,
   21
in mid-twentieth century, 95–96, 99,
   116, 185
postwar, 22–23, 113, 115–116, 119,
   121, 124–125, 229, 239
presumption against, 202
purpose of, 226
regulatory state's influence on, 119
security-oriented, 129
by states, 53
treaty law as foundation for, 66
triumph of, 124–125
in twenty-first century, 241–243
of uncivilized nations, 188

Fairman, Charles, 212
Family planning organizations, 210
FBI, 163
Federal Bureau of Investigation, 163
Federalism, 6, 31–32, 255n70
Federalist 13, 33
Feudalism, 10
Fifth Amendment, 48, 55, 137, 142,
   144, 165
   extraterritoriality of, 165, 167, 182
   Miranda warnings, 181
   torture of non-resident foreign
       nationals, 186
Filipinos, 78
Fillmore, Millard, 62
First World War
   classical legal thought after, 110
   description of, 73, 93
   effects-based extraterritoriality
       after, 111
   globalization and, 118
Fleming v. Page, 44–46, 208
Florida, 38, 45
Foreign firms, U.S. lawsuits involving,
   179

history of, 14
of Indian tribes, 39, 43
military conquests' effect on, 50
personal rights vs. state rights, 247
"standard of civilization" for
    admittance as, 14–15, 39
United States, 14–15, 33
Westphalian, 12, 23, 26–27, 35
Spain, 76
Spanish-American War, 3, 60, 86, 191
"Standard of civilization," 14–15, 19,
    39, 122
State(s)
    Cherokee Nation as, 41
    definition of, 41
    exclusive jurisdiction rights of, 53
    Indian tribes as, 41–42
    jurisdictional equality among, 12
Status of forces agreements, 21–22,
    138–140, 154, 191
Stern, Herbert, 151–152
Steyn, Lord, 190
Story, Joseph, 40, 53, 100, 171
Strict territoriality
    American Banana case as example of,
        100, 114
    coherent vision of, 65
    description of, 28, 32, 43, 52, 97
    in Japan, 65
    Ross case, 59, 61, 63–64, 67–68
    threats to, 117
    in *Verdugo* case, 179
Subic Bay, 128
Sumner, William Graham, 78–79

Taft, William Howard, 78
Takings Clause, 144
Taliban, 195–197
Tampico, Mexico, 44–46, 50, 208
Tangier, 17–18
Tariff autonomy, 17
Technological developments,
    117–118
Territorial acquisitions
    in Civil War, 51–52
    by conquest, 45, 83

Constitution's applicability to
    preexisting governments, 38
Cuba, 76–78
description of, 37–38
guano islands, 73–75
Hawaii, 75
islands, 73–75
Philippines, 37, 76, 78, 90
after Spanish-American War, 72
Supreme Court's ruling on, 44–45
by treaty, 45
Territorial commission, 164, 180
Territorial conquests, 45, 83, 128
Territorial expansion, 36–38, 43–44,
    56–57
Territorial incorporation, 83–86
Territorial presence, 55–56
Territorial security, 164, 180
Territorial sovereignty, 46
Territorial state
    consolidation of, 18–20
    history of, 8–12
Territoriality
    definition of, 5
    European objections to, 122
    history of, 8–12
    legal systems and, 5
    in seventeenth-century Europe, 12
    Story's influences on, 108
    strict. *See* Strict territoriality
    in twenty-first century, 241–243
    Westphalian. *See* Westphalian
        territoriality
Territory Clause, 33–34, 44, 47–48,
    85
Terrorism
    description of, 25, 163
    law enforcement approach to, 181
    Miranda warnings, 181
    threats of, 218
Terrorists, 25, 163
    Fifth Amendment protections, 182
    at Guantanamo Bay, 187–188,
        195–197
    offshore interrogations of, 186–188,
        197